FIGHTING IN VIETNAM

The Stackpole Military History Series

FIGHTING IN VIETNAM

The Experiences of the U.S. Soldier

James E. Westheider

STACKPOLE
BOOKS

Published in paperback in 2011 by
STACKPOLE BOOKS
5067 Ritter Road
Mechanicsburg, PA 17055
www.stackpolebooks.com

Originally published in hard cover as *The Vietnam War* by Greenwood Press, an imprint of ABC-CLIO, LLC, Santa Barbara, CA. Copyright © 2007 by James E. Westheider. Paperback edition by arrangement with ABC-CLIO, LLC, Santa Barbara, CA. All rights reserved.

Cover design by Tracy Patterson

Printed in the United States of America

10 9 8 7 6 5 4 3 2 1

Library of Congress Cataloging-in-Publication Data

Westheider, James E., 1956–
    [Vietnam War]
    Fighting in Vietnam : the experiences of the U.S. soldier / James Westheider.
        p. cm. – (Stackpole military history series)
    Originally published: Westport, Conn. : Greenwood Press, 2007.
    Includes bibliographical references and index.
    ISBN 978-0-8117-0831-9 (pbk.)
    1. Vietnam War, 1961–1975—United States. I. Title.
    DS558.W47 2011
    959.704'3373–dc22
                                    2010044894

For my father,
James E. Westheider Sr.,
who served in the Navy
in the Pacific in World War II,
and for my father-in-law,
George David Humphries,
who served as an advisor
to the Army of the
Republic of Vietnam

Contents

Preface

Vietnam was one of America's most controversial and divisive wars. It was also one of the longest. For nearly 30 years, from 1944 to 1973, the United States was either indirectly or directly involved militarily and politically in Vietnam. This involvement can be organized into three phases beginning with, first, the covert operations phase, from 1944 to 1954. The roots of U.S. involvement in Vietnam date from the last years of World War II, when Office of Strategic Services (OSS) agents made contact and began working with a little known and tiny group of revolutionaries calling themselves the Vietminh. At the time, they were allies in the war against Japan, but given the Communist influence within the organization, they would quickly be viewed as a potential threat at the end of the Second World War and the beginning of the Cold War. American involvement deepened in Vietnam during the Franco-Vietminh War as the United States supported France in its attempt to resubjugate its former colony and contain the spread of communism. By 1954, however, the French had lost, and Ho Chi Minh and his victorious Vietminh controlled at least half the country and proclaimed the establishment of the Democratic Republic of Vietnam in the north. In turn, the United States supported the creation of a rival Vietnamese state in the south, the Republic of Vietnam, and assumed the responsibility for training, arming, and advising the new South Vietnamese army, or the Army of the Republic of Vietnam (ARVN). The year 1954 marked the beginning of the second phase, the advising phase. By 1965, however, South Vietnam was collapsing politically and militarily, leading to the third phase, which was direct involvement of U.S. forces in Vietnam. The United States escalated the war in Vietnam, but after the 1968 Tet Offensive, the United States began to disengage, and by the 1973 Paris Peace Accords, the United States had withdrawn from South Vietnam. America's 30-year involvement was over. The Vietnamese civil war ended two years later in 1975, when North Vietnamese forces overran South Vietnam and reunited the nation.

ARRANGEMENT AND SCOPE

One of the questions this book seeks to answer is what it was like to have fought in Vietnam and how that experience may be compared to previous wars. Noted Australian author and Vietnam War veteran Gary McKay was once asked the old question, what was the worst war to fight in? McKay gave the standard soldier's reply: "The one you were in." Each war has its own distinctive horrors, whether it's the industrial, faceless butchery of World War I trench warfare, facing down a German King Tiger tank in World War II, or the frozen misery of the Chosin reservoir during Korea. Vietnam certainly had its own particular miseries, from the hot and humid climate and rugged mountainous or jungle-covered terrain, to a tenacious and often cruel enemy. Despite these constants of climate and enemy, within any given struggle, there are a multitude of possible assignments and experiences, so one person's personal Vietnam might differ radically from someone else's. Americans who served in Vietnam during the advising phase, from roughly 1954 to 1965, for example, had an experience quite different from those who served between 1965 and 1973.

Away from the battlefield, service during the Vietnam War also differed in many key respects from service in previous American wars of the twentieth century, particularly World War II, the war to which most conflicts involving the United States are compared. Vietnam was a very controversial struggle. Chapter 1 discusses the war's origin and U.S. involvement. Unlike Germany and Japan in World War II and, to a lesser degree, Germany in the First World War, North Vietnam and the Vietcong in South Vietnam did not pose a direct threat to the United States. Our involvement in Vietnam was shaped by the so-called Cold War between the United States and Western nations on one hand, and the Soviet Union and Communist bloc on the other, to contain the spread of communism. Vietnam, like Korea, was an undeclared and limited war, further adding to the sense of moral ambiguity.

Chapter 2 describes recruitment and training for the Vietnam War. While many Americans saw service in Vietnam as their patriotic duty, others opposed the war or did not feel like risking their lives in what they considered to be a lost cause. As with previous wars, a draft was used to supply the needed manpower, but unlike either world war, serious inequities in the Selective Service system meant that the burden of the war was carried disproportionately by minorities and working-class whites, many of whom did not want to serve.

Chapter 3 discusses soldiers' assignments during the Vietnam War era. Most military personnel serving during the period never went to Vietnam or served in combat, especially early in the American experience. Instead, many saw service throughout the vast U.S. military establishment, both stateside and overseas. A tour at Fort Lee, Virginia, for example, might be followed with one in Germany, Korea, Okinawa, or Italy. More than 2.5 million men and over 11,000 women served in Vietnam, however, and the primary focus of this book is on their experiences. While the experience of the combat soldier may be viewed as the quintessential one, most service personnel were assigned to support functions, in everything from intelligence work to vehicle maintenance, or other so-called military occupational specialties. Fighting in Vietnam entailed life at a forward fire support base or landing zone deep in the forest, or so-called Indian country, enduring heat, humidity, and insects, the boredom broken by endless patrolling, search and destroy missions, firefights, and large engagements. But life during combat periods also included times of relaxation and recreation. Chapter 3 also discusses living quarters, food, letters home, the black market in all sorts of goods, and entertainment.

Chapter 4 shows the battlefield. Much of the weaponry and equipment used by American forces in Vietnam would have been familiar to veterans of World War II or Korea, such as the Browning automatic rifle or the jeep, but Vietnam also saw the introduction of newer weapons, such as antiaircraft missiles and helicopters and a variety of new technologies to ferret out an illusive enemy, including infrared night vision equipment and human urine detectors. Evacuation of the wounded and medical care also benefited from advances in organization and technology, meaning that the average soldier in Vietnam had a much better chance of survival if wounded than did his predecessors in previous struggles.

As with previous wars of the twentieth century, the United States had allies in the struggle. Contingents from several nations, including Australia and South Korea, served in Vietnam. Most Americans appreciated their erstwhile allies, with the exception of the ARVN. "Marvin the ARVN," as many Americans derisively called him, was considered unreliable and poorly trained, led, and motivated. Most Americans, however, respected their Vietcong and North Vietnamese enemies, finding them to be dedicated, courageous, and tenacious fighters. They could also be brutal, often employing terrorist tactics, and despite any grudging admiration the two sides might have had for each other, Vietnam was a war of atrocities, revenge, torture, and cruelty. More than 800 soldiers were captured as prisoners of war and suffered greatly through torture, with some dying. Some were segregated by race, with the North Vietnamese and Vietcong attempting to exploit racial problems within the U.S. forces; they tried to get black prisoners to collaborate, though few did.

Experiences in the Vietnam era armed forces were also shaped by race, ethnicity, and gender. Women served in Vietnam, but their numbers were limited, and they were prohibited from serving in any combat capacity; they were assigned largely to service and support roles, and the vast majority were nurses. Vietnam was the first conflict since the American Revolution in which the United States entered the war with an integrated armed force, and while this eliminated numerous inequities present in the segregated military, African Americans and other minorities still had to contend with both personal and institutional racism. Chapter 5 discusses black frustration with the military, which would eventually manifest itself in the rise of black solidarity among so-called bloods, or black service personnel, and the outbreak of some instances of racial warfare within the armed forces.

Racial violence was just one indicator of the collapsing morale and effectiveness of the American military in Vietnam in the later stages of the war. Before 1968, morale among U.S. troops in Vietnam was high, and American forces were generally well disciplined, well led, and capable. That was not the case in the latter stages of the war. After the Tet Offensive in 1968, several factors, including Lyndon Johnson's virtual admission that the war had been lost, racial problems and antiwar sentiment, drug and alcohol abuse, and the breakdown of discipline and command, led to a virtual collapse of morale among U.S. personnel in Vietnam. The collapse is best illustrated by the rise of fragging in Vietnam: the murder of an officer or noncommissioned officer by his own troops.

Finally, chapter 5 also examines the lives of veterans and the problems of transition back into civilian society, including, most importantly, posttraumatic stress disorder and lack of recognition during the war. Many veterans came home with emotional or psychological problems related to the war but found a civilian society indifferent or hostile to them and a Veterans Affairs strapped of operating funds and refusing to admit that many of the problems plaguing Vietnam veterans were due to service in that country.

To provide more information, this book additionally includes a detailed chronology at the beginning, briefly explaining the events leading up to and immediately after U.S. involvement in the Vietnam War, from 1945 through 1975. The end of the book provides 100 recommended resources, including books, articles, and Web sites, for learning more about the soldiers and the history of the Vietnam War. The book concludes with a comprehensive index.

This book is based on a variety of sources, including, but not limited to, secondary sources, newspaper and other primary accounts, such as soldiers' letters to and from home, government documents, and interviews by the author with Vietnam era veterans. Mostly, I've allowed the veterans to tell their own stories, and I am indebted to all the men and women gracious enough to share their experiences so that future generations can better understand what it was like to live and serve during the Vietnam War.

Acknowledgments

Thanks to all the fine people at Greenwood whose hard work and dedication made this book possible. I owe a debt of gratitude to my colleagues at the University of Cincinnati–Clermont College, but in particular to Dan Goodman, Habtu Ghebre-Ab, Howard Todd, and Terri Premo. Special thanks goes to Fred Krome, managing editor of the Journal of the Archives of the Hebrew Union College; to Joe Fitzharris, at St. Thomas University; Don Bittner, Marine Command School, Quantico; Selika Duckworth-Lawton, University of Wisconsin, Eau Claire; David Ullrich, Ball State; and Chris Dixon, University of Newcastle, Australia. I also owe a debt of gratitude to all the veterans who were willing to share their experience in Vietnam with me, especially to Timothy Wood, Jay Williams, Alfonza Wright, and Allen Thomas, Jr. Thanks to Rosemary Young, and her excellent staff at the UC–Clermont College Library; the National Archives; the Texas Tech University Vietnam Center and Archive's Oral History Project; the University of Cincinnati Libraries; the U.S. Military History Institute at Carlisle Barracks; and the Cornell University Archives.

Finally, I thank Allen Brungs, Bill Brungs, Bernadette Dietz, Mark Herbig, Mike Tojo, Tony Saupe, Paul "Cerbel" Justice, Mike Kruse, my sister Sandy Bains, and most of all my wife, Virginia, for all of their support and encouragement.

Timeline

<table>
<tr><td>1945</td><td></td></tr>
<tr><td>Early</td><td>American involvement in Vietnam begins during World War II, when an American OSS team parachutes into Ho Chi Minh's camp in the far north of Vietnam.</td></tr>
<tr><td></td><td>A seven-man OSS team led by 28-year-old Lieutenant Colonel A. Peter Dewey, the son of a Republican congressman, arrives in Saigon. Their primary mission is to help liberate Allied prisoners of war.</td></tr>
<tr><td>September</td><td>Dewey warns his superiors in Washington that "Cochin China is burning, the French and British are finished here. We [the United States] ought to clear out of Southeast Asia."</td></tr>
<tr><td>September 26</td><td>Dewey becomes the first American killed in Vietnam when he was killed by Vietminh outside Saigon. Dewey's name is not on the Vietnam Memorial.</td></tr>
<tr><td>1947</td><td></td></tr>
<tr><td>March 12</td><td>President Harry Truman asks Congress for money to fund his just announced Truman Doctrine of aiding nations threatened by a Communist takeover, either internally or through external aggression.</td></tr>
<tr><td>July</td><td>George Kennan publishes "The Sources of Soviet Conduct" in Foreign Affairs, publicly outlining his theory of containment. The Truman Doctrine and containment will become the cornerstones of a new American foreign policy—shaped by what we perceive to be a monolithic Communist front—that will ultimately lead us into Vietnam.</td></tr>
</table>

1949

Late   The Communists, led by Mao Zedong, win the Chinese Revo-
                     lution.

                     Deputy Under Secretary of State Dean Rusk announces that
                     the resources of the United States would henceforth "be de-
                     ployed to reserve Indochina and Southeast Asia from further
                     Communist encroachment."

1950

May 8   The United States signs an agreement with France to provide
                     military aid to the French Associated States of Vietnam.

June   The Korean War begins.

August 3   An American Military Assistance Advisory Group of 35 men
                     arrives in Vietnam.

1951

September 7   The Truman administration signs an agreement with the
                     Saigon government to provide direct military aid to South
                     Vietnam.

1954

Early   The United States is now paying 80 percent of France's cost
                     for its war in Vietnam.

May   Civil Air Transport captain James B. "Earthquake McGoon"
                     McGovern and his copilot Wallace Buford are shot down and
                     killed by Vietminh over Dien Bien Phu.

July 20–21   Geneva Accords divide Vietnam temporarily at the 17th paral-
                     lel, giving the Vietminh control of the north and providing for
                     nationwide elections to elect a single government and reunify
                     Vietnam in 1956.

October 24   President Dwight Eisenhower informs Ngo Dinh Diem of
                     American support and $100 million in military aid to help
                     build up ARVN. Beginning of a direct and strong American
                     commitment to South Vietnam.

1956

July 20   The deadline for the nationwide election to unify Vietnam
                     as called for in the Geneva Accords passes without an
                     election.

1957

October   Beginning of a small-scale insurgency in South Vietnam.

1959

July 8   Major Dale R. Buis and Master Sergeant Chester M. Ovand be-
                     come the first two Americans officially killed in Vietnam when
                     they are gunned down during a Vietminh attack on Bien Hoa,
                     a town and divisional headquarters about 20 miles northeast of
                     Saigon. Buis and Ovand will become the first two Americans
                     to be listed on the Vietnam Memorial.

1960

December 20   The National Liberation Front is formed. Diem government begins to call them the Vietcong, meaning "Vietnamese Communist."

1961

January   American advisors are now being assigned to ARVN field units, but with the "understanding that they would not engage in combat except in self defense."

May   President John F. Kennedy sends Special Forces (Green Berets) to South Vietnam and authorizes covert warfare against North Vietnam and incursions into Laos.

December 11   Two U.S. helicopter companies arrive in South Vietnam to support ARVN operations, under a cover of being advisors and trainers.

1962

February 8   Military Assistance Command, Vietnam, is established, with General Paul Harkins as its first commanding officer.

December   The United States has around 10,000 military personnel in Vietnam; 109 Americans were killed or wounded in Vietnam this year.

1963

November 2   South Vietnamese president Ngo Dinh Diem and his brother Nhu are overthrown and assassinated by a group of ARVN generals led by Tran Van Don and Doung Van Minh. The coup begins on the night of November 1.

November 22   Lee Harvey Oswald assassinates President John F. Kennedy in Dallas.

December 31   There are roughly 16,500 American military personnel in South Vietnam. There are 489 American casualties this year.

1964

June 20   General William Westmoreland succeeds Harkins as first commanding officer of the Military Assistance Command, Vietnam (MACV). Henry Cabot Lodge steps down as U.S. ambassador and is replaced by Maxwell Taylor.

August 2   Gulf of Tonkin Incident: North Vietnamese torpedo boats fire on, but do not hit, an American destroyer, the USS *Maddox*.

August 4–5   A second incident involving the *Maddox* and another destroyer, the *C. Turner Joy*, is reported. No second attack is ever verified.

August 7   Congress approves and President Lyndon Johnson signs the Gulf of Tonkin Resolution.

November 1   For the first time, Vietcong forces directly target an American installation when they attack Bien Hoa Air Base. Five U.S. soldiers are killed, and six B-57 bombers are destroyed.

December 31	The United States has 23,300 military personnel in Vietnam, and most are advisors or in support and logistical roles. There are 1,278 American casualties this year.
1965	
January 27	General Khanh seizes full control of South Vietnam's government.
January 27	National Security Advisor McGeorge Bundy and Defense Secretary Robert McNamara send a memo to the president stating that America's limited military involvement in Vietnam is not succeeding and that the United States has reached a "fork in the road" in Vietnam and must either soon escalate or withdraw.
February 6	Vietcong guerrillas attack the U.S. military compound at Pleiku in the Central Highlands, killing 8 Americans, wounding 126, and destroying 10 aircraft.
February 7–8	Operation Flaming Dart, the limited bombing of North Vietnam, begins.
March 2	Rolling Thunder, a massive bombing campaign of North Vietnam, begins. Rolling Thunder will continue, with occasional pauses, until October 31, 1968.
March 6	President Johnson approves the Pentagon's request to send marines in to guard the American air base at Danang against repeated Vietcong attacks.
March 8	First American combat troops, roughly 3,500 marines, arrive in South Vietnam.
June 28–30	First major American offensive begins in War Zone D, 20 miles northeast of Saigon.
October 23–November 20	First Air Cavalry and other units fight the North Vietnamese army in the battle of the Ia Drang Valley.
December 31	There are 184,000 Americans in country. Losses for this year are 1,369 killed and 5,300 wounded.
1966	
December 31	The United States has around 385,000 troops in Vietnam. This year, 5,009 Americans are killed and 30,093 are wounded.
1967	
January 8–26	Sixteen thousand American troops participate in Operation Cedar Falls in the Iron Triangle northeast of Saigon. This is the largest operation to date.
February 22–April 1	Operation Junction City, even larger than Cedar Falls, begins in War Zone C, near the Cambodian border.
May 19	First U.S. air strike at central Hanoi.
July 30	Fifty-two percent of the American public, according to a Gallup poll, disapprove of President Johnson's Vietnam policies, and 56 percent believe that the war is a stalemate.

October 16–21	Large antidraft and antiwar protests throughout the nation, the biggest at the Army Induction Center in Oakland, California.
October 21–23	Antiwar protests in Washington, D.C., attract 50,000 demonstrators.
November 3–22	The battle of Dak To in the Central Highlands.
December 31	The United States has around 500,000 troops in Vietnam. This year, 9,353 Americans were killed, and 99,742 were wounded. The war cost around $21 billion this year.

1968

January 20	Siege of Khe Sahn begins and will last until April 14, 1968, prompting fears of an American Dien Bien Phu.
January 30	Beginning of the Tet Offensive. The Vietcong attack 5 major cities, including Saigon and Hue, 64 district capitals, 36 provincial capitals, and 50 hamlets.
February 10	Tet Offensive largely over. An estimated 33,000 of the enemy are killed. American casualties are 1,600 killed and another 8,000 wounded. Of the ARVN, 1,800 are killed.
Mid-March	Forty-nine percent of those responding to a Gallup poll said that the United States should never have become involved in Vietnam.
March 16	American soldiers under Captain Ernest Medina and Lieutenant William Calley massacre hundreds of unarmed Vietnamese villagers at the hamlet of My Lai. It would be the worst known American atrocity of the war.
March 31	In a televised speech to the nation, Johnson calls for peace talks to end the war, says he will deescalate American involvement, calls a bombing halt on North Vietnam, and calls on Ho Chi Minh to respond positively to this peace initiative. Johnson then announces that he will not seek reelection as president.
April 4	James Earle Ray assassinates Dr. Martin Luther King as he stands on the second-story balcony of the Lorraine Motel in Memphis, Tennessee.
May 10–12	Formal peace negotiations begin in Paris on May 10, and the actual peace talks begin on May 12.
June 10	General Creighton W. Abrams replaces Westmoreland as commanding officer of MACV.
June 30	Army has 354,300 troops in Vietnam.
November 5	Richard Nixon is elected president.
December 31	There are 543,000 Americans in Vietnam at the height of American involvement. This year, 14,314 Americans are killed, and 150,000 are wounded. The war has cost $30 billion.

1969

January 25	First full session of the Paris Peace Talks with both the South Vietnamese and the Vietcong represented.

May 10–20	The battle for Hamburger Hill near the A Shau Valley. U.S. forces take the hill, incurring heavy losses in the process, and only to abandon it shortly thereafter.
June 8	President Nixon announces the withdrawal of 25,000 troops from Vietnam. Vietnamization has begun.
September 3	Ho Chi Minh dies.
October 15	The Vietnam Moratorium Day: the largest antiwar demonstrations in American history occur throughout the nation.
November 15	Largest single antiwar demonstration to date occurs when 250,000 people gather in the nation's capital to protest the war.
November 16	News of the My Lai massacre appears in the public press.
December 31	The United States has 479,000 troops in Vietnam, and 9,414 Americans are killed in 1969. Signs of deteriorating morale and discipline are surfacing.
1970	
February 20	Henry Kissinger begins secret negotiations with the North Vietnamese in Paris.
May 1	Thirty thousand Americans, along with the ARVN, invade the so-called fish hook region of Cambodia; this will be the last major U.S. offensive of the war.
May 4	Antiwar war demonstrations at Kent State lead to National Guardsmen opening fire. The shootings leave 4 dead and 11 wounded.
May 6	Student protests and rioting over Cambodia and Kent State. Over 100 colleges and universities are forced to close due to the disruptions.
May 8–20	In Washington, D.C., an estimated 80,000 demonstrators, mostly young college students, demonstrate peacefully. In New York City, construction workers attack protestors near Wall Street. Later, 100,000 workers march in support of Nixon's war policies.
June 24	The Senate repeals the Gulf of Tonkin Resolution by a vote of 81 to 10.
November 11	For the first day in more than five years, no American is killed in Vietnam.
December 31	This year, there are 335,000 American troops in Vietnam, and 4,221 U.S. soldiers are killed.
1971	
March 21	Lieutenant William Calley is convicted at court-martial for the mass murders at My Lai. Calley is sentenced to life in prison but serves only three days in the stockade before President Richard Nixon orders him placed under house arrest.
April 19–23	Vietnam Veterans against the War stage a demonstration in Washington, D.C., and end by flinging their medals and ribbons on the steps of the capitol building.

November 12	President Nixon orders the remaining American troops to remain on the defensive and not conduct any further offensive operations.
December 26	Nixon resumes the bombing of North Vietnam.
December 31	The United States has around 156,800 troops in Vietnam, and 1,380 Americans are killed this year.

1972

February 21–27	President Nixon makes his historic trip to China.
March 30–April 8	A major three-pronged People's Army of Vietnam (PAVN) and Vietcong offensive leads to some of the fiercest fighting of the war with the ARVN.
April 15–20	Widespread antiwar demonstrations throughout the United States.
June 17–22	Watergate break-in and arrests and arraignments.
June 28	Nixon announces that no draftees will be sent to Vietnam unless they volunteer.
August 11	The last American combat units leave Vietnam. Only 44,000 Americans remain in country.
August 16	U.S. aircraft fly a record 370 sorties against North Vietnam, but the vast majority of aircraft involved are launched from carriers in the Gulf of Tonkin or from air bases in neighboring Thailand.
November 7	Nixon defeats his Democratic rival George McGovern and is reelected president.
November 11	The sprawling American compound at Long Binh is turned over to the ARVN, symbolizing the end of direct American involvement in the war.
December 18–31	Nixon launches the Linebacker II air campaign, or the so-called Christmas Bombings.
December 31	Only 24,000 Americans remain in South Vietnam, and 312 are killed in action this year.

1973

January 23	Henry Kissinger and Le Duc Tho sign the Paris Peace Accords, officially ending American participation in the Vietnam War.
January 27	Paris Peace Accords go into effect at 7:00 P.M. Eastern Standard Time. The draft ends, and for the first time since 1949, the United States has no conscription.
February 12–27	American prisoners of war begin to return home.
March 29	The last American troops and prisoners of war leave Vietnam. Only the U.S. Marine embassy guards remain.

1974

August 9	Nixon resigns as president. Vice President Gerald Ford is sworn in as president.

September 16   President Ford offers clemency to Vietnam era deserters and
                    draft evaders.

November 9   William Calley is paroled. His murder conviction is overturned
                    in 1999.

1975

April 30   Saigon and South Vietnam fall to PAVN forces. United States
                    evacuates 6,000 Americans and 50,000 Vietnamese.

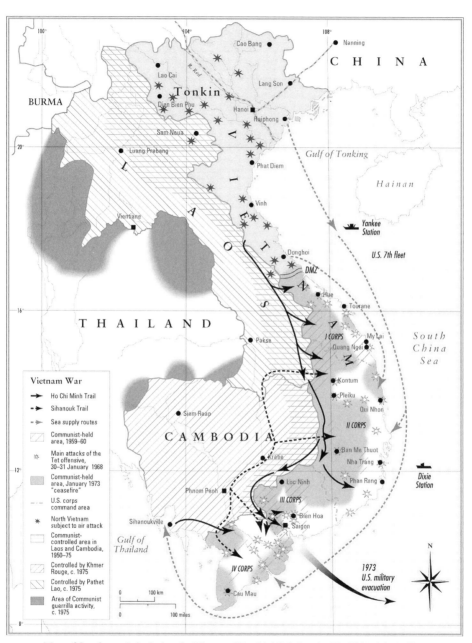

Map of Southeast Asia during the Vietnam War, highlighting the Ho Chi Minh Trail.

CHAPTER 1

The Cold War and the Origins of American Involvement in Vietnam

WORLD WAR II AND THE ROOTS OF INVOLVEMENT

The United State's involvement in Vietnam began in early 1945, the last year of World War II, when a handful of Americans parachuted into Pac Bo, in the rugged mountains in the northern part of the country. The men were led by Major Allison Thomas and were all members of the Office of Strategic Services (OSS), the forerunner of the Central Intelligence Agency (CIA). Their mission, code-named "Deer," was to link up with and help train and arm a small group of Vietnamese calling themselves the Vietminh, who were fighting Japanese occupation troops and had rescued several downed allied pilots.

The Vietminh, which was short for Viet Nam Doc Lap Dong Minh, or Vietnamese League for Independence, was founded in May 1941. It was technically an umbrella organization under which nationalist, socialist, peasant, student, and other organizations combined to fight the Japanese, who had taken control of the country from its colonial overlords, the French. In reality, the Vietminh were led by a small handful of Communists, two of whom would figure prominently in America's war in Vietnam. The first was Vo Nguyen Giap, one of the principal founders of the Vietminh and leader of its tiny military force. The other was Ho Chi Minh.

Ho Chi Minh was born either Nguyen Sinh Cung or Nguyen Tat Thanh in May 1890, in central Vietnam, and was the son of a minor court official. As a young man, he left college without taking his degree to work on a French steamship. Ho saw much of the world, including the United States. For nearly two decades, Ho, who used over two dozen aliases during his life, called himself Nguyen Ai Quoc, or Nguyen the Patriot, and was one of the leaders of the Vietnamese nationalist movement.

During World War II, Ho made contact with American OSS agents stationed in southern China. Ho had been away from Vietnam for 30 years, but as Nguyen Ai Quoc, he had become a hero in the nationalist movement, and he was eager to return to Vietnam and take control of it. But as Nguyen Ai Quoc, he also had a reputation as a professional

1

Communist operative, which undercut his viability as the leader of a nationalist movement. In 1943, he changed his name one more time to Ho Chi Minh, which means 'he who liberates' or 'he who enlightens.'

The Americans liked Ho and the Vietminh and were impressed by their enthusiasm and ability to learn quickly. They knew Ho was a Communist, but this was not an issue at the time because the United States was allied with the Communist Soviet Union in the war against Germany. If one could accept Joseph Stalin as an ally, then Ho was not a problem. The Americans also knew that Ho was first and foremost a nationalist, dedicated to freeing his country from all foreign control. During the war, that meant fighting the Japanese; after the war, it would be the French if they chose to try to reassert colonial control over Vietnam.

Ho and Giap were simultaneously fighting the Japanese, while slowly extending Vietminh political control over much of northern Vietnam. They believed that there would be a political and military vacuum in Vietnam between the time the Japanese were defeated and the French returned that they could exploit to proclaim an independent state under their control. Furthermore, Ho had the blessing of Vietnam's nominal emperor, Bao Dai, and seemed to have the support of the United States. In mid-August 1945, the Vietminh saw their chance to take power when the Japanese forces in Vietnam surrendered after the atomic bombings of Hiroshima and Nagasaki. The Vietminh seized control of Hanoi, and on August 29, 1945, formed a provisional national government. A few days later, on September 2, 1945, Ho proclaimed an independent Democratic Republic of Vietnam, with Hanoi as its capital. Americans joined in the celebrations and stood on the reviewing stand, watching units of the Vietminh parade by, with their band playing "The Star-Spangled Banner." American planes flew over the city and seemed to dip their wings in salute to the new Vietnamese flag.

But American support for the new regime was illusionary. President Franklin Roosevelt had opposed returning Vietnam to French colonial rule, but he did not necessarily support independence for Vietnam; he had suggested a United Nations protectorate, or even temporary control by China. When Roosevelt died on April 12, 1945, so did any resolve by the U.S. government to prevent a French return to Vietnam. His successor, Harry Truman, was more concerned with stability in a postwar Europe than with dismantling French colonial rule in Indochina, which, at the time, was insignificant to the United States and lacked strategic value. Before Ho had ever made his declaration of independence, which he modeled in part on the American declaration, Truman and other Allied leaders meeting at Potsdam in mid-August 1945 had agreed to temporarily divide Vietnam at the 16th parallel at the war's end. Nationalist Chinese troops would occupy the northern half of Vietnam to disarm the Japanese and maintain order, with the British performing the same function in the south, paving the way, they believed, for a peaceful return to French sovereignty.

In the north, Ho's provisional government was preoccupied with trying to stay in power and limiting the depravations of the Chinese army on the Vietnamese people. The northern Vietminh leadership also held out faint hope that they could negotiate some sort of a deal with the French for political autonomy. In the south, however, the French reoccupation of Saigon touched off hostilities between the Vietminh, under the leadership of Tran Van Giau, and the occupying Allied powers, primarily the British. The Vietminh had the support of heavily armed religious factions such as the Cao Dai, the Hoa Hao, and the Binh Xuyen, the largest and most powerful criminal organization in the south. The British, in turn, released and rearmed some of the Japanese prisoners of war (POWs) and used them to combat the insurgency.

There were also Americans in the south, but they were not involved directly in the hostilities. At the end of the war, a seven-man OSS team arrived in Saigon led by 28-year-old Lieutenant Colonel A. Peter Dewey, the son of a Republican congressman. Their primary mission was to help liberate Allied POWs, but it was inevitable that they would get caught up in the political intrigue. Dewey, who was actually somewhat of a Francophile, was accused by French authorities of being too sympathetic to the Vietminh and was ordered out of the country. In his last report from Vietnam to his superiors back in Washington, D.C., Dewey accurately predicted that "Cochin China is burning, the French and British are finished here. We [the United States] ought to clear out of Southeast Asia."[1] Dewey never made it out of Vietnam. On September 26, 1945, he was shot and killed by Vietminh outside Saigon, who, ironically, mistook him for a French officer. Dewey's body was never recovered. He was the first American killed in Vietnam.[2]

In February and March 1946, agreements were reached leading to the withdrawal of the Chinese troops and the return of French occupying forces to Vietnam. In return, the French recognized Ho's government in the north as a state within the French union and agreed to hold a referendum in the near future to determine if southern Vietnam would be reunited with the north as one country. Once the Chinese were out and the French back in, however, Paris reneged on the deal; further negotiations broke down, and in December 1946, war broke out between the Vietminh and France.

THE COLD WAR AND THE FRANCO-VIETMINH WAR

The Franco-Vietminh War coincided with a growing fear of Communism and the development of the Cold War between the Soviet Union and the United States. Communism was seen as monolithic and controlled by Joseph Stalin in Moscow. American policy makers believed that Communist insurgencies in places such as Turkey, Greece, and Vietnam were orchestrated by Moscow to further world Communism. Revolutionaries like Ho Chi Minh were no longer viewed as nationalists who happened to be Communists, but as pawns of Moscow. The Franco-Vietminh War, which, for many of its participants, began as a war of colonial liberation, now became a contest, pitting Communism against the free West.

The United States formulated a new foreign policy known as containment in response to the perceived threat: Soviet foreign policy was considered opportunistic but followed a proscribed path toward Communist domination of the world. To prevent this, the West must remain strong and firm, and Communism must be contained politically, militarily, and economically. Containment became the theoretical underpinnings of the Truman Doctrine, announced on March 27, 1947, by President Harry Truman. He stated that the United States would aid nations threatened by a Communist takeover, whether it was an internal insurgency or through external aggression. Congress responded by sending $400 million in military aid to Greece and Turkey to help combat their internal insurgencies.

After two years of fighting, France was slowly losing its war against the Vietminh. The French experienced many of the same difficulties fighting the Vietminh that the Americans would later encounter fighting the Vietcong. French advantages in technology and firepower were negated by the mobility and elusiveness of the Vietminh,

A French Foreign Legionnaire goes to war along the dry rib of a rice paddy during a sweep through communist-held areas in the Red River Delta, between Haiphong and Hanoi, c. 1954. Courtesy of the National Archives.

who were tenacious, resourceful, and learned quickly. The French had inflicted high casualties on Giap's forces and still controlled Hanoi, Haiphong, and the other major urban centers, but the countryside, especially in central and northern Vietnam, belonged to the Vietminh. The jungles and mountainous terrain that inhibited French military operations provided sanctuary and cover for the Vietminh. French attempts to pacify and hold ground in the countryside were failures. The revolutionaries also had strong support throughout the population. In March 1949, to undercut Vietminh claims that they were liberating Vietnam from colonialism, France granted nominal independence to Vietnam, Laos, and Cambodia, which all became so-called associated states within the French union. Bao Dai became head of state, but France maintained control over its former colonies' foreign affairs and defense forces. France also wanted direct American aid for their increasingly expensive and disastrous war. To reduce the high number of French casualties, the new state would also have an army to help fight the insurgents. The

French called it the "yellowing" of the army, and the result would be to help transform a war of colonial liberation into a bitter civil war.

Events occurring outside Vietnam aided the French in their quest for American military and monetary support for the Franco-Vietminh War. In September 1949, the Soviet Union exploded its first atomic bomb, and the Communists, led by Mao Zedong, won the Chinese Revolution. Alarmed, the United States extended help to the French in Indochina. Late that year, Deputy Under Secretary of State Dean Rusk announced that the resources of the United States would henceforth "be deployed to reserve Indochina and Southeast Asia from Further Communist encroachment," and on May 8, 1950, the United States signed an agreement with France to provide military aid to the French Associated States of Vietnam.[3]

On June 24, 1950, military forces from Communist North Korea invaded pro-Western South Korea in a bid to reunite the nation by force. The Truman administration committed American military forces directly to the struggle in South Korea. The wars in Korea and Vietnam were not related and were not part of a grand Communist plot, but from the vantage point of American policy makers, they certainly appeared to be. Along with direct intervention in Korea, the Truman administration increased its aid to the French and the fledgling state of Vietnam they had established in Saigon. The French also created an army for this new state, and on August 3, 1950, the first American Military Assistance Advisory Group of 35 men arrived in Vietnam to help train the newly established Vietnamese army. A little over a year later, on September 7, 1951, the Truman administration signed an agreement with the Saigon government to provide direct military aid to South Vietnam. American military personnel would serve in Vietnam for the next 25 years.

The United States took an increasingly active role in funding the Franco-Vietminh War. In September 1953, Congress approved over $900 million in military aid, and by 1954, the United States was paying 80 percent of France's costs for its war in Vietnam. Much of the money was earmarked for an operation that was supposed finally to lure the Vietminh into a trap and destroy them. In November 1953, the French established a large fortification at Dien Bien Phu in the northern mountains, hoping to interdict communications between the Vietminh and their Communist Chinese patrons. They believed that the location was of such strategic value to the Vietminh that they would be forced to attack the outpost in strength, allowing the French to bring their superior firepower to bear and decimate the Vietminh formations.

Despite the French belief, the area around Dien Bien Phu was not of vital importance to the Vietminh; there were other, if more cumbersome, supply routes to China. But Giap had spotted the weaknesses in the French position and decided to take the bait. After a month and a half of skirmishing, the battle of Dien Bien Phu began around sunset on March 13, 1954. By five o'clock the next morning, the French airstrip had been destroyed, and any resupply would now have to be airdropped. One by one, the Vietminh surrounded and overran the strongpoints surrounding the main compound. By April 2, all the eastern outposts had been lost as well as most of the strongpoints on the base's western approaches.

The French requested American air strikes on the Vietminh emplacements, including the use of tactical nuclear weapons. The Joint Chiefs of Staff formulated a plan to use three 25-kiloton atomic weapons in support of the French, code-named "Vulture." President Dwight D. Eisenhower shared the French concerns. During the siege of Dien Bien Phu, he stated that if Vietnam fell, then Communism would spread from Laos to

Cambodia to Thailand, and on to other neighboring countries, likening it to a row of dominoes toppling over. Eisenhower's domino theory quickly became a main corollary to containment and illustrates how deeply Eisenhower and other American leaders viewed the Communist threat. But he also realized that he needed to move cautiously; the Russians had just successfully tested a hydrogen bomb, and he feared that the Chinese might intervene in Vietnam, as they had in Korea. He ordered the aircraft carriers *Wasp* and *Essex* sent to Haiphong and the South China Sea, but he would not order American air strikes, especially with atomic weapons, without congressional approval.

There were Americans working with the French in Vietnam. Since late 1953, U.S.-supplied C-47 cargo planes had been supporting French operations. Most of the planes and civilian crews flew for Civil Air Transport (CAT), a CIA subsidiary and predecessor of the more famous Air America. Air Force personnel totaling 874 people serviced and loaded the planes. As the French became more desperate at Dien Bien Phu, American involvement in the siege deepened. U.S. Air Force planes flew reconnaissance missions over northern Vietnam. Another 400 Air Force personnel were brought in, and American C-19 "Flying Boxcars" with five-ton cargo loads flew resupply missions to the besieged base. The CAT pilots redoubled their efforts, braving fierce antiaircraft fire and paying a steep price. In early May, CAT captain James B. "Earthquake McGoon" McGovern and his copilot Wallace Buford were shot down and killed by Vietminh antiaircraft fire over Dien Bien Phu. Like Dewy before them, their names are not on the Vietnam Memorial. Several days later, on May 8, the Vietminh overran the last French positions, and Dien Bien Phu surrendered. The French had sustained 7,500 casualties, and another 10,000 were taken as POWs, half of whom died under Vietminh captivity. Giap's forces sustained at least 25,000 killed or wounded. Ho Chi Minh and the Vietminh were in firm control of much of northern and central Vietnam.

Vietnam's fate was settled in part at Dien Bien Phu, but events half a world away would also have tremendous impact on that nation's future. The day after Dien Bien Phu fell, delegates at the Geneva Peace Conference took up the issue of Indochina's future. Under a series of agreements known as the Geneva Accords, a cease-fire was declared on July 19, 1954, finally ending the Franco-Vietminh War. France had lost 29,605 French soldiers, 11,620 Foreign Legionnaires, and as many as 41,995 colonials killed from 1948 to 1954, about 20,000 more deaths than the United States suffered during its war in Vietnam. In 1950 dollars, the war cost the French $10 billion. The Vietminh had lost tens of thousands of men, but they had also learned how to fight a Western army with superior firepower—and win. Arguably, the most valuable lesson they learned had to do with the importance of public opinion in Western societies. When the war became unpopular back in France, the French army lost the necessary will to win; the Vietminh did not.

NGO DINH DIEM AND THE EMERGENCE OF SOUTH VIETNAM

Though the Vietminh effectively controlled over two-thirds of the country, they would be awarded only half. The Accords temporarily divided Vietnam at the 17th parallel into two so-called regroupment zones, with the Vietminh forces concentrated in the north and Bao Dai's in the south. There was no intention of creating two separate Vietnams; the regroupment zones were a temporary arrangement until a nationwide election to unify Vietnam was held within two years of the agreement. Ho accepted the deal only under intense pressure from his Chinese allies. The Eisenhower administration had not supported the conference, and the American delegation, led by Secretary of State John Foster Dulles, barely participated in any of the sessions. The United States, displeased with the results, refused to sign the Accords, but stated that it would not use force to upset the new arrangement.

The Eisenhower administration deduced correctly that having lost most of its Indochina colonies, France would quickly abandon South Vietnam. It was also equally apparent that Ho Chi Minh's Vietminh would win handily in any nationwide election. Incensed over losing northern Vietnam to Communist expansion, Eisenhower and Dulles decided to create a new state out of the southern regroupment zone as a bulwark against any further Communist expansion in the region. Bao Dai, known as the playboy emperor, was far more interested in gambling and lounging around the French Riviera with his mistress than in being an effective head of state. He was seen as weak and untrustworthy. The American choice to lead this new Republic of Vietnam was a 53-year-old expatriate named Ngo Dinh Diem. Diem seemed perfect, at first, for the job. He was a passionate nationalist who hated the French and had refused to cooperate with the Vietminh. He came out of a Mandarin family, Vietnam's traditional leadership class, and had administrative experience. Diem was also rigid, autocratic, and a Roman Catholic in a nation that was 90 percent Buddhist, but his religious affiliation and personality characteristics were not seen as a detriment at the time. Under pressure from the United States, Bao Dai named Diem premier of the Republic of Vietnam.

Diem arrived in Saigon on June 25, 1954, and found a virtually hopeless situation. The government of the state of Vietnam was corrupt and inefficient. There were an estimated 800,000 refugees—caused in part by a CIA propaganda campaign—flooding into the south from the northern Democratic Republic of Vietnam who had nowhere to live and nothing to eat. The French still exerted tremendous influence and, along with Bao Dai, attempted to undermine his government. The army chief of staff, Nguyen Van Hinh, was planning a coup. The religious sects, the Cao Dai and the Hoa Hao, had large militias armed with crew-served weapons and paid little respect to the government in Saigon. The worst threat came from the Binh Xuyen and its leader, Bay Vien, who controlled the lucrative opium, gambling, and prostitution trades. Lavish bribes by Vien to Bao Dai and corrupt officials protected the Binh Xuyen's criminal empire and bought Vien the rank of general in the Vietnamese National Army and an appointment as head of the national police.

President Eisenhower was uncomfortable giving full American backing to an untested individual in such a trying situation, and many of his advisors doubted Diem's ability to lead under such conditions. The problem was that there were no real alternatives to Diem, and American support, both public and private, was crucial to his survival. Lacking any real options, President Eisenhower, on October 24, 1954, announced American support for Diem and pledged $100 million in military aid to help build a new Army of the Republic of Vietnam (ARVN). This marked the beginning of a direct and public American commitment to South Vietnam, but American officials also worked behind the scenes to eliminate threats to Diem's rule. The most important American, and strongest backer of Diem, was Lieutenant Colonel Edward G. Landsdale, head of the CIA mission in Saigon. Under Landsdale, the CIA launched a propaganda and sabotage program in the north to keep Ho's government preoccupied from interfering in the south. Hinh was forced out of the army and into exile in France. American money helped resettle the northern refugees, three-fourths of whom were Roman Catholic, in new villages in the south, where they became strong supporters of Diem's regime.

The greatest challenge to Diem's control came in March 1955, when the Binh Xuyen, Cao Dai, and Hoa Hao, with covert French support, joined forces to destroy the Saigon government. Urged on and supported by Lansdale, Diem attacked first, and though large parts of downtown Saigon lay in ruins, and thousands of civilians had been killed or wounded, the Binh Xuyen were routed and forced to flee the city. American support had been critical to Diem's survival. U.S. military advisors had taken part in the battle against the so-called gangster warriors, and bribes from the CIA had won the allegiance, or at least the neutrality, of many of the Cao Dai and Hoa Hao leaders. Most of the leaders that refused to remain neutral or change sides were hunted down, and many of them were executed.

Diem and his brother Nhu, head of the secret police, had also used the uprising as an excuse to eradicate what was left of the Vietminh in the south. About 90,000 Vietminh and their supporters moved north during the regroupment phase, but around 10,000–15,000 cadres had remained behind to organize politically for the vote on reunification and were under strict orders from Hanoi not to oppose the southern government militarily. Nhu's brutal methods succeeded in crippling the Vietminh structure in the south, but his secret police also tortured and killed numerous innocent victims. An estimated 50,000 people were jailed, and 12,000 were executed. These vicious measures alienated many southerners from the government and convinced the southern Vietminh that they needed to fight back, despite Ho's desire to temporarily maintain the peace. Diem's opponents had been defeated, but not quite destroyed. The shattered remnants of the Vietminh, Binh Xuyen, Cao Dai, and Hoa Hao fled into the countryside, most to the Mekong delta, where the two religious sects had been most influential, to lick their wounds and reorganize.

Having crushed the military threat to his regime, Diem and the Americans now moved to remove Bao Dai, the titular head of state. Diem won a rigged election for the newly created post of president against Bao Dai in October 1955, spelling the end of Bao Dai's political career in Vietnam. It was also the end of France's attempt to cling to South Vietnam. The last French soldiers and civilian bureaucrats were gone from Saigon by March 1956. With the support of the United States, Diem also refused to hold the election mandated by the Geneva Accords, in July 1956, to reunify the country. Vietnam was now officially divided into the Democratic Republic in the north and the Republic of Vietnam in the south.

AMERICAN COMMITMENT TO SOUTH VIETNAM
AND THE BEGINNINGS OF INSURGENCY

The United States now made a massive commitment to South Vietnam's future. Vietnam received the largest single share of American foreign aid in the middle to late 1950s. Defending the new nation was considered the single biggest priority, and the primary responsibility for training and equipping ARVN fell to General Samuel T. Williams and the 342 members of the U.S. Military Assistance and Advisory Group (MAAG). It was an extremely formidable challenge. There were language barriers. Though some Americans and many Vietnamese spoke French, very few Americans spoke Vietnamese, and few Vietnamese spoke English. Some of the Americans were racist and considered the Vietnamese inferior and backward. ARVN officers were promoted based on their political connections and loyalty to Diem and not on their military capabilities, so the officer corps was rife with corruption, favoritism, and incompetence. Most had little sense of loyalty to the regime, or to Vietnam for that matter. Many, in fact, were French citizens and were more comfortable speaking French than their native Vietnamese. The chain of command was a tangled mess, with Diem and other senior officials often by-passing it to give orders directly to junior subordinates. No one was quite sure how many soldiers were actually in ARVN. The South Vietnamese army had a paper strength of around 250,000 men, but many officers padded their rolls with fake names to collect the pay and benefits. Those that actually existed were poorly trained and equipped and lacked morale and esprit de corps.

Williams and his men did the best they could. The ARVN was reduced to a more manageable 150,000 men and was reequipped with modern American weapons. American military advisors were assigned to work directly with ARVN commanders from the corps level down to battalion level, and the Combat Arms Training Organization coordinated all advisory efforts in the field. The advisors achieved some success, but they had also made a big, if inadvertent, mistake. The MAAG advisors trained ARVN to face the wrong menace. In the mid-1950s, American advisors believed that Diem had quelled any internal threats and that the greatest danger to South Vietnam was a cross-border invasion by North Vietnam, similar to what had occurred in Korea in 1950. The training emphasized conventional warfare and not what would be needed in the future: counterinsurgency training.

By 1957, American policy makers believed that their efforts to build South Vietnam into a viable, anti-Communist state were succeeding, despite the shortfalls and problems with the ARVN. But that same year, remnants of the Vietminh, against the express orders of Ho in the north, allied with survivors from the Binh Xuyen and the religious cults, began a small-scale guerilla campaign against Diem's government in the Mekong delta. The disparate groups were united only in their hatred of the Saigon government, and the insurgency at first was more of an annoyance than anything else. Diem, however, had alienated large segments of the population with his dictatorial methods, and the resistance began to pick up momentum. By 1959, the rebels had established a base of operations in the Mekong delta northwest of Saigon and had launched a campaign either to turn or assassinate Saigon government officials in the countryside.

In March 1959, faced with a growing insurgency in the south, and now convinced that Diem could not be overthrown simply through political means, the Communist leadership in Hanoi decided to aid the rebels. That spring, they established a base in the Central Highlands and began widening a series of jungle trails into South Vietnam that became famous as the Ho Chi Minh Trail. If there was going to be a revolution in the south, they wanted to influence or control it. Help, however, would be limited and indirect because Hanoi did not want to provoke American intervention.

With northern aid, the insurgency intensified. The guerillas targeted only the ARVN and South Vietnamese officials at first, hoping to avoid drawing the United States deeper into the conflict. But it was inevitable that the over 700 American advisors, many serving out in the field with South Vietnamese units, would be caught up in the fighting. On July 8, 1959, Major Dale R. Buis and Master Sergeant Chester M. Ovand became the first two Americans officially killed in Vietnam when they were gunned down during a Vietminh attack on Bien Hoa, a town and divisional headquarters about 20 miles northeast of Saigon. Buis and Ovand would become the first two Americans to be listed on the Vietnam Memorial.

Despite the growing success of the nascent rebellion, the insurgents were unorganized and lacking focus; their only general point of agreement was to overthrow Diem.

To provide coherence to the movement, on December 20, 1960, the various groups fighting Diem's government formed the National Liberation Front (NLF). Its fighting arm was the People's Liberation Armed Forces (PLAF). Diem, however, wanting to tar the insurgency with its connection to Communism, labeled the PLAF the "Vietcong," a contraction of Viet Nam Cong Sang, meaning "Vietnamese Communist." Communists did hold most of the key positions in the movement, but there were representatives from the various religious, student, and nationalist groups opposed to Diem, and most of the PLAF fighters were not Communists—and they never referred to themselves as Vietcong.

PRESIDENT KENNEDY AND A GROWING
AMERICAN COMMITMENT

The following month, January 1961, John F. Kennedy was inaugurated as president. Dwight Eisenhower had inherited a limited American involvement in Indochina from President Harry Truman, and now was passing on a much stronger commitment to South Vietnam to the new president. Kennedy was a true Cold Warrior and, like his predecessor, believed in containment and the domino theory. Faced with the growing insurgency in the south, Kennedy opted to increase U.S. aid and expand the role of American military personnel. The ARVN was equipped with new M-113 armored personnel carriers. American advisors were now directly assigned to ARVN field units, but with the "understanding that they would not engage in combat except in self defense."[4] In May, he ordered 400 Special Forces Green Berets to Vietnam to help train ARVN in counterinsurgency methods and secretly authorized covert action against North Vietnam and American excursions into neutral Laos. Kennedy also increased the number of advisors in Vietnam to around 3,200 by the end of the year.

The ARVN needed direct American combat support, and some of the men sent to Vietnam as advisors were actually there to assist in field operations. On December 11, and under cover as advisors and trainers, two U.S. helicopter companies, the 57th Transportation Company, from Fort Lewis, Washington, and the Eighth Transportation Company, from Fort Bragg, North Carolina, with 82 Shawnee helicopters and 400 men, and along with hundreds of maintenance and support personnel, arrived in South Vietnam to support ARVN operations. Twelve days later, the helicopters ferried 1,000 South Vietnamese troops into a suspected Vietcong headquarters complex about 10 miles west of Saigon during Operation Chopper, the first airmobile combat action in Vietnam. The transport helicopters proved vulnerable to Vietcong ground fire, however, so to protect them, the first 15 armed Huey helicopters were sent to Vietnam. In February 1962, MAAG was expanded into Military Assistance Command, Vietnam (MACV), with General Paul Harkins as its first commanding officer, and by year's end, the United States had around 10,000 military personnel in Vietnam, and around 16,500 by the end of 1963.

The advisors sent to Vietnam in this era were some of the best and the brightest the army had to offer. They were professional, well trained, focused, and confident. Many, like a John Paul Vann, or a Colin Powell, were already being groomed for higher command. By now, all the advisors underwent months of training before going to Vietnam. There were courses in the Vietnamese language at the Defense Language Institute in Monterrey, California, and the Military Assistance Training Advisor course at Fort Bragg, North Carolina. The army wanted as many officers and men possible exposed to combat conditions, so almost all the advisors spent a good part of their time in Vietnam out in the field with an active combat unit. Captain Colin Powell, for example, was the advisor to a 400-man infantry regiment stationed at A Shau. The increased number of advisors, and their growing role in the war, meant increased American casualties: 109 Americans were killed or wounded in Vietnam in 1962, and another 489 in 1963. In 1964, the last full year of the advising phase, there were nearly 23,300 Americans serving in Vietnam and 1,278 casualties.

The American advisors were well aware that ARVN commanding officers were under orders from Diem to keep casualties down and had to clear any major operation through the presidential palace before acting. Nonetheless, the advisors were frustrated by the South Vietnamese lack of initiative and aggressiveness and failure to follow their tactical advice. The enemy escaped or defeated ARVN troops on numerous occasions that should have resulted in a South Vietnamese victory. The quintessential example of this is the battle of Ap Bac, which occurred on January 2, 1963. What should have resulted in a major ARVN victory turned into an exercise of everything that was wrong with the South Vietnamese army. The American advisor, John Paul Vann, could not get ARVN to attack. When they finally did advance and ran into fierce Vietcong resistance, they halted and refused all orders to advance. Even a last ditch attempt by Vann to keep the Vietcong from retreating during the night by blocking their escape route with paratroopers failed when the ARVN corps commander hesitated for hours before issuing the necessary orders. The Vietcong, which had fought bravely and skillfully, slipped into the night, having suffered only 18 dead and around 40 wounded. ARVN suffered at least 61 dead and another 100 wounded. Three American advisors were dead.

Ap Bac had been a defeat for the ARVN, but the United States and South Vietnam publicly proclaimed it a victory, pinning medals on many of the South Vietnamese commanders involved. Vann was so incensed at the ineptitude and cover-up that he took the unusual and dangerous step of bypassing his superiors at MACV and writing directly to the Joint Chiefs of Staff. In language designed to get their attention, Vann characterized Ap Bac as a "miserable fucking performance, the way it always is."

The American advisors had lost faith in the ARVN, and by late summer 1963, the Kennedy administration had lost faith in Ngo Dinh Diem. The South Vietnamese president had refused to initiate meaningful land reform, curb corruption, or foster democracy. When students and Buddhist priests protested the lack of basic civil rights and self-government, Diem retaliated with prison and torture and by raiding and closing many of the nation's pagodas and temples. After repeated attempts to change Diem's behavior, and warnings that he would lose American support, the Kennedy administration reluctantly backed a coup against Diem by his own senior generals, led by the commander in chief of the ARVN, Major General Tran Van Don. The coup began on the night of November 1, 1963, and by the following morning, Diem and his brother Nhu were overthrown and assassinated by the rebellious ARVN generals. Far from bringing a more efficient and less corrupt government, the coup had severely destabilized the South Vietnamese government. Diem's successor, Lieutenant General Doung Van Minh, known as "Big Minh" because he was six feet tall, lasted only a few months, until Major General Nguyen Kahn peacefully replaced him in another coup on January 30, 1964. Khan's takeover began what historian George Donelson Moss has called the "coup season in southern Vietnam." Before the year was out, there would be five more changes in government in Saigon.[5] What President Kennedy might have done in Vietnam is open to speculation because Lee Harvey Oswald assassinated him in Dallas,

Texas, three weeks after Diem on November 22, 1963. Instead, it was up to his successor, Lyndon B. Johnson, to find a solution.

THE GULF OF TONKIN RESOLUTION

Vietnam had been a troublesome issue for Truman, Eisenhower, and Kennedy, but it had not been a crisis. In fact, numerous issues, from Korea to Cuba to the Berlin Wall, had been considered far more threatening to Johnson's predecessors than did the situation in Southeast Asia. When Johnson inherited Vietnam, however, things had reached crisis proportions, and he had fewer options in dealing with it than had previous presidents. The government in Saigon was weak, corrupt, and unstable, and the South Vietnamese military was being badly beaten in the field by the Vietcong. He was also convinced that Communist North Vietnam was aiding and probably directing the National Liberation Front's war in the south. About the only thing that could prevent a total disaster would be direct American involvement in the war. A few of his top advisors, such as Under Secretary of State George Ball, urged him to pull out of Vietnam before it was too late. In a famous quote, Ball warned Johnson against committing American ground troops to the struggle. "Once on the tiger's back, we cannot be sure of picking the place to dismount," he reminded the president.[6]

Johnson agreed and knew the dangers of further American involvement, but he feared that he was already trapped by circumstances. In a May 27, 1964, phone conversation with national security advisor McGeorge Bundy, the president referred to Vietnam as "the biggest damn mess I ever saw....I don't think it's worth fighting for." But he also added, "I don't think we can get out."[7] Johnson, like Truman, Eisenhower, and Kennedy before him, was a Cold Warrior who believed that Communism was a direct threat to American security and had to be contained. He also believed that the United States had made a promise to help South Vietnam and that it was at least partially responsible for the chaotic situation that developed after Diem's assassination. Leaving Vietnam now would tarnish the United States's reputation internationally. He had personal reasons as well, fearing Congress might impeach him if he abandoned South Vietnam. Besides, he was not going to be the first president to lose a war. Johnson chose escalation and a direct American commitment to South Vietnam.

Before he would act, however, Johnson wanted some sort of incident justifying direct involvement in the war. Johnson got his incident on August 2, 1964, when an American destroyer on an intelligence-gathering mission, the USS *Maddox,* was attacked by North Vietnamese motor torpedo boats (MTB) in the Gulf of Tonkin. Two nights later, on August 4, the *Maddox* and another destroyer, the *C. Turner Joy,* reported yet another attack. It was a rainy, foggy, and moonless night with near-zero visibility, and no one actually saw any North Vietnamese MTBs or reported the telltale sign of torpedo wakes in the water. In reality, there had been no second attack; the jittery ships' crews, anticipating more trouble on a dark and stormy night, had misinterpreted radar and sonar data as contact with the enemy. Nevertheless, Secretary of Defense Robert McNamara assured the president that it had occurred, and Johnson would use the repeated "incidents" to order retaliatory air strikes against North Vietnam and to ask Congress for broader authority to defend American interests in Southeast Asia.

On August 7, 1964, Congress passed the Gulf of Tonkin Resolution, giving President Johnson the sweeping powers he requested. The resolution stated that North Vietnam had "deliberately and repeatedly attacked United States naval vessels" in international waters and "have thereby created a serious threat to world peace." These attacks were portrayed as "part of a deliberate and systematic campaign of aggression against its neighbors" and authorized Johnson "to take all necessary measures to repel any armed attack against the forces of the United States and to prevent further aggression... and to take all necessary steps, including the use of armed force" to assist South Vietnam or any other American ally in the region "requesting assistance in defense of its freedom."[8]

Though the war they had just sanctioned would become arguably one of the most unpopular conflicts in American history, the House and Senate handed the president tremendous power with surprisingly little discussion or dissention. The House debated all of 40 minutes and then voted unanimously in favor. The vote in the Senate was 88 to 2, with only Wayne Morse of Oregon and Alaska's Ernest Gruening voting against it. The 83-year-old Gruening, who had seen his share of world conflicts, accurately labeled the Gulf of Tonkin Resolution a "predated declaration of war" and warned his Senate colleagues they were in essence abdicating their Constitutional responsibility to declare war formally.[9]

Within a year, many of the resolution's staunchest supporters, such as Senator William J. Fulbright, would come to agree with Gruening, but the votes in Congress mirrored the popularity and support the measure had with the general public. Johnson's popularity soared, his national approval rating rose from 42 to 72 percent, and he handily defeated his Republican opponent, Arizona senator Barry Goldwater, in the presidential election that November.

FLAMING DART AND ROLLING THUNDER

Johnson was still reluctant to send ground troops to Vietnam and hoped that a more peaceful solution—or at least one not involving American soldiers—could be found. Events in South Vietnam, however, would soon force his hand. The United States now had around 23,300 military personnel in Vietnam doing a variety of tasks, and many were increasingly under fire. On the first of November 1964, five U.S. soldiers had been killed during a Vietcong attack on Bien Hoa Air Base. It was an ominous development because it marked the first time that the Communist insurgents had purposely targeted an American installation. By the end of the year, the United States had suffered 1,278 men killed or wounded.

On January 27, 1965, national security advisor McGeorge Bundy and Defense Secretary Robert McNamara told the president that America's limited military involvement in Vietnam had failed and that the United States had reached a point in Vietnam where they had either to escalate the war or withdraw. Meanwhile, American casualties continued to mount. On February 6, 1965, Vietcong guerrillas attack the U.S. military compound at Pleiku in the Central Highlands, killing 8 Americans, wounding 126, and destroying 10 aircraft. In retaliation, Johnson approved Operation Flaming Dart, a series of limited air strikes, beginning with the bombing of a North Vietnamese army camp near Dong Hoi by U.S. Navy jets from the carrier *Ranger*. This was followed up a few weeks later on March 2 with the beginning of Rolling Thunder, a massive air campaign against North Vietnam designed to destroy their ability to support the Vietcong in the south. Rolling Thunder continued, with occasional pauses, until October 31, 1968.

One of the main targets for American aircraft was the Ho Chi Minh Trail, a series of trails and dirt roads leading from North Vietnam through Laos and Cambodia and into South Vietnam, by which most of the supplies for the Vietcong, and later the

North Vietnamese, flowed into the south. The trails were generally narrow and often overhung with jungle canopy, making them difficult to spot. There were occasional trucks to attack, but most of the materiel was brought in by bicycle; about 100 pounds of equipment could be strapped to a bicycle, which was then guided by hand down the trail. It was not an easy target to spot, or hit, from 5,000 feet and moving at 300 miles per hour. To make matters worse, the CIA estimated that the Vietcong could maintain the insurgency if just 10 percent of the equipment sent down from the north made it through.

American aircraft dumped more ordnance on North Vietnam than did the U.S. Air Force in World War II, but with limited results. North Vietnam had virtually no industrial base, and its infrastructure was basic, so there were few real strategic targets, and those that were damaged were often quickly repaired. Pilots also felt hampered by the restrictions placed on them by the Johnson administration. Numerous targets in North Vietnam were declared off-limits, and President Johnson personally reviewed most requests to hit politically sensitive targets. American policy makers did not want to provoke either the Soviet Union or China into entering the conflict and were aware of world opinion concerning civilian casualties. Previous presidents, such as Franklin D. Roosevelt in World War II and Harry Truman during the Korean War, to some degree also restricted possible targets. Most Vietnam veterans believed that the White House, and, to a more limited degree, the Pentagon, placed too many limitations and restrictions on the use of American forces and firepower in Southeast Asia.

THE BATTLE OF IA DRANG

Johnson was also now prepared to authorize sending the first American ground troops to Vietnam. Under what was called the "enclave strategy," a limited number of army troops and marines would be deployed to guard American bases and the major coastal cities. On March 8, 1965, 3,500 U.S. Marines arrived at Red Beach Two, in South Vietnam. Many of the marines stormed ashore from landing craft, only to be greeted by friendly civilians. They were the first of 184,000 troops deployed to Vietnam by the end of the year. They were not the only new soldiers to enter the war. At roughly the same time as the Johnson administration decided to send combat troops to Vietnam, the Communist party in North Vietnam, the Lao Dong, had reached the same decision. As American troops began arriving by ship and plane, regular soldiers of the People's Army of Vietnam (PAVN) were infiltrating the south.

The enclave strategy did not survive the spring. Contrary to the oft repeated truism, the U.S. armed forces did have a lot of experience in fighting indigenous guerillas in mountainous and in jungle conditions. The army and Marine Corps had fought in the Philippine insurrection and against the Japanese in World War II in the Pacific. The marines had also fought rebels in a host of countries, including Haiti, the Dominican Republic, and Panama. The marines had institutionalized their experiences in *The Small Wars Manual,* which was an excellent blueprint for dealing with insurgencies, and the Corps and Special Forces had already had some success with counterinsurgency programs in Vietnam. But the army was in charge of fighting in Vietnam, and while usually effective, counterinsurgency tactics took time, patience, and well-trained and disciplined troops. General William Westmoreland, who had replaced Harkins as commander in chief of American forces in Vietnam in June 1964, was a combat veteran of World War II and Korea, trained and experienced in conventional warfare, and a firm believer in aggressive action and overwhelming firepower. Counterinsurgency, he

General William C. Westmoreland, Commanding General, MACV, watches the ceremonies on the arrival of the Royal Thai Volunteer Regiment in Vietnam, 1967. Courtesy of the National Archives.

believed, would take too long at a time when the Saigon government looked to fall any day. But conventional tactics, such as taking and holding strategic locations, also did not apply very much to Vietnam. Westmoreland, and most of his advisors, settled on a strategy of attrition, namely to kill so many of the enemy that they would be incapable, or unwilling, to continue the fight.

The battle of Ia Drang in October and November 1965 was the first big test of the strategy of attrition. The Ia Drang is a valley covering around 1,500 miles of rather desolate territory, and it was there that regular units of the North Vietnamese army opposed American troops for the first time in the war in a major battle. It was also the first large-scale use of the Air Cavalry in Vietnam. The First Air Cavalry Division was based in II Corps, in the Central Highlands, north and west of Pleiku. The First had 3,600 men in assault roles, thousands in support, and 400 helicopters organic to the

Flying under radar control with a B-66 Destroyer, Air Force F-105 Thunderchief pilots bomb a military target through low clouds over the southern panhandle of North Vietnam, 1966. Courtesy of the Department of Defense.

unit, with another 450 in reserve. It could move a lot of men and firepower rapidly. The MACV had fixed the location of several regiments of North Vietnamese regulars retreating westward through the Ia Drang valley into the sanctuary of the Chu Pong Mountains along the Cambodian border. Westmoreland and First Division commander General Douglas Kennard inserted the First Air Cavalry into the Ia Drang to block the North Vietnamese army's line of retreat.

Weeks of skirmishes, ambushes, and brutal clashes followed, culminating in the battle for Landing Zone X-Ray from November 16 to 24. The battle of Ia Drang left 305 Americans dead and hundreds wounded but thoroughly decimated the three participating North Vietnamese regiments. Of the 6,000 PAVN soldiers committed to the battle, 3,561 were killed, and an estimated 1,000 were wounded. The battle of the Ia Drang convinced Westmoreland, and other senior officials, that attrition was the key to success in Vietnam.

The North Vietnamese also learned lessons at Ia Drang. The Americans were a more formidable adversary than anything the Vietcong or North Vietnamese had faced in the past. The American use of helicopters, in particular, had been a real shock to the North Vietnamese, and they could not match the foreigners' technology, control of the air, or massive firepower. Moreover, they had misjudged the enemy's fighting prowess and determination. Many of the Vietcong and PAVN were used to fighting the South Vietnamese army, and more than a few remembered the first war of liberation against the French—it was assumed that the Americans would also lack ability, discipline, and heart, but this proved to be a costly miscalculation. The Americans were well trained, disciplined, professional, and competently led. The morale of the average soldier was high, and a sense of optimism permeated the ranks. Philip Caputo was a young marine lieutenant and one of the first American combatants to go ashore in March 1965. In his highly regarded memoir, *A Rumor of War,* he expressed a common feeling among most of the early arrivals when he wrote, "We saw ourselves as the champions of 'a cause that was destined to triumph.' So, when we marched into the rice patties on that damp afternoon, we carried along with our packs and rifles, the implicit convictions that the Viet Cong would be quickly beaten and that we were doing something altogether noble and good."[10]

In response to what they learned at Ia Drang, the Communist-led forces would avoid direct clashes with the more powerful Americans, unless they had a key advantage, such as the element of surprise or overwhelming numbers. They would fight a protracted struggle, "people's warfare," they called it, using the tactics of guerilla warfare, of ambush and booby traps, and keep the initiative on when and where to fight, frustrating the policy of attrition. They would patiently bide their time, and there would only be battles on the scale of the Ia Drang from now on only if it suited their purposes.

The United States diligently pursued the policy of attrition on the ground and the Rolling Thunder bombing campaign against North Vietnam but had difficulty in finding an enemy to "find, fix, and destroy." Throughout 1966, the United States conducted nearly 350 search and destroy operations, designed to hunt down and kill enemy forces, beginning with Operation Van Buren on January 19. The U.S. and ARVN units involved claimed a lot of enemy casualties—679 for Van Buren, and a whopping 6,161 for Operation Maeng Ho, which ended in early November, just to name two examples—but proved unable to bring them to a really decisive battle because the Vietcong and North Vietnamese army stuck to their policy of avoiding large-scale encounters. Only 40 percent of the missions reported contact with the enemy, and only 20 percent, or 87 out of 350, of those resulted in so-called meaningful contact and numerous enemy dead.

By 1967, Westmoreland realized that he needed to do something more than just aggressive search and destroy missions to force the enemy into combat, and he now had the manpower to do so. He had over 385,000 troops in the country, enough to begin a series of large-scale offensives, designed to capitalize on the American advantages in mobility and firepower, against some of the more troublesome concentrations of enemy troops throughout South Vietnam.

OPERATION CEDAR FALLS AND THE BIG UNIT SWEEP

The first big unit or big battalion sweeps, which employed far more troops than did previous missions, would be against Vietcong and PAVN forces operating in the notorious Iron Triangle, a 40-square-mile patch of dense jungle. Bordered by mountains on one side and rivers on the other two, it was only 30 miles northeast of Saigon and a

Medic D. R. Howe treats the wounds of PFC D. A. Crum of the 5th Marine Regiment during Operation Hue City, a bloody twenty-six-day part of the Tet Offensive in early 1968. Courtesy of the National Archives.

major staging area for enemy attacks on the capital. It was honeycombed with miles of subterranean tunnels and chambers, some dating back to the Vietminh in World War II and capable of sheltering thousands of enemy troops. Food and other essentials could be procured from Ben Suc, a village sympathetic to the Vietcong, on a bend of the Saigon River, on the edge of the Triangle. Westmoreland wanted to eliminate Ben Suc as a haven for the Vietcong, so Operation Cedar Falls began on January 8, 1967, with hundreds of American and ARVN troops suddenly descending on the village. Despite the element of surprise, and the speed of the assault, any Vietcong in the vicinity had still managed to slip away into the jungle, but U.S. and South Vietnamese troops rounded up and forcibly evacuated all 3,500 inhabitants of the luckless village to a refugee camp 15 miles downriver. Ben Suc was methodically demolished and wiped off the map.

American forces ranged throughout the Iron Triangle hunting down Vietcong. By the time Cedar Falls ended on January 26, over 16,000 American and 14,000 ARVN troops had participated, killing an estimated 700 enemy, with a like number wounded, captured, or changing sides, under the Chieu Hoi, or 'open arms,' program, which welcomed deserters from the Communist forces. Ben Suc no longer existed, and over 12 miles of tunnel complexes housing a PLAF regional headquarters, weapons and food storage, and a hospital had been destroyed. The entire Iron Triangle was devastated and designated a so-called free fire zone, meaning that anything in the area was a legitimate target and could be attacked without warning.

Westmoreland and the MACV considered Cedar Falls to be a huge success, but it actually had achieved very little and was in some respects counterproductive. The majority of enemy troops in the Iron Triangle had dispersed and avoided confrontation or capture, waited for the end of the operation, and immediately reoccupied the area after U.S.

and ARVN forces left. The heavy-handed treatment of the villagers by the Americans and South Vietnamese did little more than create more resentment against the government in Saigon and probably more than a few new recruits for the PLAF. Nevertheless, Westmoreland was pleased, and Cedar Falls became the prototype for the numerous big unit operations that followed. From February 22 to April 1, the MACV conducted the even larger Operation Junction City, involving 34 battalions of U.S. troops in War Zone C near the Cambodian border. This time, they took measures to keep the Vietcong from slipping through the net, but despite killing, wounding, or "chieu hoi-ing" an estimated 3,000 enemy fighters, the bulk of the Communist forces melted across the border to sanctuary in neighboring Cambodia, only to return as soon as the annoying Americans left. It was a pattern largely replicated during the other big unit sweeps that year.

One solution to prevent the Vietcong from returning to areas like the Iron Triangle and resuming operations was the creation of free fire zones. Originally instituted by Commander U.S. Forces, Military Assistance Command, Vietnam (COMUS-MACV) as a geographic area for discharging unneeded ordnance, between October 1966 and 1967, the role of free fire zones changed. Free fire zones, which could cover 500 square kilometers (310.5 mi.), became areas in which the use of ordnance, including heavy artillery or airpower, was allowed without prior permission from the higher echelons of command. Military personnel could exercise such freedom in firing their weapons because most peasants were removed from, or urged to leave, the designated areas and were relocated, leaving the area free of civilians. Anyone in a free fire zone after evacuation was considered a hostile and was a legitimate target. In practice, this was virtually never the case. Many peasants, however, either refused to leave or returned after they were relocated. Because so many either returned or refused to leave, there were numerous incidents of so-called incidental friction, in which innocent civilians were targeted and attacked in a free fire zone.

Ultimately, the creation of the free fire zones and forced evacuation of the civilians was counterproductive politically and militarily. The peasants did not want to leave their ancestral lands and were resentful of the policy, creating new recruits for the NLF. American and South Vietnamese authorities had hoped that the creation of the free fire zones would remove tens of thousands of peasants from Vietcong-controlled territory; it did, but the 200,000–400,000 refugees flooded into the larger coastal cities and not to the government-controlled safe areas and relocation camps, as originally planned. The refugees also proved to be good cover for Vietcong infiltrating the cities. Additionally, the forced evacuations tipped off the Vietcong that major operations were in store in that area, so more often than not, they simply left the area.

There were two places, however, where the enemy stood and fought back. One was a Vietcong and PAVN offensive in the Central Highlands, most notably around Dak To, near the plain of Kontum. The battle for Dak To lasted for much of the month of November, but American forces finally prevailed and maintained control of the strategic Central Highlands and Plain of Kontum by the end of 1967. The other was at Khe Sahn, a marine base located near the demilitarized zone (DMZ), the border between North and South Vietnam.

KHE SAHN

Khe Sahn is located in the northwest corner of South Vietnam, roughly 6 miles east of the Laotian border and 14 miles south of the DMZ. The site overlooks Route 9, an old French road, and the main eastbound highway entering Vietnam from Laos, and had been the location of a French military base during the Franco-Vietminh War. In 1962, a Special Forces group consisting of less than a dozen Americans and around 400 Vietnamese and Montagnards established a small camp there, constructing their buildings over old French bunkers. Their mission was to guard the route and to act as a listening and surveillance post.

General Westmoreland saw Khe Sahn as a staging area for possible offensive operations in the area, aimed at interdicting the flow of men and material south along the Ho Chi Minh Trail, so in 1966, marines replaced the Green Berets and Montagnards, and the base was expanded. Late in 1967, elements of four North Vietnamese divisions began taking up positions around the encampment, but the area around Khe Sahn remained quiet until January 1968.

Gauging success in a guerilla war is never easy. Counting the number of enemy dead seemed a logical way to determine success with an attrition strategy, and in late 1966, body counts became the chief indicator of progress, or the so-called primary operational index, in Vietnam. In practice, it was not a reliable method. The CIA opposed using body counts, claiming correctly that they were too prone to inflation and inaccuracies. They preferred to use the number of enemy weapons captured or destroyed as a more reliable, if more conservative, estimate. In a one-month period in 1966, for example, American units reported 65,000 enemy killed in action but recovered only 1,800 weapons. Between July 1, 1967, and July 30, 1968, the Pentagon claimed 161,000 enemy killed but recovered only 53,000 weapons, 8,400 of which were crew served. The defense establishment chose to discount the CIA numbers based on recovered weapons as too conservative. Instead, optimism, and inflated body counts, gave COMUS-MACV the false impression that they were winning the war in late 1967.

ERODING SUPPORT FOR THE WAR ON THE HOMEFRONT

The Johnson administration had been pressuring Westmoreland, and the Defense Department, for positive results because they desperately needed good news on Vietnam. The war was costly, in both American lives and dollars. By the end of 1967, there were 500,000 American troops in Vietnam; 9,353 Americans had been killed and another 99,742 wounded that year, pushing the total of U.S. servicemen killed to date in the war to 16,021. The war cost around $21 billion in 1967, with even greater expenditures predicted for 1968. The mounting costs of the war jeopardized Johnson's ambitious domestic reform agenda, his so-called Great Society, intended to end poverty and inequality in America. Support for the war, and Johnson's popularity, had declined. A Gallup poll in July 1967 found that 52 percent of the American public disapproved of the president's Vietnam policies, and 56 percent believed that the war was a stalemate.

Johnson was very concerned about the growing antiwar movement. There was an active movement from the beginning of direct American involvement in Vietnam. On April 17, 1965, the Students for a Democratic Society helped sponsor the first mass demonstration against the war in the nation's capital. On August 6, 1966, there were large demonstrations in most major American cities, including Cleveland, Denver, Pittsburgh, and Philadelphia, to protest the Vietnam War and to mark the 21st anniversary of the dropping of the atomic bomb on Hiroshima in World War II. By 1967, the protests had increased in size and intensity. In mid-October, large antidraft and antiwar protests occurred throughout the nation, with one of the largest at the Army Induction Center in

Members of the military police keep back protesters during their sit-in at the mall entrance to the Pentagon, 1967. Courtesy of the National Archives.

Oakland, California. On October 21, 20,000 angry antiwar demonstrators marched to the Pentagon, intent on shutting it down. Two days later, on October 23, 50,000 protestors demonstrated in Washington, D.C.

The war was also costing Johnson the support of former allies, particularly in the black community. Radical African Americans, such as Malcolm X and the Black Panther Party, had opposed the war virtually from the beginning. In January 1965, a month before he was assassinated, Malcolm X denounced the Vietnam War, stating that African Americans were on the same side as "those little rice farmers" who had defeated French colonialism, and predicted a similar defeat for "Sam."[11] But the mainstream civil rights organizations, such as the National Association for the Advancement of Colored People (NAACP), the Urban League, and Dr. Martin Luther King Jr.'s Southern Christian Leadership Conference, had been reluctant to criticize Johnson on Vietnam after everything he had done for the movement, but in January 1966, the Student Nonviolent Coordinating Committee (SNCC) came out against the war, as did Dr. King in April 1967.

Johnson needed a victory in Vietnam, and based on body counts, the MACV and the Department of Defense believed that attrition was working. In late 1967, Johnson temporarily recalled Westmoreland and sent him out, along with Secretary of Defense Robert McNamara, to bolster support for the war and foretell that success was in sight.

THE SIEGE OF KHE SAHN

Despite predictions of victory, the New Year began on an ominous note. On January 2, 1968, a marine patrol at Khe Sahn spotted six men in marine uniforms outside the perimeter. When challenged, one of the men reached for a hand grenade; the patrol opened fire, killing five of the six. It was discovered that they were actually North Vietnamese officers reconnoitering the base. The incident and the troop concentrations convinced civilian and military leaders that the North Vietnamese were going to siege Khe Sahn, attempting to recreate their victory over the French base at Dien Bien Phu in 1954. Lyndon Johnson, at one Pentagon briefing, snapped at the chairman of the Joint Chiefs of Staff, General Earle Wheeler, that we didn't need "another damn din bin phoo."[12]

Westmoreland could have evacuated the base but opted to fight there instead. He believed that the siege was the opening stage of an offensive designed to conquer South Vietnam's northernmost provinces, so it was vital to hold Khe Sahn for strategic reasons. He also saw the opportunity to draw a usually elusive enemy into concentrating around Khe Sahn and then annihilate them with superior American air- and firepower.

There were some superficial similarities between the two sieges, but there were also important differences between Khe Sahn and Dien Bien Phu. Khe Sahn was easier to defend; it was a compact two square miles inside the perimeter, compared to Dien Bien Phu, which sprawled for miles. Khe Sahn was on a hill, and the French at Dien Bien Phu were in a valley. The perimeter defenses at Khe Sahn were more formidable and included seven lines of barbed wire and a minefield. Only one North Vietnamese made it through the wire and minefield, on March 1, but he was quickly killed. Unlike the isolated French, the marines could be supported and resupplied from the outside, and regular air traffic continued in and out of the base during the entire siege. The closest support base to Khe Sahn was only 12 miles away; for the French at Dien Bien Phu, the closest friendly installation was 100 miles away.

More important, the defenders at Khe Sahn had tremendous firepower at their disposal. There were approximately 250 artillery pieces available in or near Khe Sahn. On base, there were 18 105 mm howitzers, 6 155 mm howitzers, 6 4.2-inch mortars, 6 tanks, and 92 single or Ontos-mounted 106 mm recoilless rifles. In addition, two firebases, Camp Carroll, 17 miles east of Khe Sahn, and the Rockpile, 15 miles to the north, were equipped with 175 mm howitzers, capable of supporting the base. American airpower at Khe Sahn was even more decisive. During the entire 77-day siege, six B-52s flew over Khe Sahn every three hours, around the clock, along with approximately 300 sorties a day over the area by fighter-bombers and other attack aircraft. American aircraft dropped more than 100,000 tons of ordnance in the defense of Khe Sahn.

The siege of Khe Sahn began on January 21, 1968, but consisted mostly of mortaring and artillery attacks and attempts by sappers to breach the perimeter defenses. An ammunition dump on Hill 88 took a direct hit and exploded, destroying 90 percent of the ammunition available and raining debris and ammunition down all over the base, demolishing buildings and turning over helicopters. By mid-February, most of the administration buildings had been destroyed by enemy shell fire and abandoned.

PAVN trenches along the western perimeter of Khe Sanh were only 300 meters from the base.

There were minor probing attacks, but the only major attempt by the North Vietnamese to overrun the base came on the night of February 29–March 1, which was repulsed with heavy enemy casualties. The North Vietnamese did try numerous times to overrun the smaller camps and the firebases supporting Khe Sahn. On January 29, Camp Carroll was attacked, but the marine defenders held. Nineteen marines were killed and 90 wounded, and an estimated 150 PAVN were killed. Camp Carroll held out against the assault, but on February 7, a Special Forces camp at Lang Vie, nine miles southwest of the base, was overrun, forcing the 200 surviving Green Berets, South Vietnamese irregulars, and Montagnards to fight their way through enemy lines and the jungle to escape.

By the time the siege ended on April 9, the marines had suffered 205 dead and 1,600 wounded. Marine casualties during the siege were roughly 18 percent of the garrison at peak strength. The United States also lost four transport planes, two jet fighters, a spotter plane, and 17 helicopters in the Khe Sahn area. Marines recovered the bodies of 1,602 enemy dead around the base, but estimates range as high as 15,000 total North Vietnamese casualties. In June 1968, new MACV commander general Creighton Abrams ordered Khe Sahn closed and the base dismantled.

THE YEAR 1968 AND THE TET OFFENSIVE

Westmoreland was correct in that the siege of Khe Sahn figured prominently in Giap's plan for an offensive but wrong on why it was so important. Khe Sahn was not the key to Giap's planned offensive, but a diversion from his true intentions. In spring 1967, the Communist leadership decided that people's warfare was not producing the desired results and believed that a massive offensive might demoralize the Americans and lead to a general uprising throughout South Vietnam. They labeled the planned attack "General Offensive–General Uprising" and decided to target the urban areas, particularly along the heavily populated coastline. The attacks around Dak To as well as the siege at Khe Sahn were designed to distract U.S. and ARVN forces and draw them away from the intended targets, while Vietcong operatives took advantage of the flow of refugees to infiltrate the cities. They would have the element of surprise because the attack itself would begin during the biggest holiday in Southeast Asia, the Lunar New Year, or Tet, and both sides normally honored a truce during this period. The third phase, if the first two succeeded, would have been the taking of Khe Sahn.

The Tet Offensive began on January 30, 1968, with a predawn assault by 19 Vietcong sappers on the very symbol of American power in Vietnam, the U.S. Embassy. The Vietcong simultaneously attacked five major cities, including Saigon and Hue, 64 district capitals, 36 provincial capitals, and 50 hamlets. The North Vietnamese and Vietcong had achieved surprise, but the expected civilian uprising never occurred, and the allied forces reacted quickly and decisively to the threat. Throughout much of South Vietnam, the offensive was quickly defeated. Marine guards had killed all the Vietcong sappers in the embassy compound by 9:00 A.M., and much of Saigon was back in government control by the next day. There were pockets of fierce Vietcong resistance. It took three weeks and 11,000 American and ARVN troops to eliminate 1,000 Vietcong holding the Cholon district of Saigon. Civilians made up many of the casualties; at Ben Tre, nearly 1,000 civilians were killed in a fierce battle to expel 2,500 Vietcong.

Black smoke covers areas of Saigon and fire trucks rush to the scenes of fires set by the Viet Cong during the festive Tet holiday period, 1968. Courtesy of the Department of Defense.

The fiercest fighting during Tet occurred retaking the old imperial capital of Hue, in central Vietnam, from Vietcong occupiers. The battle for Hue was reminiscent of street fighting in World War II and left the once picturesque city a "shattered, stinking hulk," full of rotting bodies, by the time it was retaken from an estimated 7,500 Vietcong.

The bloodiest single week of the war for the United States occurred during Tet-68, from February 10 to 17, when 543 U.S. personnel were killed in action and over 2,500 were wounded. Altogether, 1,600 Americans were killed and another 8,000 were wounded. The ARVN, which fought skillfully and bravely in what was probably their finest hour, lost 1,800 killed. For the Vietcong, Tet was a tactical disaster. They lost an estimated 33,000 killed and ceased to be an effective fighting force. Though the North Vietnamese also sustained heavy losses, they would have to assume the bulk of the fighting until their southern allies could regroup. There had been no general uprising either, and the Saigon government had not collapsed; yet strategically, Tet-68 was their biggest and most decisive victory of the war. It may have been a huge battlefield victory for ARVN and U.S. forces, but it was also a psychological and political disaster. Tet revealed that, contrary to the pronouncements of the Johnson administration, the United States was not close to winning, and ending, the war.

The biggest single casualty of Tet-68 outside Vietnam was the presidency of Lyndon Baines Johnson. Johnson had once enjoyed the confidence of nearly 80 percent of the electorate, and his vision for a Great Society, where poverty and bigotry would forever be banished from the land, reminded some of a modern version of Roosevelt's New Deal. But the quagmire of Vietnam ruined it all. Support for the conflict, and Johnson's approval rating, had both been steadily dropping even before Tet-68, but by late 1967, his approval rating had fallen to just 48 percent. By March 1968, only 36 percent of those polled voiced confidence in the president, and his marks on handling the war were even worse: only 26 percent supported him.

On March 31, 1968, Lyndon Johnson gave a nationally televised address, but instead of starting with, "Tonight I want to talk to you about the war in Vietnam," as the speech was originally written, he changed it to, "Tonight I want to talk to you of peace in Vietnam." He said that "it was important to no longer delay the talks that could bring an end to this long and bloody war" and invited Ho Chi Minh and the North Vietnamese to meet with the United States for peace talks. To prove his sincerity, Johnson said that he would deescalate American involvement and halt the Rolling Thunder bombing campaign against North Vietnam. Johnson ended by saying that he sought nothing politically from a peace settlement and announced that he would not seek reelection as president. It was obvious that the United States would not win its war in Vietnam. Nearly 14,000 more Americans would be killed after Johnson admitted defeat in the war.

The Tet Offensive marked the beginning of one of the most tumultuous and tragic years in American history. Four days after Johnson's speech, on April 4, James Earl Ray assassinated civil rights leader Dr. Martin Luther King Jr. as he stood on the second-story balcony of the Lorraine Motel in Memphis, Tennessee. The murder touched off several days of rioting in most American cities and fed a growing resentment among some African Americans in the armed forces. Racial antagonism and racial violence would plague the armed forces for the next decade. Two months later, on June 5, Senator Robert Kennedy was assassinated shortly after winning the California Democratic primary. That August, massive antiwar demonstrations and riots marred the Democratic Convention in Chicago. On November 5, Richard Nixon was elected president over his Democratic rival, Vice President Hubert Humphrey, partially on the promise that he had a secret plan for ending the war in Vietnam and achieving "peace with honor." By the end of year, the United States had spent another $30 billion on the war and lost 14,314 killed and 150,000 wounded.

THE NIXON DOCTRINE AND VIETNAMIZATION

When Richard Nixon was sworn in as president of the United States on January 22, 1969, American involvement in Vietnam was at its height. There were 543,000 Americans in Vietnam, now under the command of General Creighton W. Abrams, who had replaced Westmoreland as commander in chief of the MACV in June 1968. Nixon and Abrams inherited a worsening situation in Vietnam. With the war all but lost, morale and discipline were deteriorating rapidly. Drug use among the enlisted ranks was rampant, and racial antagonisms and violence threatened the very cohesion of the armed forces.

Nixon had promised an end to the war and peace with honor, but his immediate steps were to follow the initiatives of his predecessor, Lyndon Johnson. In May 1968, formal peace negotiations between the United States and the Democratic Republic of Vietnam began in Paris, France. Three days after Nixon took office, the first full session to include not only representatives of the United States and North Vietnam, but the South Vietnamese and the NLF as well, opened. That spring, Nixon also announced a shift in American foreign policy. He stated that the United States would provide military, economic, and political aid to any nation resisting Communist subjection, but the United States could not be counted on to supply troops; we would help, but it would be up to the client nation to do its own fighting. In June, the White House finally revealed the first part of Nixon's plan to achieve an American withdrawal and peace with honor: so-called Vietnamization entailed the United States training the ARVN to assume sole responsibility for fighting the war, as the United States slowly disengaged from the struggle. The United States would continue to provide much-needed logistical, air, and artillery support during this period. On June 8, 1969, President Nixon announced the withdrawal of 25,000 troops from Vietnam. Vietnamization had begun.

As the number of troops declined, so did the number and scope of American operations in the war. Some, however, would still prove to be bloody and bitter affairs. From May 10 to 20, 1969, for instance, American forces fought the battle for Hamburger Hill near the A Shau Valley. U.S. forces finally took the hill, and incurred heavy losses in the process, only to abandon it shortly thereafter. The useless carnage contributed to declining morale and efficiency among U.S. forces throughout Southeast Asia. A year later, beginning on May 1, 1970, 30,000 Americans, along with the ARVN, invaded the so-called fish hook region of Cambodia to root out Vietcong. Fish hook had very limited results, and would prove to be the last major U.S. offensive of the war.

MY LAI AND KENT STATE

In 1970, the nation witnessed a series of large antiwar demonstrations, including the biggest to date on November 15, 1969, when 250,000 people gathered in the nation's capital to protest the war. Nixon's popularity, and his handling of the war, took another blow the following day, when the national press broke the story of the My Lai massacre and how U.S. troops had murdered at least 200 elderly men, women, and children in that hamlet on March 16, 1968. Both the atrocity itself and the fact that the army had suppressed news of it over a year further angered much of the American public, as did the government's handling of the case. On March 21, 1971, Lieutenant William Calley was convicted at court-martial for the mass murders at My Lai and sentenced to life in prison. He served only three days in the stockade, however, before President Richard Nixon ordered him placed under house arrest.

The invasion of Cambodia and the revelation that the United States had conducted massive bombing raids against an ostensibly neutral country led to another wave of massive antiwar protests, especially on college campuses, culminating in the killing of 4 students and the wounding of 11 others at Kent State University on May 4, 1970. Student protests and rioting over Cambodia and Kent State two days later forced over 100 colleges and universities to close due to the disruptions and demonstrations. A little over a month later, on June 24, the Senate repealed the Gulf of Tonkin Resolution by a vote of 81 to 10. On November 12, 1971, President Nixon ordered the remaining American troops not to conduct any further offensive operations and to remain on the defensive. That year, 4,221 U.S. soldiers had been killed in the war to go with the 9,414 dead in 1969.

PEACE WITH HONOR AND AMERICAN DISENGAGEMENT

As more and more veterans returned from Vietnam and attempted to rebuild their lives, the war that had cost many of them so much was winding down, at least for the Americans. There was still plenty of death and destruction to go around. On December 26, 1971, President Nixon ordered the resumption of bombing missions against North Vietnam in an attempt to force concessions out of the Democratic Republic of Vietnam at the peace table in Paris. From March 30, 1972, to April 8, 1972, a major three-pronged PAVN and Vietcong offensive led to some of the fiercest fighting of the war with the ARVN. The American presence in South Vietnam was dwindling. There were approximately 156,800 American troops still in Vietnam on December 31, 1971. On June 28, Nixon announced that draftees would no longer be sent to Vietnam unless they volunteered, but they were no longer needed anyway. On August 11, the last American combat units left Vietnam, leaving only 44,000 U.S. troops, mostly support, artillery, and air units, still in the country. Five days later, U.S. aircraft flew a record 370 sorties against North Vietnam, but the vast majority of aircraft involved were launched from carriers in the Gulf of Tonkin or from air bases in neighboring Thailand. By November 11, just days after Nixon defeated his Democratic rival George McGovern to retain the presidency—for a while at least, until Watergate caught up with him—the sprawling American compound at Long Binh was turned over to the ARVN, symbolizing the end of direct American involvement in the war.

Despite announcing that a peace accord had been reached with the North Vietnamese in late October—conveniently, right before the presidential election—Nixon unleashed one more massive air campaign against that nation beginning on December 18. Officially known as Linebacker II, the air campaign will be remembered by its colloquial name befitting the holiday season, the Christmas Bombings. The purpose of the bombings was apparently to reassure the South Vietnamese, whom we were in the process of abandoning, that we were not abandoning them and to force a few superficial concessions out of the increasingly confident North Vietnamese delegation, led by the seasoned diplomat Le Duc Tho. The United States lost 15 B-52s during the raids, more than in eight previous years of war, and achieved little more than angering the North Vietnamese and threatening the peace with honor agreed on by Le and chief American negotiator Secretary of State Henry Kissinger. By the end of 1972, 312 Americans had been killed in action, and only 24,000 remained in South Vietnam.

The peace talks resumed in early 1973, and on January 23, Henry Kissinger and Le Duc Tho signed the Paris Peace Accords, officially ending American participation in the Vietnam War. The United States would withdraw its remaining combat troops, and North Vietnam agreed to release all American POWs in enemy custody. Under the agreement, the North Vietnamese were not required to remove their troops from the south, nor was the Vietcong required to evacuate any territory they occupied. On January 28, at 7:00 P.M. Eastern Standard Time, the cease-fire between the Vietcong and the PAVN and American forces went into effect. Between February 12 and February 27, 1973, the Democratic Republic of Vietnam began releasing American POWs, and by March 29, the last American troops departed the south; the only American military left were the U.S. Marine guards at the U.S. Embassy in Saigon. For the United States, the

These young men, from all of South Vietnam's 44 provinces, will return to their native villages after 13 weeks' training at the National Training Center, c. 1970. Courtesy of the Department of Defense.

The air evacuation of siege-stricken Vietnamese from Saigon to the U.S. was conducted after the Babylift operation. Vietnamese militants and civilians await their C-141 journey during a stopover in Thailand, 1975. Courtesy of the National Archives.

war was over. The long Vietnamese civil war ended on April 30, 1975, when Saigon and South Vietnam fell to PAVN forces.

NOTES

1. Stanley Karnow, *Vietnam: A History* (New York: Viking Press, 1983), 139.

2. On May 12, 1942, an American pilot, John T. Donovan, was shot down and killed by Japanese antiaircraft fire over northern Vietnam, but his death was related to World War II and not American involvement in Vietnam.

3. Karnow, *Vietnam,* 169.

4. Department of Defense, *Annual Report for Fiscal Year 1968* (Washington, DC: U.S. Government Printing Office, 1971), 146.

5. George Donelson Moss, *Vietnam: An American Ordeal,* 3rd ed. (Upper Saddle River, NJ: Prentice Hall, 1998), 163.

6. George C. Herring, *America's Longest War: The United States and Vietnam, 1950–1975,* 3rd ed. (New York: McGraw-Hill, 1996), 139.

7. Michael Holmes, "Tapes: Vietnam 'Mess' Tortured LBJ," *The Cincinnati Enquirer,* February 15, 1997.

8. Robert J. McMahon, *Major Problems in the History of the Vietnam War,* 2nd ed. (Lexington, MA: D.C. Heath, 1995), 209–10.

9. Moss, *Vietnam,* 173.

10. Philip Caputo, *A Rumor of War* (New York: Holt, Rinehart, and Winston, 1977), xii.

11. H. Bruce Franklin, "The Antiwar Movement We Are Supposed to Forget," *The Touchstone* 10 (2000). Retrieved from http://www.rtis.com/touchstone/nov00/07anti.htm.

12. Karnow, *Vietnam,* 541.

CHAPTER 2

Recruitment, Training, and Assignment for the War in Vietnam

THE VIETNAM WAR ERA DRAFT

During the Vietnam War era, 1964–1973, roughly 8,615,000 men served in the armed forces. They entered the military in one of two ways: they either enlisted voluntarily or were drafted under the Selective Service Act. Approximately 2,215,000 men were drafted. Draftees were obligated to spend two years in the armed forces.

The use of the draft to provide much of the needed manpower for the war would be one of the more controversial aspects of the conflict, partially because of the controversial nature of the war itself, but also due to inequities in the Selective Service law, particularly in the use of deferments, which meant that while most middle- and upper-class men could avoid induction, the draft fell heaviest on minorities, the poor, and the working class.

To understand an individual's decision either to accept or refuse induction during the Vietnam War, one must recognize that the war was one of the most controversial in United States history, and one that bitterly divided the American people. Proponents of the war claimed that by defending South Vietnam, we were containing Communism and preventing its spread to neighboring nations. Opponents of the war believed that South Vietnam was not a pro-Western democracy, but a corrupt dictatorship, created and artificially sustained by American power. American troops were not protectors, but imperialists, and some were so-called baby killers, guilty of atrocities against the Vietnamese people. The fairness of the draft was also another major factor in one's decision to accept induction.

Ironically, the Vietnam era draft, which became synonymous with racism and class privilege, began as an attempt to eliminate those factors from the process. Theoretically, the Selective Service Act of 1948, which governed all aspects of the Vietnam War era draft, treated all recruits equally, regardless of race or class. All men were required to register for the draft at age 18, but after the Korean War ended in July 1953, the military neither needed nor wanted all the potential recruits, so the Pentagon took steps to limit the potential manpower pool to a more reasonable level. Draft-eligible men between 18 and 25 were in a primary draft pool, but once a registrant reached 26, he went into a secondary category, reducing the number of potential draftees. The minimum mental and physical standards for induction were also raised. The primary method employed, however, was to expand the occupational, educational, and other types of deferments allowable under the provisions of the Selective Service Act. Married men, especially fathers, were placed in a low-priority category. Undergraduate and graduate college students' deferments became virtually automatic. Those in protected industrial, agricultural, or professional occupations received a deferment. Draft boards could also grant deferments based on hardship or conscientious objection to war. Under this system, the military got enough recruits to fill the ranks each year, and the civilian economy and society suffered less disruption because those considered more productive and valuable, meaning middle- and upper-class whites, were generally spared service. The Pentagon referred to this policy as "manpower channeling," arguing that it was in the interest of the nation to exempt students and many professionals and skilled workers.

After 1953, and through the early 1960s, draft calls were relatively low; there were no major wars, and minorities and working-class whites viewed military service favorably. Allen Thomas graduated from Lincoln Grant High School in Covington, Kentucky, in 1957, only to receive his draft notice the morning of his 18th birthday. But like most other young black or working-class white men in the late 1950s, he viewed military service as an opportunity. He had a wife, a child, and no means of employment, so being drafted was "fine by me." Most of his friends also went into the military. It was "almost ritualistic, common for most of the males to leave and go into the service. The upper strata had a chance for college, but all the poor kids like me joined the service."[1] Consequently, there was little controversy regarding deferments, or the fairness of the draft in general, between the Korean and Vietnam wars. Beginning with direct American involvement in Vietnam in 1965, however, the draft calls increased significantly. In 1964, 112,386 men were drafted, but the number more than doubled to 230,991 the following year. In 1966, over 382,000 men were conscripted into the armed forces.

LOCAL DRAFT BOARDS

If called, the potential draftee had the right to appeal an existing deferment or to request one from his local draft board. During the Vietnam War, there were 4,080 local draft boards in operation. Local boards were composed of three members, and to help ensure fairness, board members were expected to be residents of a neighborhood located within their district; however, that was not always the case. The Selective Service Act stated that "if at all practicable," members of their own communities should select draftees, but the policy was neither mandated nor enforced.[2]

Most of the board members were hard-working, civic-minded people who took their duties very seriously. "I'm for anything that will seem the fairest way and with the least amount of fuss," explained Dr. William M. Springer, who chaired Board No. 53 in Hamilton County, Ohio.[3] In many cases, however, local draft boards were neither representative nor typical of the communities they served, nor of the young men that appeared before them. The average local board member was male, white, middle-aged, and middle class as working-class people seldom had the time, connections, or inclination to serve in unpaid positions. Typically, board members were military veterans, usually of World War II or Korea—although in 1966, a handful of veterans from World War I still served on draft boards.

Throughout much of the war, African Americans, in particular, were greatly under-represented on boards throughout the country. This was especially true in the South. In 1966, for example, African Americans made up 13.4 percent of the draft calls, but the 230 blacks sitting on local boards amounted to only 1.3 percent of total draft board membership. There were no black board members at all in Alabama, Arkansas, Georgia, Louisiana, Mississippi, and South Carolina.[4] Pressure by civil rights organizations did have some effect, and by 1970, there would be 1,265 African Americans serving on local draft boards nationwide, but this was still only 6.6 percent of the total.[5] The racial and often racist preconceptions that many whites held concerning African Americans was a major problem blacks faced in dealing with predominately white local draft boards. Some of the whites on the boards were avowed racists. A Grand Dragon of a Louisiana Ku Klux Klan organization, Jack Helms, was head of Local 42 in New Orleans, the largest draft board in the state, from 1957, until Hershey removed him in 1966 after protests by the NAACP.

The racial and class makeup of the local boards was extremely important because they wielded great discretionary power in determining if someone would be drafted or not. Local boards were also granted considerable latitude in making their decisions, and they were not necessarily bound by standing policies or practices; in effect, they could do pretty much as they chose. According to Selective Service regulations, the local boards had the authority to "draft or defer any person—subject to appeal—regardless of any test, exam, selective service system class standing or another means."[6]

DEFERMENTS, RACE, AND CLASS

Early in the war, most Americans were not concerned about the legitimacy of the draft, but rather about its fairness. A 1966 Harris poll found overwhelming support for the principle of selective service, with only 37 percent of those polled stating that the system was unfair. Most criticism of the Selective Service system during the war focused on the deferment system. During the Vietnam War era, over 15,410,000 draft-age men were exempted, deferred, or disqualified from military service. The vast majority of men receiving deferments were white and middle or upper class, meaning that a disproportionate number of working-class whites and minorities were drafted. Race and class were certainly powerful factors in determining who would, or would not, be called. Eighty percent of the men drafted during the Vietnam War era came from poor or working-class backgrounds.[7] Blacks made up roughly 11 percent of the draft-eligible population during the Vietnam War, for example, but they accounted for roughly 16 percent of all draftees. To put it another way, in 1964, an eligible African American had a 30 percent chance of being drafted, whereas for a white, it was only 18 percent. As the war escalated, so did one's chance of being called up, regardless of race. By 1967, almost one third of eligible whites were being drafted, but the figure for African Americans had also risen to nearly 64 percent of those eligible for induction.

Historically, the black community had overwhelmingly supported America's wars, partially to prove their military prowess and patriotism to skeptical whites, but also as a bargaining chip in the fight for equality and civil rights. Vietnam was different. While many black leaders and organizations supported the war—the NAACP, for example—numerous leaders, from Stokely Carmichael to Dr. King, opposed the war and the use of the draft to raise manpower. On January 6, 1966, for example, SNCC spokesperson

Sgt. Gerald Laird of the 101st Airborne Division fires an M60 machine gun. Known as "The Pig," the M60 was belt-fed and fired up to 550 7.62-millimeter rounds per minute. Courtesy of the U.S. Army.

John Lewis issued a statement from the organization condemning American partici-pation in the Vietnam War and the use of the draft. Lewis stated that SNCC was "in sympathy with and [in support of] the men in this country who are unwilling to respond to a military draft which would compel them to contribute their lives to United States aggression in Vietnam ... in the name of the 'freedom' we find so false in this country."[8] In April 1967, Dr. King urged draft-age men to file as conscientious objectors and re-fuse to fight. Others argued that since blacks were second-class citizens, without all the privileges of citizenship, they also did not share the same responsibilities as whites and should not be liable for the draft. SNCC activists Cleveland Sellers and Stokely Carmi-chael went a step further and claimed that the draft was actually a form of ethnic cleans-ing, calling it "black genocide" and a plan to eliminate African American men.

Another factor affecting the draft was education. A 1980 Veterans Affairs study indicated that draft-eligible men with less than a high school education appeared three times as likely to be drafted as those with a college education.[9] Middle- and upper-class whites benefited from many aspects of the Vietnam era draft, but the use of educational deferments, in particular, becomes synonymous with class privilege during the war. Educational deferments were virtually automatic, making colleges a very safe refuge from the draft. Once you were in, it was difficult to lose the exemption. You could get expelled or flunk out, but even these threats were often minimized or eliminated. Many professors opposed the war, and others did not want to be responsible for sending some-one to Vietnam, so they were reluctant to flunk draft-eligible young men.

Technically, the deferment system did not discriminate. To qualify for an educational deferment, a student had to be working full-time toward a degree that would be completed in four years, and it was just as easy for a poor or black student to get a college deferment as it was for a white student.[10] Future associate justice of the Supreme Court Clarence Thomas, for example, was a student at Holy Cross in Massachusetts during the war and received a deferment. The hard part was paying for it. College was expensive, and few working-class or black families could afford it. Consequently, only about 5 percent of draft-eligible African Americans were in college during the war. Surprisingly, most people supported the use of educational deferments, especially early in the war. Seventy percent of the respondents in a 1966 poll supported college deferments, but the results were somewhat divided according to education. Eighty-five percent of those with a college education supported it, but only 57 percent for those with only an eighth-grade education were in favor of educational exemptions.

A college deferment was seldom enough to cover an individual the entire time until he reached age 26 and was placed in a lower-priority category. Most needed or requested multiple deferments after their initial undergraduate deferment had lapsed. Many prominent men, such as future president Bill Clinton, future vice president Dick Cheney, conservative writer and columnist George Will, future secretary of education Bill Bennett, and future speaker of the house Newt Gingrich, had graduate school deferments. Cheney exhausted four student and graduate student deferments and then, as a father, was granted a paternity deferment, exempting him from the armed forces. Bill Clinton had an undergraduate deferment until 1966 and a graduate school deferment to attend Oxford University as a Rhodes Scholar. When this expired, he enrolled in the University of Arkansas Law School and its advanced Reserve Officer Training Corps (ROTC) program, gaining him a Reserve exemption. Clinton then gave up his ROTC exemption and allowed himself to be reclassified I-A, or eligible for military service, but it was late in the war by then, and his chances of actually being drafted were minimal.

Medical deferments were another popular method for escaping the draft. Numerous ailments, from flat feet to severe allergies, would disqualify someone from military service. Again, middle- and upper-class individuals, and those connected to wealth and privilege, benefited more from this than did the poor and working class. The elites had access to superior, or at least more attentive, health care, and most could find some sort of deferrable ailment. Harvard senior James Fallows remembered, "Sympathetic medical students [at Harvard] helped us search for disqualifying conditions that we...might have overlooked."[11] Military physicians were usually understaffed and overworked and usually deferred to the professional opinion of a civilian specialist. In 1966, a mentally qualified white inductee was 50 percent more likely than a mentally qualified African American to fail his preinduction physical. By 1970, over 33 percent of white inductees, but less than one out of four African Americans, failed their preinduction physicals.[12]

THE NATIONAL GUARD AND THE ARMY RESERVE

Some draft-eligible men found a way to serve, honorably, and still avoid the risk of being sent to Vietnam by joining either the National Guard or the Armed Forces Reserve. George W. Bush said that he joined the Texas Air National Guard because "I was not prepared to shoot my eardrum out with a shotgun in order to get a deferment. Nor was I willing to go to Canada.... So I chose to better myself by learning how to fly airplanes."[13] Future vice president Dan Quayle served in a headquarters unit of the Indiana National Guard, and future house minority leader Richard Gephardt served in the Missouri Air National Guard from 1965 to 1971.

Service in the National Guard or Reserve did entail military obligations. To get into the Reserve, applicants had to take the Armed Forces Qualification Test and sign up for a six-year term. They went through Active Duty for Training (ACDUTRA), normally a four-month period divided into eight weeks of basic training. This was followed by another eight weeks of specialized training as an infantryman, cook, clerk, or a variety of other military occupational specialties (MOS). The reservist is on inactive status and for five years fulfilled his obligation through periodic weekend meetings and the two-week annual ACDUTRA summer camp. Some talented reservists discharged their obligation by using their special skills or abilities on behalf of the military. Singer Jack Jones, for example, worked for Armed Forces Radio in Hollywood as his reserve duty. Guardsmen were subject to annual training and temporary call-up for duty once a year.

The Guard, and to a lesser degree the Reserve, did serve as a relatively safe haven from the war. President Lyndon Johnson did not want to risk disrupting the economy by mobilizing the Guard and Reserve, so only 38,000 National Guardsmen were called into federal service during the Vietnam War. Mostly, they were called up for riot duty. In late July 1967, over 10,000 National Guardsmen were called up as part of Task Force Detroit to help quell domestic disturbances in that city, and in 1968, 16,000 guardsmen supported police and regular troops suppressing rioters in the aftermath of Dr. King's assassination. Over 5,000 Illinois Guardsmen were called up in August 1968 during riots at the Democratic National Convention in Chicago. The chances of a National Guardsmen being sent to Vietnam were remote, however. Only 15,000 National Guardsmen went to Vietnam, and almost all in 1968, during the height of American combat involvement. All were volunteers, and most were officers, warrant officers, or noncommissioned officers (NCOs). Consequently, as early as 1966, a Pentagon study found that nearly 71 percent of all Guard enlistments appeared to be draft-motivated. The Reserve were also viewed as a reprieve from serving in Vietnam. In 1969, there were 752,000 men in the Army Reserve and the National Guard, and by 1970, the National Guard had a waiting list of over 100,000 applicants. James Cantwell, president of the National Guard Association, believed that 90 percent of all guard enlistments that year were draft-motivated.

To reduce favoritism, the Pentagon ordered that as of February 1, 1967, all Reserve vacancies were to be filled strictly in order of application, but this was not the case with the National Guard. Each state controlled its own National Guard organization and its own appointment process, which was frequently influenced by political pressure, corruption, and local considerations. An influential ally in state government, for instance, could move an applicant's name up the appointment list.[14]

Professional athletes often benefited from favoritism in securing positions in the Guard or Reserve. Some star athletes did serve in the military, and some in the war. Hiesman Trophy winner and Naval Academy graduate Roger Staubach, for example, served in Vietnam and completed his obligation to the Navy before going on to a hall of fame career with the Dallas Cowboys. Many, however, avoided active duty and Vietnam. Some, surprisingly, received medical deferments. Buffalo Bills quarterback Jack Kemp and New York Jets quarterback Joe Namath were both healthy enough to star in the National Football League but sought medical deferments from military service. Others discharged their obligation through service in the Guard or Reserve. The group with whom Bush was sworn in to the Texas Air National Guard included two congressmens' sons and several members of the Dallas Cowboys. In 1967, there were 313 professional athletes in the Army Reserve and Army National Guard, 28 in the Air Force Reserve and Air National Guard, 16 in the Marine Reserve, and 3 in the Naval Reserve; all but two of them were already professionals at the time of their enlistments.[15]

The Guard and Reserve were composed largely of middle- and upper-class whites. The Third Battalion, 385th Regiment, Second Brigade, 76th Division, U.S. Army Reserve was fairly typical in its composition of many other Reserve units during the Vietnam War. The only African American in one company was a Columbia Law School student. Most of the members of the unit had college undergraduate degrees, and some graduate degrees, including several MBAs. Another half a dozen were working on degrees in night school. Taking officers and enlisted men into account, the average salary in the battalion was around $10,000 a year. The median income for an average family was $8,274 a year.[16]

In 1965, only 5,590 men out of a total of 411,533 men in the Army National Guard were black, or less than 2 percent of the total. The racial and class injustice prevalent in securing Guard or Reserve positions during the Vietnam War angered many in the regular military. Writing years later, Colin Powell remarked, "I am angry that so many of the sons of the powerful and well-placed...managed to wangle slots in Reserve and National Guard units....Of the many tragedies of Vietnam, this raw class discrimination strikes me as the most damaging to the ideal that all Americans are created equal and owe equal allegiance to their country."[17]

CONSCIENTIOUS OBJECTORS

Many potential draftees were morally opposed to military service of any kind, and to war in general, or Vietnam in particular, and applied for conscientious objector (CO) deferments. CO status was based on guidelines established in a 1965 Supreme Court decision, *U.S. v. Seeger.* CO status could be based on either religious or moral grounds, "a given belief that is sincere and meaningful" and "occupies a place in the life of its possessor parallel to that filled by the orthodox belief in God of one who clearly qualifies for the exemption."[18] It also helped greatly to belong to a traditionally pacifistic denomination, such as the Amish, Quakers, or Mennonites. The Justice Department, for example, refused to grant CO status to black Muslims because they claimed that the Nation of Islam did not meet the criteria as a traditionally pacifistic organization because they "only objected to certain wars under certain conditions"; they were allowed to fight only if Islamic religious leaders deemed a conflict a holy war, or jihad.[19] But even non-Muslin African Americans applying for CO status were suspect in the eyes of some whites. "Few Negro boys...are true conscientious objectors," claimed a member of a Chicago draft board. "They say they object to going because of religious reasons....They pretend to believe in God and say I don't want to kill anybody, then right afterwards they go out in the streets and cut some person's throat."[20]

COs usually had to perform alternative service of some kind. Hundreds received medical training through a program at Fort Sam Houston, Texas, for example. But many resisters also refused to serve in any capacity. Robert James received a CO deferment from his Mississippi draft board but then refused to perform alternative service in a distant town. He was convicted of refusing induction and sentenced to five years in a federal prison.

AVOIDING INDUCTION

Some men chose to leave the United States rather than face either induction or jail for draft resistance. During the Vietnam War, an estimated 40,000–50,000 draft-age men sought political asylum, mostly in Canada, Sweden, and Mexico, but also in other countries. A few, for example, went to the Soviet Union. Some nations, such as Sweden, provided some assistance, but asylum in a foreign country was generally expensive, making it difficult for poor whites and most blacks to take advantage of it. But many African Americans would do so anyway, believing that the war was racist and wrong and their actions morally justifiable. One young black who went to Canada summed it up by remarking, "I'm not a draft evader. I'm a runaway slave. I left because I was not going to fight white America's war."[21]

Some sought illegal alternatives to the draft, such as forgery and bribery, to avoid induction. Many doctors, some opposed to the war, others merely for profit, were willing to fake or greatly exaggerate a medical condition to keep someone out of the service. In New York City and Cleveland, Ohio, federal authorities arrested 38 fathers and sons for buying falsified documentation to qualify for a deferment, some paying as much as $5,000 for the fake papers. A few draft board officials found that selling deferments was a quite lucrative enterprise. One New York draft board member was caught and convicted of selling deferments and exemptions for as much as $30,000.

Other resisters pursued legal means to avoid induction. Selective Service law was very complicated, and in addition to the numerous deferments, there were many loopholes that a skilled attorney could manipulate to a client's advantage. One of the most popular and successful loopholes was the so-called order of call defense. All draftees were supposed to be called up in an orderly and proscribed fashion in the same order in which their names appeared on the draft rolls. All a lawyer had to do was prove that someone had been called up before everyone else ahead of him on the list, and this automatically invalidated the induction orders. Draft rolls usually contained tens of thousands of names, and a persistent lawyer could find at least one and usually numerous names ahead of their client on the draft list that had not been called up. Though this method was usually successful, it was also expensive. Lawyers' fees usually ran around $2,500, or about half the yearly income for most working-class and minority families. There were some free—and legal—alternatives available to poor whites and minorities attempting to avoid induction: the ACLU, the NAACP, and the National Lawyers Guild were willing to provide legal assistance in many cases, and the Student Non-Violent Coordinating Committee and the Vietnam Veterans against the War/Winter Soldier Organization provided free draft counseling. Religious-based organizations, such as the American Friends Service Committee and the Catholic Peace Fellowship, provided counseling on a variety of draft- and service-related issues. The religious groups in particular had a high success rate early in the war, but almost all the agencies provided effective help.

The lawyers and legal aid organizations were successful due in part to the difficulty and time involved in prosecuting draft evaders. A draft board decision could be appealed in federal court, which often proved more lenient than local draft boards. Members of the antidraft movement had also decided to contest their inductions in court, hoping to flood and overburden the legal system with antidraft cases. The appeal process alone could often take several years, effectively preventing an individual's induction. As the war became more unpopular, many prosecutors declined to bring charges. Consequently, most draft resisters and activists were never arrested or tried for their actions. Out of an estimated 570,000 draft resisters, less than half, or around 210,000, were even accused, let alone prosecuted by federal authorities. Alex Jack, a founder the New England Resistance movement, was interrogated by the Federal Bureau of Investigation (FBI) and expelled from the Boston University School of Theology, but his local board never reclassified him I-A, and he was never called up or prosecuted. Larry Etscovitz, of the antidraft movement at Boston College, had committed a federal crime when he turned in his draft card at an antidraft rally in 1967, and then he refused to cooperate when he was called in for his preinduction physical a year later, but he was never arrested or prosecuted. In fact, his draft board simply gave him a deferment and reclassified him. Yale drama student David Clennon also destroyed his draft card and participated in the antidraft movement for a year before he was called in for induction. The board rejected his application for a CO deferment, granting him a psychological one instead.

Many activists and evaders, however, were arrested and tried. Dr. Benjamin Spock, Yale chaplain, William Sloane Coffin Jr., and three other prominent individuals in the antidraft resistance were tried and convicted in 1968 for antidraft and antiwar activities. But like many in the resistance, they never spent a day in jail. Their sentences were all reversed on appeal in 1969.[22] Many resisters were, of course, punished and spent time in prison. In 1968, David Miller was sentenced to 30 months in prison, and Tom Cornell to six months, for burning their draft cards and refusing induction. African American draft resisters often received particularly long sentences.

MUHAMMAD ALI AND GEORGE HAMILTON

Heavyweight boxer Muhammad Ali was perhaps the most famous individual to refuse to serve in the military during the Vietnam War. Ali was born Cassius Clay in Louisville, Kentucky, in 1942 and registered for the draft when he turned 18 in 1960. Clay went on to win a gold medal in boxing at the Rome Olympics that year. Two years later, in March 1962, his Louisville draft board classified him I-A, or eligible for conscription, but the rising young boxer faced little chance of being conscripted. The war in Vietnam had yet to escalate, and draft calls were low. His chances of getting drafted were further reduced when he failed the Armed Forces Qualifying Test in January 1964. A score in the 30th percentile or above was needed for induction, but the boxer managed a score only in the 16th percentile. A second exam proved that Ali had not purposely failed the first one, and he was then reclassified by his draft board as 1-Y, or mentally unfit for service. The chances of Ali being drafted now seemed very remote. A few weeks later, Ali defeated Sonny Liston for the world's heavyweight championship and then shocked the world by announcing, in February 1964, that he had joined the Nation of Islam. Furthermore, he was changing his name at the direction of the Honorable Elijah Muhammad from Cassius Marcellus Clay to Muhammad Ali.

As Ali rose in fame and in controversy, the war in Vietnam began to escalate, and the armed forces needed more draftees to help meet its manpower requirements. In 1965, the Department of Defense lowered its minimum physical and mental standards and reduced the minimum score needed for induction from 30 to 15. Ali was now eligible for conscription, and on February 17, 1966, his Louisville draft board informed the heavyweight champion that he had been reclassified back to I-A status and would be drafted. Ali knew that he would not have to fight in Vietnam if drafted. The army planned to send him on tour to promote the armed forces and to entertain the other troops, similar

Muhammad Ali, 1967. Courtesy of the Library of Congress.

to what heavyweight champion Joe Louis did in World War II. Ali was deeply religious and convinced that supporting the war would violate his principles. A month later, on March 17, he applied for CO status with his local draft board, citing his membership in the Nation of Islam. Ali was always controversial, in and out of the ring, but he hurt his own cause in an interview at his Miami home when he told reporters that he had no "personal quarrel with those Vietcongs" and that he could not serve in Vietnam because it was not a declared holy war. Ali's petition for CO status was rejected by his Kentucky draft board, so his lawyers then tried several different tactics; they filed for a CO deferment again, this one based on conscious and not his affiliation with the Nation of Islam, and requested a hardship deferment due to his alimony payments to ex-wife Sonji Clay. Like Cleveland Sellers and other black draft resisters, they also cited the absence of African Americans on local draft boards. None of the tactics worked, and all of Ali's appeals were denied by his Louisville draft board.[23] Ali still had one last chance. At a special hearing at the Justice Department in front of retired judge Lawrence Graham, Ali's lawyer Hayden Covington claimed that Ali was studying to become a minister in the Nation of Islam and requested a ministerial exemption. On August 23, 1966, Judge Graham recommended that Ali be granted CO status, but on March 6, 1967, the Appeal Board turned Ali down, apparently at the urging of Justice Department officials, who had contacted the Appeal Board and requested a negative decision. Ali was then told to report for induction in April 1967.

On April 28, 1967, Ali reported to the Houston Induction Center but refused to take the step forward indicating that he accepted induction when they called his name. To be on the safe side, the induction officer called out both Ali and Clay to make sure there was no confusion. Later that month, the World Boxing Association stripped Ali of his heavyweight title, and on June 20, 1967, he was convicted of draft evasion and sentenced to five years in prison and fined $10,000.[24]

Ali was not the only celebrity embroiled in a controversy with his local draft board. Occurring at the same time, and in stark contrast to Ali's difficult and trying ordeal, was the case of actor George Hamilton. If Ali's fight against the draft embodied the courage and determination of a black man to fight injustice, George Hamilton symbolized white privilege and much of what was wrong with the system. Like Ali, Hamilton was wealthy and successful, and like Ali, he had originally registered for the draft before the war in Vietnam escalated. In December 1961, Hamilton applied for and was granted an extreme hardship deferment by his local board in Manhattan, New York, and was classified 3-A on the basis that he was the sole support of his widowed mother. Hardship deferments were granted if the applicant was desperately needed by a dependent or dependents and was directly responsible for their personal or economic well-being. Many draft boards, especially in more affluent neighborhoods, usually granted the deferment, even if there were no real grounds for it. Hamilton's family was hardly in desperate straits. Hamilton was at the height of his career in the fall of 1966; he commanded $100,000 a movie and had made five of them in the previous 15 months. He also made money from television appearances. He drove a Rolls Royce and was often seen escorting Lynda Bird Johnson, President Lyndon Johnson's daughter. The 27-year-old actor and his mother, Mrs. Anne Potter Hamilton Hunt Spalding, lived in a 39-room mansion in Beverly Hills, California, named Greyhall, built originally by Douglas Fairbanks and Mary Pickford. He was confident and could joke about his success. When asked by a reporter if maintaining the mansion consumed most of his income, he remarked, "I'm in a business that supports my habits."[25]

Critics did not see his hardship deferment as a joke, however. Hamilton's New York City draft board reviewed and renewed his deferment at least five times between 1961 and 1966, and by then, he was over the age of 26 and automatically placed in a lower-priority category. But the heavy draft calls for Vietnam that year led Selective Service officials to believe that they may have had to call up men from this group, and that was when the public found out about the conditions surrounding Hamilton's not-so-hardship deferment. The public was outraged at this travesty of fairness. The *New York Times* referred to him as a "principal target of those disgruntled with the draft system."

On October 27, 1966, the actor was ordered by Central Manhattan Draft Board No. 8 to report for a physical examination on November 7. Selective Service officials said that Hamilton was just one of thousands of men in his age group called in for physicals. The officials admitted that the public protest over Hamilton's deferment was also a factor in their decision. Hamilton had the dubious distinction of replacing Muhammad Ali "as the chief target of angry mothers, uneasy draft-age youths, and others disgruntled with the Selective Service System," according to one official with the draft. Over the winter of 1965–1966, the Selective Service's Washington office had received "scores of letters each month" stating that Ali should be drafted, and now they were receiving scores of letters complaining about Hamilton's deferment. Letters complaining about Muhammad Ali were still arriving, but "now definitely fallen into second place" to the hate mail concerning George Hamilton.[26]

Hamilton's draft board promised to review Hamilton's status in two months, but the actor and most of the other men holding similar deferments were never called up. The system had worked to protect them from the draft, but often did little to help those who truly needed the help. George Hamilton stayed a civilian in Hollywood, but Edward Neal, an African American from Tehula, Mississippi, ended up in the army. Unlike Hamilton, his draft board turned down his request for a hardship deferment, even though he worked two jobs and was the sole supporter of his mother, disabled father, and eight siblings.

Hamilton may have been viewed as a symbol of wealth and privilege, and Ali of a principled dissenter, but they shared one important thing in common: unlike Edward Neal, neither of them had to go to Vietnam. On June 28, 1971, the Supreme Court overturned Ali's conviction, but it did so based on a legal technicality and did not use the case to decide any issues relevant to the draft and CO status. By then, the war was winding down, and a series of reforms had removed most loopholes in the draft. In 1968, Congress eliminated graduate school deferments, but the way the law was written, it effectively protected those already in graduate school until 1970. In 1969, the old system of choosing inductees was replaced with the lottery system, based on one's birthday. Each day of the year was chosen at random and assigned a number from 1 to 365. The lower the number of one's birthday, the greater the likelihood of being called up. By the time the Selective Service held its first draft lottery on December 1, 1969, however, the process of Vietnamization, or ending America's role in the war, had begun, and the draft calls for 1971 and 1972 were relatively light compared to preceding years, and a recruit's chances of being sent to Southeast Asia had diminished appreciably. Undergraduate exemptions ended in September 1971 but still covered the graduation class of 1972. The last man drafted entered the army on June 30, 1973, one of only 646 conscripted that year.

ENLISTING IN THE ARMED FORCES

One of the ironies of the Vietnam War era draft was that the socioeconomic groups most likely to be drafted supported the system more so than did middle- and upper-class whites with little chance of being drafted and sent to Vietnam. Some even joined through the volunteer draft program. A person who volunteered to be drafted was treated differently from enlistees. A volunteer draftee was liable for two years of service and had little say in where the army or marines trained and sent them. An enlistee usually signed up for three, and in some cases, four years, but often could choose from several MOS. In 1968, Gonzalo Baltazar quit school at age 17 and enlisted in the army under the volunteer draft program; his parents had to sign for him because he was underage. "I just needed a little more discipline in my life at the time because I was kind of headed the wrong direction," he recalled. Baltazar also came from a family where military service was the norm. He was one of seven brothers to serve in the military, but, as it would turn out, the only one to serve in Vietnam.[27]

Despite the controversy over the draft, the majority of young men entering the armed services during the Vietnam War era did so voluntarily. Between 1960 and 1975,

8,720,000 men enlisted in the armed forces. At the height of the war in 1968, the military drafted 343,000 men, but another 513,000 volunteered as first-time enlistees. They volunteered for a variety of reasons. Some came from military families and were idealists. Gordon Roberts joined the army a month after turning 19 and three days after graduating from high school. His father and stepfather had both served in World War II, and his brothers had recently enlisted. Roberts was influenced by President John F. Kennedy's idealism and the promise of his New Frontier. Growing up in Lebanon, Ohio, a small community north of Cincinnati, also played a part: "The citizen soldier concept was very strong. Lebanon was...a very patriotic community." It was a small, traditional, Midwestern community, with "hot dogs, mom, apple pie." Roberts believed, "It just seemed a smarter idea to do service to country first rather than pursue a college education.... I guess serving my country has always been my ideal. I have always loved the army and service to my country."[28] Some had high ideals but also looked forward to a little adventure in their lives. Philip Caputo enlisted in the Marine Corps partly to escape his safe, suburban life in Westchester, Illinois.

Many of the enlistees had deferments and did not have to serve, yet many college graduates volunteered for Vietnam, especially early in the war. Some did so for career opportunities. John Ron Ballweg had a student deferment and a good job but found civilian life and office work boring. He was not an "inside person," so he enlisted in the army in January 1964. Patriotism was not a major factor; he felt he had a chance to travel and advance himself.[29] Future senator and presidential candidate John Kerry enlisted in the navy after graduating from Yale in 1966. Kerry was typical of his graduating class. Many of the best and the brightest at Yale that year also joined up, including the future head of Federal Express, Fred Smith, who joined the marines, and Richard Pershing, the grandson of World War I hero and army general John "Blackjack" Pershing, who must have astonished his famous ancestor by also enlisting in the marines. Sixty graduates of Harvard, Yale, and Princeton who volunteered for service were killed in Vietnam. Some privileged whites, such as Kerry and Pershing, did choose to go to Vietnam, but this was more likely early in the war rather than later. By 1968, when future president George W. Bush graduated, virtually no one from his class at Yale chose to enlist in the active armed forces. David Thorne, who was a classmate of Kerry's at Yale in 1966, and, like him, also enlisted in the navy, confessed that much changed between 1966 and 1968. "If it had been '68," he admitted, "we might have made a different decision."[30]

Because the navy and air force were not as directly involved in the war as the army or marines, many draft-eligible young men often enlisted in one of these branches. This was especially true for minorities. John Brackett enlisted in the navy to avoid being drafted into the army.[31] Before the Vietnam War, African Americans made up only about 5 percent of the enlisted personnel in both the air force and navy. By 1972, African Americans were 7.3 percent of the navy's enlisted strength and 12.6 percent of the air force's.[32]

Recruiting officers from all branches of the armed forces told prospective recruits that they would get a better deal, or the ability to pick a good MOS, if they joined voluntarily. A recruiting officer told John Ballweg that he could choose his own MOS if he enlisted but that the army would send him wherever they wanted if he were drafted.[33] James Daly, a CO, enlisted in 1966 rather than be drafted because a recruiting officer promised him that he could choose a noncombat MOS, such as cooking or clerical duties, by volunteering. Anthony Preston could not find a good civilian job and knew that he would probably be drafted anyway, so he went ahead and enlisted, hoping to land in a field other than combat infantryman. In the late 1950s, Albert Childs served in the Vermont National Guard while still in high school and joined the Army Reserve while attending Paul Smith College in upstate New York but was not assigned to a particular unit. During the Lebanon crisis, he received a letter from the army stating that if he was not in a unit, he was liable to be drafted. He did not mind being drafted but wanted to get his military service out of the way before he started a career, so he enlisted.[34]

Childs, like many, enlisted because they lacked job opportunities in the civilian world. "It was just a thing, being raised in Vermont," stated Childs. "Everybody who is able goes into the service. And a very high number stay in the service and make it a career because there's no employment [in Vermont] and they have to go elsewhere."[35] Life in the armed forces meant security, decent pay, and a chance for advancement. In 1964, an E-2, a private first class, earned around $60 a week. An E-4, a rank most enlistees could hope to obtain in three years, paid $75 a week, with no food, clothing, medical, or housing expenses. Married servicepersons were eligible for even additional benefits. In 1966, married army E-3 Tim Wood, for example, made $99 a week and a dependent allotment of $40 a month.[36] Service with an elite unit, such as the paratroops, could add another $55 a month in jump pay. A tour of duty in Vietnam meant special pay and privileges such as $65 a month hostile fire pay, free postage, no customs duty on purchases under $50, and no taxes on any special pay. Officers received the same plus a $500 per month tax exclusion. The military also offered a chance for advancement and promotion, providing opportunities that usually did not exist for poor whites and minorities in the civilian world. Captain Sylvian Wailes, an African American, believed that "basically, the Army affords you as good an opportunity as you can find...there is at least a better, or more of an equal opportunity" than in the civilian world.[37]

A CAREER IN THE ARMED FORCES

Many working-class whites and African Americans left the armed forces only to return. Albert Childs originally "did not see a future for myself during my two years in the Army." He had gotten married, and his wife did not like the idea of going to Taiwan, which would have been his next assignment had he stayed in. "I got out and never dreamed that I would ever go back in the service." Childs worked construction for 11 months before returning to the army for 25 years.[38] Allen Thomas left the army in 1960, hoping to find a civilian job as a baker or in electronics, which he had learned in the Signal Corps. Allen was offered only entry-level, menial work, however, and rejoined the army 33 days after his discharge, and, like Childs, made the army a career.[39] Some returned to the armed forces but joined a different branch of the military. Gerald L. Kumpf, originally from Lexington, Nebraska, served in the U.S. Marine Corps from 1961 until 1966 and in the U.S. Air Force from 1967 until 1982. He enlisted in the Marine Corps air wing in 1961 because the army did not have anything he was interested in, and the air force and navy both required a high school diploma, which he did not have at the time.[40] Alfonza Wright left the navy and had a good job at Armco Steel in Baltimore but decided that military life offered better opportunity, and he reenlisted, this time in the army.[41]

The armed forces made a concerted effort to keep the men they already had. Gerald Kumpf and most of his unit were scheduled to get out of the marines in 1965. The unit MFA-314 was a new squadron formed four years earlier, and most of the experienced technicians would be leaving. Kumpf had only a few weeks left and was in a marine

Colin L. Powell. Courtesy of the Department of Defense.

program designed to "try and turn you back into some kind of civilized human" being—"it's like a de-conditioning program that they put you through"—when a colonel came in and told them that the marines were going into Vietnam soon and that they needed volunteers to extend their enlistments. Kumpf, now a crew chief, decided to extend for a year but considered it involuntary.[42]

Kumpf may have felt coerced, but the military had more positive enticements. They convinced men to reenlist by offering cash and other incentives. First-time reenlistees could net between $900 and $1,400 in cash bonuses, depending on rank and occupational skill.[43] Gerald Kumpf may have felt forced into extending his tour with the marines, but he did reenlist when the air force offered the Marine Corps veteran a few thousand dollars in bonuses with no basic training or tech school, and he had 30 days to report to his assignment if he would reenlist in their branch of the service. He entered as an E-3, and six weeks later, he was promoted to E-4.[44]

Many never left the armed forces. This was especially true for minorities. In 1966, 66 percent of all African Americans eligible to "re-up" did so, compared to only about

12 percent of eligible whites.[45] Private James Williams knew "a lot of brothers who will stay in the army because they're afraid to get out and face what's out there."[46] Staff Sergeant Charles Donald reenlisted in 1966 for six more years because "if I got out, I would have to take my chances," adding that there were no jobs in his native South Carolina available to blacks that would have paid as well as the military.[47] As a young lieutenant in 1961, Colin Powell recalled thinking that "if I stayed in the Army, I would soon be earning $360 a month, a magnificent $4,320 a year. I was in a profession that would allow me to go as far as my talents would take me. And for a black, no other avenue in American society offered so much opportunity."[48]

Powell also stayed because he loved army life and wanted a military career, as did many others who joined during the war. "I just wanted to join I guess," remembered David White, who enlisted in the navy after graduating from high school in 1966. White had planned to join the marines, but both times he went to the recruiting office, the Marine Corps representative was not there, but the navy recruiting officer was, and he wound up joining the navy.[49] Gerald L. Kumpf, from a farm family in Lexington, Nebraska, was in army ROTC in high school but dropped out his junior year. Kumpf entered the marines at age 17, after his parents finally consented to sign the enlistment papers. "I wanted to be a military man all my life.... I made that decision when I was probably about ten I think. I wanted to become a soldier" after the family bought its first TV set, and the first one in their county. "They used to show movies from World War II all the time, and so I was pretty well raised on those so you know a lot of John Wayne movies and what not." Like many enlistees, he had relatives that had served in the armed forces. Kumpf's father was a medal winner in World War II with the "Fighting 69th" and active in the American Legion; Kumpf grew up idolizing military veterans. "I just wanted to become a hero I guess."[50] Clifford L. Stanley wanted to be in the military all of his life. "No one could see him do anything else but join the service," his wife Rosalyn Stanley recalled. He attended the ROTC program at South Carolina State University, was the unit's guidon bearer, and was on the ceremonial rifle platoon. When he graduated in 1969 with a bachelor's degree in psychology, he immediately accepted a commission as a second lieutenant in the Marine Corps. Stanley himself said, "I just wanted to serve.... I wanted to be a Marine." The possibility of being drafted had no influence on his decision.[51]

The war in Vietnam was not a major factor in deciding to enlist for many young men. Some, like Powell or Kumpf, joined before direct American involvement. Others enlisted because they supported the war. David White's family was gung ho on Vietnam and kept up on the news. White still hedged his bets. The first person from his hometown, a relative by marriage, had already been killed in Vietnam before he enlisted, but White did not think that by joining the navy, he would end up in Vietnam.[52] Some were not paying much attention. The war in Vietnam did not influence Gonzalo Baltazar's decision to enlist. Baltazar did not pay much attention to the news on the war. "I really didn't think of me going to Vietnam.... It didn't even dawn on me that I was going in combat or even get close to Vietnam."[53]

PUNITIVE ENLISTMENT

Not all enlistments were strictly voluntary. During Vietnam, the military allowed local judges to present convicted offenders with an option of military service or jail time. The practice was known as punitive enlistment. The enlistee needed a waiver consent form, from both military and civilian authorities, and to be guilty only of relatively minor offenses.[54] Spencer E. Turner, regional supervisor of the Adult Parole Authority of Ohio, supported punitive enlistments and expressed an opinion common to other advocates of the practice: "It would do many of these men a world of good to serve in the armed forces. The old saying, 'The Army makes a man out of them,' is still true." Turner, who did parole work in World War II, when men with criminal records were liable for service, claimed, "In nearly every case, these men were better off for the experience of serving in the Army," and they made "fine soldiers."[55] Occasionally, that was true. James Hobson left Chicago a leader of the Vice Lords street gang and had served jail time for 43 offenses, including burglary and battery, before Judge Paul Epton gave him the choice of a state penitentiary or military service. Hobson returned from Vietnam a sergeant with a presidential commendation and with a new perspective on his gang days.[56]

Hobson was the exception, and not the rule. Most officers and NCOs believed that they made poor soldiers. Individuals that cannot obey the rules and regulations of civilian society could hardly be expected to accept and conform to the much more rigid discipline and expectations of the armed forces. General William Westmoreland hated punitive enlistments and believed that morale and discipline problems in the army during the Vietnam War were "heightened...by a tendency of civilian judges to forgive a man's dereliction in exchange for his enlisting in the Army, thus putting into uniform men with a penchant for trouble."[57] Several men in Gonzalo Baltazar's battalion in the 17th Infantry Division were punitive enlistments. "We had a lot of those." One man had purposely run over and killed someone with his car, but the judge still gave him the option of Vietnam or jail. He chose Vietnam, but like many punitive enlistees, he did not work out. He was one of the guys in the unit that "snapped and he couldn't handle the combat." He eventually went AWOL.[58] Some considered the practice racist and coercive. Radical black air force sergeant Clyde Taylor called punitive enlistment "a kind of modern Shanghai recruitment."[59] In 1972, the armed forces ended the practice of punitive enlistment and sent letters to numerous civilian judges and prosecutors, telling them to stop offering military service as an option to a prison sentence.[60] One of the reasons was because of Westmoreland's objections to the practice.[61]

PROJECT 100,000

Another controversial way to raise manpower for the war was what was known as Project 100,000. In August 1966, Secretary of Defense Robert McNamara announced that 100,000 young men who could not meet the military's minimum standards on the mental aptitude test would be enlisted annually in the army. McNamara called it the military version of President Lyndon Johnson's Great Society domestic reform program and promised that the inductees would receive training and educational opportunities they would not ordinarily have been able to get as civilians.[62] The Pentagon hoped to raise 140,000 "New Standards" men, as they were officially called, and the program got off to a successful start when they exceeded the 40,000-man target for 1966 by 9,000 recruits. By June 30, 1968, over 118,000 men had been accepted under the program, about half of them volunteers. All told, around 246,000 men were brought into the army under Project 100,000. Much like punitive enlistments, the New Standards men often lacked the education and discipline to make good soldiers. Less than half of the project's recruits had high school diplomas, and over one-third could not read at the fifth-grade level.

Only 90 percent of them successfully completed basic training, compared to 96 percent for all other recruits. Many considered the program racist because 41 percent of the recruits were black.[63] They were basically warm bodies for the infantry units. Thirty-seven percent were assigned to combat arms, and half of them ended up in Vietnam. Most did not receive the educational opportunities they were promised on enlistment, and most were not even allowed to reenlist because they were still unable to make the minimum test scores.[64]

YOU CAN BE BLACK, AND NAVY TOO

The armed services employed new marketing campaigns as well to attract potential recruits. In 1971, Admiral Elmo R. Zumwalt Jr., Chief of Naval Operations, announced a five-year plan to increase the percentage of minorities in the navy. Using slogans such as "You can be black, and Navy too," it was a successful effort. African Americans made up only 5 percent of the navy uniformed personnel at the beginning of the war, but by 1972, they accounted for 12 percent of the navy's manpower. In 1968, the Marine Corps created the new post of Negro Officer Selection Officer, or NOSO, which was soon changed to the equally redundant sounding Minority Officer Selection Officer (MOSO). Originally, there were 6 black captains assigned as MOSOs, but as the program showed promise, 11 more were added later and placed in cities with high black populations: Atlanta, Chicago, Kansas City, Los Angeles, New York, New Orleans, Philadelphia, Raleigh, Richmond, San Francisco, and Washington, D.C. Though the program targeted promising young African Americans, the selection officer was allowed to recruits whites.

To help ensure that the armed forces were attempting to recruit African Americans, the Department of Defense, in 1972, established a goal of 15 percent minority representation in future officer candidate school classes but found that it was a difficult goal to obtain. A college degree was usually a requirement for entry into an officer training program, but during the Vietnam War era, only about 5 percent of service-eligible black males had one, severely limiting the potential pool of recruits. The target figure was seldom met, and recruitment did not necessarily translate into 15 percent minority representation in the officer corps.

The emphasis on recruiting potential officers highlighted the fact that the military needed tens of thousands of company-grade officers for the expanded wartime military. West Point, Annapolis, and the Air Force Academy could not provide them because there were only around 9,800 cadets at the three service academies. The Pentagon also wanted to increase minority representation in the officer corps, but throughout the Vietnam War era, nonwhites were greatly underrepresented at the academies. As early as 1962, the Department of Defense announced a new program to attract minorities to the academies, but by 1968, there were only 17 black cadets at West Point and a total of only 97 African Americans at all three service academies. Annapolis, which graduated its first black midshipman only in 1949, had 26 African American midshipmen that year, enough of a boost in numbers for the navy to announce a significant increase in the enrollment of black cadets at the Naval Academy, but most black leaders were not impressed. One black critic remarked that the numbers were "hardly evidence of a successful six-year campaign" to recruit more African American cadets.[65] From 1969 to 1972, 18,782 whites, but only 105 African Americans, graduated from the three service academies.[66] It was only at the end of the war that black representation increased substantially. In 1971, 53 African Americans attended West Point, and in 1972, there were 45 blacks in the first-year class at Annapolis for a total of 150 black midshipmen at the academy; 25 African Americans were enrolled at the Air Force Academy.[67]

THE RESERVE OFFICER TRAINING CORPS

Aside from the military academies and the special programs mentioned previously, the military found the majority of needed officer candidates from a traditional source: college campuses. The ROTC was established during World War I and had successfully supplied officer candidates to the military in both world wars and Korea, so despite the antiwar sentiment prevalent on many college campuses, the Pentagon redoubled its efforts in this area. At the height of the conflict in 1968, there were ROTC programs at 256 colleges and universities, operating on 268 different campuses. A total of 165,430 students participated, and 14,176 officers were commissioned out of the ROTC program that year—only around 4,000 less than the three service academies combined would graduate in a three-year period from 1969 to 1972. At City College of New York, there were over 1,400 cadets enrolled in the ROTC that year. On graduation, they received commissions as second lieutenants and were obligated to serve for three years.[68]

ROTC was also viewed as a vehicle for increasing minority participation in the military, especially the officer corps. The Department of Defense pressured the armed services to do more to recruit promising African Americans through a variety of programs, but with an emphasis on the ROTC. The army had the highest percentage of black officers in the military, and one reason was their presence at traditionally black colleges. In addition to existing programs, such as at Tuskegee, Fisk, and Atlanta University, the army established new ROTC units at Norfolk State and Hampton. By 1970, they had ROTC programs at 14 black colleges, and 19 by 1972. In 1968, the navy established their first ROTC program at a historically black college, Prairie View A&M University. It was successful, so programs were established at Savannah State University and Southern University in 1971, and at Florida A&M University and North Carolina Central University the next year.

Declining support for the war and Vietnamization, however, led to a drastic decline in ROTC programs around the country in the early 1970s. The ROTC program at City College of New York, for example, was abolished in June 1972 because participation had dropped from a high of 1,400 students to only 81 in the final year of the program.

Reenlistment rates for men already in the armed forces also declined as the war progressed. Despite all the military's efforts, however, including bonuses and promotions, by the end of the war, reenlistment rates were low. Only 16 percent of air force personnel chose to reenlist, but even this was higher than the 14 percent for the army and 13 percent for the navy. Only half as many men in the armed forces reenlisted in 1970, compared to 1966.

REPORTING FOR INDUCTION AND BASIC TRAINING

Draftees and enlistees all had to report to a local induction center for processing when they were called up. Recruits arrived early at the center, usually at 7:00 A.M. They had to take the standard lie detector test and swear that they were not Communists or fascists nor belonged to any organization considered subversive by the Attorney General's Office. Questionable answers to any of these questions usually led to an interrogation from Army Counter Intelligence. The inductees were then lined up, and as a recruiting officer called out their names, they took one step forward, inducting them into the armed forces.

The inductees were also fingerprinted at the induction center. Afterward, they were loaded onto a bus and taken to basic training. One person on the bus, usually someone with some military training, carried the inductees' papers and orders in a sealed envelope.

Basic training was the one universal experience shared by all recruits, enlistee or draftee, regardless of service branch or MOS. It was conducted at military bases across the country. The navy had several camps, including one at San Diego, where Tennessee native David White trained, but the bulk of basic training was conducted at Great Lakes Naval Station in Illinois. Marine recruits from east of the Mississippi River usually trained at Camp Lejeune, North Carolina, and those west of the river at Camp Pendleton, California. Geography was not always the deciding factor for the army. Allen Thomas and Tim Wood both did their basic training at Fort Knox, Kentucky, only about 100 miles from their hometowns, but John Ballweg, from Baltimore, Maryland, did his basic training at Fort Jackson, South Carolina. Albert Childs, from Vermont, did his basic training at Fort Benning, Georgia.[69] Gender was a consideration, and most women in the army did their basic training at Ft. McClellan, Alabama.

From the beginning, the recruits were shouted at, terrorized, and kept psychologically off-balance. The trip to camp was usually timed so that the new recruits arrived tired and late at night. Reginald Edwards, for example, and other recruits were driven onto the Marine Corps training base in San Diego, California, along back roads and in the dark.[70] Diego Garcia remembered that when his bus stopped at Fort Ord, California, a "loud-mouthed motherfucker" who wasted no time in psychologically assaulting them met him and other recruits.[71] Typically, their recent civilian status and the trainees' manhood would be ridiculed and questioned. It usually had the desired effect. Gonzalo Baltazar expressed what most felt that first day: "I was 17, I was scared half to death once I got in there and so were the others."[72] Some began regretting their decision to join the armed forces. John Ballweg arrived at Fort Jackson, South Carolina, in early 1964. "I look back now it was nothing. At the time looking at it through my eyes it was pure hell," with all of the yelling and screaming at the recruits. He thought, "Oh my God, what did I get myself into." He also got off to a bad start when he caught pneumonia for a week and had to be recycled. He was even cursed at and harassed by his commanding officer for getting sick and having to go into the hospital.[73]

On arrival, most recruits were ordered to take a shower and "wash the civilian scum off."[74] Next, the recruits lined up, as military barbers shaved their heads. The military wanted to instill the concepts of teamwork and conformity into the recruits, and shaving their heads made them look more or less alike, reinforcing the principle. Ron Kovic remembered how the drill instructors stripped the soldiers of his platoon of their civilian clothing and shipped their belongings back to their parents' homes. Anything that might remind the trainee of his former civilian life was taken from him.[75]

Basic training in all the services was usually an eight-week course during the Vietnam War. There were, of course, exceptions. David White claimed that his navy basic training lasted "probably about twelve weeks."[76] John Ballweg did 10 weeks because he fell ill during his basic training and had to be recycled. Students in ROTC units often had an abbreviated basic training while still in college, followed by more training once they were formally inducted. Marine ROTC students, for example, did six weeks, the equivalent of basic training, at Camp Upshur, at Quantico, their first year. Training and conditioning at boot camp was as much psychological as it was physical, designed to disabuse a recruit of his civilian preconceptions and teach him to think like a soldier. There were three primary goals. The first was to identify and eliminate the weak and the unsatisfactory, or "unsats," the reasoning being that if you could not take "being shouted at and kicked in the ass once in a while," you could never survive the "rigors of combat."[77] The second goal was to get the others ready for Vietnam and combat. The abuse in boot camp was nothing compared to what faced them in Vietnam. The third major goal was to foster cohesion and unity among the recruits. Unit cohesion is often defined as learning to rely on, trust, and work efficiently with other individuals within the unit and a pride in its collective accomplishments.

Unit cohesion was the key to a unit's performance under fire or stress, and its importance cannot be underestimated. In the Marine Corps, in particular, unit cohesion would be a major factor during boot camp, subsequent training, and even in many assignments. The Marine Corps established so-called transplacement battalions, which had a cadre of proven experienced officers and NCOs that formed the nucleus of the unit, which was then filled out with enlisted personnel that had all gone through boot camp, and usually advanced individual training (AIT) together, with junior officers that had gone through Quantico together. They usually served the balance of their three-year enlistment collectively in the same battalion.[78]

THE DRILL INSTRUCTOR

Bringing the recruits together and forging the desired unit cohesion and teamwork among them was often achieved by giving trainees a universal figure to hate and unite against: the drill instructor. The drill instructors, or DIs, were the personnel assigned to train, and, if necessary, punish and abuse, the recruits. DIs shouted at, kicked, cursed, harassed, and humiliated the recruits. They would get right up in their faces, screaming abuse at them, and addressing them as scumbags, shitheads, faggots, numbnuts, shit-birds, or some other equally disparaging term. Tim Wood's DIs "were assholes. They were abusive."[79] "We were beaten up in basic," recalled Gonzalo Baltazar. "The drill sergeants were actually hitting us." On one occasion, he was hit between the eyes with a rifle butt by a DI who claimed that the gas cylinder on Baltazar's M-14 was not loose enough. It knocked him down and left a permanent scar.[80] At Camp Pendleton in 1961, the DIs in Gerald Kumpf's platoon were investigated for cruelty for punishing recruits with an unauthorized technique. The recruit would have to jump up on top or hang over the wall lockers, putting tremendous stress on the arm socket. One recruit broke his arm, fell, and cracked the back of his skull and was hospitalized.[81] Occasionally, the use of violence backfired on the instructors. There were several boxers in Gonzalo Baltazar's company, and a DI made the mistake of hitting one of them from behind for no reason. The boxer turned and decked him. Though it is a serious military offence to strike a superior officer or NCO, the DI never reported the incident because he would have to explain why he was hit, and also, it would have been embarrassing.[82]

Some recruits reported racist treatment or attitudes by their DIs. Many called black trainees boys, niggers, or coons. James Daly's DI was a white sergeant named Joiner, who complained openly that black recruits never seemed to aspire to leadership positions, such as a squad leader in boot camp, asking Daly, "So why the fuck is it that you colored guys never ask for a leadership position?"[83] In 1970, minority cadets at the

Air Force Academy protested to the Commandant and requested that instructors and white students not refer to them as boys, niggers, snowflakes, or spooks.[84] Because of such racist treatment, African Americans were often glad to see a black DI, but African American DIs could be just as tough, or even tougher, on black recruits than white DIs.

Some recruits were robbed or cheated by DIs. A sergeant swindled Albert Childs and other men in his platoon, charging them fees for nonexistent services. They learned of the deception the day of graduation; if they pressed charges, they would have had to stay, so they opted to forget about it and leave.[85] DIs in Baltazar's company stole money from the trainees, shaking them down for so-called fines and other costs, but this was not the norm. Friends in another training company, for example, had decent DIs that did not abuse them or steal from them.[86] Dishonest instructors were not the only ones taking advantage of the trainees. Tim Wood was not "shook down" for money by his DIs but stated that some cooks at Fort Knox borrowed money off the trainees and then never paid it back, knowing that the new recruits had few options for recovering it.[87]

Most of the recruits realized that the DIs were only preparing them for the future and did not feel abused. In the late 1950s, Albert Childs's DIs at Fort Benning, Georgia, were NCOs from the Third Infantry Division. They were good soldiers but "not necessarily good teachers," he recalled. The Korean War was over, and there were no other conflicts, so basic training was rather lax. There was no abuse, kicking, or hitting of the recruits by the DIs.[88] Despite his "attitude," Allen Thomas was treated well at Fort Knox during army basic training, especially by his platoon sergeant.[89] All four of former marine recruit Richard Marks's drill instructors "seem[ed] to be nice normal guys."[90] Cruel, or just "normal guys," most DIs kept their distance from the trainees. Some of John Ballweg's drill instructors, especially his platoon sergeant, an Indian with lots of overseas experience, would relate their experiences to the recruits to motivate them, but none became personal: "they wouldn't get close to you.... They were there to do a job.... They are strictly there to get into your face and get you through a course and did not care if you liked them or not. You would be gone in 8 weeks anyway."[91]

LIFE AT BOOT CAMP

The recruits had a lot in common and often bonded through their shared ordeal. Almost all of them were still young, mostly in their teens and early twenties. It was also the first time many of them had been far from home, and because many of them had come from an environment that was predominantly white, or black, or Latino, it was often the first time a recruit interacted with ethnic and cultural groups different from his or her own. Donald L. Dietrich admitted that "when I first entered the Army, I was a prejudiced young boy.... I regarded all colored people as 'niggers' although I was pretty friendly with them in person."[92] Warren Wynne was from a segregated neighborhood in Williamsburg, Virginia, attended all black Bruton High School, and "hadn't any contact" with whites until he joined the army. He became close friends with a white from Alabama during advanced infantry training in 1965. His white friend eventually confessed that he "was raised to have nothing to do" with African Americans, but Wynne "was different." Wynne thought, "It took pretty good guts to come out and say something like that... and I'm thinking, 'This is his first encounter with a black person.'"[93]

They were not paid much. A recruit in basic training at the height of the war in 1968 made only $98 a month, but he had few options for spending his meager pay.[94] Contact with friends and relatives was severely limited at first, but family of army trainees could visit them at the base after the first five weeks of training. Marine recruits were generally more isolated than army trainees and were generally restricted to base without visitors during their training. Army trainees were usually allowed off base during the later weeks of their training. After six or seven weeks of basic training, army trainees could get a weekend pass if they were not training for special duty. They had to be back in the barracks, however, no later than 10:00 P.M. Sunday night. The camps often held few comforts. Many were like marine camp Upshur, just a few Quonset huts and tin-walled buildings out in the middle of a forest.

Days at boot camp were long. A typical day started at 4:00 or 4:40 A.M. and sometimes ended as late as 10:30 P.M. Around 6:30 A.M., after physical training, or PT, the recruits headed to the mess hall for breakfast. The food was filling but bland. Tim Wood remembered that "the food was not bad" and that there was some choice and variety. Choices for breakfast might include bacon, sausage, eggs fried or scrambled, grits, and French toast. One item that was always on the menu was chipped beef on toast, or "shit on a shingle," as military personnel fondly knew it. Dinner usually featured one or two hot entrees, but not every night. The mess hall at Fort Knox had fewer cooks on duty on Sunday night, so chow usually consisted of something simple to prepare, such as chili and rice or cold cut sandwiches.[95]

The Marine Corps often regulated a recruit's food intake during boot camp, and one was fed and exercised according to whether he was overweight or underweight. At marine boot camp, near Camp Pendleton, the overweight recruits were given bread and water and ran a lot. The underweight ones, like Gerald Kumpf, who was six feet tall and only 136 pounds, were told to go through the chow lines twice. He gained nearly 50 pounds, weighing around 185 pounds by the end of boot camp.[96]

The army did not send underweight recruits through the chow line twice; in fact, authorities frowned on a soldier taking more food than he could consume, but at many installations, recruits had to perform a physical task before they were allowed to eat. At Fort Knox, trainees had to do a certain number of repetitions on a set of parallel bars set up at the entrance of the mess hall before they were allowed to get in the chow line.

The trainee had to learn all the important rudiments of military life. In the late 1950s, Albert Childs's basic at Fort Benning, Georgia, was typical of most. It included physical and mental conditioning; a lot of marching, running, push-ups, drill, military regulations, and ceremonies; and some training on the M-1 rifle.[97] John Ballweg and others reported getting some small-unit tactics training as well. Boot camp did involve a lot of physical conditioning. Shortly after arrival, the recruits were put through conditioning tests to determine how many push-ups, sit-ups, and other calisthenics they could do to see what kind of physical shape they were in. Many recruits, such as Gerald Kumpf, did not mind the physical training. He could do 100 push-ups and sit-ups with no problem before going to boot camp.[98] Most trainees hated the long and often brutal runs and marches. At Fort Knox, trainees hiked over hills named "Misery" and "Heartache." Running was the worst part of basic training for John Ballweg. They started around 4:30 A.M. and ran for two or three miles in full combat gear. Gonzalo Baltazar remembered that "they ran us to the ground all the time, to exhaustion,"[99] and Gerald Kumpf had to run through the sand with extra heavy packs on until his legs ached in pain.[100] In the summer, recruits went on punishing hikes in 90 degree heat and practiced close-order drill in heat so bad that it melted asphalt.

There was little free time. Albert Childs said that unless there was special duty or night training, they were usually left alone after 5:00 P.M. during his basic training at

Fort Benning, Georgia. But when they were not training, the recruits were usually kept busy with chores such as keeping the barracks clean and kitchen patrol, or KP. Navy basic training "kept you busy," according to David White. "You didn't have time to feel sorry for yourself." They had a week of mess cooking, and "we had to wash our clothes every night, shine our shoes and then study."[101] John Ballweg recalls peeling his "share of potatoes."[102] At Fort Knox, "everybody did KP," according to Tim Wood. "We had to show up at 3:00 A.M., to be ready for 6:30 chow time."[103] Extra duty did not mean that a recruit was excused from any drills or training. If he had done four hours of guard duty the night before, for example, he still had to report for morning call.

TRAINING AND CONDITIONING

Recruits generally considered navy and air force basic training easier than army or marine boot camp. Alfonza Wright, who served in both the navy and the army, admitted that army boot camp was more physically rigorous. David White said that his navy basic training was not all that physically rigorous. "You had a lot of marching, a lot of walking," but mostly it was preparing them for life on board ship.[104] The marine obstacle course was reputed to be the toughest of its kind in the world, but again, the test was often more psychological than physical. Gerald Kumpf had gained 50 pounds in boot camp without a corresponding increase in upper body strength. Part of the obstacle course entailed scaling a wall with a rope; the recruit ran, climbed the wall with the rope, and touched a beam at the top of the wall. Kumpf got halfway up the wall and could not make it over, but was motivated to do so when the DI approached him with a bayonet clutched between his teeth, advising Kumpf to "get your ass up there or I'm going to stick this bayonet up till you sideways [sic]." Kumpf believed he would do it because "he was a mean little SOB and I scooted right on up, touched that beam. I said, 'That's amazing, that's amazing.' It was more psychological than physical."[105]

Some recruits received tactical training in boot camp. Gerald Kumpf believed that his marine basic training helped prepare him and others for Vietnam. At Danang, he watched marines track and kill Vietcong sappers using fire maneuvers learned in basic and advanced training.[106] But basic training was not designed to prepare the trainees for guerrilla warfare in Vietnam; that would come later, in more advanced training. In fact, the instructors seldom talked about Vietnam or any other war. None of Gonzalo Baltazar's DIs in basic training had experience in Vietnam. Only his company commander did, and he never talked about it. Vietnam, or lessons from it, were seldom mentioned.[107] The trainees did learn some rudimentary tactics, usually when they went on bivouac; they did some night fighting exercises. Many trainees like Baltazar spent two weeks in basic on bivouac, living out in the desert in tents and learning some basic maneuvers.

The recruits had some weapon training. At Fort Benning, Georgia, and other basic training camps, recruits trained on the M-1 rifle, practiced grenade throwing, and underwent a live fire exercise on the infiltration course. In 1964, recruits at Fort Knox became one of the first groups to train on the new M-14 rifle. Recruits at almost every basic training facility also had bayonet practice into tire dummies and hand-to-hand combat instruction in the sand pit, under the watchful eye of the instructor.

Some veterans do not recall getting much in the way of weapon training during boot camp. The M-14 was the only weapon John Ballweg trained on in army boot camp; the rest of his weapon training came during flight school.[108] At Camp Pendleton,

As part of Operation MacArthur, Companies B and C of the 1st Battalion, 8th Infantry Regiment, 1st Brigade, 4th Infantry Division, assemble on top of Hill 742, five miles northeast of Dak To, November 1967. The purple smoke bomb was ignited to guide in a helicopter. Courtesy of the U.S. Army.

Gerald Kumpf trained only on the .45 pistol and the M-1 rifle. They spent a week on the rifle range, practicing and then qualifying with the weapon on the last day, for one of three qualifying rankings: marksman, sharpshooter, and expert.[109] David White received virtually no weapon training at navy basic; the weapon training came later at Mare Island. Gonzalo Baltazar trained with the M-14 and grenades.

Despite limited weapon training during boot camp, the military did begin to indoctrinate the trainees with the idea of the "spirit of the bayonet," described by some soldiers as the savage ability to pierce another man's flesh in close combat with the bayonet's cold steel.[110] The problem was how to overcome years of social and religious training that said that killing was wrong. Marines seemed to do a slightly better job than did the army.[111] One Vietnam veteran remarked on his basic training that "the only thing they told us about the Viet Cong was they were gooks. They were to be killed. Nobody sits around and gives you their historical and cultural background. They're the enemy. Kill, kill, kill. That's what we got in practice. Kill, kill, kill."[112] The spirit of the bayonet, and the lust to kill, would be constantly reinforced during boot camp and later training. Caputo was a platoon commandeer in the First Battalion, Third Marine Division in early 1965, stationed at Camp Schwab, Okinawa. In February 1965, his unit was sent to the Northern Training Area, a region of jungle-covered mountains, for two weeks of counterinsurgency warfare exercises. During a lesson on ambushing the enemy, one drill instructor wrote "AMBUSHES ARE MURDER. MURDER IS FUN" on the blackboard and had the class repeat it in unison.[113]

The trainees quickly learned the rudiments of military discipline and unquestioned obedience, and by the third week, recruits had learned to obey orders instantly, in unison, and without thinking. If they did not, DIs were quick to punish even the tiniest, or on occasion, fictitious, infraction. Some were innocuous and designed to teach the recruit a lesson. Soldiers that did not shave close enough were forced to dry shave before they could go to breakfast. Albert Childs said that a typical punishment involved a recruit caught chewing gum in formation. The DI put the gum on the tip of the recruit's nose and made him run up and down the street with his rifle over his head shouting, "I will not chew gum in ranks." It was a crude but normally effective method. Childs claimed that the demonstration convinced everyone in the company not to chew gum in ranks.[114] Some of the punishments inflicted on the recruits could be extremely painful. In the Marine Corps, recruits were punished with so-called Chinese push-ups, which are performed in a bent position with only the head and toes touching the floor. Some of the punishments employed, however, were dangerous and not sanctioned by the chain of command. As discussed previously, at Camp Pendleton in 1961, DIs punished recruits using an unauthorized technique. The recruit would have to jump up on top or hang over the wall lockers, putting tremendous stress on the arm socket.[115] Gonzalo Baltazar did a lot of crawling out in the desert for punishment. They would crawl until their knees were raw and bleeding. They were often disciplined for no other reason but to instill discipline.[116]

UNSATS AND REBELS AND SURVIVING BASIC TRAINING

Recruits that performed poorly in boot camp were nicknamed "unsats," for "unsatisfactory," and DIs often singled out unsats for punishment. Ron Kovic stated that the DIs usually seemed to single out one particular recruit for excessive physical discipline. On one occasion, Kovic remembered a group of DIs surrounding an unsat and "[jabbing] their tight fists into his gut" until he screamed. Extreme verbal abuse accompanied this recruit's physical punishment.[117] There was an unsat in John Ketwig's unit the instructors nicknamed "Fatso" and routinely physically and mentally abused. "I know your problem," they would yell at him. "You're fat! Fat! FAT. You're a fat, filthy, fucking pig, aren't you, boy?" "Sergeant Anderson forced Fatso to defecate on a cigarette and carry the mess off the parade field before allowing the cold recruit to dress and return to the barracks."[118]

Drill instructors picked on unsats or particular trainees for several reasons. Sometimes it was purely personal. Racism, for example, was sometimes a factor. Another reason, however, was to instill a sense of teamwork in the recruits. They wanted to get the recruits to work as a unit, not as individuals, and hoped the strong recruits would pick up and help and encourage the struggling ones. Teamwork sometimes did help a struggling trainee successfully complete boot camp, but sometimes it also meant bending a few rules. Peter Hefron writes that one Project 100,000 inductee in his unit had the mental capabilities of a 10-year-old. After a "dangerous episode on the rifle range," the soldier was put on permanent KP. He passed basic training because other soldiers in the unit used his ID card and took the necessary tests to get him qualified. He was sent to Korea, not Vietnam. Few unsats graduated boot camp, however. Even trainees with borderline performance, known as marginals, received little better treatment from the DIs than did the unsats because most of the marginals eventually fell into the unsat category and either quit or were sent home.

There were recruits who refused to conform and rebelled. Many did so for political reasons. Vietnam was an increasingly unpopular war after 1968, and many draftees would rather be thrown out of the military, rather than go to Vietnam. The armed forces was one of the most racially enlightened American institutions in the late 1950s and early 1960s, but many young black recruits viewed it as just another white-dominated, racist organization and often refused to cooperate. Getting out of the military, however, was extremely difficult. Recruits that did poorly were often recycled and forced to take the entire training course over again from the beginning. Uncooperative recruits could be severely punished or imprisoned.

Some recruits could not take the psychological pressure and humiliation. Along with the unsats, some had nervous breakdowns, and several received medical discharges. Some attempted to leave basic training and desert the military. Hitching a ride on or under a service vehicle was one method commonly attempted. One recruit at Camp Pendleton in 1961 tried to hide in a dumpster to sneak off the base.[119] A few committed suicide. One such casualty was Fatso from John Ketwig's platoon. "It is no wonder that Fatso finally broke under the psychological abuse and committed suicide." Ketwig wrote that "something went wrong at 'night fire.' It ended abruptly, and we were trucked back to the barracks. Sarge had never let up on Fatso. I guess it just got to be too much. Instead of returning, Fatso just stood behind one of the target forms and waited. 'Ready on the right? Ready on the left? Lock and load! Fire when ready.' He had been older. Once he had been a law student. He had been called to do his duty. He had a wife."[120]

Military training was generally effective, and 96 percent of all trainees eventually graduated, though the percentage varied according to service branch and basic training camp. The vast majority of recruits were fatalistic or pragmatic enough to cope, and most found ways of dealing with the trials of boot camp. The majority of recruits endured it because they did not want to be labeled an unsat and go home a failure. They worked hard to prove themselves and suffered their hardships and indignities stoically: Philip Caputo describes how soldiers thanked DIs in response to rough treatment.[121] Gerald Kumpf felt that "some people handled [the abuse] real well, some people laughed their way through it and some people cried their way through it." The abuse heaped on him by the DIs never troubled Kumpf. "My dad did that to me all my life, so it kind of rolled off, like water off a duck. It never really bothered me much." Others, however, were bothered. Kumpf could hear men crying at night in the barracks.[122] Some recruits hated basic training. "Basic was a negative for me," admitted Gonzalo Baltazar. "It was pretty tough."[123] For John Ketwig, it meant being "pushed, pulled, beaten, screamed at, humiliated, and emasculated for eight weeks."[124] Others had a much more positive experience. Gene Holliday described the later stages of basic training as "fun."[125] A select few stood out and were rewarded, such as 18-year-old marine recruit Thomas E. Henderson, named honor man of his platoon during marine recruit training at Camp Pendleton. His rewards included promotion to private first class, a free uniform, and posting to an engineering school in North Carolina.[126]

Whether a recruit hated, tolerated, or prospered, basic training was a test of his manhood, and success did instill self-confidence in the vast majority of recruits. For many, it marked a passage from adolescence to adulthood. Gerald Kumpf admitted that "they essentially brainwash you. They tear you down, make you feel worthless and then they start building you back up in the mold that they want you to be in. The biggest benefit that I got from Marine Corps basic training was the, the feeling if not the fact I could do anything. I can accomplish anything in my life, whether it be a physical, something physical, something mental, it make no difference. They instill a 'can do' attitude in you."[127]

Boot camp not only instilled discipline, teamwork, and unit cohesion in the recruits, it also began the process of turning them into soldiers, marines, sailors, or airmen, of giving them pride in belonging to a select organization. They learned and were taught to respect the history, traditions, and heroes of their particular service. Many recruits did develop a strong attachment, if not a love, for their branch of the armed forces. Marine private Richard E. Marks[128] and army trainee David Parks described the military as a fraternity, a "beautiful army" deserving great devotion and love.[129]

ADVANCED INDIVIDUAL TRAINING

After graduation from boot camp, recruits were told where to report for their advanced individual training (AIT) and were assigned a MOS, which was the job they would be trained to do during their military career. There were hundreds of MOSs, such as a 76V, which was an equipment storage foreman, or a 32C, which was a fixed station transmitter repairman. Most, but not all, of the combat specialties were in the elevens. A combat infantryman or machine gunner, for example, was an 11B, and an ammunition handler or armored vehicle driver was an 11E. A recruit was assigned a MOS based largely on his performance on a series of exams designed to determine his intelligence and general aptitude, which he took when inducted into the armed forces. All recruits took the Armed Forces Qualification Test (AFQT), which was essentially a standard intelligence quotient test, but there were also more specialized exams, such as the Army Qualification Battery (AQB), used by both the army and marines, the navy's Short Basic Test Battery, and the Airman Qualifying Examination (AQE) in the air force, to determine a recruit's aptitude and skills for specialized training in a specific field. The higher the score, the more likely a recruit would end up in the more prestigious hard-core fields, such as intelligence, or one of the technical fields.[130] For example, to enlist in the air force, a recruit needed to score a minimum of 40 on the AQE but needed a score 60 to be accepted into electronics training. The army divided recruits into five categories based on results from the AFQT and the AQB, with I being the highest classification and V the lowest. Recruits that tested into categories II and I could request or were assigned to a more prestigious hard-core MOS, and those in either III or IV could look forward to placement in a soft-core specialty, meaning a combat arm, service, or supply. Individuals that tested into category V were usually considered mentally unfit for service.

Because of better access to good schools and a probable institutionalized racial bias in the test battery, whites tended to do appreciably better on the AFQT and other exams than did minorities. In the early 1970s, among army personnel with between 19 and 24 months' service, about 25 percent of whites, but nearly 75 percent of African Americans, scored 30 or less on the exams, placing them in category IV.[131] As a consequence, whites were overrepresented in assignments to the more technical or intellectual fields, as were minorities in the combat arms and other soft-core specialties. African Americans constituted more than 12 percent of the army's enlisted strength during much of the Vietnam War, for example, but accounted for less than 5 percent of the military's electronics equipment technicians and only 7 percent of the armed forces communications and intelligence specialists. Conversely, blacks made up 16.3 percent of enlisted personnel assigned to combat specialties and nearly 20 percent of the service and supply troops.[132] In the air force, which was probably the most technical of the armed services, whites predominated in the technical fields and in the more prestigious ones, such as fighters or bomber pilots, whereas blacks were overrepresented in administration, the air police, food service, supply, and transportation.

A good score on the exams did give an individual a certain amount of choice and flexibility. John Ballweg originally trained for intelligence work, but then applied for and was accepted into flight school and became a helicopter pilot instead.[133] The military also provided educational opportunities and allowed recruits to switch their MOSs if they improved their scores. Gerald Kumpf earned his GED in the marines and passed the examinations for flight school, only to be turned down because of poor night eyesight. Ironically, his two friends that were accepted both died in Vietnam. Kumpf was trained as an avionics technician, basically an electrician's mate, at Jacksonville, Florida, graduating at the top of his class. He was allowed to choose his first assignment and chose MFA-314, a marine F-4 fighter unit stationed at El Toro, California. Then he became a plane captain, the person responsible for the preflight check and for strapping the pilot into the cockpit.[134] Most recruits, however, had little choice in their MOSs. No one asked Gonzalo Baltazar or his fellow trainees during basic training if they were interested in applying for certain jobs or MOSs. He found out he was slated for the infantry when he started his advanced infantry training at Camp Crockett, at Fort Gordon.[135]

A recruit learned his MOS at AIT, and, depending on the MOS, in more advanced schools afterward. AIT generally lasted around eight weeks, but it varied according to the specialty involved. Early in the Vietnam War era, someone would likely do his basic training at one base and his AIT at another. Gonzalo Baltazar did his basic training at Fort Bliss, Texas, but his AIT at Fort Gordon, Georgia,[136] and John Ballweg did his basic at Fort Jackson, South Carolina, and his AIT at Fort Holibird, Maryland, to name two examples.[137] Beginning in 1970–1971, the army introduced one station unit training, which combined basic training and AIT at the same location for most military personnel. There were, of course, exceptions. At the same time, Fort Knox began training women with a clerical MOS for the first time at its AIT schools. Some specialized training was still available only at certain bases, such as the Army Chaplain School at Fort Hamilton, New York.

For many army veterans, AIT seemed easy compared to basic training. John Ballweg said that army AIT was far less an ordeal than basic. Reveille was still at 5:30 A.M., and they still had to do some PT, but it was not as grueling. Ballweg was training for intelligence work, so most of AIT involved classroom work, such as learning photo and document analysis.[138] "It was a lot of good training, good information," recalled Gonzalo Baltazar. "It was a lot different from basic and we were treated pretty good."[139]

Navy advanced training was often very technically oriented, involving a lot of class work, and physical training was not very rigorous. At navy AIT for patrol boat river (PBR) sailors, trainees spent three months at the PBR School at Mare Island, California. The routine included 15 minutes of calisthenics in the morning, followed by a two- to three-mile jog. Then it was class work. Trainees learned to do every job on the boat, except overhauling the engines, including driving the boat and operating the radio. Part of the program included a week of survival training and a week or two of Vietnamese language school. They also heard lectures from former Korean War POWs on what to expect and how to act if captured by the enemy.[140]

Marine advanced training, however, was often more physically grueling than basic training, and trainees had to run the Hill Trail twice a week in full pack and equipment. The Hill Trail ran over a range of seven, steep, rolling hills. Marines went on to advanced training immediately after finishing boot camp, but for the ROTC candidates, however, this was two years after basic, and most had been softened by a return to college and campus life.

AIT for those training in a combat MOS was geared to replace peacetime civilian values with military values and behaviors and reinforce the principles of the spirit of the bayonet. One way to do this was through pugil-stick fights. A pugil-stick is a long pole with padded ends, used in the armed forces to simulate bayonet fighting.[141] Two men would square off and fight with the clubs, urged on by the instructor helping to inculcate the spirit of the bayonet into the trainees.

WEAPON AND TACTICAL TRAINING

There was also a lot of weapon training at AIT and officer candidate schools (OCS). Gonzalo Baltazar first trained on the M-16 at AIT and also familiarized himself with the M-72 LAW, the M-60 machine gun, claymore mines, and other weapons he would need to know how to use in Vietnam.[142] The Marine Corps, in particular, placed a lot of emphasis on weapon and tactics training during AIT and OCS. Every marine is a rifleman first and foremost, and even marine aviators are trained as infantry before being sent to flight school. Because of this, there was a great deal of emphasis on weapon training and small-unit tactics for new officers and enlisted trainees. They learned such things as how to properly attack a hill, by either frontal assault or envelopment, and how to hold it once captured. They trained with the M-14, the standard rifle at the time in the Marine Corps, and learned how to deliver searching or traversing fire with the M-60 machine gun.[143]

Amtracs coming into the LPD during training exercises involving the 1st Amphibious Tractor Battalion, 1968. Courtesy of the National Archives.

Many veterans believed that AIT and the more advanced service schools did not adequately prepare men for the guerrilla and counterinsurgency warfare they were likely to experience in Vietnam. As early as 1956, the U.S. Army Intelligence School acquired part of the battery area around Fort Howard, Maryland, to serve as a field training area for counterinsurgency tactics. They built a Vietnamese village named "Duc Huc" for training and familiarizing troops headed to Vietnam.[144] But few troops actually got to benefit from this program. General Wallace H. Nutting, who served two tours in Vietnam commanding armored cavalry units—first a squadron in 1966–1967, and then the 11th Armored Cavalry Regiment from 1970 to 1971—claimed, "I can't say that in the school system I recall any personal preparation for or attention to this difficult form of combat" (guerilla warfare).[145] Sometimes it depended on just which service school one attended. Counterinsurgency warfare was addressed at US Army Combined Arms Center at Leavenworth in the early 1960s, for example, but Nutting attended the Naval War College as an exchange student, and counterinsurgency was not a major issue for the navy or a topic for study at their premier school in 1962–1963.[146]

A few were lucky enough to be stationed to a tropical posting and received jungle training before being sent to Vietnam. Some marine platoon commanders received two weeks' counterinsurgency training in the mountainous and jungle-covered Northern Training Area on Okinawa. Some of it proved useful. They became acquainted with the numerous miseries of jungle warfare: the heat, the humidity, the leeches and mosquitoes, and the darkness and claustrophobic environment created by thick, triple-canopy jungle. Instructors emphasized the need to be aggressive and ruthless in jungle warfare and the need to kill every enemy soldier who entered the killing zone in an ambush. First burst of fire should be at waist level, the second at ankle level to finish off anyone who survived the first volley. Many of the officers that went through the program did not find it particularly useful; it was based largely on the British experience fighting guerillas in Malaya, which bore only a superficial resemblance to conditions in Vietnam. Albert Childs had nearly a decade of experience in the army before going to Vietnam for his first tour in 1968. He had been stationed in Panama in 1964, "and by this time Vietnam was starting to build up so all of our training over there was in the jungle anyway, but then since Vietnam was building up, it was all geared towards Vietnam. So we were either in the jungle being trained or we were detailed to assist others." Childs spent two years in Panama with an infantry unit and also eight months at the language school before serving in Vietnam.[147]

The degree of training also depended on when one attended AIT or a service school. A recruit was far more likely to get training on guerrilla and counterinsurgency warfare later in the war, rather than earlier. Anthony Zinni was in officer training for the Marine Corps at Quantico when the first marines were landing in Vietnam in spring 1965 and said that his training was based largely on the lessons learned during the Second World War and Korea. But counterinsurgency warfare was fashionable in the marines and Army Special Forces, and it was obvious that the next war would be in Southeast Asia: Congress had just passed the Gulf of Tonkin Resolution, and though Kennedy was now dead, his enthusiasm and support for counterinsurgency warfare lived on. As a result, new officers usually received counterinsurgency training at the Marine Officers' Basic School. Many of the instructors had little practical experience. One senior first lieutenant instructor in counterinsurgency warfare had spent only 30 days in Vietnam as an observer, which did not inspire much confidence in his knowledge. He did have a Purple Heart from his short stint in Vietnam, though hardly earned under heroic circumstances: he had been hit in the buttocks while squatting over a latrine. The instructors taught that counterrevolutionary warfare was a highly specialized art, with complex tactics. They were taught so-called hammer and anvil tactics, designed to trap and smash enemy forces, and how to stage a minuet ambush and repel attacks with a triangular defense. In addition, many young officers studied and read more on counterinsurgency and revolutionary doctrines themselves in addition to the training they received.

By 1968, many of the DIs at AIT or other training facilities had service in Vietnam longer than the mere 30 days some instructors had, and many in combat. They shared their experiences with their trainees, stressing that the trainees needed to pay attention and be team players, or they would die in Vietnam.[148] John Ballweg, for example, served a tour of duty in Vietnam and stayed another 15 months in the army. He was assigned as a helicopter instructor at Fort Walters, Texas, and spent another year there after leaving the army as a civilian instructor. Though he had it easy, and only worked about five hours a day, he knew his trainees were eventually headed for Vietnam; the instructors were even told they were not allowed to wash anybody out. Ballweg did his best to prepare them. He talked about Vietnam with them and tried to incorporate what he had learned over there into his lessons.[149]

"We had excellent training" in 1968, recalled David White of his navy AIT. He became familiar with the boat and the weapons he would use in Vietnam. Many of the instructors at the navy's PBR School at Mare Island were veterans of naval riverboats in Vietnam. For example, White learned that in Vietnam, they had restricted or unrestricted firing zones, and his instructors stressed that under fire, you might have only one or two seconds to make up your mind to decide if you are going to shoot back or get out, lessons White would later apply during his tour of duty in the war.[150]

Gonzalo Baltazar said that a good number of the instructors, and even some of the trainees, during advanced training for a rapid reaction aero-rifle platoon had Vietnam experience and gave excellent advice. Some of the trainees were learning a new skill and preparing themselves for their second or even third tour. Baltazar stated that the veterans, both instructors and fellow students, shared their knowledge and experience with the uninitiated. It was good and realistic training because the Vietnam veterans had been there and knew what to expect. His instructors divided the trainees up on maneuvers into Americans and Vietcong to teach them counterinsurgency methods. Baltazar was a Vietcong on one maneuver and had to plan a surprise attack on the American camp. "It was pretty good training." They also conducted night raids.[151] Some of the lessons were more subtle and unintentional. Baltazar noticed that while some of the veterans during his specialized training referred to the enemy as "dinks" or "gooks," it was far more common to refer to them as Vietcong, VC, or most frequently, just "Charlie," indicating a certain level of respect for the enemy in Vietnam.[152]

Though most of the trainees were likely to go to Vietnam, they were told little about the Geneva Convention and the treatment of civilians in a war zone. Each soldier was given a wallet-sized card summarizing the rules. Few soldiers received any more training on the topic after that, though some received a one-time brief introduction to the Geneva Convention and the treatment of civilian noncombatants and POWs, usually by a young lieutenant "reading from a prepared script."[153]

For incoming members of the marines' Platoon Leader's Class, advanced training was also their OCS. Marine OCS was located at Quantico, Virginia, near Fredericksburg.

Candidates received 13 weeks OCS in the Marine Corps, the first 6 weeks being the equivalent of basic training for enlisted personnel. Candidates were all members of the Platoon Leader's Class, the marine equivalent of ROTC. They did six weeks of basic training and then did an advanced course the summer before graduation from college. Much like they had been in basic, the candidates were subjected to intense indoctrination that emphasized the glories of the Marine Corps and the bonds of affection the officer candidates should feel for the institution. Candidates attended history courses on the Marine Corps, and on parade, they chanted, "Hut-two-three-four, I love the Marine Corps." The candidates praised the Marine Corps before each meal as the most invincible fighting force in the world since 1775, ending with a rousing "Gung ho! Gung ho! Pray for war." The indoctrination was somewhat effective. Even those participants who might have found such ceremonies and sayings hackneyed were drawn in and became true believers.

Caputo graduated in August 1963 and was commissioned a second lieutenant on February 2, 1964. There were 700 men in Caputo's class when they started the advanced training/OCS, but only around 500 finished. Numerous field-grade officers and civilians, mostly friends and family of the graduates, attended the graduation ceremony. There were awards given out, the customary congratulations, and speeches about duty and honor. Then, "eyes right," and the graduating class marched past the reviewing stand as the band played the "Marine Corps Hymn."[154]

Graduates from AIT and OCS were usually granted up to 30 days leave before they had to report to their next assignment. For many of them, it would entail even more schooling. Albert Childs was sent to Nike Ajax missile training at Fort Bliss, Texas. Gonzalo Baltazar was given his orders for Vietnam in the fall of 1968 but was sent to train another eight months, until February 1969, as a member of a rapid reaction aero-rifle platoon, whose main job was to rescue downed pilots and do some reconnaissance. They learned how to repel out of a helicopter: "McGuire, we were trained McGuireing." And they were also trained as door gunners in case of an emergency, learned how to operate a radio and the proper language to use, and some more night exercises.[155]

After leave, the new officers returned to Quantico in May 1964 for the mandatory six-month apprenticeship for new second lieutenants at the Officers' Basic School before being sent out to their first commands. The purpose of the school was to turn them into professional officers. Being marines, there was still an emphasis on physical training, and they went on hikes of 30 miles with 40-pound packs on their backs, but Officers' Basic School was pleasant compared to OCS. The housing was comfortable. The fresh lieutenants lived in bachelor officers quarters (BOQ), which looked like a modern dormitory in two-man rooms. The best part was that the DIs now had to call them sir and could not physically or verbally abuse them, though the very sight of a DI still filled most of them with dread.[156]

Classroom work at the Officers' Basic School was boring for young men seeking romance and adventure. Instead of Homer, or *Guadalcanal Diary,* they read material more germane to their craft and lives, such as the German military theoretician Clausewitz, with emphasis on his nine principles of war.[157]

Field exercises took up about half of the training schedule at the Officers' Basic School, but it was not always the most exciting way to learn. Most of the information learned during exercises was dry and methodological, about how things were done—the language being more out of a technical journal than a rousing military treatise.[158]

Learning to compose battle orders was particularly confusing for many of them. The new officers learned to write the standard five-paragraph attack order, but many of them found it a complex and arcane lesson. They learned the language of the military, with its abstract jargon and love of acronyms and abbreviations. A battle was a "combat situation." A helicopter assault was a "vertical envelopment." An M-14 rifle was a "hand-held, gas-operated, magazine-fed, semiautomatic shoulder weapon."

The field exercises were designed to simulate battlefield conditions and teach the new officers how to apply the lessons they learned in the classroom, and to develop a spirit of aggressiveness and innovation in the young officers. The Marine Corps believed in an offensive doctrine. The emphasis in training was on élan and the offensive. They were taught only the rudiments of defensive warfare, and retreat, or a "retrograde maneuver," was hardly mentioned. When it was, it was in disdain. The army retreated, not the marines. The frontal assault was the essence of aggressive warfare and marine doctrine. The instructors often used blank round fire and other devices to simulate battlefield conditions. The young officers took these exercises seriously and believed at the time that they were a close approximation to what they might face in real combat. But in reality, they "bore about as much similarity to the real thing as shadowboxing does to street-fighting."[159]

Training was as broad as possible and covered the mostly likely scenarios in which the young officers might someday find themselves. Part of their training included a week at the Amphibious Warfare School, in Norfolk, Virginia, and schooling in urban warfare techniques such as house-to-house fighting. They also received night fighting training. Their education in the military arts, moreover, changed the way young officers like Caputo viewed the world around them. The landscape, for example, was no longer scenery, something to look at and enjoy; rather, it was terrain, something to study for cover and concealment, for lines of fire or possible avenues of escape, something now viewed for tactical rather than aesthetic reasons. New officers were also taught how to be officers and gentlemen. There was still a lot of emphasis on the ceremonial side of military life. They learned how to put on reviews, how to flourish a sword, and how to behave at social functions, including "Mess Night," an ancient tradition handed down from the British Royal Marines.

FIRST ASSIGNMENTS

After completing Officers' Basic School, graduates received a month's leave before reporting to their first commands. The new officers were required to serve 90 days in a command billet to qualify for their MOSs. Those that proved themselves were often then permanently assigned to that unit.

Most of the new enlisted personnel and officers did not immediately receive orders for Vietnam. Most of John Ballweg's graduating class from helicopter flight school went to Korea, and some to Germany, but none went directly to Vietnam. Most, however, would end up there. In early spring 1966, Ballweg and his unit were informed that they were being sent to Vietnam. He reported in Vietnam in August 1966.[160] Gonzalo Baltazar graduated from AIT in July 1969, but because he was still only 17, he was not sent directly to Vietnam. Instead, he spent two months with an armament company at Fort Hood, Texas. "I had it easy for two months." Then, like many in the armed forces in that era, his orders came down for Vietnam.[161]

NOTES

1. James E. Westheider, "Sgt. Allen Thomas, Jr.: A Black Soldier in Vietnam," in *Portraits of African American Life Since 1865*, ed. Nina Mjagkij (Wilmington, DE: Scholarly Resources, 2003), 221.

2. Gene Stephens, "Some Draft Board Members Live outside Jurisdictions," *The Cincinnati Enquirer*, August 8, 1966, 1.

3. Emil Dansker, "Boards 'Want Best for Boys," *The Cincinnati Enquirer*, March 6, 1967, 5.

4. "The Marshall Commission Report," *Current History*, July 1968, 49.

5. "First for Alabama," Roundup, *Sepia*, May 1968, 32.

6. Gene Stephens, "The Ins and Outs of the Draft," *The Cincinnati Enquirer*, August 18, 1966, 4.

7. Russell F. Weigley, *Putting the Poor in Uniform, The New York Times*, April 11, 1993, 12.

8. "Viet Rebuke Stirs Storm," *The Baltimore Afro-American*, January 22, 1966, 14, and John Lewis, "SNCC Statement on Vietnam," *Freedomways* 6 (1966): 6–7.

9. Committee on Veteran Affairs, *Veteran's Administration, Myths and Realities: A Study of Attitudes toward Vietnam Era Veterans*, 96th Cong., 2nd sess. (Washington, DC: U.S. Government Printing Office, 1980), 6.

10. U.S. Department of Defense, *Black Americans in Defense of Our Nation* (Washington, DC: U.S. Department of Defense), 43, and "Abuse of the Draft," *The Baltimore Afro-American*, January, 15, 1966, 4, and "Lottery-Draft Won't Alter Race Ratio," *The Pittsburgh Courier*, May, 24, 1969, 3.

11. Robert J. McMahon, *Major Problems in the History of the Vietnam War*, 2nd ed. (Lexington, MA: D. C. Heath, 1995), 437.

12. Lawrence M. Baskir and William Strauss, *Chance and Circumstance: The Draft, the War, and the Vietnam Generation* (New York: Random House, 1978), 47; Paul T. Murray, "Blacks and the Draft: A History of Institutional Racism," *Journal of Black Studies*, September, 1971, 70.

13. Evan Thomas, "War Stories," *Newsweek*, February 23, 2004, 24–31.

14. Ibid., and "360 Pros Reported Exempt from Draft," *The New York Times*, April 8, 1967, 23.

15. "360 Pros," 23.

16. Richard Todd, "Life with the Conscientious Acceptors," *The New York Times Magazine*, October 12, 1969, 27.

17. Colin Powell with Joseph E. Persico, *My American Journey* (New York: Random House, 1995), 148.

18. "The Marshall Commission Report," *Current History*, July, 1968, 46–49, and Edward Fisk, "On Conscientious Objection to This War," *The New York Times*, February, 5, 1967, section IV, 5.

19. Baskir and Strauss, *Chance and Circumstance*, 97, and Martin Waldron, "Clay Guilty in Draft Case; Gets Five Years in Prison," *The New York Times*, June 21, 1967, 1.

20. L. Deckel McLean, "The Black Man and the Draft," *Ebony*, August, 1968, 64.

21. "Vietnam Veterans against the War, Position Paper on Amnesty" (Placitas, NM: Vietnam Veterans against the War, 1973), 5. Citizen Soldier File #7037, Box #1, File #1, Cornell University Libraries, Dept. of Manuscripts and University Archives, Ithaca, New York.

22. Michael S. Foley, *Confronting the War Machine: Draft Resistance during the Vietnam War* (Chapel Hill: University of North Carolina Press, 2003).

23. "Cassius Faces March Draft," *The Baltimore Afro-American*, February 19, 1966, 1, and "Board in Kentucky Refuses to Reclassify Clay As Conscientious Objector," *The New York Times*, January 11, 1967, 62, and "Clay Draft Plea Denied by Board," *The New York Times*, February 1, 1967, 3.

24. "Clay Guilty in Draft Case; Gets Five Years in Prison," *New York Times*, June 21, 1967, 1, and David E. Rosenbaum, "Ali Wins in Draft Case Appeal," *The New York Times*, June 29, 1971, 1.

25. "Draft Exam Ordered for George Hamilton," *The New York Times*, October 28, 1966, 17, and "Good by to Civilian Life," *Ebony*, August 1968, 46.

26. "Draft Exam Ordered," 17.

27. Gonzalo Baltazar, *Oral History Project*, The Vietnam Archive at Texas Tech University. Interviewed by Steve Maxner, March 23, 2001. Retrieved from http://www.virtualarchive.vietnam.ttu.edu/cgi-bin/starfetch. exe?3qUevQOjUtg2mDgIBOhT3hQ7wvenAzlebd@qMS7Av.N9BF7TSM9wvr@vB2M4o7sdoJfUBL5. U3WHS1XkROhq2hvFxK3tPSLj/OH0152.pdf, 1.

28. Lew Moores, "Soldier Devotes Life to Country," *The Cincinnati Enquirer*, November 10, 1997, A-1, A-4.

29. Ron Ballweg, Oral History Project, The Vietnam Archive at Texas Tech University. Interviewed by Richard Verrone, May 19, 2003. Retrieved from http://www.virtualarchive.vietnam.ttu.edu/cgi-bin/starfetch. exe?8ef.0OThTHlw@ovB@bMAIW5KtMcM31GAZwYqlEtpvVWLEnlWMsbO6qa0zk8nerqkpky0E2@3. AAMn2RrUMjKQM1MI39jwXFA/OH0296.pdf.

30. Thomas, "War Stories," 24–31.

31. James E. Westheider, *Fighting on Two Fronts: African Americans and the Vietnam War* (New York: New York University Press, 1997), 34.

32. Office of the Assistant Secretary of Defense, *Task Force on the Administration of Military Justice in the Armed Forces* (Washington, DC: U.S. Government Printing Office, 1972), 1:55.

33. Ballweg, *Oral History Project.*

34. Albert Childs, *Oral History Project,* The Vietnam Archive at Texas Tech University. Interviewed by Steve Maxner, February 3, 2003. Retrieved from http://www.virtualarchive.vietnam.ttu.edu/cgi-bin/starfetch. exe?px@DCzXFmOuNx2T6g1RlUxXU5JKU.VHLnKVjhB5A.zu78Y18RLhkxS@8DT4FUZiZFMSEp2vq jMbGIa4Bk5SPT9GKohPkmUno/OH0095.pdf, 1.

35. Ibid., 2.

36. Timothy R. Wood, in discussion with the author, Cincinnati, Ohio, June 2, 2006.

37. Gene Grove, "The Army and the Negro," *The New York Times Magazine,* July 24, 1966, 7, and James E. Westheider, "African Americans and the Vietnam War," in *The Blackwell Companion to the Vietnam War,* eds. Marilyn Young and Robert Buzzanco (Boston: Blackwell, 2002), 333.

38. Childs, *Oral History Project,* 1.

39. Allen Thomas Jr., in discussion with the author, Erlanger, Kentucky, July 25, 2000.

40. Gerald Kumpf, *Oral History Project,* The Vietnam Archive at Texas Tech University. Interviewed by Richard Verrone, March 10, 2003. Retrieved from http://www.virtualarchive.vietnam.ttu.edu/cgi-bin/starfetch. exe?EWoAfq.tJEBzwDooKsGN8mxwA2X3@q8.Y4@lpzu0qrpNanzPx0Zh6@ZwMPIxL.ex6Y3AV. nGBn7aUH1WFP4otrIS5b2nFx1OwsFzXQ8FRlo/OH0276-1.pdf, 5.

41. Westheider, *Fighting on Two Fronts,* 22.

42. Kumpf, *Oral History Project,* 16.

43. David Llorens, "Why Negroes Re-enlist," *Ebony,* August 1968, 88.

44. Kumpf, *Oral History Project,* 44–45.

45. Jack D. Foner, *Blacks and the Military in American History* (New York: Praeger, 1974), 208.

46. Sol Stern, "When the Black GI Comes Back from Vietnam," *The New York Times Magazine,* March 24, 1968, 2.

47. Ibid.

48. Powell, *My American Journey,* 61.

49. David White, *Oral History Project,* The Vietnam Archive at Texas Tech University. Interviewed by Richard Verrone, n.d. Retrieved from http://www.virtualarchive.vietnam.ttu.edu/cgi-bin/starfetch.exe?71mIafe P3JsUwk7rv@lU9xasA5uYhgjKNAyaDpYf5Nk.Blkuvd69i.GoLp0Gl4jSbk8HMOoS284C0l6iWWadecNnjn. SRsiy/OH0227.pdf, 3.

50. Kumpf, *Oral History Project,* 1–2, 5.

51. Captain Gabrielle Chapin, "Trading His Sword for Penn," *The Quantico Sentry,* September 19, 2002, 1.

52. White, *Oral History Project.*

53. Baltazar, *Oral History Project,* 2.

54. Office of the Assistant Secretary of Defense, *Task Force on Military Justice,* 1:44.

55. Gene Stephens, "Military Doesn't Want Men with Criminal Records," *The Cincinnati Enquirer,* August 17, 1966, 4.

56. "Tough Chicago Gang Leader Returns from War a Hero," *The Baltimore Afro-American,* January, 24, 1970, 3.

57. General William C. Westmoreland, *A Soldier Reports* (Garden City, NY: Doubleday, 1976), 372.

58. Baltazar, *Oral History Project,* 10–11.

59. Clyde Taylor, "Black Consciousness and the Vietnam War," *The Black Scholar,* October 1973, 7.

60. General William C. Westmoreland, *Report of the Chief of Staff of the United States Army, 1 July 1968—30 June, 1972* (Washington, DC: Department of the Army, 1977), 10, 68.

61. Ibid.

62. Stern, "When the Black GI," 37, and Martin Binkin and Mark J. Eitelberg, *Blacks and the Military* (Washington DC: The Brookings Institute, 1982), 34.

63. Binkin and Eitelberg, *Blacks and the Military,* 34, and U.S. Department of Defense, *Department of Defense Annual Report for Fiscal Year 1968* (Washington, DC: U.S. Government Printing Office, 1971), 73.

64. Johnny Bowles, "A 41% Black G.I. Deal: Fight But Can't Re-up" *The Baltimore Afro-American,* February 21, 1970, 6, and Office of the Assistant Secretary of Defense for Manpower and Reserve Affairs, *Project*

One Hundred Thousand: Characteristics and Performance of "New Standards" Men (Washington, DC: U.S. Government Printing Office, 1969).

65. Alex Poinsett, "The Negro Officer," *Ebony,* August, 1968, 138.

66. Honorable Louis Stokes, "Racism in the Military: The Congressional Black Caucus Report, 15 May, 1972," 82nd Cong., 2nd sess., *Congressional Record 118,* part 27, (October 14, 1972): 36,585.

67. Westmoreland, *Report of the Chief of Staff,* 65, and Foner, *Blacks and the Military,* 240, and Brigadier General Daniel James, Jr., "Rapping with Chappie," *Air University Review,* July, 1972,12.

68. Philip Caputo, *A Rumor of War* (New York: Holt, Rinehart, and Winston, 1977), 7.

69. Childs, *Oral History Project.*

70. Brandon Johnson, and Robert A. Goldberg, "Boot Camp Violence: Abuse in Vietnam War-era Basic Training," *The University of Utah's Journal of Undergraduate Research* 6(1) 7–15.

71. Ibid.

72. Baltazar, *Oral History Project,* 3.

73. Ballweg, *Oral History Project,* 4.

74. Johnson and Goldberg, "Boot Camp Violence," 8.

75. Ibid.

76. White, *Oral History Project,* 4.

77. Caputo, *A Rumor of War,* 10.

78. Ibid., 32.

79. Timothy R. Wood, in discussion with the author.

80. Baltazar, *Oral History Project,* 3.

81. Kumpf, *Oral History Project,* 9.

82. Baltazar, *Oral History Project,* 4.

83. James A. Daly and Lee Bergman, *Black Prisoner of War: A Conscientious Objector's Vietnam Memoir* (Lawrence: University Press of Kansas, 2000), 12.

84. Black Cadets, "An Answer to Wing Staff's Request" (MS: U.S. Air Force Academy, 1970), 1–3, Citizen Soldier Files, #7033, Box 8 File 54, Cornell University Archives.

85. Childs, *Oral History Project,* 7.

86. Baltazar, *Oral History Project,* 4.

87. Timothy R. Wood, in discussion with the author.

88. Childs, *Oral History Project,* 2, 7.

89. Allen Thomas Jr., in discussion with the author.

90. Johnson and Goldberg, "Boot Camp Violence," 7.

91. Ballweg, *Oral History Project,* 5.

92. Hank Lovelady, "Our Men in Vietnam," *Sepia,* July 1968, 75.

93. William H. McMichael, "A War on Two Fronts," *Newport News–Hampton, Virginia Daily Press,* Williamsburg edition, July 27, 1998, 1, A4–A6.

94. Baltazar, *Oral History Project,* 4.

95. Timothy R. Wood, in discussion with the author.

96. Kumpf, *Oral History Project,* 7.

97. Childs, *Oral History Project,* 2.

98. Kumpf, *Oral History Project,* 7.

99. Baltazar, *Oral History Project,* 3.

100. Kumpf, *Oral History Project,* 8.

101. White, *Oral History Project,* 4.

102. Ballweg, *Oral History Project,* 4.

103. Timothy R. Wood, in discussion with the author.

104. White, *Oral History Project,* 4.

105. Kumpf, *Oral History Project,* 7–8.

106. Ibid., 11.

107. Baltazar, *Oral History Project,* 7.

108. Ballweg, *Oral History Project.*

109. Kumpf, *Oral History Project,* 8.

110. Caputo, *A Rumor of War,* 12.

111. Johnson and Goldberg, "Boot Camp Violence."

112. Christian G. Appy, *Working-Class War: American Combat Soldiers and Vietnam* (Chapel Hill: University of North Carolina Press, 1993), 107, and Joe Allen, "Vietnam: The War the U.S. Lost; From the

Overthrow of Diem to the Tet Offensive," *International Socialist Review* 33 (2004), online edition, n.p., http://www.isreview.org/issues/33/vietnam2.shtml,

113. Caputo, *A Rumor of War,* xii, 36.
114. Childs, *Oral History Project*, 7.
115. Kumpf, *Oral History Project*, 9.
116. Baltazar, *Oral History Project*, 3–4.
117. Johnson and Goldberg, "Boot Camp Violence."
118. Ibid.
119. Kumpf, *Oral History Project*, 9.
120. Johnson and Goldberg, "Boot Camp Violence," 8.
121. Caputo, *A Rumor of War,* 10.
122. Kumpf, *Oral History Project*, 9.
123. Baltazar, *Oral History Project*, 3.
124. Johnson and Goldberg, "Boot Camp Violence," 8.
125. Ibid.
126. Allen Thomas Jr., in discussion with the author.
127. Kumpf, *Oral History Project*, 7.
128. Richard E. Marks, *The Letters o/pfc. Richard E. Marks, USMC* (Philadelphia: J. B. Lippincott, 1967), 12, and David Parks, *GI Diary* (New York: Harper and Row, 1968), 14.
129. Johnson and Goldberg, "Boot Camp Violence," 9.
130. Office of the Assistant Secretary of Defense, *Task Force on Military Justice,* 2:11–13, and NAACP, *The Search for Military Justice* (New York: NAACP Special Contributions Fund, 1971), 1.
131. NAACP, *Search for Military Justice,* 1.
132. Stokes, "Black Caucus Report," *118,* 36,583.
133. Ballweg, *Oral History Project*.
134. Kumpf, *Oral History Project*, 12–13.
135. Baltazar, *Oral History Project*, 2–3.
136. Ibid., 3.
137. Ballweg, *Oral History Project*, 4.
138. Ibid., 5.
139. Baltazar, *Oral History Project*, 6.
140. White, *Oral History Project*, 5–6.
141. "Pugil stick," *The Free Dictionary by Farlex.* Retrieved from http://www.thefreedictionary.com/pugil+stick
142. Baltazar, *Oral History Project*, 6.
143. Caputo, *A Rumor of War,* 14.
144. Merle T. Cole and Scott S. Sheads, *Fort McHenry and Baltimore's Harbor Defenses* (Charleston, SC: Arcadia, 2001).
145. General Wallace H. Nutting Interview, *Senior Officer Oral History Project,* U.S. Military History Institute: Carlisle Barracks, PA, 1989, 9, 109.
146. Ibid., 9.
147. Childs, *Oral History Project*, 5.
148. Baltazar, *Oral History Project*, 6.
149. Ballweg, *Oral History Project*, 43.
150. David White, 5–7, 9.
151. Baltazar, *Oral History Project*, 8.
152. Ibid.
153. Peter O. Hefron, "Memories of a U.S. Army Replacement Battalion: Service and Disservice to the Vietnam War Effort" (paper presented at The Vietnam War, Thirty Years On, Memories, Legacies, and Echoes Conference, Newcastle, Australia, April 14–15, 2005).
154. Caputo, *A Rumor of War,* 13.
155. Baltazar, *Oral History Project*, 8.
156. Caputo, *A Rumor of War,* 14.
157. Ibid.
158. Ibid.
159. Ibid., 16.
160. Ballweg, *Oral History Project*.
161. Baltazar, *Oral History Project*, 7.

CHAPTER 3

Assignment Vietnam and Life in the Field

TOUR OF DUTY

American military personnel served in Vietnam from 1945 until 1975. Vietnam was different from previous twentieth-century wars when it came to the length of assignment. In both World War I and World War II, men served for the duration of the war. A rotation policy was introduced in Korea, but men in noncombat units had a longer tour of duty than those in combat units. In Vietnam, army and air force personnel served a 12-month tour of duty, and a marine served for 13 months. Unless one was killed or wounded, everyone knew his DEROS, or "date expected to return overseas," the exact date he could leave Vietnam and go home.

Not everyone served the standard 12- or 13-month tour of duty in Vietnam. In 1965, the marines decided to rotate as many people through Vietnam as possible. Marine air units, such as Gerald Kumpf's unit, MFA-314, were split in half, with each half of the squadron serving six months in Vietnam with part of another squadron, MFA-115, and the other half serving in Japan. Later, when he was in the air force, Kumpf earned his flight wings and was assigned to a transportation unit in Okinawa that spent 30 days every three months in Vietnam. They would fly cargo in C-130s, usually fresh fruits and vegetables, stay for a month, and rotate back out.[1]

Some of the first troops to be sent to Vietnam did not know that they were going until the last minute. On February 15, 1965, Marine Corps officials denied rumors that a marine regiment stationed on Okinawa would be sent to Vietnam and said that the unit would leave for either the Philippines or Hong Kong within the week. They were sent to Vietnam instead, and with only 24 hours' notice.[2] Sergeant Allen Thomas Jr., who did three tours of duty in Vietnam, was assigned to Southeast Asia for the first time in 1965. "First time I went I didn't even know where the hell I was going," he recalled. "I got an APO for San Francisco, not my eventual destination."[3]

Most had some sort of advance warning, and soldiers assigned to Vietnam were usually given a 30-day leave before they were due to report. Albert Childs knew over eight months in advance that he was going to Vietnam. Lieutenant Colonel Arthur Gregg knew that the 96th Quartermaster Battalion at Fort Riley, Kansas, was headed for Vietnam before he assumed command of the unit in January 1966.[4] In early spring 1966, John Ballweg and his unit were informed that they were being sent to Vietnam in August.[5] Gonzalo Baltazar and his training class were told about a week before they finished training. For some, it was a rude shock; they were told to have their insurance papers and wills filled out because the majority of them would be going to Vietnam. "It was a rude awakening that maybe you weren't going to be coming back."[6]

VOLUNTEERING FOR VIETNAM

Despite the popular image, not every soldier sent to Vietnam was a reluctant draftee. Many American military personnel volunteered and looked forward to service in Vietnam, especially in the early years of the war. For many, it was a mixture of patriotism and adventure. David White volunteered because he really believed in the war and because "everybody secretly...wants to know what combat's like." Also, shipboard life was "a little blasé."[7] Men and women continued to volunteer for Vietnam after the war had become unpopular. Many of the more elite formations remained all or nearly all volunteers. All of the navy PBR crews were volunteers, for example. Officers and career NCOs volunteered because service in a war zone generally led to more rapid promotion and advancement. It was known as getting your ticket punched. John Ballweg claimed that Vietnam was full of officers "trying to obtain medals, trying to obtain that recognition while they had the chance in a war zone to further their career after the war."[8]

One or more tours in Vietnam did help an aspiring officer's or NCO's career. Arthur J. Gregg was assigned to command a quartermaster battalion in Vietnam a few days after he turned down a chance to attend the Armed Forces Staff College. Gregg was told up front that his assignment to Vietnam was not in retaliation for him turning down the Staff College, but rather a chance for him to command at the lieutenant colonel level, the rank to which he had just been promoted. Gregg never felt that he received orders for Vietnam because he disagreed with his superiors.[9] Colin Powell served two tours of duty in Vietnam. In 1962, as a captain, he was an advisor to an ARVN infantry battalion and returned as a major in 1968, as a battalion executive officer. Powell's performance in Vietnam earned him 11 medals and more rapid promotions. After his second tour, his superiors purposely groomed him for higher rank and responsibilities. It was the same for NCOs. Albert Childs went to Vietnam in June 1968. As a career soldier, an NCO going to Vietnam "was the thing to do, to go get some combat time," if one wanted to remain competitive and receive promotions.[10]

Patriotism and devotion to the military were other reasons men and women volunteered for Vietnam. Allen Thomas "was brainwashed...anti-Communist, pretty much supported the war. You have to remember this was in the early sixties, before all hell broke loose. We were still patriotic, and I thought I was up to the job.... What did I know!"[11] In 1970, Medal of Honor recipient and combat medic Lawrence Joel voluntarily returned for a second tour of duty in Vietnam because "I want to do what I can here, to serve my country as best I can."[12]

AFRICAN AMERICANS AND SERVICE IN VIETNAM

Between 1957 and 1973, over 300,000 African Americans served in Vietnam and accounted for roughly 9–10 percent of military personnel assigned to Vietnam. Approximately 448,000 marines were sent to Vietnam, for example, and about 41,000 of them were black. African Americans making a career out of the military often sought service in Vietnam for a mixture of reasons. Like their white compatriots, they were often fiercely anti-Communist, very patriotic, and wanted to serve their country. First Lieutenant Gasanove Stephens was "dedicated to this country to suppress any type of aggression or any threat of communism against it or its allies.... I'm a soldier dedicated to keeping my country free."[13] Colonel Daniel "Chappie" James believed he "couldn't live long enough to pay this country what I owe it. I've fought in three wars, and three more wouldn't be too many to defend my country. I love America, and if she has weaknesses and ills, I'll hold her hand." On another occasion, the 48-year-old fighter pilot remarked, "I'd go back to Vietnam if they'd let me, and it wouldn't take me but about fifteen minutes to pack."[14]

Many African Americans were dedicated and loyal to the armed forces for giving them opportunities not generally available in civilian life. Vietnam, they believed, was a level playing field, where blacks served equally with whites and a person rose on his skills and merits, not the color of his skin. "The brother does all right here," remarked an unnamed black officer, assigned as an advisor to an ARVN unit. "You see it's just about the first time in his life that he finds he can compete with whites on an equal—or very close to equal basis. He tries hard in this kind of situation and does well." Army major Beauregard Brown believed that service in Vietnam represented the best chance for advancement, anywhere, for a black career officer.[15]

Vietnam was also yet another chance to dispel the old myth that whites made superior soldiers to African Americans. The father of marine Medal of Honor recipient Milton Olive Jr. believed that his son's sacrifice and "the service the colored soldier has given in Vietnam has erased for all time the disparaging statements made about him."[16] It was a reputation paid for in blood. "I feel good about it," remarked African American army lieutenant colonel George Shoffer in 1968 about the disproportionately high casualty rate among blacks in Vietnam. "Not that I like the bloodshed, but the performance of the Negro in Vietnam tends to offset the fact that the Negro wasn't considered worthy of being a front-line soldier in other wars."[17]

For many African Americans, service in Vietnam was yet another way to demand the civil rights they deserved as American citizens. Sergeant Willie E. Burney Jr. believed that African Americans were "earning the right to call the United States 'our' country, and when we return home, we will earn the right to keep it 'ours.'... We now fight two separate wars in Vietnam, and as long as we share a predominately white society we will always fight two wars—one for freedom, the other for equality. We therefore will return from Vietnam still 'fighting men.'"[18] Lawrence E. Waggoner stated with pride that "the Negro warrior has distinguished himself in Vietnam. This is to be looked on with pride and committed to memory as he presses on to distinguish himself in his own country." In Vietnam "there are no color lines—I am a marine, period."[19]

It was so important that some risked their careers and family relationships for a chance to serve in Vietnam. Major General Frederic E. Davison had to convince both the army and his skeptical family. He "wanted to go very badly," despite the fact that the military had no plans to send him. "And I god damn nearly lost my family—lost my family because they couldn't see why the hell I had to volunteer to go to Vietnam."[20]

WOMEN IN VIETNAM

Women also served in Vietnam, some even before American combat troops arrived. In 1956, the first three army nurses arrived in Vietnam on temporary duty assignments, attached to the U.S. Army Medical Training Team. They were sent to train South Vietnamese nurses, not to care for wounded Americans, but soon became part of the American Dispensary, Saigon, that was in charge of health care for Americans in Vietnam.[21] Relatively few women, however, served in Vietnam. Between 1962 and 1973, the Defense Department claims that roughly 7,500 women served in Vietnam, but Veterans Affairs puts the figure somewhat higher, at over 11,500 women.[22]

Roughly 90 percent of the women were nurses, 5,000 of them army nurses. Most of the nurses were single, but some were married, and the Pentagon made an effort to station married couples together, or near each other, but could not always do so. Married nurses who became pregnant were generally sent back to the United States, but several of them completed their tours before returning home to give birth.

Another 1,300 women served in nonmedical occupations, and almost all were with the Women's Army Corps (WAC). The first nonnurse woman to be assigned to Vietnam was Major Anna M. Doering, a WAC officer at MACV in 1962. About half of the 1,300 nonmedical army women in Vietnam were enlisted.[23] Women from the other services served in Vietnam, but in much smaller numbers. There were 771 women in the air force (WAFs), 421 from the navy, and 36 female marines. By 1965, women in the army were represented in 36 of 61 noncombat MOSs, and women officers in 35 out of 46, and

Basic trainees march in company formation at the WAC training Center at Fort McClellan, 1968. Courtesy of the National Archives.

this was apparent in Vietnam. Though 90 percent of the enlisted women and 75 percent of the officers were in traditionally feminine fields, such as nursing or clerical work, women were also engaged in a variety of occupations, including maintenance, intelligence, secretarial, photo interpretation, administration, meteorology, and other fields. One even became the first woman to give briefings on air strikes to senior officers. Despite these accomplishments, there were never that many WAC women in Vietnam at any one time. Peak strength for WACs in Vietnam was reached in January 1970, but it was only 20 officers and 139 enlisted women.

The women volunteered for duty in Vietnam for mostly the same reasons the men did: patriotism, adventure, or career opportunities. Colonel Mary C. Quinn said, "I wanted to be an Army nurse and combat is where the soldier is."[24] Major Marion Davis went because "there were American troops there that needed help. They needed the things that I could give them in my nursing profession."[25]

ASSIGNED TO VIETNAM

Many individuals did not necessarily want to go to Vietnam but still accepted assignment there as part of their professional duty. Sergeant C. Nelson Williams Jr. served as a military fire chief at an airfield, and "to tell the truth, I did not want to come here, nor did I volunteer to come, but the Army saw fit to send me here and I will do my job as a man for my country." Williams added that he was not sorry he was sent to Vietnam because it's "been more than educational."[26] Corporal Lawrence E. Waggoner also did not volunteer for Vietnam, but he "did volunteer for the Marine Corps and any place they saw fit to send me." Like Williams, he was "not one bit sorry I am here. Believe me, it has been more than educational."[27]

Given the controversial nature of the war, and the draft, there were many men who refused to serve in Vietnam. Two men from Gonzalo Baltazar's F (B) Troop of the Second Battalion, 17th Division, for example, went AWOL the night before they were supposed to leave for Vietnam.[28] But if the men were caught, the price they paid for desertion or refusal was steep. The fate of army private Ronald Lockman was typical. In January 1968, Lockman was convicted of refusal to obey a lawful order and sentenced to two and a half years at the Presidio in San Francisco.[29] Army privates James Johnson, Dennis Mora, and David Samas, collectively known as the Fort Hood Three, refused to go to Vietnam and were court-martialed and imprisoned. West Point graduate Captain Richard Steinke went to Vietnam but refused a combat assignment, stating that the war was not worth a single American life, leading to his court-martial and dismissal from the army.

THE TRIP TO VIETNAM

During the initial phase of American buildup, most troops went to Vietnam as part of a unit. The 3,500 marines in the first two battalion landing teams sent to Vietnam in March 1965 arrived at Danang together on four ships after a stormy six-week voyage from Japan. Even later in the war, entire units were being rotated into Vietnam. Gonzalo Baltazar's entire 400-man battalion went over together in early 1969.

Most of the equipment and a lot of the personnel during the initial buildup of U.S. forces in 1965–1966 arrived in Vietnam by ship. The 96th Quartermaster Battalion was one of the units to deploy to Vietnam by ship. Standard practice was to ship a unit's equipment, but the personnel were flown in by air because it took weeks or even months from a port in the United States to sail to Cam Ranh Bay.[30] The equipment for the 11th Armored Cavalry Regiment, for example, was shipped to Vietnam in July 1966 and did not arrive until September. The equipment for the Second Battalion, 17th Division, was shipped to Vietnam, but most of the 400 men in the battalion were flown to Vietnam in a couple of civilian airliners. A few men from a unit were always detailed to the ship to accompany a unit's equipment.

A lot of military personnel flew into Vietnam in military transport, especially in the early phases of American involvement. Special Forces enlisted man Adam Smith recalled that "a Southeast Asia trip in 1955 was exotic; it meant riding in a military transport—metal bucket seats, no heat—from Hawaii to Guam to Wake Island to Japan to Hong Kong to Saigon."[31] Ten years later, the trip was not much better. In August 1966, John Ballweg flew a military C-141 out of Dulles airport outside Washington, DC, and rode in "troop seats all the way." The trip took 24 hours and was "not a comfortable ride." The plane's route took it to Alaska to Japan to Saigon.[32]

After the buildup was complete, most were assigned to Vietnam on an individual basis. Later in the war, when the Pentagon was rotating tens of thousands of men through Vietnam each year, the military often used chartered civilian airliners, complete with stewardesses, to transport troops to Vietnam.[33] The men on board often had something in common, such as all being NCOs, for example. In the summer of 1968, navy patrol boat veteran David White flew to Vietnam on a Transworld Airlines chartered flight, and most of the men on board were headed to PBR duty. The route was San Francisco to Honolulu to Saigon, and it was more comfortable, but it was still a 12-hour trip. The journey could take longer if there were any complications. William Calley stated that Charlie Company was up at 4:00 A.M. the morning they departed for Vietnam in 1968 but did not board the busses until 1:00 P.M. because of antiwar protestors at the airport in Honolulu.[34]

ARRIVING IN VIETNAM

Arriving in Vietnam for the first time was always an experience. The port of Cam Ranh Bay was so busy because of the American buildup that ships could not get close enough to the general dock. The men of the 96th Quartermaster Battalion had to disembark by climbing down nets, just like in World War II.[35] Aircraft often went into steep dives coming in to land to avoid enemy antiaircraft fire and mortars. Army nurse Kathleen Trew flew from Travis Air Force Base on a cargo plane to Anchorage, Alaska, to Yakota, Japan, and then to Vietnam. Her plane had to circle and wait until the enemy was finished mortaring the airstrip before they could land.

Most personnel assigned to Vietnam had some idea of what the country was like before they arrived. Normal procedure during the advising phase was to send officers and senior NCOs headed to Vietnam as advisors to the six-week Military Assistance Training Agency course, at the U.S. Army Special Warfare School at Fort Bragg, North Carolina. There they learned about the culture, history, politics, and geography of Vietnam as well as the organization and capabilities of ARVN and some basic language instruction. Albert Childs attended the army language school at Fort Bliss, Texas, before being sent to Vietnam. They also learned something of the people and culture of Vietnam because the sons and daughters of refugees that had fled northern Vietnam in 1954 taught the courses at Fort Bliss.

The newly arriving personnel had been briefed on the climate, and most thought they understood what a jungle environment was like, some having served in the tropics before, but for the vast majority, disembarking the plane was an eye-opening experience. One of the first things new arrivals noted was the intense tropical heat, which many of them described as like stepping into an oven, and the strange smells that permeated the cabin when the plane's doors opened. "We got off the plane and it was hot," remembered Gonzalo Baltazar.[36] John Ballweg remembers it being "hot, it was miserably hot." They were all drenched in sweat within 20 minutes of disembarking from the plane.[37]

The abundance of insect life was another not so pleasant surprise. Kathleen Trew stated that the plane was sprayed with bug spray before they opened the door to let them out. David White flew into Tan Son Nhut airport and was amazed at how big Saigon was and all the fortifications around the airport. After disembarking the airplane, they were bussed to the Montana Hotel for the night. White remembered it as a stately French building with substandard toilets and showers, and fortified. He was used to the big-city noise, and the lack of air-conditioning did not really bother him, but he really hated the mosquitoes.[38]

Once you were on the ground, you were "in country." Everything outside of Vietnam was "the world." The difference between the two was instantly obvious to the new arrivals. The fact that they had flown into an active war zone was inescapable for many of the new arrivals. The busses that picked them up at the airport had small wire screens on the windows so grenades, or homemade bombs, could not be thrown through. Many were a bit apprehensive on their first night in country. On the basis of what he had heard, Gonzalo Baltazar feared he would have to "get off the plane fighting" and run for cover. They were at Danang. Later that night, he heard M-60 machine guns in the distance, bombs, and fighting, and all he could think was that the battalion's weapons were still on board the ship, and they were defenseless if the base was overrun. A few days later, they went up to Camp Eagle, near Hue, and were reunited with their equipment, much to Baltazar's relief.[39]

Others, however, were self-confident, and morale was excellent among the marines in Vietnam in 1965–1966. "We were going to kick ass," recalled Gerald Kumpf. "We were there doing our duty and doing it well. It was the entire atmosphere was different at that time. We were there doing our duty and people were supporting us, the newspapers, everybody was supporting us. The protestors hadn't gotten the public eye at that time yet."[40]

Some were just cocky and immature. Lieutenant William Calley remembered acting "asinine." He believed that "we're going to end this whole damn war tomorrow!" He was "standing there in a trailer truck like the meanest, the most tremendous, the most dangerous weapon there is. My rifle swung low. My helmet pulled down. I was scowling even! I realize now, I couldn't have impressed the Vietnamese less."[41]

ASSIGNMENT AND ORIENTATION

In most cases, troops heading for Vietnam did not get their assignments until after they arrived in country.[42] Two U.S. Army replacement battalions operating in South Vietnam made the vast majority of assignments: the 22nd Replacement Battalion was located at Cam Ranh Bay near Danang and the 90th Replacement Battalion at Bien Hoa Air Base at Long Binh, near Saigon. There were some exceptions, usually based on a specialized MOS. Nurses, for example, either reported to the 90th Replacement Battalion or the 178th Replacement Company at Camp Alpha.

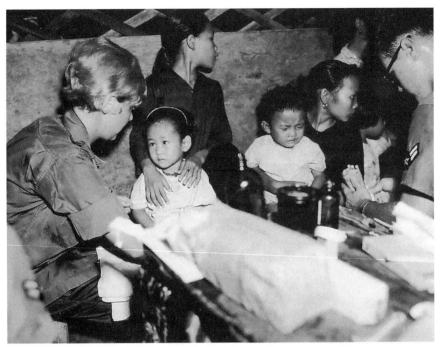

Second Lieutenant Kathleen M. Sullivan treats a Vietnamese child during Operation MED CAP, a U.S. Air Force civic action program in which a team of doctors, nurses, and aides traveled to Vietnamese villages, treated the sick, and taught villagers the basics of sanitation and cleanliness, 1967. Courtesy of the National Archives.

At the replacement battalion, all incoming troops were given a 30-minute lecture by a staff sergeant/E-6 on Vietnamese culture, U.S. troop deployment in country, and how the in-country assignment process worked. Most soldiers did not think much of the orientation, and it was nicknamed "charm school" by the troops. The talk probably had little impact on the new arrivals, most of whom were tired after a long plane ride, anxious as to their new assignments, and some still in a bit of shock from their arrival in country.[43] They were also given a standard pocket guide to Vietnam. The guide informed them that the United States was in Vietnam by invitation of the government to help protect them from Communist aggression. "If you are bound for Vietnam," the booklet read, "it is for the deeply serious business of helping a brave nation repel Communist aggression." They were warned that the Vietcong would attempt to turn the local population against them, but they were to remember that they were there as friends and allies of the South Vietnamese people. It contained a language guide, a short history of Vietnam and its culture, and an overview of the various ethnic groups in the country. Since Vietnam was on the metric system, it also contained charts for converting miles into kilometers and gallons into liters.[44]

A group of specialists known as the assignment team made the actual unit assignments for most incoming personnel. Because there was some flexibility in assignments, there were attempts by some personnel to secure a more favorable job, or preferably, a noncombat position, through bribery or favoritism. One's actual assignment, however, was often luck of the draw, and you went where your MOS was needed. One day, that might be a combat unit; the next, it could be an assignment in Saigon.[45] Sometimes your particular MOS did not matter. In 1972, Albert Childs went back for a second tour in Vietnam. He was sent to Pleiku, but because the war was winding down, they did not have an assignment for him at first, so they put him in II Corps G-2, or intelligence. He had nothing to do with actual intelligence, just administrative duties.[46] The new assignments were normally announced at the following morning's formation. If you arrived after morning formation, you usually waited around for a few days until your orders became official.[47]

It normally took a week or so for a fresh arrival to be processed, assigned, and then transported to his new unit. David White spent a few days in Saigon, got another round of shots, and then was bussed to Nha Be, a small town a few miles outside Saigon. He waited another few days until the chief of a boat asked him if he would like to be a gunner's mate, and within a week, he had been assigned to the boat crew.[48]

Sometimes a new arrival was sent to an established unit for some in-country training before being ordered to his permanent assignment. Some had to learn a new skill or job quickly. Many of the men assigned to armored personnel carrier crews, for example, had no training on the M113, or any other armored personnel carrier (APC), so MACV mandated a weeklong in-country training course for all new APC crewmen. Even well-trained personnel needed to learn how things actually worked in Vietnam. Though John Ballweg was already an experienced helicopter pilot, he spent his first two weeks in Vietnam doing in-country training with an air unit of Bien Hoa. Then he was with a maintenance unit out of Phou Loi whose mission was to recover downed or wrecked choppers. He served with them for two weeks. His unit was finally assembled and based at Camp Black Horse near Xuan Loc, out in the jungle.[49]

Getting an assignment and then getting to that assignment could sometimes be a bit of an ordeal. Albert Childs went to Vietnam in 1968 and spent his first week in Vietnam in processing in Saigon, then boarded a C-130 for more processing at an unidentified base in the north. Finally, he caught a helicopter headed south for Ban Me Thout. When he arrived, "and I got off there at East field," there "was not a soul around, except apparently some Montagnards." Then a jeep with a Vietnamese driver and an American lieutenant pulled up. Childs attempted to present his orders, but the officer tersely ordered him into the jeep and told him that the driver would take him where he had to go. Attempting to converse with the driver in his native language, Child's was told, "Come on man, give me a break! Speak English!" Childs was assigned to the 23rd ARVN Division, but there were so many interpreters around, and so many of the Vietnamese spoke fluent English, that he seldom needed to speak any Vietnamese.[50]

Most of the personnel assigned to Vietnam were not combat troops, but the ratio of combat to support personnel fluctuated during the war and depended, to a degree, on one's definition of *combat*. General William Westmoreland stated in his memoirs that during the initial buildup, priority was on combat troops, but afterward, the emphasis shifted somewhat to support units. He claimed that the number of support troops in Vietnam never exceeded 45 percent of U.S. total troop strength and, by 1968, was down to about 40 percent of total American manpower in Vietnam.[51] This would have been similar to both World War II and Korea, where roughly 43 percent of all military personnel were support troops.

Others, however, argue for a much higher ratio of noncombat to combat personnel. Ultimately, probably only about 10–20 percent of the U.S. soldiers in Vietnam were there to fight, and the rest were in support roles. There were large numbers of noncombat enlisted personnel and lots of officers at the huge base camps. One officer from a replacement battalion estimated that 88 percent of the troops they processed were non-combat personnel, a figure that dovetails nicely with Henry Kissinger's criticism in 1975 that the United States had over half a million troops in Vietnam, but only 100,000 were combat troops. At the height of American involvement in 1968, for example, there were 543,000 American military personnel in Vietnam, but only 80,000 were considered combat troops.[52]

In Vietnam, the lines between combat and noncombat personnel were often very blurred. Allen Thomas Jr. was a member of the Signal Corps and held a noncombat MOS, but he still engaged in fighting the enemy. Military police in Vietnam carried out the customary functions for police such as maintaining law and order, security, traffic control, and serving as guards at the various military brigs and stockades. But they also served as so-called tunnel rats and patrolled the jungles and villages near Long Binh and in other areas throughout Vietnam and engaged the enemy in firefights.[53] The 96th Quartermaster Battalion, a support unit, had the "usual amount of tactical training" according to Lieutenant Colonel Arthur Gregg. They had done some fieldwork and received some defensive training before leaving Fort Riley, Kansas. All the men in the battalion had received infantry training and helped guard the base perimeter in Vietnam.[54]

Sometimes new arrivals were pressed into service in an area where there was a shortage of trained personnel. Many of the men assigned to logistics units had no particular training in that field. Gregg was sent replacements trained as bakers and laundry operators and had to retrain them in depot and supply operations.[55] Others started off in support positions, only to be reassigned to ones in combat. Men with a clerk typist MOS, for example, were sent out into the field as radio telephone operators, despite no training with the equipment. Sp/4 Joe Roberson Jr. started his tour of duty in Vietnam as a supply clerk, "one of the easiest jobs to have over here." But since his MOS was 11B, or combat infantryman, he found himself reassigned to one of the more dangerous jobs after his first few months. "My job now is a door gunner. It's rough, but I like it. My aircraft has been shot up several times, but so far I haven't been hit."[56]

NONCOMBAT ASSIGNMENTS AND REMFS

Many of the noncombat personnel stationed in Vietnam never saw combat or the enemy. Airman Richard W. Harper was a self-styled "Saigon Warrior" and "one of the lucky guys that got stationed in Saigon." Harper said that contrary to what the "mud-stompers" may think, "we in Saigon don't have such an easy life." Twenty-year-old Airman Harper was relatively safe. "I can't tell you any shocking war stories because the only battles I see are on Monday nights when I watch *Combat* [a World War II drama on ABC] on television."[57] Likewise, Peter Hefron never saw any combat when he served in Vietnam from May 1969 to April 1970 as an information specialist for the 90th Replacement Battalion.[58]

Men in combat units often derided noncombat personnel and had a litany of disparaging names for them. Collectively, they were "base camp commandos," or, worse, "REMFS," for "rear echelon motherfuckers." There were also terms for individual service and support occupations. A clerk, or anyone who carried a typewriter for a living, was a "Smith-Corona Commando" or a "Remington Raider." Combat soldiers had their own language separating them from noncombat personnel. Field soldiers called the collection of track blocks on a tracked vehicle "tracks," but REMFs referred to them as "treads," for example. "Spooky" was field radio code for the AC-47 gunship, known to reporters and rear echelon personnel as "Puff."

NO FRONT LINES

Vietnam, however, differed from most previous wars in that there were no front lines, and no place was truly safe from enemy attack. Most installations, even large ones, were subject to mortar fire or booby traps. Nurse Eddie Meeks, stationed at the Third Field Hospital, was told when she first arrived in Saigon not to kick any cans she saw in the street because the Vietcong often booby-trapped them.[59] Because army field hospitals were located as far north as Quang Tri, just 35 kilometers (21.7 mi.) from the DMZ, and deep in the Mekong delta at Can Tho, nurses were often assigned to active combat areas. Many nurses carried sidearms in the field and used them on more than one occasion, especially during Tet-68. Gerald Kumpf said that at Danang, "you can't really call it combat because it's kind of a one-sided thing, they used to lob mortars in all the time." They would lob a few in and then retreat. Often, they would infiltrate snipers down from a hill called "Monkey Mountain" at the end of the runway and take shots at the guys on the runway. For protection, the men would be taken out to the flight line in large, protected cattle cars, but one morning, as Kumpf sat in the car reading on his way out to the flight line, he heard a large noise like a thunderclap directly above him. He looked up and realized that an exploding mortar had missed him by only a few inches.[60]

The farther out into the jungle, or "Indian country," the greater the likelihood of attack. The enemy routinely mortared John Ballweg's helicopter unit, stationed at base camp Black Horse. Ballweg claimed that they seldom hit anything, though. The defenses at his base camp reflected their nonchalant attitude toward enemy mortaring. The holes had been dug, for example, but the unit's bunkers were never completed. They did not think they needed them because their living quarters, or "hooches," were located so far in the interior of the compound that when a mortar attack occurred, they just turned off the lights and continued partying. Ballweg claimed that they were not really worried about getting mortared and believed that the round that took out the washbasin in front of his quarters was simply a lucky hit.[61] Duc Lop was a small army camp near the Cambodian border that the Vietcong camp across the border mortared every afternoon at precisely 5:00 P.M. They never hit anything, and for the men in the camp, it was usually the signal to go have dinner in the mess tent.

WORK AND VIETNAM

Most everyone, regardless of MOS, worked hard. Many of the first large units sent to Vietnam were not ready to be deployed, necessitating near-round-the-clock work by a unit's personnel. The 96th Quartermaster Battalion was due to deploy to Vietnam in May 1966, but as late as March, it was still not ready. Other units already sent to Vietnam had taken most of the battalion's equipment, and the battalion had the lowest readiness rating possible, a C-4. The 800 officers and men worked hard, and the battalion was ready to deploy on time.[62] Once in Vietnam, Arthur Gregg said that the battalion routinely worked 12 hours a day, seven days a week.[63] That was a typical work schedule for most units. "My unit was working," recalled Bruce Cary, captain of a transportation company stationed at Tam My in 1970–1971. "The guys were kept extremely busy for twelve hours a day and we were pretty tired at night and have a couple of beers and go to bed."[64] Gonzalo Baltazar and the Second Battalion, 17th Division, arrived at Camp Eagle near Hue in early 1969 and were assigned newly built hooches, and "the first week or so consisted of nothing but filling sandbags and putting them up on our hooch, building our bunkers. We were pretty busy."[65] Captain Robert Arnold's frontline ordinance company at Camp Eagle also had a "good work schedule," which kept the men busy.[66]

In the early years of direct American involvement in Vietnam, much of the hard work and effort was directed toward building the huge infrastructure needed to accommodate and support hundreds of thousands of troops. The navy alone, for example, built massive installations at Saigon, Da Nang, and Cam Ranh Bay, turning them into major logistical bases, and Qui Nhon, Nha Trang, Phan Rang, Chu Lai, Phu Bai, and Vung Tau into minor support bases. In Vietnam, First Logistics' Command near Saigon was the main logistical command, and all other depots and service centers in Vietnam were subordinate to it. Materiel flowed out of the First Logistics' Command to the regional depots, and then to the service centers. The only exception to this system was aerial resupply, which was handled by the 96th Battalion at Cam Ranh Bay.[67]

Combat operations in particular dictated long stretches of work. The average sailor on a combat vessel deployed off the Vietnamese coast worked 18-hour days. Between December 4, 1966, and April 28, 1967, the aircraft carrier USS *Kitty Hawk,* stationed off the South Vietnamese coast, launched 4,544 combat sorties, and another 2,150 in April and May 1968, spending a record 61 days on the line. It was not just the carriers. Crews on most ships were kept very busy, and each sailor had multiple duties on board a ship at sea. On the troop carrier USS *Monticello,* which carried marines up and down the South Vietnamese coastline, David White stood gun watch during the day at his gun and served as helmsman during his ship watch. The so-called brown water navy in Vietnam also kept a rigorous workday. PBR crews had a schedule of 12 hours on patrol, 12 hours on call, then 24 hours off. This was followed by two days of patrols, then off 24 hours, then two night patrols. In August 1968, his first full month on the job, David White made 25 patrols.

Nurses at base or field hospitals normally worked 12 hours a day, six days a week, but in an emergency, everyone worked. Gerald Kumpf worked "long hours" the entire time he was in Vietnam. "Just constantly working. I don't ever remember sleeping." Once he was on the flight line working virtually nonstop for three weeks, eating nothing but C rations. A normal day was a 12-hour shift, six days a week. Commanders tried to give personnel one day a week off, but it didn't always work out that way. Kumpf worked a similar schedule later, when he was in the air force.[68]

John Ballweg's helicopter unit was stationed at base camp Black Horse. Ballweg had breakfast at 6:00 A.M. and then went to make sure his clerk was doing his job. The pilots that had to fly that day would then go on their missions. There were two briefings every day, one in the morning and the other in the evening. The unit flew mostly medivac and resupply missions, often into hot areas, carrying such things as ammunition, fuel, and spare parts, but also mail and hot meals for the troops. They also flew psyops missions and supported other units, such as the First Infantry and 25th Infantry divisions, when they were in the field. A typical operation might last two or three weeks, with a typical day being around 10–12 hours, flying and refueling every two hours. They would hot refuel, meaning one pilot would get out and stretch his legs, while the other manned the controls in case they needed an immediate take off. This routine went on seven days a week, and the pilots spent a lot of time in the air. During his tour of duty in

Vietnam, John Ballweg logged around 4,000 total flying hours; about 1,000 of them, or 25 percent, were during night flights.

Not many provisions were made for exhausted pilots, who routinely flew seven days a week. The flight surgeon would monitor how many flying hours they put in; once they reached 90 hours in a month, he would call them in for consultation and see how they felt. The typical result was that the pilot was cleared for another 30 hours' flight time. The flight surgeon might order what was known as a crew rest, but that was only eight hours off for rest. A flight surgeon could ground a pilot for a week but rarely did so.[69]

A lack of trained personnel often meant that many servicepersons had to do more than one job. In addition to his full-time job as a combat helicopter pilot, Warrant Officer John Ballweg also worked in a tech supply unit at headquarters.[70] At Danang, and other installations in 1965–1966, personnel also did guard duty at night. During the day, the guard posts were not usually manned, but a standing patrol guarded the perimeter. At night, there would be two men out in each bunker watching. Both were supposed to be alert, but usually, one would catch a nap, while the other one watched. "You are apprehensive because most of the sapper activity and mortaring occurs at night," recalled Gerald Kumpf.[71]

Some worked hard at questionable assignments. Lieutenant William Calley and Charlie Company were sent to Landing Zone Carrington, 200 kilometers (124.2 mi.) south of Danang. They spent 30 days there attempting to blow up wells. The colonel in command believed that he could deprive Vietcong of water supplies but had no idea how difficult it was to blow up a well. They would throw 20 pounds of TNT down the well, creating a small rainstorm when it exploded, but the well almost inevitably just filled back up again.[72]

"LITTLE AMERICA"

In 1968, the Department of Defense boasted that "by any standards, the American soldier is better paid, fed, and clothed today than his predecessor of any generation, and the provisions made for his support in the case of sickness or disability are unequaled even in modern times. Beyond that, any neglect of his mental or religious needs has long since been rectified."[73] The Pentagon did make a concerted effort to provide a "little America" overseas and make life as comfortable as possible, and to provide as many amenities as they could for the men and women serving at military installations all over the world, but particularly those stationed in Vietnam. The quality of life, however, depended a lot on when someone was in Vietnam, what type of work he did, where an individual was stationed, and the chain of command, from MACV down to platoon level.

HOUSING AND LIVING QUARTERS

Living conditions for American service personnel in Vietnam ranged from primitive to luxurious. Many of the first troops to arrive lived in tents, as did the 96th Quartermaster Battalion, which arrived in Cam Rahn Bay, Vietnam, in 1966. They then constructed cement or wooden floors and added wooden louvers so that they could raise or lower the canvas sides of the tent let more air through. They put in cement sidewalks and eventually even planted some bushes and trees around the area as well. They tried to create a "comfortable living environment" throughout the camp, including dining facilities, and even supply tents.[74]

Until 1967, army nurses also lived in tents. Afterward, most were quartered in Quonset huts or, occasionally, air-conditioned trailers. Most had small but private rooms, though some roomed dormitory-style in open bays. They still lived in tents, however, when moving or establishing a new hospital.

Gerald Kumpf and MFA-314 were also quartered in tents when they arrived in Danang in 1965. The plywood flooring had rotted in the tropical environment, so Kumpf and some of his friends drove over to an air force base and requisitioned some fresh plywood with phony papers. Ultimately, it really did not matter very much because he didn't spend much time in his tent, except to sleep. The rest of the facility was equally primitive. "When we first got there, it was one runway, one taxiway, one big Quonset hut for a hanger, a bunch of tents and foxholes.... We didn't even have any sandbags at the time; we're waiting for those to come in. They made us dig foxholes and stuff for a defensive perimeter, and if it rained, they'd just cave in. So it was rather primitive at the time, but we had done that before in different exercises, so we were kind of used to it."[75]

John Ballweg had a similar experience when his unit was transferred to Xuan Loc and had to carve their base camp out of the jungle. "We had to go in and just clear it all. We had to build a runway. We had to build the revetments for the aircraft to sit in. We had to fix our tents up as much as we could." They lived in tents with plywood floors and screened sides for the entire year, but the army never sent them any wabtocs, which was a wooden frame kit that you would assemble and then put the tent over. Ballweg was a warrant officer but lived four to a general purpose (GP), large tent, with each man getting a quarter of the tent. He had his bunk and a wall locker, and their tent happened to be the location of the company officers' bar. "But of course we had our bar. Everybody had a bar over there. We just happened to be the ones to get the bar."[76]

The large installations all had purpose built or Quonset hut barracks, and many had private or semiprivate rooms for officers and NCOs. John Ballweg's housing inside the compound at Long Binh when he first arrived in Vietnam in August 1966 was typical of quarters on many of the large bases. "Private rooms almost like a motel."[77] In Vietnam, most troops lived in hooches. Hooches were basically any living quarters more permanent than a tent. They could be constructed from a variety of materials; there was at least one made out of Falstaff beer cans. At more exposed installations, they were usually reenforced bunkers, with three or more feet of earth piled on the aluminum roofs and the sides of the structure reinforced with sandbags. Hooches and Quonset huts could be hot, humid, noisy, leaky, and bug infested, but usually, they were an improvement over tents. Some could be comfortable. David White was stationed out in the Mekong delta at Nha Be. The barracks had rooms petitioned off, with two men assigned to each room. White had his own small refrigerator, though the mess hall across the street stayed open 24 hours a day, and his own stereo.[78] In many units, men were allowed to choose their own hooch mates. In 1967, Dan Furman's helicopter support team at Danang was quartered in aluminum-roofed hooches, and "we were not told where to set up," so "we stayed in whatever hooch we wanted to."[79]

High-ranking officers normally had good housing, but occasionally, enlisted personnel would get lucky. In 1968, while serving as an advisor to the 23rd ARVN Division, Albert Childs was stationed at a hunting compound at Ban Me Thout once owned by the former emperor Bao Dai. It looked like a big Swiss chalet.[80] Later in the war, Gerald Kumpf worked for Air America, which flew out of CIA Air America headquarters at Takhli, Thailand, and into Cambodia and Vietnam in support of Montagnard and Hmong tribesmen. The entire base was surrounded by lush jungle, and he stayed in a "beautiful little compound," more civilian than military. They had a swimming pool, clubhouse, and theater, and a French-trained chef in a "beautiful chow hall," where "they had some of the best chow in the world."[81]

Taking over an existing camp or firebase was no guarantee that there would be decent living quarters. Troops leaving a particular camp sometimes left the living quarters in a shambles for the troops arriving to relive them. Nathaniel Tripp's unit found "a revolting mess" when they first arrived at Camp Alpha. "The red clay knoll was strewn with garbage and infested with rats. The fighting holes were collapsing and filled with putrid water." Tripp could not believe what he saw, and "it was hard to imagine an infantry outfit so demoralized and undisciplined that they could live like that. Within our first week there we had rebuilt the base, hiring local kids to help fill the sandbags. Then we went on to design elaborate sleeping quarters, command centers and clubhouses, all with the mandatory three feet of earth on the roof."[82]

All large installations had ample shower and washing facilities, but almost all camps and bases had some sort of shower facility. At Gerald Kumpf's camp, the showers were located about 700 yards from the living quarters, a typical arrangement. But bathing conditions could be basic out in the field. There was a water stand right in front of John Ballweg's tent, where everyone would line up to fill his GI can: "That was our washstand."[83] In most remote camps, the showers were just wooden stalls with old fuel tanks from jets, or other large containers, perched on top. They would fill them up with water in the morning and let the sun heat it all day, and by evening, they could enjoy a hot shower.[84]

RELIGIOUS AND SPIRITUAL NEEDS

The military also tried to provide for the religious needs of personnel stationed in Vietnam. The first army chaplain, John A. Lindvall, arrived in Vietnam on February 26, 1962, and by 1967, there were over 300 army chaplains serving throughout Vietnam. Chaplains were assigned to a territory and not a specific unit, but all large bases, and most small ones, and most navy ships had chapels and chaplains. The chapels were nondenominational, and the chaplain might be a Protestant minister, Roman Catholic priest, or Jewish rabbi, but he was trained to perform key rituals for most major denominations. Helicopters choppered them out to remote firebases to conduct services. David White remembered that there was "actually quite a bit" of religious activity at the PBR base at Nha Be, and they usually had some sort of religious service on Sundays. When someone from the base was killed, a military chaplain, usually a navy one, would come in and say a memorial church service for him.[85] Chaplains also served as counselors and advised men seeking CO status.

The chaplains shared the discomforts and dangers of war with the men and women to whom they ministered. The first chaplain to die in Vietnam was Rabbi Meir Engel, who suffered a fatal heart attack in 1964, and in 1966, William J. Barragy became the first to be killed in combat. Chaplain Michael J. Quealy administered last rites to one soldier and was then killed while tending another wounded man. In all, 82 chaplains would be casualties, and 13 would die, in Vietnam. They would also win their share of medals for courage. Charlie Watters, posthumously, and Angelo Liteky were Medal of Honor recipients. In all, chaplains were awarded 26 Silver Stars, 719 Bronze Stars, 318 Air Medals, 586 Army Commendation Medals, 66 Legions of Merit, and 82 Purple Hearts.

Religious faith helped many get through their tour of duty. In 1968, Sp/4 Willie L. Christian thanked "the Lord every day for helping me this far. I have only 71 days left in this place and I pray every day that I make it back home safely—for without him, I know I could never make it back alive."[86] Many attended religious services whenever possible. John Ballweg was raised Roman Catholic, and it stayed with him in Vietnam. He never missed Sunday Mass, unless he was out on a mission, and was just as spiritual after serving in Vietnam as he was before.[87] Despite the old saying that there were no atheists in foxholes, many of the men serving in Vietnam were not particularly religious or lost their faith because of the war. "I was an atheist then, I'm still an atheist now," stated Gerald Kumpf. What he saw in Vietnam "probably reaffirmed it. I couldn't believe the stuff that was going on, no god out there could allow that."[88]

FOOD AND NUTRITION

Food was another matter of great importance to military personnel stationed in Southeast Asia. Much of what was served was standard military fare, such as the ubiquitous chipped beef on toast, but at major installations and remote base camps, soldiers ate a variety of foods, from steak and potatoes washed down with beer to Vietnamese dishes in local eateries. A wide variety of American food was usually available. Within 30 minutes of his arrival in Vietnam, for example, someone offered Peter Hefron a frozen custard cone.

The quality of American food available to military personnel in Vietnam often varied according to location and branch of service. Gonzalo Baltazar claimed that both the marines and the air force had really good food, better than the army's, and rear echelon personnel could get steaks, hamburgers, and other American foods.[89] Gerald Kumpf, however, was not pleased with the quality of the food at the chow hall at Danang. It was not very good, "a whole lot of green eggs and World War II hotdogs, which were green too. It was terrible chow in the chow hall, just atrocious." He remembered only two occasions when the food was decent, and that's when movie stars John Wayne and Ann Margaret visited the base. The food was so bad in his opinion that Kumpf preferred to stay on the flight line and eat C rations for lunch.[90] Sometimes the food was good, but the drinking water was another matter. At Nha Be, the water evaporator left a "salt water tinge" to the drinking water, making it unpalatable for many. The only way David White could drink it was to make coffee out of it, but it still had an "old brown flavor" to it. A lot of the sailors drank soft drinks or beer instead.[91]

The military made an effort to make sure that decent food and a few amenities, such as soft drinks or beer, were available to service personnel wherever possible, including those stationed out in remote areas. Beer and Coca-Cola were available at almost every base. Joseph DeFrancisco's field artillery battery stationed out at Phan Thiet from August 1970 to January 1971 also had good living conditions, and at the end of each long workday, the men could purchase either two cans of American beer at 50 cents a can or two cans of Coke at only 15 cents apiece. David White was stationed out in the Mekong delta, but "life at Nha Be was pretty nice." The base had a nice chow hall, which had fresh milk and a long sandwich line, open 24 hours a day. "You could get about anything you want to eat, excellent food."[92]

At other bases, however, the menu was more limited. At Camp Black Horse, each squadron had its own mess tent. The food was "okay," recalled John Ballweg. "We had fairly decent food ... nothing to write home about. They weren't like going to Outback or something like that. They were passable."[93] White could get fresh milk, but Ballweg could not. The "only thing that stuck" in Ballweg's "crawl" was the fact that they never had any fresh milk, only reconstituted milk.[94] Ballweg also learned to drink his coffee black because the climate was so hot that it would turn the sugar rancid.[95] Sometimes standards such as Coca-Cola were unavailable, and substitutes from neighboring countries were brought in, such as F&N soda imported from Malaysia. It came in two flavors, lemonade and ginger beer. There were also locally bottled soft drinks, such as Bireley's orange soda and Vietnamese Coca-Cola, which tasted sweeter than the American version and could cost as much as a dollar a can.

The men out in the field were often a bit jealous of the amenities enjoyed by their comrades back at base or in one of the coastal cities. Gonzalo Baltazar did not get steak or hamburgers out at base camp; he only saw food like that when he was on R & R in Saigon or Cam Rahn Bay. "Man, they treat these guys good when we're out there fighting in the jungles," recalled Baltazar, "but we were kind of envious of those guys because they were eating good and we were just eating powdered eggs and C-rations."[96]

The army tried to get at least one hot meal a day, known as an A ration, out to troops in the field. The food would be cooked back at base camp and then taken in thermite containers out into the field by helicopters. Nathaniel Tripp was glad he was stationed at An Loc, the capital of Binh Long province, because "after the bad times we'd been through down south, this outpost was like heaven. Hot meals were flown in to us by helicopter twice a day from brigade headquarters in nearby Quan Loi and dished out of big green thermos containers. We were awash in C ration sundry packs; cartons of cigarettes, chewing gum, candy bars and toothpaste."[97]

There was a lot of equipment needed, however, to preserve and prepare the A rations properly. Because much of the food was prepared fresh, refrigeration facilities were necessary. The equipment needed for cooking and serving the food included a field range, a small detachment cooking outfit, a field bake oven, insulated food containers, and cafeteria trays.[98] B rations could be used when there was access to kitchen facilities, but not refrigeration. The basic difference was that in the B ration, the fresh foods in the A ration were replaced with nonperishable substitutes. The B rations were relatively compact and easy for the cooks to prepare. Six boxes held everything needed to feed 100 men, including disposable eating ware. Some equipment was still needed to cook the food, and the meals were not nutritionally complete without the addition of fresh bread and milk, which was often unobtainable. Preparing and getting the A rations or B rations out to the men in the field was not always possible, and as a result, the troops ate a lot of C rations.

C rations, or "meal, combat, individual," were first developed in 1938, made famous in World War II, and used by the Department of Defense until they were replaced in 1983 by the MRE, or "meal, ready to eat." Each C ration contained a complete meal of packaged and precooked foods that could be eaten hot or cold. Each one provided 1,200 calories, and the daily ration of three large C rations provided the minimum of 3,600 calories needed each day to sustain the average soldier. Each ration contained a meat item; a vegetable, fruit, or bread food; and an accessory pack. There was a decent variety of choices, including beans and wieners, spaghetti and meatballs, beefsteak, potatoes and gravy, ham and lima beans, and meatballs and beans. Smaller C rations featured meatloaf, boned chicken, or chicken and noodles. Some featured breakfast cereal or fruit. The rations also included bread or four crackers, processed cheese spread or jam, and a dessert item, such as pound or fruitcake, cookies, or a pecan roll.

The B or accessory packet contained many handy things such as a hot beverage mix, usually cocoa or coffee, salt and sugar packets, chewing gum, a plastic spoon, matches, and several sheets of toilet paper. Until 1975, they also contained four cigarettes, usually popular brands such as Kools, Marlboros, Pall Malls, or Camels.

The accessory pack also contained one of the most useful and beloved items ever issued by the military, the P-38 can opener. The P-38, nicknamed the "John Wayne" in the navy, was originally issued in World War II. It was a key chain–sized, hinged piece of metal, with a blade on one side to serve as a handle and a tooth in the middle of the other to pierce and open the can.[99] It had a thousand uses, including can opener, screwdriver, or blade. Marines in Vietnam claimed that they needed no other weapon than a P-38 to kill the enemy, and some troops used them to decorate Christmas trees in lieu of real ornaments.

Many soldiers complained about taste and quality. C rations were "dog food left over from WWII and canned for GIs in Nam," according to one veteran. One of the worst was ham and lima beans, nicknamed "ham and motherfuckers" by those forced to eat it. Some were arguably better tasting than others. The potted ham was not bad, and spaghetti and meatballs was another favorite. Most had their favorite. Gerald Kumpf, for example, liked the fruitcake. Like soldiers throughout history, the grunts that served in Vietnam knew how to cook the food to make it tastier, or at least more palatable. Since the food at the mess hall in Danang was terrible, Kumpf and the men in his unit would pool their C rations and cook them up. Kumpf and his friends would take the cracker, or hardtack, soak it to soften it up, and mix it in a helmet with some of the powdered cream that came for the coffee and, if possible, some dried fruit; they would then bake it in small stoves using blocks of C-4, an explosive, as fuel. C-4 was perfect for cooking because fire would not cause it to explode, and it burned hot and smooth. Even the awful-tasting ham and lima beans could be dressed up. A recipe for "outstanding ham and mothers" called for adding one can of cheese spread to the ham and lima beans once they were hot and stirring until all the cheese was melted. Next, you crumbled four crackers into it and stirred the concoction thoroughly. It was ready to eat when the crackers had absorbed all the excess moisture in the mix.

In addition to the bad or bland taste, many grunts complained about the weight and bulk the rations added to their already heavy load of equipment. C rations were heavy, weighing around five and a half pounds each. Many soldiers bemoaned the extra weight that food added and often carried the minimum amount they needed until the next scheduled resupply drop. Not infrequently, they came up short. Like armies throughout history, individual soldiers often augmented their diet by scavenging or buying rice, fish, or other locally obtainable foods.

Some Americans bought food from local Vietnamese. Nathaniel Tripp's unit's daytime duty was to sweep Highway 13 south from An Loc each morning looking for mines. There were never any mines, and "our sweeps were accompanied by vendors with pushcarts selling Coke and French bread."[100] Albert Childs recalled, "We got a lot of our food from the local economy. We even had a fisherman who brought us shrimp and lobster. The thing that I remember about those shrimp, the first time we had shrimp, three shrimp without the heads or tails filled a dinner plate."[101] Vietnam had around 480 traditional dishes, and there were Vietnamese restaurants near every large base. There were obvious cultural differences. Vietnamese ate noodle soup, and not bacon and eggs, for breakfast, for example. Many Americans enjoyed the local cuisine, but others could not stand it, especially dishes made with nuoc mam, a very pungent fish sauce, which has been described as smelling like a combination of ripe Limburger cheese and over-ripe sardines.

REST AND RELAXATION

Rest and relaxation were very important and necessary to keeping one's sanity, particularly after a difficult day. "Little America" meant providing the comforts and reminders of home, and every major base in Vietnam offered a wide range of amenities and luxuries to make the military personnel feel a bit more like they were back in the States. The facilities at Long Binh, for example, were typical of what you would find on any large American installation in Vietnam, or around the world for that matter. Long Binh had a snack bar, an officers' club and an enlisted men's (EM) club, a post exchange, or PX, which was a department, and usually, a grocery store, a barbershop, a souvenir store selling Vietnamese and Thai souvenirs, a swimming pool, pool tables, a recreation center with musical instruments one could borrow, a library, and even a portrait photographer and a Thai custom tailor. By the spring of 1970, there was also a post office and medical clinic and a Korean massage parlor.

There were officers' and EM clubs on all the large installations and most of the smaller ones, and these were often the center of any social life there was on the base. Off duty personnel could enjoy American food, beer, or soft drinks, shoot pool, watch TV, listen to music, or just relax. Air Force F-4 Phantom pilot Johnny Hobbs, a veteran of 100 combat missions over Vietnam, recalled that at Ubon Royal Thai Air Force Base in Thailand, "all we had was the mission and the club. You did everything in the club but sleep."[102] Sometimes the officers' or EM clubs were little more than tents. Camp Black Horse, for example, had a PX and an officers' club in tents.[103]

Some camps did not offer much in the way of diversion. Gonzalo Baltazar said that where he was stationed, as far as recreation in camp, there was none, but they did have movies at night at an outdoor theater. Gerald Kumpf also remembered an outdoor theater at Danang in 1965: "They had an outdoor theater right in the middle of the tent area where all the support crews lived and it was just nothing but actually a big sheet between a couple of posts and shacks sitting out there to protect it from the rain. We used to sit out in the rain, matter of fact the movie would be better in the rain because once the screen became wet it got a little shinier and you could see the picture better."[104] John Ballweg said that at his base, movies were shown at night, and occasionally, small shows would come in, but Ballweg said that the pilots were usually too exhausted after a day's work to go to any entertainment.

Even the more remote base camps and firebases boasted some comforts. Albert Childs and the other Americans working with the 23rd ARVN Division at Ban Me Thout used part of the large "Swiss chalet" as a movie theater every night, and the post also had a small PX and library. There were various forms of entertainment available at Nha Be, according to David White. Like most units, they had movies, television, and music; they gambled, played cards, and drank. Poker was a major diversion for many. At Danang, in 1965, there were several tents with poker tables in them and, usually, a nonstop game going on at one of them. Gerald Kumpf spent a lot of his off duty time playing poker, as did David White down in the Mekong delta.

Like their ancestors in earlier wars, many of the servicepersons or units in Vietnam kept pets and mascots. Monkeys were a popular choice. John Ballweg had a pet rhesus monkey he called "Baby John," which he inherited from another flyer. He normally kept the monkey tied up in front of the tent because when it got loose, it tore things up. Once it got loose and made a complete mess out of the officers' club. Ballweg had to keep the monkey out of sight because the commanding officer was looking for the owner. After about three months, the monkey got loose and escaped into the jungle, and they never saw it again. Gerald Kumpf recalled one man who owned a monkey "which used to love to hop on somebody's head and screw them in the air."[105] Albert Childs's unit at Pleiku in 1972 had a dog named "Farto" because its vocal cords had been damaged in an explosion, and the only noise it could make was when it was passing gas. A few others in Kumpf's outfit had "dogs, puppies, whatever was around," but he does not remember anyone having a cat.[106]

Reading was another way to pass some leisure hours. The larger bases usually had libraries, and the PX carried a wide range of American magazines, though sometimes they were somewhat late. Sergeant J. M. Wright could get *Sepia,* a black-oriented magazine, at the base PX in Vietnam, but it was usually a month late. Out in the more remote areas, popular magazines were passed from one reader to another. "Every time a soul brother over here gets an *Ebony* or a *Jet* magazine, there is a waiting line of at least 30–50 soul brothers throughout our troop waiting to read it," wrote one black army private to *Ebony* in 1968, adding a very grateful, "The black people back in the U.S. don't know what it means to a black soldier to have magazines such as *Ebony* and *Jet* to call their own."[107] In many areas, current reading materials were scarce. Gerald Kumpf said that he could not keep up with the news at home. Stateside newspapers were rare where he was stationed, and they mostly read the *Stars and Stripes.*

TV, RADIO, AND MUSIC

Radio and music were popular diversions virtually anywhere in Vietnam. A lot of men owned transistor radios and some reel-to-reel tape recorders, though they only used them when they were at their base camps and did not take them out in the field so that they could maintain sound discipline. Gerald Kumpf, like many, listened to a lot of Armed Forces Radio because he liked the music, and they usually got good reception. Many men in Vietnam, however, did not always trust the news they heard on Armed Forces Radio, which had a tendency to minimize American or ARVN setbacks. Stateside news broadcasts replayed on Armed Forces Radio seldom were critical of the war or of the government. The British Broadcasting Company was considered the most objective source for news but was often very difficult to tune in.

Many of them enjoyed listening to enemy broadcasts on Radio Hanoi and Liberation Radio. One of their favorites was Hanoi Hannah, who could be heard throughout most of South Vietnam, usually at night, around 10:30, on Radio Hanoi. Ken Watkins was a marine stationed in Vietnam in 1966 and recalled that "Hanoi Hannah didn't necessarily make sense and there was a certain awkwardness; she used American English, but really didn't speak our language in spite of her hip expressions and hit tunes, even tunes that were banned on U.S. Army radio. The best thing going for her was that she was female and had a nice soft voice."[108]

Like Tokyo Rose from World War II, Hannah was not one person, but actually several women playing the part on the radio, though Thu Houng, whose name means "the fragrance of autumn," was the senior announcer. The show was a mixture of propaganda, scare tactics, and music, ranging from Connie Stevens to Eric Burdon and the Animals. "How are you, GI Joe?" began a typical broadcast on June 16, 1967. "It seems to me that most of you are poorly informed about the going of the war, to say nothing about a correct explanation of your presence over here. Nothing is more confused than to be ordered into a war to die or to be maimed for life without the faintest idea of what's going on."[109]

Hannah, or her counterpart on Liberation Radio, Saigon Sally, often mentioned and directed messages to specific units, a tactic enjoyed by many servicepersons. Jim Maciolek, who was with the First Division in 1966, recalled, "When we heard Hannah mention our unit we would give a toast to her and throw our beer cans at the radio." But Hannah's familiarity with American names and unit locations also scared a lot of them. Hannah would often broadcast the names and hometowns of Americans recently killed in battle, sometimes only hours after an engagement, leaving everyone wondering where she got her information. "Whenever she named our unit, the First Marines, and where we were, that always stands out in my mind," explained Watkins. "Some of us thought she had spies everywhere or a crystal ball." In reality, Hannah got her information from such open sources as the AP and UPI wire networks and the *Stars and Stripes*. What often made it seem so inexplicable to the men in the field was the tendency of Armed Forces Radio and TV to suppress the same information. "Armed Forces Radio was on constantly, too," explained Jim Maciolek. "It was run by the U.S. military so we heard what they wanted us to hear. I think I would have liked to hear about opposition to the war that was being staged back home. That way I would have been better prepared when I got back home ... seeing hippies, people chanting slogans, people with black arm bands.... That was all new to me."[110]

Much of the propaganda was aimed at particular groups, such as draftees or those disaffected with the war, and she would urge enlisted personnel to frag, or murder, their officers or encourage them to go AWOL or defect to the Communist side. The North Vietnamese and Vietcong paid close attention to events in the United States and within U.S. forces in Vietnam and were well aware that both were experiencing racial problems, so much of their efforts were devoted to African Americans. Black activists that visited North Vietnam during the war were often asked to make propaganda broadcasts to black troops serving in the war. Civil rights and antiwar activist Diane Nash Bevel, for example, addressed her "Black brothers" over Radio Hanoi, telling them, "The Vietnam War is a colonialist war. If you fight in it, you are fighting Asian brothers who are determined to prevent their country from becoming owned and managed by racist-capitalist white men."[111] In August 1970, Black Panther Party minister of information Eldridge Cleaver appeared on the radio twice "to proclaim to the entire world the absolute, unequivocal and enthusiastic support and solidarity of black people of the U.S. for our Vietnamese comrades."

Most Americans thought that the clumsy propaganda efforts were humorous, but some were not amused, believing that the propaganda efforts hurt morale. In August 1965, First Lieutenant Patrick Graves "listened to Radio Peking and the distorted news this morning. I wish it were possible for that certain group at home in the United States that is responsible for our many domestic troubles, for them to hear the use made of it in the Communist news.... The only news that is broadcast concerns our racial troubles and the few, very few who protest openly our involvement in Vietnam."[112] Despite Graves's pessimism, North Vietnamese attempts to turn black military personnel against the war, and the United States, generally failed. A/1C Clarence Thrower's reaction to Carmichael's trip to Hanoi was typical of many African Americans fighting in Vietnam: "I was reading ... where Stokely Carmichael ... was in North Vietnam.... Mr. Carmichael doesn't seem to realize there are many black people dying in Vietnam so he will be free to do as he pleases.... People like these are the kinds that get others hurt or killed."[113]

Television was another way the military brought "little America" to Vietnam. At Nha Be, like many bases, there was a recreation room in the barracks with a TV in it. Armed Forces Network (AFN) showed programs from all three of the national networks, ABC, CBS, and NBC, and college football games. The games were a week late, but they were broadcast throughout the week.[114]

AFN TV also aired programming originating in Vietnam. One of the most popular was "the bubbling, bundle of barometric brilliance," Bobbie the Weather Girl, on AFN TV from 1967 to 1969. She was Bobbie Keith, who originally went to Vietnam as a secretary for the U.S. Agency for International Development. She did the weather nightly at 7:00 P.M., accompanied by a bit of music and comedy, such as dousing her with water when she predicted rain. One Halloween, she rode around the studio on a broomstick. Marine Evan Morgan, stationed at Chu Lai, recalled that he and other men "stayed glued to our TV's in our hooches waiting to enjoy her weather show. She shocked it to us all with kicks and gimmicks and danced to songs like Proud Mary. Often, she extended greetings to guys who had written in or to the units she had visited. Bobbie closed each show with a wink and wished 'everyone a pleasant evening weather-wise and good wishes for other-wise.'"[115] Bobbie visited the troops out in the field and posed for photographs on helicopters, boats, armored personnel carriers, and with servicemen.

One of the things that endeared Bobbie to the servicemen was the fact that she usually wore miniskirts, or even a bikini on occasion, on TV or when visiting the troops. "My favorite was when she appeared in a bikini with the temperatures painted on her body," recalled Evan Morgan. Men of the First Air Cavalry said that she was "a miniskirted heat wave who raised troops' temperatures" and wore a camouflage bikini in a pinup photograph for the Green Berets at Nha Trang. AFN TV studio in Saigon received hundreds of requests for photos of Bobbie in a bikini.

Bobbie the Weather Girl was not the only female to capture the hearts of servicemen fighting in Vietnam. One of the most popular shows worldwide on Armed Forces Radio was "A Date with Chris," starring actress Chris Noel. Noel also wore a miniskirt when she visited the men out in the field, singing and dancing for tens of thousands of troops, even on remote outposts, from 1964 to 1970.

SEX AND THE COMPANY OF WOMEN

The soldiers' adoration of Bobbie the Weather Girl and Chris Noel underscored how much most of them missed the company of women, specifically so-called round-eyes, or non-Asian women. Though women were integrated into every branch of the armed forces, relatively few served in Vietnam, and war was still largely a male prerogative. Only around 33,000–55,000 American civilian and military women worked in Vietnam between 1962 and 1975. Doris I. "Lucki" Allen estimated that there were 300 men to every woman when she was stationed at Long Binh, for example. "I saw two roundeyes the entire time that I was in Danang," stated Gerald Kumpf, and that was due to a plane malfunction. The women were airline stewardesses from a civilian airliner that was bringing troops in and that had developed mechanical problems. The stewardesses and the flight crew had to walk down the flight line leaving the aircraft.[116] The average enlisted man in Vietnam was young—usually in his early twenties—single, and lonely. Any reminder of women, therefore, was of tremendous importance to the male personnel stationed in Vietnam.

There were plenty of prostitutes, of course. Prostitutes were called "boom-boom girls," and having sex was "boom-boom," and the cost was often relatively cheap. Many of the girls would stand emotionless on the street, wearing the traditional *ao dai* and giving passing soldiers the finger, meaning that they were available. Some of them did not wait for their customers to be off duty. Nathaniel Tripp remembered "the 'short-time' girls who came around at night; Butch and Nancy and the others with Americanized names and hair cut short. The lucky men assigned to listening posts just outside the wire got to share the warmth of their poncho liners with them for a few dollars. Often, while I scanned our defensive perimeter with a starlight scope, I would be startled by the image of a pale white ass bobbing up and down against a hazy background of brush and tree line."[117] There were also the bar girls, who would sit patiently with a soldier or sailor, listening to him, flirting with him, and drinking very expensive glasses of Saigon tea.

Pornography was very popular, but many of the young men missed women who reminded them of the wives and girlfriends they had left behind back in the States. Mainstream magazines that featured such women were very popular. Sergeant J. M. Wright wrote *Sepia* from Vietnam to thank them for a rather popular feature article titled "Mini-Skirts and Morals" in the November 1967 issue. Though the morals part didn't seem to be particularly important to the men of the "Red Horse" Squadron, the mini-skirt part was. Getting pictures of the girls for pinups was very important to the troops. Wright wrote to the magazine because the so-called Soul Patrol of his unit had "selected one of your fine models, Miss Yvonne Anderson, as our 'Soul Sister Pinup.' We would appreciate any information about Miss Anderson that you are able to forward." Getting a picture of a popular or famous woman was all the better. Bobbie the Weather Girl was obviously one of the favorites and was featured as a pinup for many units. She was photographed in a Christmas bikini, for example, for the December 1968 pinup, or so-called Hawk Honey, for the *First Aviation Brigade Magazine*.

LETTERS FROM HOME

Most were just young men a long way from home and feeling very much alone. Most of the men spent the majority of their free time writing letters home, and most wrote every day, according to John Ballweg. "This is a letter from a lonely Marine," began a typical letter. "Sometimes I sit down and wonder what the people are doing back in the world. Suddenly, I get homesick. A lot of guys over here feel the same way."[118] Like soldiers in most previous wars, they did not write a lot about what it was like to fight in Vietnam, believing that the people back home would have no idea what they were talking about or going through.

John Ballweg's unit, like many, received mail almost daily; the letters from home were extremely important to the men in Vietnam because the letters were their precious link with the real world. Some obviously received more mail than others. Gerald Kumpf received, on average, only one letter from home a month. He also received two care packages, one at Christmas and one at Easter. Many of the servicemen in Vietnam had wives or girlfriends back in the United States, and letters from a sweetheart were very essential. Conversely, bad news could be disastrous to a serviceman's morale, and no news from home could be devastating. "I have seen with my own eyes men crying because they didn't get a letter from their wives, even cracking up in Vietnam due to all the confusion and tension on their minds," observed Sp/4 Willie L. Christian. They were also there for each other when the news from home was bad, especially when it was a Dear John letter, informing the poor recipient that a wife or girlfriend back home was leaving him, often for someone else. "Girls, take heed to what I say. Stand by your man," Christian begged, and pointed out the consequences of a Dear John letter to a soldier in a war zone. "Without you, he is nothing, and you could very well be the cause of another man's death.... I speak of the man that pulls the pin on a grenade and blows his head off—all because of a letter he got from home."[119]

Advances in technology meant that personnel in Vietnam could talk to their friends and family back in the United States courtesy of MARS, a system that routed phone calls from Vietnam through volunteer Hamm radio operators in the United States. The person talking had to say over when he was finished speaking, like on a radio, but the signal was usually very good and clear, and there was only a nominal charge for the phone calls. The number of calls home varied from individual to individual. John Ballweg made six MARS calls home during his tour in Vietnam, whereas Gerald Kumpf made only one, and that was to tell his family that he was headed home from Vietnam.

The Red Cross was active in Vietnam through its Supplemental Recreational Activities Overseas program. The Red Cross ran canteens and camp centers and sent trucks or helicopters to remote firebases and camps with donuts, coffee, and Kool-aid for the troops. Young, college-educated women, nicknamed "donut dollies," staffed both the vans and the canteens.

THE USO

As they had in World War II and Korea, the United Service Organizations (USO) provided entertainment to personnel stationed in Vietnam. President Franklin Delano Roosevelt created the USO in 1941 during World War II, combining the efforts of the six member organizations, the YMCA, YWCA, the Jewish Welfare Board, the Salvation Army, Traveler's Aid, and National Catholic Community Services, into one coordinated association. The USO was in Vietnam before the first combat troops arrived; the first USO club opened in Saigon in April 1963. At the height of the war, there would be 17 USO clubs operating in Vietnam, and six in Thailand, serving upward of a million service personnel a month. The USO slogan was "a home away from home," and much like the armed forces, it tried to bring a little America to Vietnam. Volunteer American civilians, who did 18-month tours, staffed the clubs. The young women wore miniskirts—no slacks were allowed. Each USO club had a snack bar, gift shops, a barbershop, photo developing, overseas telephone lines, and hot showers.

Many of the clubs, such as the ones at Danang and Vung Tua, were on the beach. The USO stayed in Vietnam almost as long as the military, with the last club closing in June 1972.

In addition to operating clubs, the USO also sponsored entertainment tours, some by big-name stars, throughout Vietnam. There were a total of 5,559 USO performances in Vietnam during the war years, featuring a variety of entertainers, from Martha Raye to Playboy playmates of the month. Some were superstars or Hollywood legends such as John Wayne, Rachel Welch, and Ann Margaret. Sports stars also visited Southeast Asia. Beginning in 1966, the National Football League (NFL), working with the USO, sent players and former stars to Vietnam; the first group included future hall of famers Sam Huff, Johnny Unitas, Frank Gifford, and Willie Davis. This collaboration marked the

Comedian and actor Bob Hope performs with dancers Harold and Fayard Nicholas for sailors aboard the USS *Ticonderoga* during the Vietnam War, 1965. Courtesy of the National Archives.

first time a sports league had ever worked with the USO in this capacity, and between 1966 and 1973, dozens of NFL players, including Don Meredith, Larry Csonka, Floyd Little, and Jack Snow, visited American forces stationed in South Vietnam—including remote firebases—Guam, Thailand, Japan, and on ships stationed out at sea. The tours generally lasted three and a half weeks.

Many of the entertainers and athletes were part of the annual USO Christmas Tour headlined and organized by comedian Bob Hope. Hope was an icon of the USO and a tireless trooper who was one of the USO's top entertainers since its inception in World War II. As he had in previous wars, Hope toured the war zone at Christmas. His first USO Christmas Tour of Vietnam was in 1964, and it was the first of eight in a row, ending only in 1972.

Hope's humor was seldom controversial or offensive; much of it was aimed at himself, often, for example, at the expense of his golf game. "I set out to play golf with the intention of shooting my age, but I shot my weight instead," he would deadpan. "I asked my good friend Arnold Palmer how I could improve my game. He advised me to cheat!" Even Hope's political jokes were nothing more than innocuous jabs at the president. Of Lyndon Johnson, he cracked, "You can tell he used to be a rancher. He squeezes Republicans like he's milking a cow." Even controversial material, such as Watergate, was handled innocently enough: "I told Nixon to burn the [Watergate] tapes," Hope cracked. "He told me to burn my golf clubs."

The visits by the stars meant a lot to the men and women in Vietnam. It was not just the entertainment; it meant that they were not forgotten that far away from home. The tours made a deep impression on the stars as well. Singer and actress Connie Stevens remembered her 1969 Christmas Tour with Bob Hope to Vietnam. She decided to go despite the fact she had two children both under the age of two. She remembered that it was incredibly hot performing out in the jungle. At night, while flying from one show to another, the celebrities would often speak by radio to remote bases or to a ship out at sea. Stevens recalled "flying over the ocean, dead asleep." Someone would wake her and take her to the cockpit, where Bob Hope would be waiting. He would explain that he "was talking to a ship that hasn't been home for months, they're out in the middle of this dark ocean and the speakers are on. Connie, why don't you go talk to them? I'd hardly even be awake, and I'd suddenly be talking to 2,700 young men in the dead of night, over a black ocean." Sometimes they would make up a little song about how they were appreciated and sing it to them a cappella. The entertainers were greatly appreciated by the soldiers and sailors. Veterans were still stopping her and thanking her for visiting Vietnam and entertaining them over 30 years later.[120]

The USO made a concerted effort to bring shows to military personnel stationed throughout Vietnam, but there were many limitations. Many of the entertainers and celebrities braved the dangers and visited men stationed out at small firebases and camps. Chris Noel and many of the professional football players, among others, made a point of visiting the more remote outposts, but normally, the largest shows and biggest stars played only at the big installations. Shows starring Martha Rae, Hank Williams, and Nancy Sinatra played Camp Black Horse, for example, but USO shows did not travel to the relatively isolated PBR base at Nha Be in the Mekong delta; the only USO show David White saw during the war was Flip Wilson and Rodney Dangerfield in San Diego, California.[121] Even when the stars came to a base, however, not everyone could see them. Gerald Kumpf got to see Arthur Godfrey but saw his idol John Wayne only from a distance, when he visited Danang, and missed Ann Margaret altogether because he had to work.[122]

The military also provided entertainment, and bands composed of military personnel toured Vietnam, often playing the smaller and more remote bases. One of the more popular was Phase Three and singer Priscilla Mosby. Though she went to Vietnam as a stenographer, the E-4 spent most of her time touring and entertaining the troops after the military discovered her singing talents. They played a variety of songs and musical styles, from such standard white artists as Frank Sinatra and Barbra Streisand to their own original tunes. More often than not, they were forced to improvise. About half the time, they did not have electricity for their musical instruments, Mosby recalled. "So we had to just rough it, and that was even more fun.... If you played bass, you would stand up there and go 'Da-Dom-Dom-Dom' and make the sound with your mouth. It was beautiful." It was beautiful, but it was also dangerous. Mosby had to sign a waver before the army would allow her to perform in a combat zone. As military personnel,

Mosby and the band members were well aware of the inherent dangers. The name of her nine-piece backing band, Phase Three, was an allusion to the soldiers' belief that "there are four phases before you die. If you're out in the field, you're in phase 3. You're hanging on—you may make it and you may not." Mosby was rare among women veterans in serving two tours in Vietnam, at Long Binh from March to June 1970, and in the Mekong delta from August 1971 to April 1972. Mosby returned home safely from Vietnam, but Phase Three did not. The entire band was killed at Bihn Thuy in the Mekong delta by a mortar hit on their bunker.[123]

ALCOHOL

For a lot of the men in Vietnam, alcohol was the principal form of recreation and the best way to forget unwelcome news from home or the scarcity of women. When John Ballweg first arrived in Vietnam in 1966, the pilots had a routine reminiscent of World War II in that they would go out and fly their missions by day and spend their nights at the officers' club. After a tough day, especially after medivac missions, the men of Ballweg's helicopter unit needed to unwind. "We'd just sit around. We didn't have TV over there. We had radio and have a few beers. Just totally become loose. If you have kept it in day in and day out you would have been a basket case."[124] Army reconnaissance veteran Jim Stone said, "It was great to come back after a hard day of slogging thru the paddies and woodlines along Hwy 4, to come 'home' to our schoolhouse and find a chilled-down crock of beer and soda. I used to reach way down to the bottom of that crock and grab a couple of nice cold cans of beer and crack them both open with my church key...one hole to vent and a double wide for pouring. I would then 'shoot' the first one to slake my thirst, then sip the second one while relaxing and cleaning my machine gun and getting ready for chow. Man, it was about as close to heaven as a low down dirty grunt could experience, without sex or drugs!"[125]

Beer was normally the drink of choice and is so associated with the Vietnam experience that during an army cavalry punch ceremony—where an alcoholic beverage symbolic of each particular war is mixed together in a large punch bowl—beer is used to symbolize that war. Alcohol was "a big thing, everybody was drinking beer," recalled Gerald Kumpf.[126] Baltazar drank beer, but many of the others drank hard alcohol. "The alcoholism was the big thing. Everybody drank heavily, to forget the problems, forget the war." No one said anything about it because with the exception of a handful of officers, everyone drank to excess. "Us infantry guys, we were a bunch of alcoholics."[127]

There were a variety beers available, including American-made Ballantine's, Budweiser, Carling Black Label, Falstaff, Pabst Blue Ribbon, and Schlitz, and some foreign brews such as San Miguel from the Philippines or Australia's Fosters Lager. Though pop-top cans were available, most of the beer shipped to Vietnam was in the old-style cans that still required a can opener. Another problem out in the more remote camps was keeping the beer cold. Jim Stone's Recon Company would pool their money and send an NCO into town on a beer run. They would buy ice, rapped in rice husk containers to keep cool, from local Vietnamese children. They requisitioned a large "water crock from a native hooch. This was a red clay pot about 2–3' tall and about as round. We used to load up this crock with beer and soda cans in the bottom and fill it with ice cracked from the big blocks that the kids would deliver," remembered Stone.[128]

American beer was usually available, but there were shortages. For several months after Tet-68, for example, it was unavailable in many places throughout Vietnam, but they could still get Western beer. Two Australian beers, Fosters and Reschs, for example, were shipped in. Some, however, did not like the beer available. Gerald Kumpf could not stand the Carling Black Label beer available at his installation, claiming that two cans of it "made you puke for the day."[129] Jim Stone said that Fosters was OK "but that Reschs was crap...real bitter, as I recall."[130] Many preferred hard liquor to beer, but it was often unavailable on base to most enlisted personnel. Kumpf could not get hard liquor but said that the officers had it flown in for their use. The only time he could get liquor was at a Danang bar, and then it was normally a local product bolstered with formaldehyde.[131]

Alcohol was available at the numerous bars around most military bases. Much of it was of local production, such as Ba Mui Ba, also known as Biere 33, which came in a 12-ounce bottle like American beers, or the more famous Biere Larue, better known as Tiger beer, which came in one-liter bottles. As Kumpf pointed out, Vietnamese beer was often bolstered or aged with ingredients such as formaldehyde. Vietnam veteran Jim Stone remembered that Tiger beer "was very inconsistent in quality. Some bottles tasted bitter, some like formaldehyde, and even vinegar! But occasionally (about once out of 3 or 4) you hit one bottle that was about as good tasting as you could ever find."[132]

THE BLACK MARKET

Enterprising Vietnamese made sure that luxuries such as Tiger beer were available to the soldiers and followed the movement of the American military throughout Vietnam, creating instant towns near large U.S. installations. "The First Cav is so big it creates a town wherever it goes," observed an unnamed Special Forces captain. "A week after it arrives, there will be shanties all around it, the locals trading for cigarettes and flashlights."[133] American goods, either stolen from an American installation or bought cheaply from a corrupt South Vietnamese official or ARVN officer, accounted for much of the merchandise sold by the street vendors. The black market was obvious the minute you left Long Binh. There were stalls along National Highway 1, the main north-south highway along coastal Vietnam into Saigon, selling all sorts of goods stolen from the American bases: soft drinks, cigarettes, liquor, laundry detergent, fruits, vegetables, meats stolen from the mess halls. American toilet paper, in particular, was a very big item on the black market. Getting the pilfered items off base was easy. Because there were so many Vietnamese working on the American installations, the security guards at the gates seldom checked them for stolen items. Someone stole Gerald Kumpf's boots when he made the mistake of taking them off one night before going to sleep in the transient barracks at Tan Son Nhut Air Base. He tried for four days to get replacement boots through the air force but ended up buying a pair for $6 or $7 at the black market.

Military authorities took several measures attempting to curtail illegal and subversive activities. Service personnel in Vietnam were issued military script, officially known as military payment certificates, or "funny money" to the troops, and not U.S. dollars in the hope that this would help curtail the black market, but all it normally did was create a speculative market in script. In an attempt to limit theft and spying, many base commanders did not allow or restricted the number of Vietnamese allowed on an American installation. Because of that, some Americans had limited contact with the South Vietnamese. Gerald Kumpf saw few Vietnamese working on base at Danang in 1965–1966. John Ballweg, for example, did not have much contact with the Vietnamese people when he was stationed at Bien Hoa because his regimental commander did not allow them on base. Instead of local women, his unit used Korean girls, associated with a Republic of Korea (ROK) unit stationed nearby, for laundry and cleaning.

Many Vietnamese could make far more money working on an American installation than they could through the local economy, and despite the fact that some base commanders prohibited their employment, most bases had dozens if not hundreds of Vietnamese working on them because they did jobs, such as laundry and cleaning, that the Americans did not want to do themselves. Many also worked as laborers or in the PX. Peter Hefron stated that for most people in his battalion, the 90th Replacement, relations with the Vietnamese were work related. Vietnamese worked on base cleaning the hooches, barracks, and latrines, and some worked as cashiers in the PX.[134]

Sometimes a unit's mission meant that they needed to stay at base. Gonzalo Baltazar did not have much interaction with local Vietnamese people because his unit was usually at their base camp or out in the jungle. Their commanding officer normally did not allow them to go into the local village when they did have some time off because the unit was always on standby to rescue downed pilots. Many base commanders, however, were distrustful that local Vietnamese might be Vietcong, spies, or dishonest and placed local towns off-limits to base personnel. Gerald Kumpf recalled that the local village, northwest of the base and not far from the living quarters, was off-limits 90 percent of the time.

Some officers found creative solutions to keep their men from visiting unauthorized places of entertainment. To reduce the venereal disease rate and interracial fighting among his men, Captain James Love set up a whorehouse for his men, which he admitted "may or may not have been legal," but it did help alleviate both problems.[135]

Most personnel, however, were able to visit local towns or villages on occasion. When the men in Gonzalo Baltazar's unit were allowed to go into town, they were warned to stay away from the women because they might be spies, Vietcong, or have venereal disease. The advice usually fell on deaf ears. The bars in the towns near the military bases provided the entertainment that many of the grunts in Vietnam missed, and for that reason, it was difficult to enforce the off-limits regulations. Many base commanders allowed their personnel to go into town but, because of Vietcong activity at night, restricted the hours the men could spend there. David White said that if you were not on patrol, you were allowed to go into the town of Nha Be between 4:00 P.M. and 8:00 P.M.[136] At Danang, in 1965–1966, when the nearby town was not off-limits, Gerald Kumpf and his friends "would go on out there … bar after bar after bar, whorehouse after whorehouse and that's where you would find your women." Kumpf said that the one street village "belonged to us during the day and to Charlie at night." When they were allowed to go into town, however, they went armed. "It's funny, you would be sitting around like a bunch of guys in the Old West, your rifle in your lap or your pistol strapped to your hip drinking beer, petting the women."[137]

REST AND RECUPERATION LEAVE

In addition to the occasional and unscheduled time off, personnel in Vietnam did get regular leave. After six months in country, all service personnel were eligible for two weeks of R & R during his or her one-year tour of duty in Vietnam. Anyone who agreed to extend his or her tour of duty in Vietnam by six months was given a 30-day leave with free transportation. About 46,000 soldiers chose to extend their tours in fiscal year 1968.[138]

Surfing judges Captain Rodney Bothelo and Miss Elli Vade Bon Cowur, are shown with Private First Class Robert D. Binkley, who took first place in the event; Corporal Tim A. Crowder, second place winner, and Lance Corporal Steven C. Richardson, third place winner, 1966. Courtesy of the National Archives.

Many did so they could make the long trip back to the United States to see loved ones. Everyone got at least one five-day R & R outside Vietnam, but even personnel with two weeks' leave generally did not make the journey back to the continental United States. Instead, many servicemen met loved ones at a much closer location, Hawaii being the most popular destination. John Ballweg, for example, spent a week R & R in Honolulu with his wife, who met him there. Other popular destinations for service personnel while on leave included Hong Kong, Taipei, Bangkok, Manila, Tokyo, Singapore, Penang, and Sydney.

Vietnam was a beautiful country, with miles of sandy beaches, and many Americans chose to spend all or part of their leave in Vietnam. The beaches at Cam Ranh Bay were very popular, partially because they had the added attraction of off duty army nurses. Eagle Beach near Hue on the South China Sea was a popular spot. Gonzalo Baltazar's entire platoon had two days R & R at Eagle Beach. Albert Childs got three days off and went to Nha Tran when he was stationed at Pleiku in 1972. Vung Tao was another popular in country rest and relaxation destination. It was considered the "French Riviera of the Orient" because it was located right on the South China Sea and boasted some great French restaurants. John Ballweg took a weekend R & R at Vung Tao, for example. For many servicemen on leave, R & R was referred to as "I & I" for "intercourse and intoxication,"[139] but many just needed to unwind and forget about the war for a while. David White took a week of R & R in November 1968 and spent his time drinking, walking along the beach, and just relaxing.

By far the most popular destination was the capital of South Vietnam, Saigon. The French called Saigon the "Paris of the Orient," and it was a beautiful city, with wide, tree-lined boulevards and French architecture. Getting around Saigon was cheap and relatively easy. It could also be fun. You could get a pedicab, which was similar to a rickshaw and powered by a human being. Like many GIs, Gerald Kumpf enjoyed riding around Saigon in what they nicknamed a "shit scoop," a tricycle motorcycle with a small awning over it that could accommodate one or two passengers.[140] There were numerous bars and restaurants to cater to any individual taste. The Continental Hotel in downtown Saigon was one of the most popular meeting places for journalists, dignitaries, and high-ranking military officers. Most personnel on leave, particularly whites, frequented Tu Do Street, lined with brothels and bars. Many of the bars featured American rock or country and western music, either taped or played live by Vietnamese singers and bands.

African Americans generally avoided To Do, considering it too white and too expensive. Racism was also a factor. Donald Duncan remembered, "In Saigon, Na Trang, and Ua Nang and some of the other larger towns, colored persons do not go into white bars except at the risk of being ejected. I have seen more than one incident where a colored newcomer has made a 'mistake' and walked into the wrong bar. If insulting catcalls weren't enough to make him leave, he was thrown out bodily."[141] Many African Americans did not like the choice of music available at the To Do clubs and bars. Instead, they usually preferred to party along Trinh Minh Street, located in the Khanh Hoi district. One black soldier explained that he preferred Trinh Minh because "I get so tired of the goddamn hillbilly music," but there were other enticements for blacks.[142] African Americans nicknamed Trinh Minh "Soul Alley" because the establishments catered to a black clientele, playing rhythm and blues or so-called soul music, and restaurants such as the L&M and the C.M.G. Guest House served real soul food such as turnips, barbequed ribs, and chitterlings. Interestingly, the Khanh Hoi district had once been a popular leisure area for black Senegalese troops during the Franco-Vietminh war. Half Vietnamese and Senegalese children and teenagers were common in the district, and the women working in Soul Alley tended to be of Cambodian and Senegalese-Asian heritage.[143]

AMERICAN INTERACTION WITH THE VIETNAMESE

Much of the interaction between Americans and Vietnamese was of a commercial nature, but a lot of Americans fell in love with Vietnam and its people. Many Americans considered Vietnam to be the most beautiful place they had ever seen, with colors—especially green—so vivid that they appeared to shimmer in the sunlight. Many Americans also understood that years of war had negatively impacted the Vietnamese and helped shape their attitude toward foreigners in general. John Ballweg felt sorry for the children around Bien Hoa because they were so "rag-tag" and would give them candy and chewing gum: "If you threw it they chased after it like a pack of dogs." Ballweg also thought the women were pretty when they were young but that they were forced to grow up fast.[144]

David White said that most "were pretty nice people." White appreciated their patience. During the day, his PBR stopped junks and sampans checking for contraband and checking identification cards. There was a curfew from 6:00 P.M. to 6:00 A.M. on most Vietnamese rivers, so on night patrols, they patrolled for curfew violators. The local Vietnamese expected to be stopped and searched and treated it as routine. "You know it's sort of like you standing in the line at the airport. You don't like it, but there's not very much you can do about it." They were sort of passive but good people.[145]

There was a natural curiosity about each other. There were some obvious superficial differences, such as ethnicity and physique. The average Vietnamese adult was around 5'2" and weighed around 105 pounds, and by comparison, the average American was a giant. They were also somewhat hairier. The children of a Vietnamese sergeant Gerald Kumpf befriended, for example, were fascinated by the hair on his arms and loved to pull on it because the Vietnamese had relatively little body hair compared to the average American.[146]

Like armies in a foreign land throughout history, the Americans and Vietnamese quickly devised ways of communicating with each other. The barriers were somewhat formidable. Some of the early advisors attended language school before going to Vietnam, but few Americans spoke Vietnamese, and few Vietnamese spoke English. Even those Americans that went to language school had a hard time communicating because of the different regional dialects. French could often bridge the gap, especially with the upper-class Vietnamese, but most common soldiers and Vietnamese quickly developed a pidgin language incorporating English, Vietnamese, a bit of French, and army slang. Some of the terms and language were imported from outside of Vietnam. On Okinawa, and in Vietnam, for example, anything that was "number 1" was good, and anything that was "number 10" was very bad. Americans picked up and used Vietnamese phrases such as *dee dee,* which means "to leave," *la dai,* meaning "come here," *no bic,* "I don't understand," and *tee tee,* which means "very little," to name a few examples.

There was, of course, a lot of positive interaction with the Vietnamese. American personnel participated in Civic Action Programs and Medical Civil Action Program (MEDCAP) visits to nearby villages and orphanages. Peter Hefron did get to see meet more Vietnamese and see more of the countryside as a participant in his battalion's Civic Action Program and MEDCAP visits to nearby villages and orphanages.[147] At Danang, in 1965–1966, members of MFA-314 often went out and dug wells for local villages. The water table was pretty high, and you only had to dig down around 16 feet before you hit water. They also brought electricity to the countryside as well as helping to build a new school. They were welcomed at first by the villagers. "Yes, the people were actually glad to see us, and contrary to everything you always hear that they hated us and didn't want us around and all that," said Gerald Kumpf. "When I was there initially, the people were really glad to have us. Of course we had money to spend, to spread around."[148]

By Vietnamese standards, the average American was rich and the United States a land of unbelievable plenty; to many Vietnamese, the United States was known as the Big PX. The American dollar or U.S. military–issued script could buy a lot of piasters, the basic South Vietnamese monetary unit. In late 1968, for example, one U.S. dollar equaled 100 piasters. Alternately, the average peasant was poor, and some Americans were shocked at the standard of living for most Vietnamese. Gerald Kumpf was surprised at what he considered to be the primitive living conditions of the people in the countryside. Danang "wasn't so bad," but even in the urban areas, the infrastructure and such things as sanitation were crude and elementary. "It was kind of a mix, half civilized and half stone age," Kumpf recalled. "Most of their villages and stuff were grass huts and it was very alien to us, no electrification or water or anything like that. That was really strange to us."[149]

The standard of living was so low for the average Vietnamese that even the things Americans threw away were valuable to them. They took old coke cans, for example, cut off both ends, flattened them, and used them for shingles on their roofs. John Ballweg watched Vietnamese peasants take American beer cans, flatten them out, and use them to build houses, using the flattened beer cans for roofing and siding. At most American installations, locals would go through the garbage cans on base and retrieve nearly empty cans of deodorant, shaving cream, and toothpaste. They would even cut the zippers and buttons off of discarded clothing.

Vietnamese eating customs also shocked and perplexed the Americans. Vietnamese ate many things that Americans would not, including dog and rat. Peter Hefron claims that his battalion lost three mascot dogs to someone's stew pot. Americans would set poison traps for rats along the perimeter; the Vietnamese would come along and take the dead rats and eat them, and often then get sick from the poison. Hefron claims that the base commander at Long Binh changed the traps so that the rats were captured alive.

The Americans also noticed differences in hygiene. Some Americans were shocked at the Vietnamese habit of relieving oneself out in the open by the side of the road if one had to go to the bathroom, and John Ballweg claimed that they used rocks to clean themselves with. "Hygiene was non-existent. The rivers over there, I never did see clear river." Ballweg thought the rivers were brown and muddy due to sewage.[150]

Many Americans were convinced that the local Vietnamese were just interested in making money off them. Though he was told that Americans were "guests," in Vietnam, John Ballweg "felt like...all they wanted to do was to take my money." He rarely went into town because he felt like there was nothing for him there.[151] Many Americans believed that the Vietnamese were profiteering from the war and not bearing their fair share of the fighting. Private First Class Willie Watkins Jr. claimed that "first of all, the major part of the men here are not fighting for the country of Vietnam itself, for 75 percent of the people don't care one way or another who is ruling them....All the people here want is our money to keep their skinny little bodies well fed."[152] Lance Corporal Charles Smith believed that "the Vietnamese live better than we do and are making a fortune off the troops for little things like Cokes and ice and most of all, pot."[153] Sp/4 Ray Ambrose expressed an opinion common to many Americans: "I must say, with all due respect, that I don't think that a young man with so much to live for should come over here and die for a country that is so worthless and unconcerned. The only reason I don't mind coming over here is to help keep the United States and its people free from Communism."[154]

Many Americans had racist preconceptions and believed that the Vietnamese were inferior. Lieutenant William Calley admitted that when he arrived in Vietnam, "I felt superior to these people....I'm the American from across the sea. I can really sock it to these people."[155] It came as a shock, therefore, for Americans to discover that many Vietnamese, particularly the upper classes, considered the Americans to be naïve and inferior. This was particularly true for black Americans stationed in Vietnam. Some African Americans had an affinity and empathy for the Vietnamese as another people of color exploited by white imperialists. Many, however, felt that the Vietnamese were as racist, or more so, than the average white American. "The women with babies wouldn't let colored soldiers touch them because the V.C. told them Negroes are cannibals that are hired from Africa to eat babies as their reward for fighting in Viet Nam," Sp/4 David M. King of the First Air Cavalry explained. "They have also been told Negroes grow tails like monkeys at night, and the Vietnamese believe every word of it."[156] Lance Corporal

Charles Smith found that he was "not the only black man that has fought over there and feels that this country isn't worth the lives being lost.... I've been called 'Blackie' by the Vietnamese after coming off patrol protecting their lives."[157] Sp/4 Hank Lovelady, during his tour as a medic in Vietnam, "tried to learn the language" but became disillusioned with the people he had met. "The things the people call the Negro G.I. over here—and get away with—you wouldn't let your closest friend get away with."[158]

Vietnamese culture was 2,000 years old and, by comparison, considered Americans to be unsophisticated and lacking subtlety, ignorant in understanding the subtleties and the often byzantine nature of South Vietnamese politics. Because most Americans did not, in fact, understand Vietnamese culture, one very important concept, that of the mandate of heaven, often eluded their comprehension of events and why the Vietnamese so often appeared to be duplicitous to many Westerners. Many Vietnamese still believed that leaders were ordained by a higher entity. It is similar to the European divine right of kings, but with some important differences. One does not have to be royalty to have the mandate, and one can lose the mandate. During times of confusion, it was incumbent on the individual to determine who had the mandate. If you were following the wrong person, it was considered wise to switch allegiance to the holder of the mandate. What Westerners saw as treason, duplicity, and dishonesty, the Vietnamese saw as pragmatic—why go down with a loser, when you can prosper by supporting the winner? Some Vietnamese saw no problem in switching sides several times.

Not every American believed that lying and duplicity were Vietnamese character traits. Gerald Kumpf observed that some of the Vietnamese people could be spies, and undoubtedly some were, "but for the most part, I trusted them. I thought that they were no different than any other people in the world."[159] Most Americans, however, considered it too dangerous to put much trust in the Vietnamese. There was no national identification system in South Vietnam, so anyone could be a spy or Vietcong. Albert Childs compared telling a Vietcong from an innocent civilian to telling a Democrat from a Republican.[160] The Vietcong uniform was essentially the same clothes worn by the average farmer, and there was no way to tell friend from enemy. "Well, they looked like they were teenagers," explained John Ballweg. "They would be our friends during the day and then at night they were the ones shooting at us. They blended very well. They never wore what you called uniforms. They wore the black pajamas. So many other ones wore them too. You just couldn't say, 'Oh, there's one.' Unless he was carrying a rifle, you wouldn't know it. It was just a situation that you just couldn't know who was who."[161] They especially mistrusted the Vietnamese that worked on American installations as possible Vietcong spies or terrorists. Gerald Kumpf believed that "there were more spies than people with guns out there."[162] John Ballweg heard about a 14-year-old girl that worked as a cleaning lady for several months at another installation who walked in one day and blew up herself and several GIs.[163]

The Vietnamese civilians working on or near American bases were in a good position to gather all sorts of intelligence on U.S. and ARVN operations. Many of the bar girls working at the very popular Continental Hotel in Saigon, frequented by high-ranking officers, were actually Vietcong spies.[164] Nathaniel Tripp believed almost fatalistically that At An Loc, his reconnaissance unit, had "doubtless made friends with lots of Viet Cong already. Not only were their kids filling sandbags, wandering around our base all day, but there were also mamasans cooking dinners to order and passing them to us through the concertina wire, and a host of other vendors."[165] Albert Childs said that the Americans always knew when the Vietcong were going to attack their compound because the mamasans would not show up for work that day.[166] Even the laundry the Americans sent out provided vital clues to the enemy. Troopers sent their fatigues out to Vietnamese women to be laundered, telling them that they needed them back by Tuesday, for example, and the laundresses would then inform the local Vietcong that a big sweep was beginning on Wednesday, so the enemy units just faded away from the area before the "surprise" American attack ever occurred—a phenomenon the Americans would become all too accustomed to in staging offensive operations against a very elusive enemy.[167]

NOTES

1. Gerald Kumpf, *Oral History Project,* The Vietnam Archive at Texas Tech University. Interviewed by Richard Verrone, March 10, 2003. Retrieved from http://www.virtualarchive.vietnam.ttu.edu/cgi-bin/star fetch.exe?EWoAfq.tJEBzwDooKsGN8mxwA2X3@q8.Y4@lpzu0qrpNanzPx0Zh6@ZwMPIxL.ex6Y3AV. nGBn7aUH1WFP4otrIS5b2nFx1OwsFzXQ8FRlo/OH0276-1.pdf, 18, 52.

2. Philip Caputo, *A Rumor of War* (New York: Holt, Rinehart, and Winston, 1977), 37–38.

3. Allen Thomas Jr., in discussion with the author, Erlanger, Kentucky, July 25, 2000.

4. Lieutenant General Arthur J. Gregg, *Senior Officer Oral History Project,* U.S. Army Military History Institute, Carlisle Barracks, PA, 1997.

5. Ron Ballweg, *Oral History Project,* The Vietnam Archive at Texas Tech University. Interviewed by Richard Verrone, May 19, 2003. Retrieved from http://www.virtualarchive.vietnam.ttu.edu/cgi-bin/ starfetch.exe?8ef.0OThTHlw@ovB@bMAIW5KtMcM31GAZwYqlEtpvVWLEnlWMsbO6qa0zk 8nerqkpky0E2@3.AAMn2RrUMjKQM1MI39jwXFA/OH0296.pdf.

6. Gonzalo Baltazar, *Oral History Project,* The Vietnam Archive at Texas Tech University. Interviewed by Steve Maxner, March 23, 2001. Retrieved from http://www.virtualarchive.vietnam.ttu.edu/cgi-bin/starfetch. exe?3qUevQOjUtg2mDgIBOhT3hQ7wvenAzlebd@qMS7Av.N9BF7TSM9wvr@vB2M4o7sdoJfUBL5. U3WHS1XkROhq2hvFxK3tPSLj/OH0152.pdf, 6.

7. David White, *Oral History Project,* The Vietnam Archive at Texas Tech University. Interviewed by Richard Verrone, n.d. Retrieved from http://www.virtualarchive.vietnam.ttu.edu/cgi-bin/starfetch. exe?71mIafeP3JsUwk7rv@lU9xasA5uYhgjKNAyaDpYf5Nk.Blkuvd69i.GoLp0Gl4jSbk8HMOoS284 C0l6iWWadecNnjn.SRsiy/OH0227.pdf, 5–6.

8. Ballweg, *Oral History Project,* 28.

9. Gregg, *Senior Officer Oral History Project.*

10. Albert Childs, *Oral History Project,* The Vietnam Archive at Texas Tech University. Interviewed by Steve Maxner, February 3, 2003. Retrieved from http://www.virtualarchive.vietnam.ttu.edu/cgi-bin/starfetch. exe?px@DCzXFmOuNx2T6g1RlUxXU5JKU.VHLnKVjhB5A.zu78Y18RLhkxS@8DT4FUZiZFMSEp2vq jMbGIa4Bk5SPT9GKohPkmUno/OH0095.pdf, 9.

11. Allen Thomas Jr., in discussion with the author.

12. Conrad Clark, "This Is Vietnam," *The Baltimore Afro-American,* January 10, 1970, 22.

13. First Lieutenant Gasanove Stephens, "Our Men in Vietnam," *Sepia,* June 1968, 58.

14. "Big Man with a Big Message," *Sepia,* April 1968, 64.

15. Thomas Johnson, "Negroes in the Nam," *Ebony,* August 1968, 31–34.

16. "U.S. Gives First Medal of Honor to a Negro Marine," *The New York Times,* August 22, 1968, 4.

17. Sol Stern, "When the Black GI Comes Back from Vietnam," *New York Times Magazine,* March 24, 1968, 37.

18. Sergeant Willie E. Burney Jr., "Our Men in Vietnam," *Sepia,* August 1968, 69.

19. Corporal Lawrence E. Waggoner, "Our Men in Vietnam," *Sepia,* March 1968, 77.

20. Major General Frederic E. Davison Interview, Senior Officer *Oral History Project,* Blacks in the Armed Forces Series, U.S. Military History Institute, Carlisle Barracks, PA, 1977, 26.

21. Vietnam Women's Memorial Project, *Celebration of Patriotism and Courage: Dedication of the Vietnam Women's Memorial, November 10–12, 1993* (Washington, DC: Vietnam Women's Memorial Project, 1993), 35.

22. Kathryn Marshall, *In the Combat Zone: An Oral History of American Women in Vietnam* (Boston: Little, Brown, 1987), 4.

23. Ibid., 7.

24. Vietnam Women's Memorial Project, *Celebration,* 36.

25. Ibid.

26. Sergeant C. Nelson Williams Jr., "Our Men in Vietnam," *Sepia,* August 1968, 69.

27. Waggoner, "Our Men in Vietnam," 77.

28. Baltazar, *Oral History Project,* 10–11.

29. "People Who Make the World Go Round," *Sepia,* January 1968, 9.

30. Gregg, *Senior Officer Oral History Project.*

31. Adam Smith, "Lessons in Firepower," *Esquire,* December 1981, 13.

32. Ballweg, *Oral History Project,* 12.

33. John Sacks, "The Education of a Young Lieutenant," *Esquire,* June 1983, 260–262.

34. Ibid.

35. Gregg, Senior Officer *Oral History Project.*

36. Baltazar, *Oral History Project,* 12.

37. Ballweg, *Oral History Project,* 12.

38. White, *Oral History Project,* 8–9.

39. Baltazar, *Oral History Project,* 44.

40. Kumpf, *Oral History Project,* 28.

41. Sacks, "Education," 260.

42. Peter O. Hefron, "Memories of a U.S. Army Replacement Battalion: Service and Disservice to the Vietnam War Effort" (paper presented at The Vietnam War, Thirty Years On, Memories, Legacies, and Echoes Conference, Newcastle, Australia, April 14–15, 2005).

43. Hefron, "Memories."

44. U.S. Department of Defense, *A Pocket Guide to Vietnam* (Washington, DC: Office of Information for the Armed Forces, 1971), 1.

45. Hefron, "Memories."

46. Childs, *Oral History Project,* 18.

47. Hefron, "Memories."

48. White, *Oral History Project,* 9.

49. Ballweg, *Oral History Project,* 17.

50. Childs, *Oral History Project,* 6–7.

51. General William C. Westmoreland, *A Soldier Reports* (Garden City, NY: Doubleday, 1976), 186.

52. Paul L. Savage and Richard A. Gabriel, "Cohesion and Disintegration in the American Army: An Alternative Perspective," in *The Military in American from the Colonial Era to the Present,* ed. Peter Kartsen (New York: MacMillan, 1980), 413.

53. "US Army MP's in Vietnam, 1962–75," http://home.mweb.co.za/re/redcap/vietnam.htm.

54. Gregg, *Senior Officer Oral History Project.*

55. Ibid.

56. Sp/4 Joe Roberson Jr., "Our Men in Vietnam," *Sepia,* June 1968, 58.

57. Airman Richard W. Harper, "Our Men in Vietnam," *Sepia,* January 1968, 79.

58. Hefron, "Memories."

59. Eddie Meeks, "Nursing the Dying," *Newsweek,* March 8, 1999, 61.

60. Kumpf, *Oral History Project,* 33.

61. Ballweg, *Oral History Project,* 6.

62. Gregg, *Senior Officer Oral History Project.*

63. Ibid.

64. Major Bruce B. Cary Interview, Senior Officer *Oral History Project,* U.S. Army Military History Institute, Carlisle Barracks, PA, 1982, 7.

65. Baltazar, *Oral History Project,* 13.

66. Major Robert Arnold Interview, Senior Officer *Oral History Project,* U.S. Army Military History Institute, Carlisle Barracks, PA, 1982, 6.

67. Gregg, *Senior Officer Oral History Project,* 50.

68. Kumpf, *Oral History Project,* 19, 22.

69. Ballweg, *Oral History Project,* 19–20.

70. Ibid., 13.

71. Kumpf, *Oral History Project,* 35.

72. Sacks, "Education," 260.

73. U.S. Department of Defense, *Annual Report for Fiscal Year 1968* (Washington, DC: U.S. Government Printing Office, 1971), 180.

74. Gregg, *Senior Officer Oral History Project.*

75. Kumpf, *Oral History Project*, 19, 21.

76. Ballweg, *Oral History Project*, 18.

77. Ibid., 13, 17–18.

78. White, *Oral History Project*, 22.

79. William H. McMichael, "A War on Two Fronts," *Newport News–Hampton, Virginia Daily Press,* Williamsburg ed., July 27, 1998, 1, A4–A6.

80. Childs, *Oral History Project*, 14.

81. Kumpf, *Oral History Project*, 60.

82. Nathaniel Tripp, "Father, Soldier, Son: Memoir of a Platoon Leader in Vietnam," 1996. Retrieved from *washingtonpost.com,* http://www.washingtonpost.com/wpsrv/style/longterm/books/chap1/fathersoldier son.htm, n.p.

83. Ballweg, *Oral History Project*, 18.

84. Ibid.

85. White, *Oral History Project*, 20.

86. Sp/4 Willie L. Christian, "Our Men in Vietnam," *Sepia,* July 1968, 74.

87. Ballweg, *Oral History Project*, 38.

88. Kumpf, *Oral History Project*, 38.

89. Baltazar, *Oral History Project*, 36.

90. Kumpf, *Oral History Project*, 25.

91. White, *Oral History Project*, 16.

92. Ibid,, 18, 20–21.

93. Ballweg, *Oral History Project*, 19.

94. Ibid.

95. Ibid.

96. Baltazar, *Oral History Project*, 36.

97. Tripp, "Father, Soldier, Son."

98. Army Quartermaster Foundation, Inc. Website, "Rations: Conference Notes," January 1949, http://www.qmfound.com/history_of_rations.htm.

99. Major Renita Foster, "The Greatest Army Invention Ever," 1986. Retrieved from *DogTagsRus,* http://www.dogtagsrus.com/army%20greatest%20invention.htm.

100. Tripp, "Father, Soldier, Son."

101. Childs, *Oral History Project*, 25.

102. McMichael, "A War on Two Fronts."

103. Ballweg, *Oral History Project*, 20.

104. Kumpf, *Oral History Project*, 22.

105. Ibid, 39.

106. Childs, *Oral History Project*, 20.

107. "Letters to the Editor," *Ebony,* August 1968, 15.

108. Don North, "The Search for Hanoi Hannah," *The Sixties Project,* 1991. Retrieved from *The Psywarrior: Psychological Operations,* http://www.psywarrior.com/hannah.html, n.p.

109. Ibid.

110. Ibid.

111. Diane Nash "Black Woman Views Genocidal War in Vietnam," *The Black Liberator,* May 1969, 2.

112. Diary of First Lieutenant Patrick Graves, entry for August 10, 1965, 55. Patrick Graves File #7047, Box #1, Cornell University Archives, Ithaca, NY.

113. A/1C Clarence Thrower, "Our Men in Vietnam," *Sepia,* July 1968, 75.

114. White, *Oral History Project*, 18, 20–21.

115. Evan Morgan, "Bobbie the Weather Girl—AFVN TV Saigon, Weather-wise and Other-wise," 1998. Retrieved from *Stealth Volunteers: About Women Who Served in Vietnam,* http://www.illyria.com/women/vn wweather.html.

116. Kumpf, *Oral History Project*, 29.

117. Tripp, "Father, Soldier, Son," 118.

118. L/Corp. Winston McElrath, "Our Men in Vietnam," *Sepia,* July 1968, 75.

119. Christian, "Our Men in Vietnam," 74.

120. Connie Stevens, "A Voice in the Dark," *Newsweek,* March 8, 1999, 62.

121. White, *Oral History Project*, 22.

122. Kumpf, *Oral History Project*, 26.

123. "Unarmed and Under Fire: An Oral History of Female Vietnam Vets," *Salon.com*, http://www.salon.com/mwt/feature/1999/11/11/women/index1.html.

124. Ballweg, *Oral History Project*, 23.

125. Jim Stone, "Beer and Soda Available during the Vietnam War: A Welcome Break from the Hardships," March 15, 2003. Retrieved from the *Mobile Riverine Force Association,* http://www.mrfa.org/Beer.Soda.htm.

126. Kumpf, *Oral History Project*, 38.

127. Baltazar, *Oral History Project*, 31.

128. Jim Stone, "Beer and Soda."

129. Kumpf, *Oral History Project*, 15.

130. Stone, "Beer and Soda."

131. Kumpf, *Oral History Project*, 15.

132. Stone, "Beer and Soda."

133. Adam Smith, "Lessons in Firepower."

134. Hefron, "Memories."

135. Major James Love Interview, *Senior Officer Oral History Project,* U.S. Army Military History Institute, Carlisle Barracks, PA, 1982 6.

136. White, *Oral History Project*, 18, 20–21.

137. Kumpf, *Oral History Project*, 29.

138. U.S. Department of Defense, *Annual Report for 1968,* 15.

139. Kumpf, *Oral History Project*, 51–52.

140. Ibid.52,

141. "Viet Hero Sees Racial Bias In Big Lie," *The Baltimore Afro-American,* February 26, 1966, 20, and NAACP, *The Search for Military Justice* (New York: NAACP, 1971), 18, and "Air Force Jim Crow," *The Crisis,* June–July, 1970, 229.

142. Thomas Johnson, "The U.S. Negro in Vietnam," *The New York Times,* April 29, 1968, 16, and Johnson, "Negroes in the Nam," 39, and Zalin B.Grant, "Whites against Blacks in Vietnam," *New Republic,* January 18, 1969, 16.

143. Ibid.

144. Ballweg, *Oral History Project*, 15.

145. White, *Oral History Project*, 11–12.

146. Kumpf, *Oral History Project*, 31.

147. Hefron, "Memories."

148. Kumpf, *Oral History Project*, 30.

149. Ibid., 29–32.

150. Ballweg, *Oral History Project*, 15.

151. Ibid.

152. Private First Class Willie Watkins Jr., "Our Men in Vietnam," *Sepia,* March 1968, 77.

153. Lance Corporal Charles Smith, "Our Men In Vietnam," *Sepia,* January 1968, 79.

154. Sp/4 Ray Ambrose, "Our Men In Vietnam," *Sepia,* February 1968, 71.

155. Sacks, "Education," 260.

156. Sp/4 David M. King, "Our Men in Vietnam," *Sepia,* March 1968, 77.

157. Lance Corporal Charles Smith , "Our Men in Vietnam," *Sepia,* January 1968, 79.

158. Sp/4 Hank Lovelady "Our Men in Vietnam," *Sepia,* February 1968, 71.

159. Kumpf, *Oral History Project*, 32.

160. Childs, *Oral History Project*, 33.

161. Ballweg, *Oral History Project*, 30.

162. Kumpf, *Oral History Project*, 29.

163. Ballweg, *Oral History Project*, 46.

164. Kumpf, *Oral History Project*, 29.

165. Tripp, "Father, Soldier, Son."

166. Childs, *Oral History Project*, 33.

167. Smith, "Lessons in Firepower," 14.

CHAPTER 4

Fighting in Vietnam

GRUNTS

The goal of the United States was to prevent a Communist takeover of South Vietnam by the Vietcong and the North Vietnamese. To accomplish this goal, General William Westmoreland and his senior officers at MACV decided on a policy of attrition: basically, to kill so many of the enemy that they were either unwilling or incapable of continuing the war. Offensive sweeps would locate, concentrate, and fix the enemy, and then use the overwhelming advantage in firepower American forces enjoyed to destroy them. Though there were various types of combat during the war, including set piece battles and urban warfare, most of the fighting would be done by company- to battalion-sized units, and the Vietcong and North Vietnamese would pit surprise, ambush, and a disciplined tenacity against the United States's tremendous advantages in technology, infrastructure, and firepower.

The basic element in either an army or Marine Corps unit was the 11B, the MOS for a combat infantryman or, as they called themselves in Vietnam, "grunts." The average age of an infantryman fighting in Vietnam was 22, and not 19 as often stated. This is still younger than either World War I or II, where the average infantryman was approximately 26 years old.

The American military in Vietnam was organized along conventional lines, and the size of specific units varied according to function and branch of the armed services. In the army and Marine Corps, however, unit structure was roughly equivalent, though there were exceptions. Marine rifle companies in 1965 had four platoons, whereas there were three in an army company, for example. There were nine infantrymen in a squad, commanded by a sergeant. Three or four squads, totaling 30–50 men, made up a platoon, led by a lieutenant. A captain normally commanded a company, which was made up of several platoons and could vary in size from 100 to 190 men. Three or four companies made up a battalion of 500–900 men, usually with a lieutenant colonel in charge. The size of certain units also changed as the war progressed. In 1968, for example, army infantry battalions were reorganized to provide a fourth rifle company, giving the infantry battalion an overall strength of 920 men. A brigade contained approximately

3,000–4,000 men, organized into several battalions and supporting units. The Ninth Marine Expeditionary Brigade, the first to go ashore on March 8, 1965, for example, contained around 3,500 men.[1] It was normally commanded by a colonel if part of a division, or by a brigadier general if it was operating independently. Two to four brigades made up a division, commanded by a major general.

A division could be anywhere from 10,000 to 20,000 men strong, and it was the smallest unit to have everything necessary for sustained warfare and to be able to function autonomously; it was, in essence, a small army. Each division operated in a corps area. Operationally, South Vietnam was divided into four regional commands or corps areas, designated I–IV and under the command of a lieutenant general. I Corps was farthest north and was largely the responsibility of the Marine Corps, and IV Corps was farthest south, encompassing much of the Mekong delta.

BATTLEFIELD SOUTH VIETNAM

Vietnam is roughly the size of the state of New Mexico, covering 127,000 square miles. All of Vietnam lies in the tropic zone, but there are variations of climate and topography. As in most wars, weather also influenced the fighting, with the heaviest combat occurring in the dry season. From November to April was the winter monsoon, a period of cool and relatively dry weather for much of the country. Some places, such as the Mekong delta, however, were hot all year round, with temperatures in January ranging from a low in the fifties, to highs in the nineties. The summer monsoon, from

Two battle weary Leathernecks of the 26th Marine Regiment take a break during Operation Bold Mariner, 1969. The cordon operation on the Batangan Peninsula in Quang Ngai Province was aimed at uncovering and destroying the Viet Cong. Courtesy of the National Archives.

May to October, brought an average of six feet of rain, often leading to swollen rivers and flooding, and stifling heat and humidity, with daytime temperatures soaring above 100 degrees.

Conducting military operations during the summer monsoon was difficult and often more dangerous because of the adverse weather conditions. The combination of torrential downpours, fog, and high winds often made flying a dangerous occupation, for example. Being on the ground was hardly any better. Troops in Vietnam had to contend with torrential rains, swollen rivers, and muddy quagmires, making life out in the field during bad weather miserable. Winston McElrath's unit would "go on all-night ambush. It'll be raining and you'll shiver from the cold rain that continues to roll down your back. Suddenly you say to yourself 'I wish I were dead.'"[2] "We had to sit through one rain in the month of April of '69 and it rained either 78 or 82 inches in one month," recalled Gonzalo Baltazar. "We had a hard time with that. It was sleeping in water and all that. A lot of people don't realize what we had to go through besides combat. You had all the other elements like the tigers and scorpions and all that. We had a lot of outdoor elements you had to battle, the rain, the cold nights out in the jungle in the rain and all that stuff."[3]

Vietnam teemed with all sorts of animal life, from leeches and snakes in the rivers, to mosquitoes, snakes, scorpions, and tigers on land. The mosquitoes were terrible, and everywhere, and according to Gerald Kumpf, "God, they used to eat you alive."[4] Larger life forms also posed a threat, especially encounters with Vietnamese tigers. Stumbling on a tiger in the jungle was not only dangerous, but it could also lead to confusion. *Tiger* was code for an ambush, so when a chopper pilot radioed Gonzalo Baltazar and a search party he was leading that there was a tiger up ahead, they originally assumed an ambush. Luckily, Baltazar and his party drove the tiger off.[5]

Some of the animal attacks fell into the strange category, and Gonzalo Baltazar seemed to have more than his share of animal encounters in Vietnam. Monkeys attacked Baltazar's unit once when they were out on patrol. They had inadvertently made their camp right below a group of trees the monkeys were living in, "and for some reason during the night, about one in the morning, we were attacked by them. That was quite an experience. They scared the heck out of us obviously. All you can do is fight them off and grab them because you really couldn't see, and the jungle's pitch black. We couldn't see a thing. So, it was a scary situation. We didn't know what was happening."[6]

The terrain in South Vietnam ranged from lowland rice paddies along the coast, the Mekong delta in the south, and mountains in the west, running the length of Vietnam's border with neighboring Laos and Cambodia. Much of the country, including most of the interior, was jungle. Most of the ethnic Vietnamese population, who made up 85 percent of the inhabitants, lived along the coastal plain and the rich Mekong delta. Vietnam also had a large population of ethnic Chinese, roughly a million or so, and most lived in the coastal cities, often in their own enclaves. The Cholon district of Saigon, for example, was the Chinese section of town. The mountains were inhabited largely by the so-called Montagnards, a generic term for various tribes of mountain peoples such as the Hmong, Hre, Rhade, or Nung. Most were of Polynesian extraction and were the indigenous inhabitants before the ethnic Vietnamese arrived. Some of the tribes, such as the Renago, with 10,000 members, or the Nung, with around 15,000, were modest in size, but others were quite numerous. There were at least 110,000 Hre, for example, and more than 120,000 Rhade.

Vietnam is a veritable tropical paradise, but paradise can be an awfully difficult place in which to operate. Triple-canopy jungle obscures light and wind and muffles sound, and it is dark on the ground because the foliage is so thick. Albert Childs said that the jungle was so dark and thick, "you could step off a road, go twenty-five feet into the jungle and you can become completely disorientated."[7] At ground level, movement is difficult because of grasses eight feet high, and stands of saw grass, in particular, with leaves aptly named because they are so sharp that they can cut right through clothing. The United States had the ability to move large numbers of men and equipment throughout Vietnam by air, usually at a moment's notice, but once on the ground, out in the bush, their mobility became greatly restricted. Moving 100 meters an hour was making good time in the bush.

THE WEAPONS OF WAR

Most of the equipment carried by soldiers in Vietnam, especially early in the war, was ill suited for jungle fighting or a tropical environment. The steel helmet, or "pot," provided some protection from bullets or shrapnel, but it was heavy and very hot. Many soldiers chose to wear floppy fabric hats in the field rather than endure the discomfort of the helmet. The intense heat and humidity were also the reasons many men chose not to wear a protective flak jacket. The jackets did give some protection against shrapnel and small arms fire, but they were hot, heavy, and cumbersome, and many soldiers weighed the chance of getting hit without one to catching heat stroke while wearing a flak jacket and steel helmet.

The standard-issue uniform was another case in point. In hot, humid jungle climates, the standard-issue cotton uniforms quickly disintegrated. As the war progressed, the Pentagon introduced newer equipment, albeit in some cases, it was not a great deal better. The military developed new fatigues for jungle use that incorporated ripstop nylon, but it was not much of an improvement. The military did learn from many of its mistakes. At the beginning of the war, the standard black leather combat boots were hot and rotted easily in the hot, wet climate. The military introduced new jungle boots, which included cooler nylon-mesh uppers and drain holes that allowed water to escape. The boots also had reinforced soles to protect against the sharpened bamboo stakes, or punji spikes, used as booby traps by enemy soldiers.

Many critics blame Secretary of Defense Robert McNamara's policy of cost-effectiveness for the military purchasing inferior equipment. McNamara wanted to save money, so the Defense Department standardized equipment as much as possible between the various service branches and purchased it as inexpensively as possible. All the services had to adopt the same basic battle uniform, for example. In the first few years of American involvement in Vietnam, the new standard battle uniform was a failure. It was cheaply made, and its generic design meant that it was not adapted to the needs of the men in the field. Unlike the old one, the new uniform did not have fly fronts or extra pockets, or buttons on the sleeves, and they quickly fell apart under jungle conditions. Footgear is extremely important to an infantryman, but McNamara's cost-effectiveness policies also led to cheaply made boots that quickly fell apart. In addition, to save money, the Pentagon eliminated half sizes, which made a big difference to the men that required them. Private First Class James Hebron, with the First Battalion, 26th Marine Division, who was a fire team leader at only 18 years old, recalled being issued size 12 jungle boots, despite the fact that he wore a size 10. "My foot is still fucked up from that today."[8]

"Doe" Morris moves through heavy grass in a deserted rice paddy while on patrol during operation Kentucky V with A Company, 1st Battalion, 4th Marines, 1967. Courtesy of the National Archives.

Infantrymen carried their gear in canvas field packs. In 1965, a marine field transport pack contained a haversack, knapsack, blanket, shelter half, poncho, tent pegs, ridge pole, guy line, an extra pair of boots, extra socks and underwear, a spare uniform, a shaving kit, a mess kit, and an entrenching tool. Marines also carried a helmet, two canteens, a sidearm, a flak jacket, field glasses, a compass, a knife, and rations. The entire kit weighed 65 pounds. Spare clothes increased the weight of field packs. Soldiers prized extra socks but often carried only the clothes they wore, along with rain ponchos, which also served as bedrolls. Each individual carried three C ration meals while on operations, adding even more extra weight to the backpack. When filled to capacity, an army pack weighed 90 pounds or more. Adding to the discomfort, the straps cut into the shoulders, sometimes rendering the arms numb. Many Americans solved the problem by using enemy equipment. Some GIs, for example, favored Vietnamese packs, which were taken from captured or killed North Vietnamese.

Whatever the initial shortcomings of some of the equipment, the U.S. military could deliver a lot of firepower. At the height of the war in mid-1968, the United States had approximately 540,000 troops in Vietnam, and they were armed with some of the most advanced and lethal weapons in the world. The first troops assigned to Vietnam were armed with M-14 rifles. They weighed a little over eight and one-half pounds and fired a 7.62 mm round and could be set either to single shot or semiautomatic. Unlike the old M-1 Garand, which carried only eight shots, the M-14 was fed from a 20-round box magazine. Gerald Kumpf actually preferred the earlier World War II era M-1, which was still in use in the early phases of the war. "The M-14 was a big botch. I hated the sucking rifle." He hated it because his jammed all the time. Luckily, for Kumpf, the only time he used it in Vietnam was on the rifle range. He never fired it in anger.[9] Despite Kumpf's low opinion of the weapon, many combat veterans favored the M-14, finding it to be more durable and reliable than its replacement, the M-16.

In 1966, the M-16 rifle became the standard weapon for infantrymen. At roughly six and one-half pounds, it was lighter than the M-14 and fired a .223 caliber/5.56 mm bullet at a rate of 750–900 rounds per minute on automatic setting, or as fast as a soldier could pull the trigger on semiautomatic, and had an effective range of about 430 meters. Like a lot of American equipment, the M-16 had problems early on, and before a late 1966 redesign, the rifle jammed easily under wet, dirty field conditions. Marines were issued M-16s beginning in early 1967, but as late as the siege of Khe Sahn, they still complained that the weapon jammed too much. The M-16 did have its advantages. The gun was light, easy to operate, and the cartridges came in 20- or 30-round clips, which could be quickly popped in and out of the rifle's loading port during firefights. Many soldiers taped two of them back to back with duct tape for even quicker reloading.

Each rifleman in a company was armed with an M-16 rifle, 400 rounds of ammunition, two smoke grenades, and two fragmentary grenades. A grenade could be thrown about 30 yards or propelled accurately at distances of about 150 yards using a rifle-mounted launcher. Carrying grenades through thick jungle was a hazardous proposition. Fuse pins sometimes could catch on undergrowth and pull from grenades, resulting in unintentional and deadly explosions. Out in the field, the equipment carried by an individual trooper varied according to taste. Many carried extra canteens, but others preferred extra ammunition. Gordon Roberts, who fought in the Ashau Valley in July 1969, carried 600 rounds of ammunition for his M-16 and anywhere from 6 to 10 grenades.[10] Although extra magazines added weight to the soldier's gear, the danger of running out of ammunition during a firefight caused many grunts to carry as many clips as possible when they went into the field.

In addition to a soldier's personal weapons, each squad had two M79 grenade launchers with 45 rounds each and at least two claymore mines. The M18A1 Claymore antipersonnel mine was portable, versatile, and tripod mounted and could be detonated by a trip wire or a manually operated lanyard. When triggered, it released over 700 steel balls in a 60-degree arc in an effective range of around 50 meters.

The company as a whole was equipped with three 81 mm mortars with 30 rounds per mortar. Many also used the M19 60 mm mortar, which was lighter, more portable, and easy to use. It could be operated from a handheld position or mounted on the ground using a steel base plate, and fired as many as 30 high explosive, smoke, or illumination rounds per minute, with an effective range of approximately 45–2,000 meters. All companies were armed with M60 general purpose machine guns. They were light enough to be carried on patrol and deadly in a firefight, firing up to 550 high-velocity bullets from a gas-powered, belt-fed system at a range of over 1,900 meters. The M60 could be fired from a bipod, a tripod, or even from the hip. The M60's only real drawback was its heavy cartridge belt, which limited the amount of ammunition that could be carried into the field. A two-man crew usually tended it. Bill Beck, for example, was an assistant machine gunner and served with the army at Ia Drang. He crewed the machine gun with his friend Russ Adams and traded off manning the weapon every other day.

Many units were equipped with M113 armored personnel carriers (APCs). The vehicles ran on aluminum tank treads, could go as fast as 40 miles per hour, and carried up to 11 soldiers. They could serve as personnel transport or reconnaissance vehicles and provided fire support with .50 caliber Browning machine guns. Some M113s also carried two optional M60 60 mm machine guns. The APC was lightly armored, however, and the 12 and 38 millimeters of armor on each vehicle provided little protection for the occupants. Sometimes older, proven technology worked best. One of the most popular and reliable vehicles used in Vietnam was the World War II era jeep. The four-wheel-drive jeep was rugged, dependable, and capable of traversing some of the roughest roads and terrain.

The diesel-powered M-48 was the most common American tank employed in the war. It could go up to 30 miles per hour and was armed with a 90 mm gun capable of transversing 360 degrees and two machine guns, a 7.62 mm and a .50 caliber. Vietnam was not a tank war; the jungles and mountainous terrain were ill suited to armored warfare, and the Vietcong and North Vietnamese army possessed few tanks themselves. But tanks were still useful in Vietnam for guarding convoys, securing roadways, and supporting troops in combat. At night, for example, tanks and APCs could be circled around a camp in a defensive position known as a lager.

American units could normally count on massive air and artillery support to aid them or extricate them in a tight situation. The armed forces used a variety of artillery in Vietnam; the navy even brought the battleship *New Jersey* out of mothballs temporarily to provide artillery support along the coastline from September 1968 to April 1969. One of the largest guns used by the army was the self-propelled 175 mm gun, with a maximum range of around 32,600 meters and a crew of five. The workhorse of the artillery was the 105 mm howitzer, which had first seen action in World War II. Modified for use in Vietnam to make it more mobile, the gun performed admirably. It had a range of about 12,500 meters and could be towed into place by truck or helicopter, and its eight-man crew could fire between three and eight rounds a minute of high-explosive, shrapnel, or beehive cartridges, which contained thousands of small, sharpened darts.

HELICOPTERS AND FIXED WING AIRCRAFT

The military employed a variety of helicopters in Vietnam, including the CH-47 Chinook, or the Hughes 500C, and Bell Jetranger; both were a Loach, or light observation helicopter. If any one weapon defined the battlefield in Vietnam, it was the helicopter, particularly the Bell UH-1 helicopter, or Huey. The first element of 15 armed Hueys was deployed to Vietnam in September 1962, and over 12,000 helicopters of various types would serve in the war. The Huey had a crew of one or two and usually a tail gunner. Armament varied but often included one or two M60 7.62 mm machine guns, a XM157 rocket launcher with high explosive or phosphorus rockets, or 40 mm grenade launchers. Pilots carried a .45 caliber automatic, but John Ballweg never used his. Many pilots also carried nonissue weapons they had acquired one way or another.

The Huey had a cruising speed of 115 miles per hour, a maximum speed of 140 miles per hour, and a service ceiling of 24,830 feet. It could carry up to 225 gallons of fuel, but most pilots only carried 175 gallons due to weight restrictions, giving it a range of about 330 miles. Fully loaded, one could carry around 3,000 pounds, which worked out to up to six fully armed Americans or eight fully armed ARVN.

Hueys were excellent aircraft, but they did have their drawbacks. They were not armored. Soldiers riding in them often sat on their helmets to provide some protection for their backsides. Crews would often put a flak jacket in the chin bubble, and even though the seats were armored, many of them sat on a flak jacket as well. John Ballweg kept his .45 between his legs more to deflect bullets or shrapnel than as an offensive weapon. Above 3,000 feet, the helicopters were relatively safe from enemy ground fire, the one big exception being the .50 caliber machine gun, but the choppers often had to operate much closer to the ground, making them vulnerable to various types of enemy ground fire, and there were numerous places on the aircraft that, if hit, could bring it down. During the Vietnam War, enemy ground fire downed 4,865 U.S. helicopters. At a cost of about $250,000 each, the losses cost the United States roughly $1.2 billion.

Ballweg considered the Huey "a beautiful aircraft," but it wasn't built for a tropical climate, and the heat and humidity affected its performance; in particular, it made landings and takeoffs more difficult. Despite these problems, Ballweg stated, "It was still a Cadillac in my eyes. I loved that aircraft. Very dependable. It could take a beating."[11]

The United States also operated thousands of fixed wing aircraft. At the height of the war, in 1968, there were 1,121 American fixed wing fighter and ground attack aircraft operating in Vietnam. One of the most important and versatile was the F-4 Phantom. The Phantom had a crew of two and first went into service in 1963 with both the navy and air force, proving versatile enough to fill a variety of roles, including fighter, bomber, reconnaissance, and ground attack. It had a service ceiling of 59,600 feet, a top speed of 1,400 miles per hour, and a range of 1,750 miles at a cruising speed of 590 miles per hour. It was originally armed with missiles only, but pilots finally convinced the Defense Department to install a 20 mm cannon as well. Externally, it could carry up to 16,000 pounds of bombs, rockets, or missiles.

The Phantom also had its faults. It was nearly impossible to pull the navy version out of a tailspin, and it was not as nimble as its MIG adversary. Like most high-performance jet aircraft, it was temperamental and needed a lot of maintenance. Gerald Kumpf, an avionics technician, judged the F-4 to be "powerful, fast, and reliable in the air, when its working. It doesn't, it's got a terrible maintenance record... you have to disassemble the airplane anytime you want to fix it and it was really terrible for that." He estimated that there were 40 hours of down maintenance time for every hour of flight time with the F-4. But the plane was a workhorse and could absorb a lot of punishment.[12]

The North Vietnamese air force was tiny and posed little threat to American forces operating in South Vietnam, so most of the U.S. aircraft were involved in supporting ground operations. One of the most appreciated was the AC-47 gunship. Known to the troops as either Puff or Spooky, the plane was usually armed with two 7.62 mm Gatling guns, capable of saturating an area the size of a football field with deadly fire in a few seconds. The use of illumination flares allowed it to operate at night as well.

Perhaps the most feared weapon in the American arsenal was the B-52 bomber. Though the B-52 proved to be an excellent weapon platform in Vietnam, it was not intended for conventional bombing operations. It was originally designed in the late 1940s for long-range nuclear strikes against the Soviet Union and was reconfigured to handle conventional munitions. It could carry nearly 60,000 pounds of ordinance, either in its cavernous bomb bay or on pylons attached under the wings. It was not particularly fast, having a maximum speed of only 595 miles per hour, but it had a ceiling of 46,000 feet. Because they could operate so high, the enemy in the field had no way to shoot one down and could not hear the approaching planes, or bombs, until they began exploding. The North Vietnamese and the Vietcong hated the B-52 and nicknamed it the "whispering death" because of this combination of surprise and massive destructive power. The Vietcong and North Vietnamese army could not even get to the planes when they were on the ground: the plane's tremendous cruising range of over 8,400 miles meant that the aircraft could be based safely in Thailand and Guam, and not in Vietnam.

RIVERINE FORCES

Vietnam was primarily a land war, but with its thousands of miles of coastline, numerous rivers, and wide deltas, there was a need for small, fast attack and patrol boats. The river patrol boat, or PBR, was a small, fast, lightweight craft and served as the main vessel of riverine operations. PBRs, or "swift boats," as many of them were designated, were powered by a 220-horsepower General Motors engine and propelled by a Jacuzzi Brothers water jet—the fiberglass-hulled PBR could reach 28.5 knots. It was powerfully armed with twin .50 caliber machine guns, a 7.62 mm machine gun, a Mark 18 grenade launcher, and, occasionally, a 20 mm cannon. Ceramic armor protected the conning station and the machine gun positions. In 1967, the navy deployed the new Ashville class patrol gunboat in Vietnamese waters. The 165-foot-long Ashvilles, with their shallow draft and 37-knot speed, were designed for coastal operations in the developing world and were heavily armed with a three-inch 50. caliber gun forward and one 40 mm gun aft, with four .50 caliber machine guns distributed along the sides of the boat. Less successful were the hydrofoils the navy introduced late in the war to replace the Ashville class. Revolutionary in concept, the hydrofoils proved difficult to maintain at the facilities in Vietnam and unsuited to the rough seas off the coast.

By 1968, the navy operated 331 watercraft of various types in South Vietnam, organized into special riverine task forces designed primarily to disrupt weapon shipments in areas such as the Mekong delta. Beginning that year, the naval coastal and riverine forces were reinforced by 26 WPB 82-foot cutters operated by the U.S. Coast Guard.

Neither the North Vietnamese nor the Vietcong had armed riverine forces in the south similar to the American swift boats, but boats were important for transportation of men and materiel, and enemy forces shipped supplies through coastal and riverine areas using thousands of small watercraft. The principal watercraft was the junk, a traditional Chinese vessel dating back thousands of years. Some junks were steel hulled and displaced 100 tons, but most were made of wood and were usually powered by sail, although motors were also used. With the exception of weapons carried by their crews, the junks were unarmed. Therefore a typical day for a swift boat, gunboat, or Coast Guard crew included stopping and checking sampans, junks, and other river craft for contraband and checking identification cards. There was a curfew on most South Vietnamese rivers from 6:00 P.M. to 6:00 A.M., so swift or gunboats, usually operating in pairs, hunted for curfew violators at night. The river and coastal forces also exchanged gunfire with shore-based enemies and helped transport troops rapidly up and down the coastline. The troop carrier USS *Monticello,* for example, carried 400–500 marines and could deliver them where needed along the South Vietnamese coast.

The ability to move troops rapidly by sea or air, combined with massive firepower, were key American advantages in the war, and the Huey, in particular, proved a nasty surprise for the Vietcong and their North Vietnamese allies early in the war. "At first your helicopters and aircraft were hard to fight. They go fast," recalled North Vietnamese army colonel Dang Viet Mai. "So much rocket, bomb and artillery fire scared our fighters. But we learned. We set ambushes. We knew you would run out of aircraft and bombs before we ran out of spirit."[13]

THE VIETCONG AND THE PEOPLES ARMY OF VIETNAM

The United States and South Vietnam faced two enemies in the war. The largely indigenous forces were under the auspices of the NLF, an umbrella organization dominated by the Communists but encompassing all the South Vietnamese revolutionary groups opposed to the American-backed regime in Saigon. The Americans and South

A Vietcong soldier crouches in a bunker with an SKS rifle, 1968.
Courtesy of the National Archives.

Vietnamese called them Vietcong—short for "Vietnamese Communists"—but it was a term they never applied to themselves as they were members of the National Liberation Armed Forces. Because of the use of phonetic pronunciations for each specific letter—*alpha* for *A* or *India* for *I*—the Vietcong, or VC, were also known as Victor Charles, or just plain Charlie to the grunt in the field. Charlie's allies were troops from the Democratic Republic of Vietnam, or North Vietnam. Again, the allies tended to call their military personnel something different than their official name, referring to them as the North Vietnamese army, or NVA. Their proper name, however, was the Peoples Army of Vietnam, or PAVN.

The PAVN units fighting in the south were conventional military units, and their soldiers some of the best light infantry in the world. The Vietcong were organized along both conventional, and unconventional lines. Main force Vietcong units were uniformed, full-time soldiers, organized into conventional formations, such as companies, battalions, and divisions, and were used to launch large-scale offensives over a wide area. The recruits were relatively well trained, receiving about a month's worth of advanced instruction. As early as spring 1965, there were approximately 12 Vietcong main force regiments, each around 1200–1500 men, but with little coordination between the various units. Regional forces were also full-time but operated only within their own districts. When necessary, small regional units would unite for large-scale attacks. If enemy pressure became too great, they would break down into smaller units and scatter. There were also the part-time and often poorly trained local forces. Most were young teenagers, and while many were motivated by patriotism, others had been pressured or shamed into joining the Vietcong. They also had legitimate doubts about their ability to fight heavily armed and well-trained American soldiers. Local guerrillas were given only basic infantry training, but there were also dozens of hidden centers all over South Vietnam for squad and platoon leader, weapon, and radio training. To ensure that the guerrillas understood why they were fighting, all training courses included political instruction.

North Vietnamese soldiers wore a variety of headgear, the most common a pith-type helmet made from pressed paper, or sometimes plastic, and decorated with a five-pointed star insignia. Vietcong troops usually wore a floppy cotton hat in the field. The North Vietnamese wore a simple, green, canvas uniform, while the Vietcong preferred the black pajama-type garb worn by the peasantry. Many NVA soldiers wore standard-issue, jungle-type boots, but they often wore the same footwear as their Vietcong counterparts, which tended to be simple cloth sandals with soles made from recycled tire treads, known to Americans as Ho Chi Minh sandals. Some Vietcong fought barefoot. Unlike the Americans, who relied on an extensive logistics system to feed their troops, the dietary needs of the enemy combatants was simpler and often easy to obtain. The typical ration for either a Vietcong or NVA regular was usually a ball of rice wrapped in cabbage leaves, sometimes with a little rat or dog meat, and some fish sauce. Supplies were often easily obtainable from local villages, which either voluntarily, or out of fear, supplied them.

The Vietcong, and to a much lesser degree, the North Vietnamese, often carried arms captured in previous wars from the French and even the Japanese, or homemade or improvised weapons, but much of their equipment and weaponry came from the Soviet Union and the People's Republic of China. By the mid-1960s, most main force Vietcong troops were armed with Chinese versions of the Russian AK-47 submachine gun. The AK-47 was almost the perfect weapon for a peasant warrior because it was simple to use, rugged, and easy to maintain. Nor was it as temperamental as the M-16. The AK-47 seldom jammed, even after being dropped in mud or exposed to other climatic hazards.

It fired a 7.62 mm round, either automatically or semiautomatically, from a 30-round clip at a rate of up to about 600 rounds per minute. It was not as accurate as the M-16, but a good marksman could hit a target as far away as 430 meters. Communist troops also used the SKS carbine, or "Chicom," a semiautomatic rifle that also fired 7.62 mm ammunition. It had a 10-round clip but a slightly greater range than the AK-47.

They also used a range of effective Soviet and Chinese light and medium machine guns. The North Vietnamese used the Russian-designed DP light machine gun as their squad-level automatic support weapon. It was fed by a pan magazine or belt and fired the standard 7.62 mm round, with an effective range of about 875 meters. They also, but more infrequently, used heavy machine guns. In particular, heavy machine guns were valued for defense against American helicopters.

The Vietcong and North Vietnamese had highly effective rocket-propelled grenades and recoilless rifles for destroying armored vehicles or bunkers. The 122 mm rocket launcher was a weapon feared and hated by the Americans fighting in Vietnam, not so much because of its lethality, but largely because the NVA and Vietcong operators had a hard time aiming the weapon. Albert Childs remembered, "They have a launcher for it which they can use to point it with some degree of accuracy, but normally the troops in the field jammed a couple of pieces of bamboo in the ground to make a cross and they just laid it in there (and fired it). The beauty of it to them was, you didn't know where it was going to land," making taking cover far more problematical.[14] Mortars were also available in large numbers and had the advantage of being very easy to transport.

In addition to Chinese and Soviet mines, both the Vietcong and NVA soldiers employed an assortment of antipersonnel devices, many handmade or obtained from U.S. forces. Dud American bombs could leave more than 20,000 tons of explosives scattered around the Vietnamese countryside a year, which were retrieved by volunteer Vietcong. Their soldiers dug up and reused American land mines, took Claymore mines from their tripods, and even cut open unexploded bombs to harvest components for their handmade weapons. Many Vietcong soldiers lost their lives in accidental explosions at low-tech bomb factories attempting to convert the stolen components into workable devices.

The Vietcong, but also the North Vietnamese, commonly employed homemade booby traps. These included punji sticks, which were sharpened sticks of bamboo, often smeared with animal or human excrement to cause infection, concealed in hidden pits and designed to pierce the feet of enemy soldiers. They also made such medieval but effective weapons as bamboo maces, which swung down onto soldiers who triggered trip wires, trip wire–operated crossbows, and boards studded with nails. These devices were more a component of psychological warfare as they were not necessarily designed to kill an enemy, but to maim and wound him and cause morale problems.

The NVA did not employ tanks in large numbers, and its main battle tank was the Soviet T-54/55, which, like most Russian-made armor, was a good tank. It had a four-man crew and a top speed of about 50 miles per hour. It was well armored and armed with a powerful 100 mm, turret-mounted main gun, capable of firing armor-piercing and high-explosive rounds at a range of about 16,000 meters. The few tanks available to the Vietcong were generally Russian light tanks.

The Soviet-made BTR armored personnel carrier was the North Vietnamese equivalent of the M113. Several different models of the BTR series were used, including the BTR 60P, an eight-wheeled amphibious vehicle with a crew of two, which carried up to 16 soldiers. The BTR 60 traveled on land at speeds of up to 50 miles per hour and in water at about 10 miles per hour. The BTR offered better protection than the American M113, with the sides of the vehicle protected by 10 mm of armor, but it was roofless, with no protection from attack from above.

The Vietcong did not have an air force, but North Vietnam had a small one. Like the rest of its advanced equipment, their aircraft were all of Soviet design, with the Soviet-made MiG-21 as the primary fighter aircraft for the North Vietnamese air force. Like most Russian equipment, it was a good fit for a developing nation because it was easy to maintain and could operate from unimproved airfields. It was a very capable aircraft that could fly more than twice the speed of sound, had a ceiling of 50,000 feet, and was well armed with air-to-air missiles and a 30 mm cannon. It was more maneuverable than an F-4 Phantom and could be dangerous in a dogfight, especially in the hands of an experienced and skilled pilot. In fact, many American F-4s encountered MIGs with volunteer Russian, eastern bloc, or Chinese pilots. An earlier MIG design, the MIG-17, also saw service in the war as a fighter and interceptor, but it was markedly inferior to its American adversaries.

Early in the war, the air defenses in North Vietnam consisted mostly of World War II era antiaircraft guns and a few Russian surface-to-air (SAM) missiles. As the war progressed, the Russians sold the North Vietnamese increasingly capable SAM systems. By the early 1970s, Hanoi boasted what was probably the best air defense system for any city in the world, and American pilots over North Vietnam encountered a lethal barrage of radar-guided, base-stationed antiaircraft fire. In the south, one of the biggest threats to American aircraft was the SA7 Grail. A shoulder-fired, portable weapon, the Grail could be moved quickly and concealed easily, making it difficult to deter. Grail missiles downed numerous American planes and helicopters.

The first American combat troops sent to Vietnam originally thought that the enemy would be quickly beaten; after all, the United States had never lost a war. Because the level of training varied widely among Vietcong units, many of the men in local or provisional units were not particularly adept at fighting. At Danang, in 1965–1966, Gerald Kumpf felt that the Vietcong "were rather inept as far as their trying to become sappers or throwing in mortar rounds" because they would fire four or five rounds and seldom hit anything.[15] Many referred to them derisively as "gooks," or "dinks." Most American combat soldiers, however, learned to respect the Vietcong and PAVN as worthy adversaries; they were brave, tenacious, daring, resourceful, and dedicated. They were also elusive. Kumpf saw only five or six Vietcong during his tour of duty, and four of them were already dead.[16] John Ballweg was in Vietnam from August 1966 to August 1967 and never saw, or fought against, to his knowledge, any North Vietnamese regulars.

Most Americans were impressed by the enemy's sheer desire to win and their willingness to sacrifice for their cause. Vietcong private Nguyen Van An, who lost a leg in March 1969 fighting David Hackworth's battalion, "slapped on a wooden leg, and proudly fought for five more years."[17] Even Gerald Kumpf admitted that they were "persevering little fucks, I'll give them that. Yes, they wouldn't give up."[18] This dedication and courage, along with misguided preconceived notions of the Asian view on existence, led most Americans to believe that the Vietcong and NVA did not value life as much as did Westerners. Many writers state that to achieve his objectives, General Vo Nguyen Giap was willing to take casualties that would have appalled most Western generals of his day, and Giap did claim that the Vietnamese were willing to fight another 20 or 100 years if necessary. But his willingness to take casualties to win was not that much different from generals in the American Civil War, World War I, or World War II.

REVOLUTION AND CIVIL WAR

War in Vietnam combined two of the most bitter forms of warfare—revolution and civil war—with the ferocity of jungle and guerilla warfare. Vietnam was a vicious war by any standard, similar in many respects to the war without mercy fought between Americans and Japanese in World War II. The Vietnamese had been in a near-constant state of hostilities for decades: fighting the Japanese in World War II, the French in the first Franco-Vietminh War, and then ARVN and the Americans. Decades of warfare and atrocities had left many of the Vietnamese callous to suffering and death.

Both sides in the war used cruelty, atrocity, and torture. "Twenty years of terrorism and fratricide had obliterated most reference points from the country's moral compass," reflected Philip Caputo. "Communist and government forces alike considered ruthlessness a necessity if not a virtue. Whether committed in the name of principles or our of vengeance, atrocities were as common to the Vietnamese battlefields as shell craters and barbed wire."[19] Civilians were considered fair game in this type of environment. Saigon government officials routinely tortured or summarily executed suspected Vietcong, and the NLF used torture and assassination enthusiastically to achieve its goals. Mass graves of thousands of civilians massacred by the Vietcong were discovered after Hue was retaken during Tet-68, for example, and at Ben Tre, over 1,000 civilians were killed in a fierce battle to expel the 2,500 Vietcong holding the city.

Communist soldiers were often brutal and cruel to prisoners, sometimes torturing and executing captured Americans. Some captured soldiers were skinned alive and staked out for patrolling Americans to find. American GIs became embroiled in the culture of violence, with its body counts, death's head playing cards, atrocities, revenge for dead comrades, and taking trophies in the form of fingers, ears, or other body parts.[20] Philip Caputo argued that the savagery of the Vietnam War distinguished it from every other American conflict and turned otherwise decent American men into merciless killers. War can "arouse a psychopathic violence in men of seemingly normal impulse."[21] Isolation from the accepted norms of society contributed to the transformation.

Americans may have been reacting to the realities of war in Vietnam, but many harbored racist preconceptions that contributed to their behavior toward the Vietnamese people. A soldier from the First Infantry Division told journalist Michael Herr matter-of-factly that they treated the Vietnamese like animals. "Well, you know what we do to animals...kill 'em and hurt 'em and beat on 'em so's we can train 'em....We don't treat the Dinks no different than that." Herr said that the young soldier was not making a moral judgment, or even particularly upset about it; it was just something the young man had observed.[22] David Parks admitted that the villagers in the delta region, where his company operated, considered the GIs murderers and admitted that some men in his unit raped and murdered civilians.

War has its gray areas, Vietnam probably more than most. It was difficult, if not impossible, to always tell enemy insurgent from innocent peasant, and many people could be either, depending on place and circumstance. Nevertheless, all Americans sent to Vietnam were supposed to adhere to certain basic rules of conduct in dealing with both civilians and captured POWs. The reasons for treating both civilian and POWs humanely were practical ones. The United States was not only waging war against the insurgents, but also attempting to win over the peasant population to the American-backed government in Saigon. Murdering and raping the civilian population obviously undermined these goals and provided valuable propaganda and recruiting incentive for the enemy. Torturing and killing prisoners was also counterproductive. The United States and the Republic of Vietnam were interested in convincing Vietcong and North Vietnamese to switch sides under the Chieu Hoi, or "open arms," program. Many were willing to cooperate and provide valuable information if treated humanely. Gonzalo Baltazar's rapid reaction company captured numerous prisoners, including enemy nurses, soldiers, and some high-ranking officers, principally during operations in the A Shau Valley from May to August 1969. The Americans at the scene did not beat or mistreat the prisoners, and most of them, especially the officers, cooperated. "They were willing to go." They loaded them on the helicopters, and that was the last they ever saw of them. Baltazar and the others did not know what happened to the prisoners after that.[23]

FRIENDS AND ALLIES

The United States had allies in Vietnam, principally the South Vietnamese army, or ARVN, and troops from the ROK, Thailand, the Philippines, Australia, and New Zealand. Some of the allied contingents were sizable. Between 1962 and 1973, nearly 50,000 Australians, and several thousand New Zealanders, brigaded together in the Australian and New Zealand Army Corps (ANZAC), would serve in Vietnam. The ANZACs, or "Diggers," as they called themselves, had their own area of responsibility around Phuoc Tuy, but they often crossed paths with the Americans socially and worked with them out in the field. Gerald Kumpf's unit at Danang worked occasionally with an Australian helicopter unit stationed nearby. Most Americans liked and respected the Aussies. John Ballweg, for example, thought that the Australians and New Zealanders were decent guys, but some Americans, such as Kumpf, did not have a particularly high opinion of them. He thought Americans were crazy until he met the Australians, which he characterized as arrogant, and "thought they could control the world."[24] The Australians may have been a bit cocky because they were all highly trained professionals and volunteers. Australia had a draft, but conscripts had the right to refuse service in Vietnam. The diggers were rotated into Vietnam by unit, not individually, so there was a high degree of unit cohesion.

Interestingly, many Australians criticized the performance of American units in Vietnam. Major Jerry Taylor, who served in Vietnam in 1967–1968, said that there was excellent cooperation between the Americans and Australians, and "there was certainly nothing wrong with their physical courage," but overall, he found American units to "be rather patchy in quality, and many exhibited severe disciplinary problems." Second Lieutenant Kevin Byres worked very closely with American units in Vietnam and said that many of them were first class. He also added, however, that there was a wide disparity between the best and the worst U.S. formations. One American platoon was so noisy and undisciplined out in the field that the Australians refused to camp with them: "If you really wanted to telegraph to the Vietcong where you were you just stayed with this unit—if you really wanted trouble."[25] The Australians were impressed, however, with the performance of American air force and army helicopter pilots and at the sheer magnitude of the American war effort in Vietnam.

Most Americans also thought highly of the South Koreans, who had two infantry divisions and a marine brigade in Vietnam. Officially, they were "Republic of Korea" troops, so most Americans commonly called them ROKs. Ballweg considered the

A contingent of the Royal Australian Air Force arrives at Tan Son Nhut Airport, Saigon, to work with the South Vietnamese and U.S. air forces in transporting soldiers and supplies to combat areas in South Vietnam, 1964. Courtesy of the National Archives.

ROKs to be crack soldiers, and Kumpf had a higher opinion of the Koreans than he did of the troops from down under. "They were good, I mean, the South Koreans were really disciplined."[26]

ARVN

The American combat soldier in Vietnam may have held his Communist opponent in high regard but did not hold some of his own allies in the same esteem. ARVN had many crack units, such as the ARVN Rangers, and capable officers, and some Americans respected and befriended them. As an advisor to the 23rd ARVN Infantry Division, Albert Childs had more contact with ARVN men and officers than did most Americans. Many of the ARVN officers and men Childs worked with were "super. They were really good."[27] But many more would have agreed with John Ballweg's assessment that ARVN was "worthless." Even someone generally favorable, such as Childs, also admitted that many of them did not want to fight and that the stereotype was often true.[28]

The average ARVN soldier was a poorly trained and badly motivated conscript, whose officers frequently were more interested in profiting from corruption and the political intrigues in Saigon than in confronting a skilled and determined enemy. "Marvin the ARVN," as Americans nicknamed him, was underpaid and treated poorly; consequently, most appeared more interested in the everyday aspects of life than in fighting the enemy. ARVN soldiers stationed at Danang brought their families with them, a common practice. There was an antiaircraft battery about 60 yards from Gerald Kumpf's location, and "they lived right outside where the gun was at; it was embanked, in places. Surrounded, and they lived right outside of that emplacement with their kids and their wives... their pigs and their goats and all that."[29] Helicopters would drop off an ARVN unit for a search and destroy mission and return later that day to pick them up. John Ballweg claimed that instead of dead Vietcong, "they'd all have dead chickens hanging around their shoulders. It was big game to them."[30] In addition to being unreliable, Americans often did not trust ARVN soldiers because many of them were playing both sides or were actually Vietcong. Two of the Kit Carson scouts in Gonzalo Baltazar's unit defected back to the NVA during a bitter firefight on hill 376, for example.[31]

Unlike the Vietcong and PAVN, the average ARVN soldier had little stomach for a fight. Americans nicknamed ARVN tanks "voting machines" because the only time you saw one was during another political coup. One ARVN soldier refused to leave the helicopter during one insertion, and Ballweg had to threaten him with a pistol to get him to disembark on the next trip.[32] "We hated the ARVN. We had watched them shuffle and sniffle through too many operations while 'searching and avoiding' the VC," stated David Hackworth. "Our opponent we held in the highest esteem."[33]

THE IMPORTANCE OF LEADERSHIP

Whether it was a large battalion sweep or a few men on patrol, good leadership was naturally a key to any unit's effectiveness and survivability. In summing up the importance of a capable leader, Lieutenant Colonel K. E. Hamburger found that "successful leaders required aggressiveness, audacity, and vigorous execution by their subordinates, and both they and their soldiers refuse to accept defeat. They were ingenious in overcoming obstacles, and in desperate situations, they often took irrational, even foolhardy action to forestall failure." The well-led unit would persevere despite casualties, lost equipment, or a shortage of supplies. Surrender was never an option.[34]

Good leadership was also the key in forging unit cohesion. Hamburger found that units commanded by successful leaders took on their "confidence and spirit.... It is no exaggeration to say that the leader was the most decisive factor in building unit cohesion."[35]

Successful commanders were visible to their men. As a lieutenant colonel commanding the 96th Quartermaster Battalion in Vietnam, Arthur Gregg spent little time at his command post. He believed it was important to be out among his men. "I spent my time out visiting the troops. I believed then and I believe now that a constant presence with the troops makes a difference." He recognized that the vast majority of the officers and men in his command worked hard, but they were young and inexperienced, and it helped to have the presence of a confident senior officer in charge, reassuring them that what they did was important and that their efforts were recognized. Gregg stressed that a good officer recognized excellence quickly and rewarded it.[36]

There were problems with the command system, however. Most officers served only six months in combat units as platoon or company officers, then automatically rotated to administrative or staff positions at the battalion or divisional level. Policy was aimed at creating well-rounded officers with both combat and staff experience and also at rotating as many career officers through Vietnam as possible. By the time someone had become a seasoned combat veteran and leader, and, more importantly, knew the men under his command, he was transferred out, and a new, less experienced, and usually less capable officer took his place. Walter Nutting served two tours in Vietnam commanding armored cavalry units. During his first tour, in 1966–1967, he led a squadron for the first six months, and then served as operation officer for the First Field Force. In his second tour, he commanded the 11th Armored Cavalry Regiment from 1970 to 1971. There were exceptions to the rule. In 1966–1967, Lieutenant Colonel Arthur Gregg commanded the 96th Quartermaster Battalion in Vietnam for his entire one-year tour of duty.

Compounding the problem was the fact that novice officers often did not have an experienced NCO to guide and teach them. Though many NCOs served multiple tours in Vietnam, career NCOs that had already served a year in Vietnam could choose their assignment to any unit if they volunteered to go back within a year. Most chose to go to noncombat units, so while there were many experienced NCOs in Vietnam, there was a shortage of them in combat units. The military's solution was to send graduates from combat AIT that had either a college education or had done well on the military aptitude tests to an eight-week fast track course in leadership and in squad and platoon tactics. Recruits arrived as private/E-2 and left the course promoted to sergeant/E-5, or squad leader, or staff sergeant/ E-6, or platoon sergeant.

SEARCH AND DESTROY

The most common operations conducted by American forces in Vietnam were so-called search and destroy missions: offensive patrolling, ostensibly to flush out the enemy and kill them. They could be a large-scale big battalion sweep, such as the 22,000 troops in Operation Attleboro in late 1966, or Cedar Falls, involving thousands of soldiers and hundreds of helicopters, fixed winged aircraft, and vehicles, but more likely, they were platoon- or company-sized patrols. Units were usually inserted by helicopter transport into Indian country. If a landing zone did not exist, one was made through the use of a so-called daisy cutter, a 15,000-pound BLU-82 bomb, dropped by C130, which literally blew a hole in the jungle or bush large enough to set a helicopter down in. Once on the ground, troops would further clear and secure the area. Initially, the Vietcong contested the troop landings, stationing themselves in the nearest tree line, preferably about 100 meters from the landing zone (LZ). Bill Beck was an assistant machine gunner and served with the army at Ia Drang. Beck and the other men in his unit came under fire the minute they got off the helicopters. "We barely had time to get our bearings when we came under heavy fire. And when the firing started, it wasn't like a sniper shot or anything. It was bullets and bombs and grenades and everything going off simultaneously. And all at once, everyone around me is getting shot. My friend Jerry Kirsch was right in front of me and he got machine gunned right across the stomach. He dropped at my feet and was screaming for his mom. It was something in a movie. You just can't believe your eyes, or your ears."[37]

After disembarking the helicopter and taking up a defensive position, Bill Beck was stunned to see dead soldiers still in firing position. "So that scared the hell out of me. At that moment, my instincts and adrenaline just took over." Beck's friend Russell Adams had a serious head wound. Beck manned the machine gun and fired into the enemy approaching not more than 10–20 yards away. He could not see how many were behind them because the jungle was so thick. It went on for three days and sleepless nights. "I didn't think I would ever get out. Many of the guys in my unit—kids I'd grown up with—never did."[38]

Men of H Company, 2nd Battalion, 7th Marines, move along rice paddy dikes in pursuit of the Viet Cong, 1965. Courtesy of the National Archives.

But attacking the LZ brought great risks to the Vietcong or NVA; it gave away the enemy's position and brought artillery and helicopter gunships down on them immediately. By 1966, the Vietcong had changed tactics and no longer routinely contested the landings. Instead, they pulled their units back well over 250–500 meters, leaving only a few snipers behind, and waited to see if any opportunity to attack would develop. Once the LZ was secure, troops could be brought in very rapidly. During the initial phase of Cedar Falls, for example, 60 helicopters landed the entire First Battalion, Second Infantry, in only five minutes.

At Ia Drang, and other early encounters, the Vietcong and NVA regulars learned to appreciate the American forces' tremendous firepower and discipline and tended to shun set piece engagements with American units unless it was unavoidable or they had some sort of advantage such as surprise or superior numbers. They kept the initiative but, more often than not, chose not to fight, fading into the jungle and disappearing from the approaching Americans. Only one Vietcong main force battalion chose to stand and fight on the first day of Cedar Falls, for example. According to an after action report from the U.S. Second Brigade, "this was the only incident during the entire operation in which the Viet Cong elected to fight."[39] This meant that allied units had to go looking for the enemy, which was usually very unrewarding and frustrating work. David Hackworth, who commanded the 439th Infantry, Ninth Infantry Division, remembered that his "troopers were not fighting to take critical ground. They were just rolling the dice, looking for 'Cong'—as were more than 100 other U.S. grunt battalions that beat the bush in the flawed strategy called 'Search and Destroy.'"[40] Military historian Russell Weigley described a typical mission: "The soldiers seemed to 'hump the boonies' endlessly, prowl through jungles, marshes, savannahs and mountains, parched by heat." The men were often so thirsty that when they found water, they drank it, despite contamination by mud and dead insects, without using their disinfectant pills. "All the while they were fighting off leeches; at best, they were half-sick and dog-tired long before" they encountered any enemy soldiers.[41]

Some jobs while out on patrol carried more inherent dangers than others. A unit on patrol following normal procedure would have men out on the flanks and at least one man "waking point" anywhere from a few to 100 meters in front of the main body. The point man was to be on guard for both ambushes and booby traps. In the army and marines, more experienced men with a knack for it were usually put out on point. "If a man is an outstanding squad leader point man, he'll be on the point every time," explained marine sergeant Thomas A. Roberson. "Some guys have a sixth sense about finding the enemy." The marines had a tendency, however, to put newcomers out there to initiate them from time to time, but it was never a good idea to leave someone out on point that could not do the assignment. Roberson "never seen a man who asked to be taken off point who wasn't taken off. If he's asking to be taken off, he's not a good point man anymore."[42] Walking point may have been dangerous, but at times it could be safer than being back with the main body. The Vietcong and PAVN often allowed the point man or men through before springing an ambush so as not to alert the bulk of the troops following behind. But this was not always the case; in many ambushes, the men at point were the first casualties.

Officers foolish enough to wear visible insignia of rank often ended up casualties. Another favorite target for the enemy were radio operators. The heavy radio set and antenna made them stand out on a battlefield, and killing the radio man impeded a unit's communications ability. Infantryman Jack Smith reported seeing Richards, a radio operator in Charlie Company, First Battalion, First Air Cavalry, shot through the heart by a sniper. "Just as I looked back, he moaned softly and fell to the ground. I knelt down and looked at him, and he shuddered and started to gurgle deep in his stomach. His eyes and tongue popped out, and he died. He had a hole straight through his heart."[43]

Forward observer (FO) for a mortar platoon was another unwanted assignment. Many grunts in Vietnam said that FO actually stood for "fucked over" because they carried a radio set, making them preferred targets for enemy fire. They also went out on patrol more frequently than most men in the unit because most missions required one, and there were only a few FOs in each company.

TUNNELS AND TUNNEL RATS

Many of the patrols searched for tunnel complexes used by the Vietcong. The first tunnels, mostly located in the Cu Chi district, were constructed by the Vietminh during the Franco-Vietminh War. By war's end, the Vietminh had dug over 45 miles of tunnels in Cu Chi alone. Years later, the need to hide from overwhelming American firepower made them extremely useful to the Vietcong. In the early 1960s, the Vietcong began expanding the tunnels, directing villagers in areas they controlled to dig at least three feet of tunnel a day. By the time the United States escalated the war, there were over 200 miles of tunnels in the Cu Chi district. Another large system existed in the Iron Triangle, but numerous systems both large and small honeycombed the country. One tunnel complex even reached Saigon and ran directly under the U.S. Army First Division Command Headquarters.

The larger complexes contained large storage rooms, hospital and command facilities, sleeping quarters, and training and conference rooms. One American unit found a complete M-48 tank in one and a jeep in another. Almost all had numerous exits and entryways, some large enough for bringing in supplies, others so small a human being could barely squeeze in. At Ben Suc, American soldiers found a series of interconnected tunnels and underground rooms that was representative of many of the complexes dug by the Vietcong. "Building #1 was approximately 9 feet wide by 18 feet long and 10 feet below the surface of the ground. The building had cement on all four

An infantryman is lowered into a tunnel by members of the reconnaissance platoon during Operation "Oregon," a search and destroy mission conducted by an infantry platoon of Troop B, three kilometers (1.9 mi.) west of Duc Pho, Quang Ngai Province, 1967. Courtesy of the National Archives.

sides and flooring about 5 inches thick. The only overhead protection was afforded by sheets of tin. On the northwest corner was a bunker with no overhead protection. Beds and tables were on the floor. Building #2 was approximately 9 feet wide by 12 feet long and 10 feet below the surface. It had concrete identical to Building #1. Overhead cover over one-half of the structure consisted of 5 inch logs and 3 feet of packed dirt. There were no fighting positions located near the building and beds were located on the 1st floor and on top of the overhead protection."[44]

Many of the tunnels were also connected to fortified and often well-hidden bunkers on the surface. The after action report of the Big Red One's Second Brigade during Operation Cedar Falls, in mid-January 1967, described a typical tunnel and bunker complex: "The second level tunnel going north was made so that at every 10–15m it came to a dead end; and a trap door on the floor connected with a tunnel which went down, around and back up to the other side and on the same level with the fake dead end. There were two small holes in the dead end permitting one man to observe and fire through the tunnel."[45]

The U.S. Army had little previous experience in tunnel fighting and had to learn and improvise methods as they went along. Initially, they were interested in destroying the tunnel and killing anyone hiding inside. Standard procedure was to drop several grenades or blocks of explosives down into the tunnel or clean it out with a flamethrower. They quickly discovered, however, that most of the systems were too extensive to destroy by either aboveground bombing or underground explosives. They also learned that the tunnels often contained valuable intelligence or other important material, so it was worthwhile exploring the tunnels before demolishing them. The army developed special four-man teams dubbed "tunnel rats" to explore and then destroy tunnel complexes. Most of the original tunnel teams were recruited out of the 25th Infantry Division, but all the tunnel rats were volunteers and had the right to transfer back to a conventional unit at any time. Volunteers had to have the right psychological makeup to go into a dark, claustrophobic tunnel. Size was also a factor. Being short helped, but some lead men were as much as six foot tall, and there were no height restrictions for surface team members.

Each major unit had a four-man tunnel rat team, and generally, two men went into the tunnel, with the other two serving as a surface support team. The first man in carried a flashlight and a knife and checked for booby traps. The second man followed about 10 feet behind with a radio, sending coordinates to a team member on the surface so that they could map the tunnel. The best time to enter a tunnel was in the early morning, when the heat on the surface was still tolerable. Temperatures underground were usually a lot cooler. While the temperature aboveground might reach 120 degrees on the surface, it was a more comfortable 75 degrees below. The team brought everything they needed because the operations often took all day, and the tunnels were so big that it was unfeasible to go back to the surface to get necessary equipment.

The tunnels were full of dangers, both man-made and natural. Experienced tunnel rats learned to tape up their shirt sleeves and cuffs to keep out scorpions and fire ants. The fire ants in particular were such a nuisance that team members often wore gas masks and carried canisters of CS gas or, preferably, DDT bombs in case they encountered any of them. The ants attacked very quickly, and the best defense involved putting on a gas mask and stabbing a DDT canister with a bayonet to make it explode, filling the chamber with the deadly gas.

The tunnels were usually booby trapped; one favorite method was to tie a poisonous snake to bamboo stakes stuck in the roof. The grunts referred to them as "one step" snakes because allegedly, if they bit you, you were dead after a single step, but because the snakes wiggled, a tunnel rat could usually spot one before it did any damage. The Vietcong also spread shards of broken glass, coated with human urine and feces to cause infection, around the floors of the tunnels or booby-trapped dead bodies with grenades under them.

The tunnels were used as barracks, unit headquarters, and hospitals, and the Vietcong often defended them, but in many cases, they simply abandoned and closed off the section of tunnel that had been discovered and invaded by the Americans. The abandoned tunnel, however, could still yield significant intelligence. In their haste to escape a major tunnel complex on the outskirts of Saigon under attack by American troops, the Vietcong abandoned medical supplies, weapons, maps, and even diagrams of U.S. billets in Saigon. One of the documents detailed a plan for a December 4 raid on Tan Son Nhut Air Base. The operation's commanding officer, Brigadier General Richard Knowles, was convinced that they had found the headquarters for all Vietcong activity in the Saigon region. "This is by far the most important one yet," said Knowles. "This was his headquarters."[46]

No matter what the objective, most operations failed to make contact with the enemy. Only 40 percent of the sweep and clear missions conducted in 1966 reported contact with the enemy, and only 20 percent, or 87 out of 350, of those resulted in meaningful contact and many enemy dead. Lieutenant William Calley and Charlie Company were sent to Landing Zone Carrington, 200 kilometers (124.2 mi.) south of Danang. There were no Vietcong in the area, and Charlie Company did not fire in anger the entire 30 days it was there.[47] Calley became adept at setting up ambushes, and at another LZ, often went out on one every other night. He eventually became depressed and frustrated, however, because he did not see a single Vietcong on 20 straight nights spent on ambush.

Of course, some units saw a lot of action. Gonzalo Baltazar's rapid reaction aerorifle platoon's main job was to rescue downed pilots and do some reconnaissance. His unit would often spend a week or two weeks out in the jungle on patrol. Out in the bush, they were in a position to respond immediately if there was a pilot down in their area, and they often were the blockade during army or marine sweeps of the enemy. In that capacity, they encountered numerous enemy troops. "We'd catch them as they were coming down, running away from the sweeping. We did a lot of that, a lot of recon." Baltazar's unit saw a lot of action, particularly when they were going in to rescue downed pilots because a downed aircraft attracted the enemy. "We'd always get in a firefight, short firefights, some long firefights. . . . It was always hot." It wasn't like a regular infantry unit: "They go out and they hump the jungle for weeks at a time and then they run into a battle. Ours was a lot different. We was always encountering some kind of battle, always running into NVA or VC."[48]

THE BODY COUNT

The all-important primary operational index of the body count determined the success of any particular engagement, but there were usually problems in ascertaining how many of the enemy were actually killed. Especially after small-scale engagements, both the Vietcong and North Vietnamese tried to take their dead with them when they disappeared back into the bush, so there might not be an enemy body to count in the first place. More often than not, the actual count was inflated. Most important, there was heavy institutional pressure from above for results. Score sheets were often put up in command posts down to the platoon level for keeping score. Commanding officers often gave rewards, from cases of cold beer to three days R & R, for the unit with the highest body count. Troops in the field had a tendency to be overly optimistic about their achievements anyway, and the weapons of war—napalm, artillery, and heavy machine gun fire in particular—can shred or blow an individual into numerous pieces, making it difficult to determine just how many bodies are present. It was easier, and often more rewarding, just to count parts and estimate. It was difficult to determine the political orientation of a corpse: was the victim a Vietcong or an innocent peasant caught in the fire? For the sake of convenience, the rule of thumb in the field was that if it was dead and Vietnamese, it was Vietcong. David Hackworth said that in the Ninth Army Division, "the military imperative was body count." The division's commanding general was called the "Delta Butcher" because "civilians counted along with soldiers" in tallying up the unit's body count.[49] In 1969, the area around the town of Cai Be in the delta, for example, had 30,000 killed during the war, 26,000 of them civilians.

Some soldiers took body parts from the enemy, either as a trophy or as evidence of a kill, a practice encouraged by some commanders to get a more accurate body count. Ears, in particular, which were nicknamed "apricots" because of their appearance when they dried, were a favorite trophy and proof of a kill. Some soldiers wore strings of them around their necks to indicate their personal prowess on the battlefield. The desire to bring back proof of a kill sometimes put American lives in jeopardy. Gonzalo Baltazar recalled the first time he was in combat, and his unit killed one Vietcong and wounded another. The wounded enemy escaped, and the platoon began taking heavy enemy fire as it retreated back to the landing zone, but Baltazar's company commander, hovering overhead in a helicopter, was adamant that they bring the dead Vietcong along as proof for the body count. Under fire, Baltazar and his platoon lieutenant dragged the dead Vietcong back to the LZ, nearly sinking in the rice paddies, under the covering fire of cobra gunships overhead. Only later did they discover that an entire company of NVA had been chasing them. Retrieving an enemy body slowed up the entire platoon and put everyone at risk. "It [the body count] wasn't a big deal to us, but it was a big thing to our higher ups.... To them it was a big thing: to us, it was nothing."[50]

AMBUSH AND HIT-AND-RUN

Many of the grunts believed that the patrols really served as bait to lure the Vietcong or North Vietnamese into attacking, and then allowing the MACV to use its superior air and firepower to destroy them. It often worked out that way. More often than not, the Vietcong or NVA initiated contact by ambushing the patrolling Americans. MACV considered Operation Attleboro, for example, to be a great success, but according to David Hackworth, "Over and over during Attleboro, the VC lured our troops into well-laid killing zones and consumed them at close range."[51] Most ambushes were of the hit-and-run variety, lasted only seconds or moments, and involved up to company-sized units. Normally, the enemy would set up a posed ambush, normally L-shaped to maximize fire, but also to prevent deadly cross fire from killing their own men. The Vietcong and NVA usually let the point man through and then hit the main body. There was a short, very intense firefight, but the enemy seldom followed it up with an assault.

A well-laid surprise attack was quite deadly. On January 20, 1968, for example, a marine company was ambushed while on patrol outside Khe Sahn from an enemy position on Hill 881, leaving 20 men killed or wounded in 30 seconds.[52] Jack Smith saw 20 men dropped in a few seconds when his platoon was ambushed. It began when a soldier named Richards was shot and killed by a sniper. Smith said that only a minute or two had elapsed since Richards was shot and the ambush hit. Bill Beck recalled the aftermath of another ambush: "The dead were all around. In such a short time I saw so many guys shot and killed and maimed and screaming in pain and misery. It was horrifying. It was disgusting. And for me it's as real today as it was back in 1965."[53]

Sometimes the enemy would stay and press the attack if the situation was to their advantage. David Hackworth described a company from the Ninth Infantry Division that was caught and ambushed in a 300-meter-long rice paddy near the village of My Hiep in the Mekong delta. When Hackworth "got to the paddy at noon, I saw point scouts Tran Doi and Earl Hayes sprawled on their backs. I knew they were dead; a wounded man's instinct is to lie face down to protect his belly. Jim Fabrizio and Don Wallace were pinned down within yards of the Vietcong guns, unable to move either forward or back. I felt like a fire chief arriving at a burning building after the roof falls in."[54]

Sometimes if the cohesion of a unit was broken, the fighting could continue for hours and degenerate into a massacre. Along with Jack Smith's outfit, the rest of Charlie Company and other units were also ambushed that day. Smith's account is typical of what it was like to be caught in a protracted enemy ambush. He recalled that confusion reigned in his platoon after the initial ambush. Men were huddled together in small groups in the thick elephant grass; wounded men were screaming, mortars, machine gun fire, lots of noise. Many of the soldiers were confused and did not know where the fire was coming from and opened fire on their own men. Several men around him were wounded, one by a grenade, another by a bullet in the spine, and the executive officer had all his toes on one foot blown off. Wounded men lay all over the place in the tall elephant grass with no one to help them. Many of the wounded, especially those with stomach wounds, were screaming in agony and begging for help—if not to kill the pain, then to kill them. The Vietcong were doing just that: going through the tall grass and killing any wounded Americans they found. Smith and virtually everyone else in the platoon was killed or wounded; at one point he was surrounded by a dozen PAVN troops literally right on top of him, but they thought that he and two other wounded Americans were already dead, and they were preoccupied with setting up a machine gun against an American mortar platoon. M-79s from the platoon killed all the enemy troops but also the two wounded soldiers with Smith. The rest of Jack Smith's day was filled with bullets, blood, artillery, smoke, screaming, and enemy soldiers "screeching with glee when they found one of us alive."[55]

THE REALITIES OF COMBAT

For many, combat was a terrifying experience. Many soldiers urinated or defecated on themselves; others were paralyzed by fear. During an ambush in March 1969 in the Mekong delta, David Hackworth saw a company commander "go literally mad; his babbling tied up the radio until he was relieved."[56] Jack Smith states that some soldiers could not take it and committed suicide. Some, however, displayed superior courage and often made the ultimate sacrifice. In February 1967, Vietcong near Cam Lo ambushed marine private James Anderson's platoon. Anderson's Medal of Honor citation reads, "The platoon reacted swiftly, getting on line as best they could in the thick terrain, and began returning fire. Pfc. Anderson found himself tightly bunched together with the other members of the platoon only 20 meters from the enemy positions. As the firefight continued several of the men were wounded by the deadly enemy assault. Suddenly, an enemy grenade landed in the midst of the marines and rolled alongside Pfc. Anderson's head. Unhesitatingly and with complete disregard for his personal safety, he reached out, grasped the grenade, pulled it to his chest and curled around it as it went off. Although several marines received shrapnel from the grenade, his body absorbed the major force of the explosion. In this singularly heroic act, Pfc. Anderson saved his comrades from serious injury and possible death. His personal heroism, extraordinary valor, and inspirational supreme self-sacrifice reflected great credit upon himself and the Marine Corps and upheld the highest traditions of the U.S. Naval Service. He gallantly gave his life for his country."[57] Anderson was one of 237 Medal of Honor recipients during the Vietnam War.

For most soldiers in Vietnam, the first taste of combat was also very confusing. Baltazar was the radioman for his rapid reaction aero-rifle platoon, and in his first combat, a pilot radioed, "You have a Victor Charlie up ahead. We spotted a Victor Charlie," or Vietcong, to which the green radio operator replied, "A what?" He repeated Victor Charlie, to which Baltazar replied, "What's that?" The pilot told him, "You know, the enemy." Baltazar recalled, "Because I was only 17, and then realizing that we were going to have our first encounter with the enemy. I was kind of like, 'holy cow' this is the real thing now."[58] Time seemed to either slow down or speed up in combat. Under fire, Gordon Roberts "felt as if he was set in fast motion, for what seemed so fast and so long that it was like driving a car at fast speed. Time slowed even if the car didn't."[59]

Soldiers carry a wounded comrade through a swampy area, 1969. Courtesy of the National Archives.

Reporter Michael Herr, who was under fire several times covering the war in Vietnam, including at Khe Sahn and at the battle for Hue during Tet, said that during a firefight, "your vision blurring, images jumping and falling as though they were being received by a dropped camera, hearing a hundred horrible sounds at once; screams, sobs, hysterical shouting, a throbbing inside your head that threatened to take over, quavering voices trying to get the orders out, the dulls and sharps of the weapons going off, the thud of helicopter rotors, the tinny, clouded voice coming over the radio, 'Uh, that's a Rog, we mark your position over.' And out. Far out."[60]

Despite the dangers, combat could be a thrilling experience. Allen Thomas Jr. said that in combat, you were never more scared, but you also never felt more alive. For Philip Caputo, the monotony of offensive patrolling was relieved by the occasional search-and-destroy operation, and the thrill of riding the lead helicopter into a landing zone.

American units could normally count on massive air and artillery support to aid them or extricate them in a tight situation. When used properly, it could be devastating and inflict terrible casualties on the enemy. The Vietcong learned to negate the American advantage in firepower somewhat by "hugging the belt," or closing rapidly with their enemy and fighting at close range to neutralize American firepower.[61] Some commanders, their units in danger of being overrun, often called it in anyway. The lieutenant commanding Jack Smith's ambushed platoon called artillery fire down around his own position, killing several of the Vietcong and scaring off the rest. Americans kept up artillery fire about every half hour throughout the night. Some of it was so close to their position that the shrapnel flew only a few feet above their heads.

Reinforcements were also usually available to send in to help rescue an ambushed unit. Gonzalo Baltazar's platoon was scrambled on short notice and given only the barest of information, such as a chopper down or a unit trapped at a certain location. They usually did not know the size of the enemy force they were likely to encounter. "They knew there was enemy out there but they wouldn't know how many or who was NVA or VC. You went in blind. It could have been a couple hundred, it could be two. We didn't ever know."[62] Sometimes, however, the relief patrols were also ambushed.

Often, an ambushed unit was trapped out in the field for the night. Around dusk, a few helicopters tried landing in the LZ to extricate Smith's shattered unit, but whenever they came within about 100 feet of the ground, they were driven off by heavy machine gun fire, leaving the men of the ambushed patrol to fend for themselves for the night.[63] Smith was hit by shrapnel and wounded again, this time in the thigh, and as he lay screaming in pain, he thought he was going to die. There were no clumps of Americans, just individuals scattered throughout the elephant grass. In the last dim light of the day, the Vietcong pulled back into the woods. There was no longer any worry about attacks from American aircraft, but the artillery kept up the barrage and also fired illumination flares; as long as there was some light over the field, the enemy was not likely to attempt an assault to wipe out the remaining Americans. As night fell, the North Vietnamese began mortaring the Americans still trapped in the elephant grass, using mortars they had captured that day from the Americans.

Smith had gone all afternoon and evening without water and was terribly thirsty. He risked smoking a cigarette; he knew it was dangerous, but he did not care anymore. He tore off the end of the cigarette before lighting it because it was soaked in blood. By then, the small arms fire had quieted down and almost ceased entirely. After nightfall, Smith crawled over to where a few other survivors had grouped. He found a canteen of water that was "about one third blood" but drank it anyway and passed it around the group. There was a heavy concentration of small arms around their position about an hour after nightfall. It lasted around five minutes and was repeated at intervals throughout the night. Ironically, it was protective fire from the battalion, but they were right in the path of it, and bullets were ricocheting around the woods and hitting Americans.

Around midnight, the temperature had dropped to around 50 degrees, which was typical for the highlands for that time of year, leaving Smith shivering. Smith heard men coming through the grass and assumed it was the Vietcong coming to finish them off. Most of the men by that point were either unconscious or had died quietly. He had his grenade out waiting to pull the pin when he heard soft whistling noises and realized that it was an army patrol of around 15 men, sent out to look for wounded. Smith told them that he could walk back since they only had four stretchers, but he passed out cold the minute he stood up. Despite his wounds and fatigue, Smith would still have to wait to be evacuated. When he woke up, they had taken the most seriously wounded with them and promised to return in a few hours for the rest of them. They had left their medic behind to treat the wounded, but Smith still could not get medications or fresh bandages for his wounds because the medic had not seen him in the darkness and had already used up his limited supplies on the other men.

The men on the ground were still in danger. Smith had his hand grenade and a .45 with three bullets. There were about eight other wounded men along with Smith huddled under some trees. One of them was Lieutenant Sheldon, wounded in the thighbone, kneecap, and ankle but talking to the company commander on the one operational radio left in the company. Sometime after midnight, a Vietcong patrol was heard coming through the grass. The men huddled together with their few weapons, hoping to make a stand. Some of the men were too weak to cock their weapons, but luckily, the Vietcong heard them and decided not to charge. Small groups of Vietcong were still combing through parts of the woods and grass looking for wounded Americans to kill. Throughout the night, Smith and the others heard Vietcong yelling for their buddies and wounded Americans screaming for mercy, then silenced by bursts of gunfire. American artillery ceased about an hour before dawn, except for the occasional shell, but the American small arms fire picked up again. There was a large group of GIs about a mile away methodically clearing the area of Vietcong and moving in their direction. The bullets were cracking and thudding all around them.

Smith and the other survivors expected to be massacred by a human wave attack when the sun came up, but the enemy had pulled out during the night, leaving behind only a few so-called suicide squads and some wounded. With the light of dawn, Smith could see the carnage around him; it looked like the "devil's butcher shop." He realized that the dead body he had rested his head on that night was his friend Burgess, a professional saxophone player with only two weeks left in Vietnam. He hardly recognized his friend, or any of the other dead; most were unrecognizable and had already begun to smell. His wounds were bleeding again, the heat was rising, and ants were tormenting them. There were dead Vietcong all over the place and several dead snipers hanging out of the trees.

Smith was finally medivaced out to Pleiku in the late morning. The ambush had started shortly after noon the previous day. The enemy had suffered over 500 dead in the ambush, but Smith's battalion had been hard hit. They suffered 150 dead, and only 84 returned to base camp a few days later out of 500 men. Charlie Company had suffered 93 percent casualties, with half of those dead.[64]

CASUALTIES

Smith, like most men who served in Vietnam, had wondered what it would be like to be wounded. When he was wounded in the head by shrapnel from an American M-79 grenade launcher, "it felt as if a white-hot sledge hammer had hit the right side of my face. Then something hot and stinging hit my left leg. I lost consciousness for a few seconds. I came out of it feeling intense pain in my leg and numbness in my head. I didn't dare feel my face, I thought the whole side of it had gone."[65] Smith was actually relieved after it had happened; he knew what it was like to be wounded now, and he was still alive. "Blood was pouring down my forehead and filling the hollow of my eyeglasses. It was also pouring out of my mouth. I slapped a bandage on the side of my face and tied it around my head. I was numbed, but I suddenly felt better. It had happened, and I was still alive."[66] His relief was short lived. Shortly after dark, Smith was wounded again in a North Vietnamese mortar attack. Something big went off behind him and he felt "something white-hot go into my right thigh." The pain was terrible; he kept screaming, "My legs, God, my legs" over and over again. Smith could feel the blood pouring out of the wound. He ripped the bandage off his face and tried to apply it to his new injury, but it did not fit.[67]

Most military personnel who served in Vietnam were not seriously wounded. Unlike most Medal of Honor recipients, who usually receive the medal posthumously, for example, Gordon Roberts was not wounded. In three tours of duty, Allen Thomas did not

A young American lieutenant, his leg burned by an exploding Viet Cong white phosphorus booby trap, is treated by a medic. 1966. Courtesy of the National Archives.

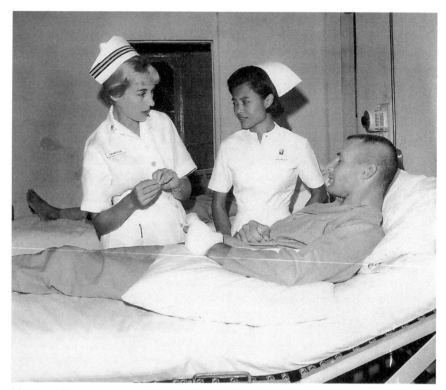

Lieutenant Frances Crumpton and Miss Nangnoi Tongkim, a Thai nurse, talk with an American soldier in the Navy hospital in Saigon, 1966. Courtesy of the National Archives.

lose a single man under his command in combat. Thomas was never seriously wounded. "Got blowed up twice," he recalled, but it was nothing serious. Survival depended partly on skill and experience, and often on sheer luck. Sergeant Thomas remembered putting on his helmet, "and I never wore my helmet," seconds before the two-and-one-half-ton truck he was riding in struck a mine. "Blew the whole front of the truck off," but Thomas escaped with only minor injuries.[68]

Some ignored the danger. Like many military professionals, Albert Childs never really thought about getting killed or maimed.[69] The odds were in his favor. A soldier assigned to Vietnam had a 1 in 10 chance of ending up a casualty during his tour of duty. Out of 2.59 million men and women who served in Vietnam, 58,169 were killed, and 304,000 were wounded. By comparison, the French lost 41,225 French and Foreign Legionnaires killed and as many as 41,995 colonials killed from 1948 to 1954. In both World War II and Korea, shrapnel from mortar fire, rockets, and artillery was the primary cause of casualties. Only 32 percent of those killed in World War II died in small arms fire. In Vietnam, however, small arms fire accounted for over half the Americans killed or wounded, with booby traps and pungi sticks accounting for 11 percent of those killed and 17 percent of the wounded.

The common perception of Vietnam as a war without a front line and a war in which anyone could be attacked is true, but the vast majority of casualties in Vietnam were still suffered by combat and combat support units. For example, all six men aboard David White's PBR were killed or wounded during an enemy rocket attack in 1968 in the Mekong delta. From December 1968 through February 1969, during Operation Giant Slingshot, White's PBR unit, which normally had around 18 men on the rivers at any one time, sustained 35–40 wounded and 3 or 4 killed in that period. In the spring of 1969, Gonzalo Baltazar's platoon was overstrength with 52 men, but a friendly fire attack quickly reduced them to only 28. Soon they were down to 22 men. Ironically, the casualties were not replaced because they discovered that they could move faster and more efficiently rescuing downed pilots with fewer men. When one served in Vietnam also affected his chances for survival. Between 1968 and 1973, deaths due to hostile action declined steadily for an overall four-year decline of 84.6 percent.

Draftees also had a better chance of ending up casualties than did regular army volunteers. In 1968, draftees made up 42 percent of the military in Vietnam but accounted for 58 percent of the casualties; for volunteers, however, the ratio is reversed. In 1970, draftees were only 39 percent of U.S. forces in Vietnam but accounted for a staggering 65 percent of the casualties. There were several reasons for the disparity. Lifers, or those that made a profession out of the military, usually received more consideration in choice of schooling and MOS, and many chose a noncombat MOS. NCOs, for example, that had already served one tour of duty in Vietnam could usually choose their next assignment in Vietnam, subject to availability and qualification, and most chose noncombat assignments. In addition, reenlisting or extending one's tour of duty in Vietnam often came with a promise, not always honored, of a noncombat assignment.

Enlisted men were also more likely to become casualties than the officers leading them. Compared to World War II, 34 percent more enlisted men died in action than did general officers, and 54 percent more than colonels. Again, there were several reasons for this. Officers only spent 6 of their 12- or 13-month tours of duty in Vietnam with a combat unit, lowering their chances of becoming casualties. Most enlisted personnel in combat units had to serve their entire tour of duty in harm's way. The low officer-to-enlisted ratio in casualties was not the norm for twentieth-century wars. The state of Israel lost 2,500 killed in action in the 1973 Yom Kippur War, for example, but only 85 of them were privates; 95 percent of the dead were officers, which accounted for 26 percent of the total, and NCOs.

Some of the battlefield casualties were self-inflicted. Battlefields cover a large area and are confusing environments, and artillery or air support meant for the enemy can fall on one's own troops in the form of so-called friendly fire. In spring 1969, Gonzalo Baltazar's platoon was out on patrol near Camp Eagle, when a colonel in a small observation helicopter flying overhead mistook them for the enemy and called artillery fire down on them. Several men were killed and at least 15 wounded.

On the battlefield, it was the job of the medic to administer to the wounded. Though usually nicknamed "doc," medics had emergency medical and trauma training but were not physicians. They did have one of the most dangerous jobs on the battlefield and often proved to be some of the bravest men under fire. David Hackworth "watched medics Dan Evans and Rick Hudson drag troopers across that bullet-swept field, inch by bloody inch" during a Vietcong ambush of an American company in March 1969.[70] Army medic Lawrence Joel won his Medal of Honor in Vietnam in 1965 for demonstrating "indomitable courage, determination, and professional skill" after a larger group of Vietcong ambushed his unit, leaving every man in the forward squad either dead or wounded. Joel was wounded twice himself as he moved about the wounded men and enemy gunfire, shouting encouragement and treating the injured.[71]

Vietnam was just as deadly as earlier twentieth-century American wars, but advances in medicine, transportation, and technology meant that your chances of survival if wounded were much better than in earlier conflicts. The key to quick treatment and survival of the wounded was the helicopter. Air ambulance units, or medivacs, were known as dust off units, and medivac helicopters flew nearly 500,000 missions, airlifting over 900,000 patients, nearly half of whom were American, to hospital facilities. Medivac units could usually get a wounded soldier to a field hospital in less than one hour and to a fully equipped hospital in less than three hours. As a result, less than 1 percent of all Americans wounded who survived the first 24 hours died.

Some medivac units were dedicated, but others flew dust offs as one of their many normal duties. John Ballweg's helicopter unit flew medivac missions in addition to their other duties. Because time was of the essence, they did not keep a crew on call— whoever got to the helicopter first when the alarm came in flew the mission. Medivac pilots seldom found out if the wounded men they had carried to safety survived or not because they were usually rushing to go back and retrieve more.

Sometimes enemy action or weather made it impossible to evacuate the wounded, and medics were forced to improvise until help arrived. During the battle of Ia Drang, the First Battalion, First Air Cavalry, was in continuous fighting for nearly four days and could not dust off all their wounded. Wounded men lay all over the place, with no one to help them. When the fire died down and the medics could tend to the wounded, there was often little they could do. Smith described wounded men lying around, bandaged up with filthy shirts and bandages, smoking cigarettes or lying in a coma with plasma bottles hanging above the stretcher.

Once at a hospital, the doctors and nurses often faced a daunting task. The high velocity of modern rifles, and close proximately of ambush weapons such as mines and booby traps, caused multiple wounds. Infections were a serious problem and were likely to develop in an untreated wound. Wounded men that made it to a hospital still breathing, however, usually survived. The hospital mortality rate during the Vietnam War was 2.6 percent of those hospitalized, compared to 4.5 percent for World War II. One's chances for a relatively full recovery were good, but not as high as one's chances for survival. Between January 1, 1965, and June 30, 1968, for example, 161,000 U.S. personnel were wounded in Vietnam, and 89 percent were either returned to duty or restored to health and discharged. Some returned to duty only to be wounded again. David White was wounded twice while serving on a PBR in 1968 in the Mekong delta: once by shrapnel and fiberglass fragments in a rocket attack that killed or wounded all six men on board the boat, and the second time during an ambush in which an enemy rocket left him temporarily blind, a gash down his forehead and shrapnel in his left hand and right arm. The right side of his face was burned, and most of his hair, including eyebrows and eyelashes, was burned off. Luckily for White, the rocket apparently had been a dud, and the warhead never detonated, or he would have been killed.

About 5 percent of those wounded received disability discharges. Those that did not fully recover, however, were often left with crippling disabilities and amputations. Crippling wounds were 300 percent higher in Vietnam than in World War II. In all, around 75,000 Vietnam veterans returned home severely disabled. Army Sergeant James Rush, for example, who considered himself a "pro and a damn good one," was forced to retire from 14 years in the military after losing his right arm in a mortar attack.[72]

Wounded who could be returned to duty within 30 days, on the opinion of the attending physician, were treated in country. The smaller field hospitals and MASH units were capable of stabilizing a patient, and the larger base hospitals and hospital ships were equipped for major surgery. The armed forces had established medical facilities throughout South Vietnam, and some of them predated the presence of American combat troops. As early as April 1956, the first three army nurses arrived in Vietnam on temporary duty assignments attached to the U.S. Army Medical Training Team. They were sent to train South Vietnamese nurses, not care for wounded Americans, but soon became part of the American Dispensary, Saigon, which was in charge of health care for Americans in Vietnam.[73] In March 1962, the Eighth Field Hospital, staffed by army nurses, opened in Nha Trang, and the following year, the navy assumed responsibility from the embassy for providing medical care to American personnel. By January 1965, the army had 15 nurses and 113 hospital beds in Vietnam. The arrival of large numbers of combat troops in early 1965 also meant an expansion of hospital facilities in Southeast Asia. In January 1966, the U.S. navy hospital ship, the USS *Repose,* took up station offshore near Hue-Phu Bai and remained on duty until May 1970. A sister ship, the USS *Sanctuary,* arrived in April 1967 and stayed until November 1972. By December 1968, there were 900 army nurses working in Vietnam at 23 army hospitals and 1 convalescent center, with a total capacity of 5,283 beds. The nurses were some of the first military personnel to arrive, and they were also some of the last to go: the last nurse left Vietnam in March 1973.

To wounded young men in Vietnam, the nurses were angels in white, even if many of them did not wear traditional nurses' uniforms. Nurses at the 3rd, 8th, and 17th Field Hospitals wore the traditional white duty uniforms, but nurses at other hospitals in the field with a medical unit, self contained, transportable (MUST) wore lightweight olive drab fatigues. The nurses preferred fatigues because of the difficulty of keeping the white uniforms clean in a tropical environment. Army nurses came in all specialties, but the most common in Vietnam were surgical intensive care, recovery room, emergency room, and medical-surgical care. The nurses treated all U.S. personnel, civilian or military, allied troops, and Vietnamese, and many volunteered on their off days staffing free clinics and visiting villages and orphanages. Like the wounded they cared for, most nurses were young; the average age of an army nurse in Vietnam was 23.6 years. Some of them were male, but four out of every five nurses in Vietnam were female. Most were regular army, but some were reserves, and only 35 percent had more than two years' nursing experience.

As in previous wars, casualties by disease outnumbered casualties by combat. From 1965 to 1969, disease accounted for 69 percent of admissions to army hospital facilities. The most common diseases to plague American servicemen were malaria; viral hepatitis; typhus; typhoid; a variety of diarrheal diseases; several tropical fevers, including dengue fever, known and unknown; skin maladies; and the ever popular venereal diseases.

Lieutenant Colonel Ruth Sidisin, who was stationed at the air base at Danang, recalled seeing "diseases they'd told us people hardly got anymore."[74]

Insects were yet another major medical problem in Vietnam. Gerald Kumpf was stung in the arm by a wasp and lost strength in the arm for three to four weeks. The doctors really did not know how to treat it. While out on recon in the jungle in spring 1969, a scorpion bit Gonzalo Baltazar on the eye. He got really sick from it, and his eye swelled up to the size of a golf ball, so he had to be medivaced out. "It was pretty amazing, they took a picture of it because they'd never seen anything like it."[75]

Accidents also accounted for killed or wounded. Battlefield injuries made up 17 percent of hospital admissions, while accidents accounted for another 14 percent. Some were due to negligence in handling ordinance, and many men were killed trying to mechanically disarm claymores or by the accidental discharge of a firearm.

Carrier operations were inherently dangerous. Vietnam era American aircraft carriers were massive vessels. Some, like the USS *Kitty Hawk,* were over 1,000 feet long and displaced over 80,000 tons. There were over 4,200 officers and men in the crew, and they operated an air wing of 85 aircraft, which was more powerful than many nations' air forces. Gerald Kumpf compared working aboard an aircraft carrier to "choreographed mayhem." You are "working aircraft on the hanger deck and moving around on top of the flight deck, you know within inches of each other, aircraft running all over the place, people running all over the place ... it's a wonder anybody survives, it really is."[76]

There were numerous major accidents involving carriers during the war. In addition to losses among the aircrew caused by enemy fire or mechanical failure, three separate accidents killed or injured several crewmen on board the *Kitty Hawk* when it was deployed off Vietnam. In December 1965, a flash fire in a machinery room during combat operations killed two sailors and wounded 29 others. Four months later, in April 1966, two more crew members died during a helicopter malfunction on deck, which sprayed the deck of the ship with deadly fragments from the chopper's rotor blades. No one was killed, but over 125 sailors were injured during a shipboard fire in December 1967. The accidents on board the *Kitty Hawk* were typical of the everyday dangers in just working on an aircraft carrier. On October 24, 1972, *Kitty Hawk* raced to the assistance of another carrier, USS *Midway,* after a serious fire on that ship killed five sailors and injured 23. Probably the worst accident at sea during the war occurred aboard the USS *Forrestal* on July 29, 1967, when a rocket accidentally discharged from a Phantom, striking an A-4E Skyhawk on the flight deck occupied by pilot John McCain. McCain escaped from the flaming wreckage with shrapnel wounds in his chest and legs, but the ensuing blast and fire killed 134 sailors, destroyed 20 aircraft, and threatened to sink the ship.

The accidental deaths could be as or more gruesome than those caused by war. Gerald Kumpf witnessed a man being run over and killed by a tug, a large vehicle used to tow aircraft. "He stepped off the airplane, his first day in Vietnam, walked right in front of a tug which this guy was driving backwards and wasn't watching where he was going and just peeled him like a grape.... It was more horrifying than watching the enemy killed." He also witnessed an F-105 come in too low and clip the wheel shack, a small observation shed where someone with binoculars checked to make sure that the landing gear retracted correctly on outgoing planes, killing the pilot. A C-147 stalled on takeoff and crashed, killing all seven on board. During Kumpf's tour of duty at Danang, MFA-314 sustained more casualties from accidents than from enemy action.[77]

Many men were hospitalized in Vietnam on several different occasions because of wounds, disease, or accident. Marine Corps officer Anthony Zinni contracted malaria, hepatitis, and mononucleosis near the end of his first tour in Vietnam, and was wounded.[78] After Gonzalo Baltazar was bitten in the eye by the scorpion, he was wounded in a friendly fire artillery barrage.

Historically, more soldiers die of disease in any given war than from combat, a ratio that changed only with the Second World War. In World War II and Korea, approximately three Americans died in combat for every two that were killed by other causes.[79] In Vietnam, the ratio of soldiers killed in battle versus those that died of other causes was almost five to one, with accidents, suicide, and illness accounting for 10,700 of the over 58,000 American dead in Vietnam.[80]

Despite the old adage, dying was neither sweet nor noble. It could be swift in many cases, but too often, it was prolonged and agonizing. David Hackworth witnessed an ammunition helicopter go down, trapping its crew chief inside the metal inferno, and Hackworth "heard his screams until death ended his agony."[81] Jack P. Smith recalled Sergeant Gale, from his platoon, who was hit in the stomach during an ambush. He thrashed around in agony, alternately begging for a medic, for something to take away the pain, or for someone to shoot him. But there were no medical supplies, no one could move, and no one would shoot him, so Gale suffered for six hours before he finally died.

A body was normally embalmed before it was shipped back to the United States. There was a hanger at Tan Son Nhut Air Base used as a mortuary, and it was usually filled to capacity. The embalmers worked practically around the clock. John Ballweg said that you could hear them work as you walked by. There were silver metal caskets stacked up in front of the building.[82]

Draftees may have had a better chance of becoming casualties, but it was deadlier to be an enlistee. Most of those killed in action had enlisted voluntarily, but 17,675 of the dead were draftees. Only 9 of the draftees killed were commissioned officers, but 7,819 officers, including chief warrant officers, died in Vietnam.[83] Despite the Army Reserve's reputation as a haven from the war zone, 5,741 military Reserve personnel were killed in Vietnam. Because most were specialist and volunteers, the death total for the Reserve included 5,118 officers, but only 623 Reserve enlisted personnel were killed. Several thousand volunteers from the National Guard also served in Vietnam. The National Guard lost 97 men in Vietnam, 28 of whom were officers.

Buis and Ovand were the first two Americans officially killed in Vietnam on July 8, 1959, when they were gunned down during a Vietminh attack on Bien Hoa, and Lieutenant William B. Nolde was the last official casualty of the war, when an artillery shell at An Loc killed him just 11 hours before the final truce and cease-fire took effect on January 28, 1973, at 8:05 A.M. On April 29, 1975, Corporal Charles McMahon Jr. and Lance Corporal Darwin Judge, U.S. Marine Corps, became the last U.S. military personnel killed in Vietnam, during a rocket attack at the U.S. Embassy in Saigon, during the fall of South Vietnam in April 1975.

To some degree, age was a determinant of your chances of getting killed. War is normally a young man's pursuit, and the death totals from Vietnam reflected that, with the average age of all personnel killed in Vietnam at 23.11 years; for officers, it was slightly more than 28 years old. The youngest American killed in Vietnam was 15-year-old marine Dan Bullock, but at least five others were only 16 years old, and 12 more were only 17 years old. Another 3,108 dead were only 18 years old. In all 35,168 of the American dead in the war were between the ages of 17 and 21. Ninety-one of the American casualties in Vietnam were aged 51 or older, and the oldest to die was 62.[84]

So was race. African Americans were the biggest single minority in the armed forces and accounted for the largest number of nonwhite deaths. Blacks made up around 11 percent of the draft-aged population and around 10 percent of U.S. forces in Vietnam, but by late July 1966, basically the first full year of combat for U.S. forces, they accounted for 22 percent of American casualties and 14 percent of all combat fatalities by the end of 1967. The black casualty rate did begin to drop after 1967. By 1975, the 7,257 African Americans killed in Vietnam represented around 12.6 percent of the total American dead in that war. Most were enlistees, but 131 were officers, and another 16 were warrant officers. The highest-ranking blacks to be killed in Vietnam were five air force colonels. By comparison, 226 Native Americans, including nine officers, none higher than the rank of captain, and 114 Asian Americans, including 18 officers, were listed as killed in Vietnam. But the dubious honor of having the second highest death total for a minority group in Vietnam belongs to Malayan Americans, who lost 253 during the war. There were also 221 Americans of unknown race killed in Vietnam.

During Vietnam, West Virginia had the highest casualty rate for any state in the nation, according to the U.S. Department of Defense. The state had 711 casualties, or 39.9 deaths per 100,000 people. Oklahoma had the second highest casualty rate. Beallsville, Ohio, with a population of only 475, suffered the largest per capita loss of life of any American town in the war, losing six young men between 1966 and 1971.

Many of America's allies also paid a high price in lives. South Korea lost 4,407 servicemen killed in action. Australia suffered 520 dead and another 2,398 wounded, while Thailand lost 351 dead. In comparison to U.S. losses, it is extremely difficult to gauge what the war cost the Vietnamese people in terms of lives. Historian Stanley Karnow cites a figure of an estimated 600,000 enemy dead. For the population as a whole, the head of the Vietnamese Institute of Military History, General Nguyen Dinh Uoc, claimed in a September 1995 article that there were 3.6 million Vietnamese dead in the war. Many Western analysts put the total at three million for the period 1947–1975.

PRISONERS OF WAR

In addition to the killed and wounded, at least 839 Americans were taken prisoner by the North Vietnamese and Vietcong during the war. Some got lost and simply fell into enemy hands. Marine corporal Robert Garwood was captured on September 28, 1965, as he was driving a jeep in Quang Nam Province, unsuspecting that the enemy was even near. Many were taken when their position was overrun by the enemy. Captain William "Ike" Eisenbraun was serving as a senior advisor at the MACV Headquarters, U.S. Army Special Forces, during his fourth tour of duty in Vietnam at Ba Gia, near Quang Ngai, when an estimated 1,000–1,500 Vietcong overran the isolated jungle outpost and its 180 defenders. Jose Agosto-Santos was captured when his unit was overrun in Quang Nam Province on May 12, 1967. A large number of the POWs were pilots shot down over Vietnam. Air force captain Norman A. McDaniel arrived in Southeast Asia in February 1966 and by July 20 was flying his 51st mission in his Douglas EB66C Skywarrior, an electronic warfare aircraft, when the plane was shot down over North Vietnam, and he was taken prisoner. John McCain was a young navy aviator when he was shot down over Hanoi in October 1967. McCain bailed out but landed in Hanoi's Truc Bach Lake.

Like many of the POWs, McCain was injured when he was captured. He had broken his arm in the crash. Agosto-Santos had been wounded in the stomach and back. Many had their lives saved by their captors. The Vietcong spent a month nursing Agosto-Santo back to health in a cave before moving him. Dazed and badly hurt, McCain would have drowned in the 16-foot-deep, cold waters of the lake if not for a 50-year-old factory worker and veteran of the People's Army named Mai Van On, who rescued him. Initial

U.S Army's Brigadier General Stan McClellan and Viet Cong and North Vietnamese members of the Four Power Joint Military Commission discuss the release of their respective prisoners of war, 1973. Courtesy of the Department of Defense.

capture did not mean safety or humane treatment. American bombs were still falling on Hanoi, and an angry crowd wanted to kill McCain. He was bayoneted in his foot, and someone hit him with a rifle butt against his already broken arm. On stepped in once again and stopped the mob until soldiers came and took McCain away.[85]

Prisoners were moved around a lot to avoid detection by American forces and were often housed among possible military targets, meaning that POWs were often caught in the middle of U.S. air strikes, especially those that were being held in or near Hanoi. The North Vietnamese and Vietcong often segregated their prisoners according to rank. Most officers, especially the pilots, were almost always sent to imprisonment in the north, in part because most of them had been shot down over North Vietnam. McCain and McDaniel, for example, were both shot down over North Vietnam and taken to the infamous "Hanoi Hilton" prison.[86] Most enlisted personnel were captured in the south and generally were interned there by the Vietcong.

The psychological aspects of imprisonment were devastating. Many POWs were extremely depressed and felt alone, isolated, and forgotten. Because communication from remote parts of South Vietnam was difficult, and because the North Vietnamese and Vietcong did not always admit when they had taken an American prisoner, the fate of the missing serviceman was often initially unknown by the Defense Department or the family back home. Some POWs were initially reported as missing or killed in action. Captain Ike Eisenbraun, for example, was initially reported as killed in action, until two ARVN who managed to escape the ambush told American authorities that he was being held as a prisoner.

Some prisoners reported acts of kindness by their captors. When James Daly claimed that when he could not walk due to jungle rot and his wounds, his Vietcong captors

After a brief refueling stop, the first group of prisoners of war (POW) released in Hanoi by North Vietnam walk on the red carpet toward their waiting aircraft. The POWs were enroute from Clark Air Base, Philippines, to Travis Air Force Base, CA. They would then be reunited with their families in the states. February 1, 1973. Courtesy of the Department of Defense.

carried him on a litter and gave him penicillin every three hours, which was an extremely precious commodity to the Vietcong. For the vast majority of POWs, like John McCain or Norman McDaniel, however, the pain and torture were just beginning. The overwhelming majority of American prisoners of war reported harsh, brutal, and inhumane treatment by their Vietcong or North Vietnamese captors during most of their incarceration. Torture was common, especially for the pilots, whom their Vietnamese captors labeled criminals. In 1998, McDaniel described his ordeal for reporter Millicent Rothrock. "Sometimes, his Vietnamese captors bent him backward, tightly bound his ankles to his wrists, hurled him onto a hook in the ceiling and hung him upside down," she wrote. "They left him there for hours while his circulation weakened, his body swelled and he blacked out. For days at a time the enemy sat him on a small, concrete seat and dared him to sleep. When he nodded off, they slapped him and kicked him around. Once, they beat and interrogated him for so many days that he lost track of time."[87]

POWs would be brutalized and tortured for any minor infraction, including conversation with other POWs, and the Vietnamese were particularly adept at both psychological and physical torture. "American POWs brought back stories of having been buried; held for days in a cage with no protection from insects and the environment; having had water and food withheld; being shackled and beaten."[88] Captain William "Ike" Eisenbraun, who died in a POW camp, was probably tortured to death for resisting his captors and attempting to escape.

Everyday living in a POW camp was an ordeal, even without torture. Many prisoners were kept in isolation, and communication between POWs in different cells was usually forbidden, and punished harshly if a transgressor was caught. Despite the dangers, however, prisoners developed a tap code based on Morse code for communication back and forth.

Normally, the prisoners were fed twice a day, and the meals usually consisted of a "small bowl with about an inch and a half of rice, a smaller bowl of watery swamp soup or some kind of greens or bamboo shoots. Sometimes you'd get what they called a side dish, a little bit of pork fat or a smattering of chopped up chicken with the bones." The only variation from this might be some "old cod-type fish with scales and heads and something we called swamp weeds because they grew them in the wet marsh area." The food was so bad that it nauseated many of the prisoners. Part of the reason the Americans were underfed had to due with the fact that rations in the Vietcong or PAVN were usually smaller than the American equivalent because the Vietnamese are smaller people, averaging about 105 pounds. Sometimes the lack of food was due to the exigencies of war and not simply cruelty on the part of their captors. American air strikes often cut the supply lines to the camps, meaning that everyone, POWs and guards alike, went on short rations and suffered. If the POWs were able to remain in one location for a while, their Vietnamese captors would often let them grow vegetable crops and keep some small animals to supplement their meager standard diet of rice and what they could forage from the jungle. Whatever the combination of reasons, malnutrition was a major problem for the vast majority of POWs. Most prisoners were severely malnourished and lost considerable weight. Norman McDaniel weighed 155 pounds when he was captured and at one point was down to only 115. He felt lucky. It "wasn't bad," he said. "Some of the guys dropped from 190, 200 pounds down to 110, 115 pounds."[89] Malnutrition and lack of adequate health care meant that diseases such as dysentery, edema, skin fungus, eczema, malaria, beriberi, and dysentery were common.

The earliest years of the war were the worst for those in captivity. McDaniel and others stated that after the death of Ho Chi Minh in September 1969, their treatment and diet improved, and by the time he was released, he had regained most of his lost weight. The prisoners were also given clean clothes and decent food when foreign delegations came to visit, especially when the guests were from the United States. Numerous Americans visited North Vietnam during the war, but the most infamous was by actress Jane Fonda. Contrary to myth, Fonda did not turn messages handed her by the POWs over to the North Vietnamese guards, and she did not call the prisoners baby killers or war criminals. She asked them how they were being treated and did bring letters home from some of the POWs to their families. She did pose on an antiaircraft gun, denounced the American war effort, and was friendly with her North Vietnamese hosts, who played her for maximum propaganda value, earning her the hatred of most Vietnam veterans even 30 years after the end of the war.

The NVA and Vietcong also segregated many of their prisoners by race in an attempt to exploit racial animosities within U.S. forces and possibly convince black prisoners to collaborate. They spoke of so-called special treatment for African Americans, claiming that blacks were not their enemy and were being forced to kill other people of color in the name of white imperialism. Occasionally, the Communists would make a gesture attempting to show their good will to Americans of color. Lance Corporal Jose Agosto-Santos and Private First Class Luis Antonio Ortiz-Rivera of the Marine Corps, for example, were released as a propaganda move by their Vietnamese captors on January 23, 1968.[90]

Most African Americans, however, refused to cooperate. "They even tried to play the race card with me," Norman McDaniel recalled. "They'd say, you're a black man, we're colored people and the United States is waging a war of genocide against colored people. They knew enough about the Black Panthers, officers being fragged by enlisted people in South Vietnam and the friction between black and white GIs in Europe to throw them in my face saying, 'You must agree with us, help us,'" he said. "They wanted me to make propaganda appearances." Instead, McDaniel was defiant and argued with his captors. This simply made them madder. Failure to cooperate had painful consequences. "When I did that, I'd get slapped around, kicked around," McDaniel said. "They called me an Uncle Tom, lackey and all that, but I wasn't about" to cooperate with them.[91]

Some prisoners, however, proved willing to cooperate. The majority of Americans held in prison camps in the south were enlisted men who, as a rule, did not maintain military discipline and a chain of command as did their counterparts being held in the north. They also proved more susceptible to collaboration with the enemy. James Daly became friendly with his captors and willingly collaborated with the Vietcong and North Vietnamese, writing letters denouncing the war. He even asked to join PAVN in April 1972, after American B-52 raids on Hanoi.[92] A few, such as marine corporal Robert Garwood, went beyond writing propaganda letters and essentially did join their captors. American POWs reported Garwood as being armed and having the free run of the camp. Those that did cooperate received favorable treatment. They were not tortured and were generally well fed and housed by the North Vietnamese.

Over 2,200 servicemen remain unaccounted for from the Vietnam War, leading many to believe that at least some of the men classified as missing in action (MIA) were POWs and that some were held by the enemy after the war had ended. Vietnam veteran and writer David Hackworth claimed in 1993, "Of all the issues, the POW/MIA one packs the most political wallop. But it's a bogus issue." Hackworth had "no doubt that POWs were held after 1973 and that some American officials knew this. I was told this repeatedly by insiders who also said that some prisoners, such as B-52 crewman and electronic warfare specialists, were probably transferred to the Soviet Union and China because they knew America's nuclear weapons capabilities." But none remain alive in Vietnam today. "Members of our recovery teams have chased down every rumor. Most of them believe it is highly unlikely that any living POWs remain in Southeast Asia. The same goes for every qualified military expert or jungle-wise American and Vietnamese veteran I have interviewed....It is doubtful that Americans could survive decades of Asian style imprisonment—disease, malnutrition and insanity would have killed them long ago."[93]

LEARNING TO FIGHT

Combat was a cruel but effective teacher, and both sides learned quickly, often changing tactics in response to an enemy initiative. In Vietnam, for example, Americans learned that if you are taking fire from several places, or from indeterminate locations, do not charge in without knowing what lies ahead. You send scouts ahead to check out the situation and try to maneuver the rest of the unit out of the ambush area.[94] Helicopter pilots quickly learned not to land, but to hover a few feet off the ground, when dropping off or picking up personnel during daylight hours because a helicopter sitting on the ground took longer to take off and was more vulnerable. The same precaution was not advisable at night, however. Night landings could be as "dark as a pocket," according to John Ballweg, making night landings "hairy." The pilots quickly learned not to hover three feet off the ground before landing, but to land immediately, because hovering kicked up a huge cloud of dust, known as a brown out, especially in the dry season.[95]

Learning and innovation could keep one alive. Men riding in convoys learned to be very wary of mines; even roads that had been swept in the morning could be mined again by that afternoon. Men assigned to drive APCs learned to sit on two full sandbags to compensate for inadequate armor on the vehicle's underside. The more experienced looked for the telltale blue and orange wires leading back from the mine to the battery and detonator. One had to look above as well as below for booby traps. The Vietcong fixed them in tree branches, and they were detonated when caught in a vehicles radio antenna. Men on patrol avoided booby traps by looking for Vietcong markers such as pieces of string tied near or around the danger area or by bamboo sticks pointing in the direction of the booby trap.

Of course, the enemy also proved adept at learning quickly and often used American standard operational procedures against their adversary. Air strike targets were sometimes marked as much as an hour ahead of time, giving the Vietcong and NVA plenty of time to evacuate the area. Circling helicopters were also another indicator of an impending strike. John Ballweg said that the enemy monitored American radio frequencies and knew what color smoke markers were used for dust off or other operations, and would use captured ones to sow confusion. In one case, Ballweg was told to look for purple smoke because the Vietcong had popped off the standard yellow one used for a dust off. Another time, the pilot requested red markers, and before the men at the LZ could set one off, two had already been popped off by the enemy.[96] The Vietcong watched American units when they occupied an area to learn their patterns before booby-trapping an area. According to Albert Childs, though the Vietcong and PAVN hated the B-52s, they also knew that once the Americans had bombed an area, the B-52s were not likely to be back soon, so the safest place to camp was often in newly created bomb craters.[97]

FRUSTRATION AND RESTRICTIONS

Most Vietnam veterans were willing to credit the skill and resourcefulness of the enemy, but they also believed that the White House, and, to a more limited degree, the Pentagon, placed too many limitations and restrictions on the use of American forces and firepower in Southeast Asia. Some understood the political reasons behind the decision. David White "didn't have much respect for U.S. policy at the time. Actually what I think is they were scared they were going to get another" intervention by China. "It's disheartening to think you've got an excellent military, you think you're doing an excellent job and they put a leash on you."[98] The average soldier did not understand why the Americans did not pursue the enemy into their sanctuaries in Laos and Cambodia or invade North Vietnam. John Ballweg agreed with Barry Goldwater's stance in 1964 that we should have just massed at the demilitarized zone (DMZ) and moved north—anyone ahead of us was an enemy, anyone behind was a friend.[99]

Others wondered why, if Americans could not invade North Vietnam, they did not bomb it more effectively. Despite all the bomb tonnage dropped on North Vietnam during Rolling Thunder and Linebacker I and II, the general feeling was that the United States was wasting its efforts. Gerald Kumpf, echoing an opinion held by many veterans, believed "that whole bombing routine was just a wasted exercise, a waste of money and time." They were restricted in the targets they could hit and were ordered to hit the same targets repeatedly. The joke among B-52 crews was that they were off to make the rubble bounce. Most argued that if Americans were going to bomb them, they should mimick the strategic bombing of World War II: "Let's bomb the hell out of their cities, kill all of the civilian population."[100]

Of course, Americans were operating in Laos and Cambodia, but the operations were usually top secret, and few of the grunts on the ground were aware of them. Beginning in 1963, White Star teams, combining South Vietnamese and Americans together in the same unit, operated in Laos. There were only about 100 Americans and 500–800 Viets involved, but the teams proved very valuable. Between October 1965 and March 1966, intelligence gathered by White Star teams led to highly effective air interdiction missions into Laos, codenamed "Barrel Roll." In 1970, Richard Nixon not only ordered secret B-52 bombing missions over the two ostensibly neutral countries, he authorized a joint US-ARVN mission into the so-called Parrot's Beak area of Laos.

The CIA was heavily involved in Laos and Cambodia. Between 1957 and 1975, the CIA sponsored a so-called Secret Army composed primarily of Laotians and tribesmen, which operated in Laos along that country's mountainous spine. Again, there were few Americans involved, but apparently about a dozen of them were killed. CIA-owned Grey Birds, armed aircraft with no national insignia of any kind on them, supported the ground missions. Later in the war, when he was working for Air America, Gerald Kumpf routinely flew out of Takhli, Thailand, headquarters for the CIA and Air America, and into Cambodia and Vietnam in support of Montagnard and Hmong tribesmen. The C-130 hauled food, usually rice. The plane was stripped of all its American and military markings, and the crew dressed in civilian clothes with orders to bury their military IDs if threatened with capture. They had to sign a secrecy agreement and could not even use the term *E-flight,* which was the operational term for the missions.[101]

Most combat military personnel in Vietnam believed that there were too many restrictions on fighting the enemy, even in South Vietnam, and that it gave the enemy an unfair advantage. "I mean here you are...trying to win a war and there are all these restrictions, all these rules, yet the Viet Cong, they don't have any rules. The North Vietnamese soldiers who are fighting the south, they don't have any rules." As an advisor with the 23rd ARVN Division in 1968–1969, Childs had a "laundry list of things we had to check" before allowing heavy artillery or B-52 support such as checking to see if there were friendly troops in the area, civilians, or things of a religious or cultural nature. There were 12–15 things they had to check, and they spent a lot of time getting clearances.[102] Under the rules of engagement, the helicopter pilots could return fire if fired on if the target was in the open. He related the story of some fellow pilots who said that some Vietcong opened fire on them and then ran into a warehouse, so they were no longer in the open. The pilot needed to radio back to his unit for permission to fire on the warehouse. In turn, they then called the MACV advisor in Saigon for permission, and he checked with his ARVN counterpart sitting across from him at his desk, but permission to attack was denied, and later they found out that a cousin of the ARVN officer who denied permission to fire owned the warehouse.[103]

FEELING ABANDONED BACK HOME

Many soldiers in Vietnam felt abandoned and blamed both the government and the people back home for what they considered halfhearted support of the war effort. Airman Richard W. Harper, 20 years old and stationed in Saigon, expressed feelings typical of many young men in Vietnam: "We should stand firm when fighting for a just cause, and the cause of peace and freedom is exactly that.... The eyes of the world are on the United States. We have to succeed where France failed. It's up to the people to make our government finish this war" by winning it. Harper believed that the soldiers in Vietnam were pawns in a political chess game, frustrated at government policy and lack of support back home. "I can understand why a Vietnamese hospital might be a 'hands-off' target, but why does our government fail to see the necessity of destroying such strategic targets as Haiphong Harbor and Hanoi?" Harper "does not appreciate the fact that Americans are being killed, while our government at home is making half an effort to win this war.... We need more motivation from our fellow Americans back home, and we also need to 'go ahead' to fight this war like it should be fought." Harper knew why we were in Vietnam; he just didn't understand why we had been there so long. And, like many in Vietnam, he was "counting the lives of fathers, brothers, and close friends being lost each day."[104]

The antiwar movement was also heavily criticized by military personnel in Vietnam and was blamed in part for the government's lack of will in prosecuting the war. Others felt that the protestors actually prolonged the war. Private First Class Michael O. Brown just wanted "all the people back home to know that protesting the war will do no good. It's too late to protest, so stop marching and give us a little more support."[105] Private First Class Floyd Evans really wished "the people back in the states would cut out some of that protesting against the war. Everybody should get together and give us men a helping hand over here. I think the war will be over much sooner than they think it will, and then everybody—son, husband, and father—can be back home with their families and we all can be happy again."[106]

THE MEDIA

The media was another favorite scapegoat. Many soldiers blamed what they considered to be biased reporting for influencing the general public, and ultimately, the government, into believing that the war was unwinnable. John Ballweg thought that media coverage of the war was "totally, totally slanted" against the war effort. Reporters went with them on missions and then would write what they wanted to about the war.[107]

The war was covered by hundreds of journalists and photographers, with most of them working for a specific journal, newspaper, or television network. Some media outlets had several reporters in South Vietnam; *Time* magazine had five or six reporters or photographers in Vietnam at any one time covering the war. Some were freelancers selling their work to several publications, like photographer Sean Flynn or writer Michael Herr. Herr was nominally on assignment for *Esquire* magazine, but in his own words, "My ties to New York were as slight as my assignment was vague."[108] Many of the reporters were highly respected journalists, such as Neil Sheehan, David Halberstam, and Bernie Weinraub, while others could best be described as colorful oddities. A Korean cameraman covering the war had spent four years in Spain as a matador and spoke fluent Castilian. Michael Herr mentioned a Portuguese writer who showed up at Khe Sahn in sports clothes and a plaid suitcase, believing he could buy equipment and fatigues at the embattled base.[109]

One valid criticism of the media was that many reporters rarely left the relatively safe confines of Saigon. Albert Childs, who had a more balanced view of the media in Vietnam than many of his compatriots, remarked, "Well, a lot of it was good." But there were reporters who never left Saigon and wrote about the war as if they were in a

Walter Cronkite reporting on the Ford-Carter presidential debate, 1976. Courtesy of the Library of Congress.

combat zone, but using file footage of combat in their stories. Childs, like many veterans, also thought that some of the reporters revealed too much information to the enemy and believed that censorship is a "very necessary part of war."[110] Ironically, much of the information came directly from official military sources. Journalists stationed in Saigon relied largely on the Joint U.S. Public Affairs Office (JUSPAO), headed by journalist Barry Zorthian. Most reporters considered the information given out by JUSPAO to be unreliable and dubbed the daily 5:00 P.M. news briefings the "five o'clock follies." Michael Herr observed wryly that the JUSPAO was "created to handle press relations and psychological warfare, and I never met anyone there that seemed to realize that there was a difference."[111]

Senior print media and television executives would occasionally go to Vietnam on fact-finding missions to see for themselves if their reporters in the field were guilty of bias in their reporting of the war. Usually, the MACV gave them the VIP treatment and sent them on guided tours of safe areas, often not far from the comforts of Saigon. Occasionally, "news chiefs and network vice-presidents and foreign editors would dress up in their Abercrombie & Fitch combat gear and come by for a first hand look," commented Herr, "and after three days of high-level briefings and helicopter rides, they'd go home convinced that the war was over, that their men in the field were damned good men but a little too close to the story."[112]

In many respects, journalists found Vietnam to be an easy war to cover, and the better and more aggressive reporters did go out into the field. There were virtually no travel restrictions for the media, and a reporter was generally free to follow the troops;

Herr, for example, went to Khe Sahn during the siege on a Huey with a group of marines. Normally, there was little or no friction between reporters and troops out in the field, and many units welcomed reporters. The military even provided free transportation, and reporters often hitched rides on military transport. More than a few journalists acquired their own transportation, such as photographers Tim Paige, Sean Flynn, and Rick Merron, who used Honda motorcycles to get around the combat zones. When military or personal transportation was not available, reporters could hire South Vietnamese to take them to a combat zone. "The war was oddly accessible," recalled *New York Times* correspondent David Halberstam. "You could hire a cab in Saigon for a few dollars and drive to My Tho, go to the war if you wanted, and it was there every day."[113]

Many of the reporters, such as Herr, followed in the great tradition of Ernie Pyle and focused on the experiences of the common soldier. Herr's classic work on the war, *Dispatches,* is famous for capturing the surreal quality of the Vietnam War, but it is also a sympathetic portrayal of the average grunt in Vietnam. Covering a war was by definition dangerous, and some, such as noted journalist and historian Bernard Fall and photographer Sean Flynn, lost their lives.

Much has been made about the influence of the press, and next to the limitations placed on combat operations by officials in Washington, many critics blame the press for a climate of defeatism over Vietnam. Many journalists did voice criticism of the war, including TV newscaster Walter Cronkite, probably the most trusted and respected news commentator in America. But like Cronkite, most journalists had originally been strong supporters of the war; it was only in the later stages of Vietnam, especially after Tet-68, that most began criticizing and questioning the war.

Many Vietnam veterans blamed the politicians, and the restrictions they placed on American forces, for losing the war. One study found that 82 percent of Vietnam veterans who saw combat "strongly believe the war was lost because of lack of political will."[114] John Ballweg thought, "The military leadership, the upper level was too political. No one was allowed to do anything without permission as far as firing on anything....The leadership was, for lack of a better word, too milk toast because the politicians were running that war. It was being run from Washington." Ballweg did not see it at the time; it was only after he returned home and talked with other pilots that he decided that the restrictions cost us the war.[115] There were a lot of reasons the United States did not achieve its goals in Vietnam. The restrictions certainly compromised the ability of American forces to prosecute the war, but no war is fought in a political vacuum, and there are restrictions placed on the military in virtually every conflict. It was true that the Americans had to learn to fight an unconventional war in Vietnam as well.

BECOMING A GOOD SOLDIER

During the first two months of a combat tour, a soldier in Vietnam was still learning how to survive and was often more of a liability than an asset to the unit; 997 men were killed on their first day in country, for example. They were often referred to derisively as a "cherry" or an FNG, for "fucking new guy." Many arrived thinking war was a glorious adventure or that they could defeat the enemy single-handedly, and most were quickly disabused of these notions. The first combat troops arrived in Vietnam in March 1965 full of optimism, but by that fall, most were just fighting to survive their tour of duty. Michael Herr observed that a few "grunts would run around during a fight when they knew there was a television crew nearby, they were actually making war movies in their heads...for the networks." But this was an exception to the rule. "Most combat troops stopped thinking about the war as an adventure after their first few firefights."[116] The more time he spent in Vietnam, the more Gonzalo Baltazar realized that he was "just fighting to stay alive until your time was up and hopefully you made it back."[117]

Virtually all troops arriving in Vietnam had received some sort of jungle or counterinsurgency training, but as conditions and tactics changed, they had to learn how to fight and stay alive as they went along. After completing AIT, Gonzalo Baltazar "thought I was and most guys around there thought they were trained well enough" to be "combat ready, and you kind of get brained washed into that, that you're a real fighting machine, a soldier. Realistically you weren't ready for it. You knew how to use all your weapons, your booby traps, your claymores, all your big weapons. You knew how to do all that. In actual combat, it was a totally different story. You just didn't go by the book anymore. You learn as you went along in Vietnam."[118]

The novices also discovered that actually fighting a war was infinitely more difficult than training for one. William Calley had been in Vietnam less than a month when he led his first ambush patrol. "I thought I would slay one or two hundred enemy between the hours of sunset and sunrise and I might end the war," he recalled. "I didn't want to go after dark, though, and I talked to C.O. into letting us out during daylight hours."

Calley had problems from the very beginning. There was nothing but cornfields in the area, and he could not find a suitable place for his ambush. Setting up their ambush position in the cornfield, they discovered that the stalks made a huge racket and spooked nearby water buffalo, leaving the callow lieutenant apprehensive that any moment, they would be overrun by herds of water buffalo. More importantly, he was "waking the VC nation up" with all the noise. He was taught at officer candidate school (OCS) that the key to successful ambush was to be as quiet as possible: ties things up so they would not rattle, fill up one canteen rather than have water sloshing around in a couple of half empty ones. In training, he never realized how difficult it was to remain quiet. How do you drink out of your canteen if you don't want water sloshing around, for example? His machine gunner got lost and came crashing through the cornstalks, calling out for them. They had thought he was a Vietcong. Then, in setting up the machine gun, they made a lot of noise. Loading the M-60, there is a *clink, clink, clink,* followed by a louder *clank, clank, clank,* and then the heavy *clank* of the bolt closing. Another one of his men suddenly got up screaming; they thought he had been shot or gone crazy, but it turned out to be ants. Calley was thinking to himself that if there was "a V.C. within ten miles of us, I bet he was listening and laughing himself to death."

Calley kept going around to his men periodically, patting them on the back and encouraging them, but by midnight, he was frustrated. They had been in ambush position and relatively quiet for three hours, and still no enemy had stumbled by. "I got disappointed, and I got annoyed! Never at O.C.S. had we had to wait three hours: at O.C.S. the enemy had stumbled upon us promptly." Calley began to fear that the reason he had not seen any enemy was that he had made so much noise that the Vietcong knew where he was, and they were sneaking up to ambush him. He called the nearby mortar platoon and requested continuous illumination. For an hour and a half, yellow flares went up into the sky, bathing everything for miles around in their light. Finally, Calley received a call on the radio from his commanding officer, Captain Ernest Medina, who asked angrily, "Charlie One. What in the goddamn hell are you doing out there?" Calley attempted to explain, but Medina cut him off: "You nitwit. You are without a doubt the stupidest second lieutenant on the face of the earth." Calley agreed with his commanding officer's assessment of his intellectual abilities. "Yes, sir! I know sir! I am stupid sir. What shall I do?" Medina's curt reply was, "Turn off them goddamned lights." The sun came up fours hours later. Calley said the night was "a comedy of errors, but it didn't matter much: we weren't dead, and we had lived and learned.... The second time I took an ambush out, I knew how to do it. From that day on, I pulled ambushes every other night."[119]

Many learned the skills that could keep them alive on the job from more experienced soldiers. Gordon Roberts credited the sergeants in his platoon for his winning the Medal of Honor for his action in the Ashau Valley in July 1969. "I listened very, very closely when I was a private to my sergeants. When we were in battle, I just did what they told me to do. This guy must have been a good infantryman is all I can say."[120] In 1969, before Baltazar and his rapid reaction unit went out into the field, they received briefings and a bit more training from some Green Berets on booby traps and jungle warfare, and more on booby traps from some Kit Carson scouts, who were former Vietcong that had switched sides.[121] After they arrived in Vietnam, the helicopter pilots for the 11th Armored Cavalry Regiment were sent to other units for two weeks of in-country training. They flew missions every day. Ballweg listened and learned from the more experienced pilots. To escape enemy fire, for example, "you take off running and then you just climb like a homesick angel."[122]

Some replacements did not like taking advice from the more veteran soldiers, especially if the new man was an officer or NCO. "A couple of sergeants just couldn't figure out why we had to tell them how to fight this war, and we'd get into heated arguments and end up fist fighting," explained Gonzalo Baltazar.[123] Baltazar's platoon was decimated after Hill 376, and down to only 11 or 12 men, they were reinforced with a few veterans from other companies, but most of their replacements were new, including several so-called shake and bake sergeants. The instant sergeants did not want to listen to Baltazar, an E-4, or the other veterans in the unit. They preferred to do things by the book, the way they were taught back in the States. "So we explained to them that, 'everything you learned back in the States from a book, forget about it. It's a new ballgame out here. This is combat. Either you listen to us or you're not going to make it back.' They didn't like the idea and some listened to us and a couple of them wouldn't.... Obviously a couple of those guys didn't make it back because they wanted to do it by the book and they didn't make it back." Most of the new men, however, did learn to take advice from the veterans. "You know what, at the end, we were all good buddies," Baltazar remembered. "It just happened that we had to make them understand and after their first big firefight they woke up and pretty soon we were good buddies and we learned how to depend on each other."[124]

By the third or fourth month of a combat tour, the average soldier was experienced and knowledgeable enough to be efficient and contribute to the unit. Gordon Roberts, for example, had been in country for three months when he earned his Medal of Honor in Vietnam. Men with combat experience learned to judge how close a bullet or shell was likely to land to you by the sound. Michael Herr said that close bullets whistled, and really close bullets cracked.[125] The Vietcong usually fired random mortar rounds and were more interested in firing quickly than accurately. The Vietcong seldom repositioned the mortar after firing a round, meaning that the next one would fall about 15–20 yards away from where the first one hit. At Danang, in 1965–1966, a young, inexperienced lieutenant was shocked when Gerald Kumpf got up after the first round of a mortar attack and went back to work. Experience had taught Kumpf that the rounds were moving away from them.[126]

Soldiers in their 9th and 10th months were seasoned veterans operating at their peak efficiency and were most combat-effective. Because of the rotation policy, however, a soldier's desire to face the enemy and overall efficiency declined in the last two months of his tour, when he became a short-timer. There were literally hundreds of short-timer jokes and sayings: "I'm so short I can walk under a pregnant amoeba" or "I'm so short they use my height to measure jungle boot tread" and "I'm so short I have to jump up to look down!" Many lampooned the military, such as "I'm so short I have to look *up* to a second lieutenant" or "I'm so short they don't even reprimand me for dragging ass!" One in particular incorporated both a parody of the acronyms the military is apparently so fond of along with the sense of longing most short-timers felt when they got really short, and in language the average grunt in Vietnam would appreciate: "I'm so short I'm FIGMO—Fuck it, got my orders!" Many men kept calendars, or "short-timer's sticks," adding a notch for each day in country. Many began the countdown the day they arrived in Vietnam. John Ballweg thought to himself after combat, "Not bad, it was like one more day down. That's the way we started counting. Yes we started short-timer's counters as soon as we got there."[127]

A soldier with only a few months left on his tour had to worry about so-called short-timer's disease, losing your concentration out in the field and getting hurt or killed because you were daydreaming about going home. Though the practice was far from universal, it was common in many outfits to give short-timers with only a few weeks or days left in country noncombat duties or to withhold them from offensive patrolling. Gonzalo Baltazar said it was standard procedure in his unit to put men with 10 days left on restricted duty. "When you get close to leaving Vietnam, ending your tour, you get very nervous. They—the chain of command—would usually pull you out of the field because they knew you were nervous, more focused on getting out alive than performing the mission."[128] Unit policy in John Ballweg's outfit was to put short-timers on restricted duty a week before they went home. They were given administrative duties or safe runs. They also flew their pilots back to the replacement depot when they were going home, rather than having them take the bus, which was standard procedure. Despite efforts by some company commanders to rotate short-timers out of harm's way, 1,448 men were killed on their last day in country.

Men placed on restricted duty were sometimes forced by circumstances to go on, or they volunteered for, one last mission. With only five days left in country, and on restricted duty, Baltazar agreed to go out one more time to help rescue the company's executive officer, David Livingston, whose light observation helicopter was shot down, and he was shot in the head. Baltazar was one of the few skilled rappellers available and liked and admired Livingston. The jungle proved deeper than they thought, and several members of the rescue team, including Baltazar, ran out of rope before they reached the jungle floor. One broke an ankle, and another had his head split open by a box of hand grenades. They extracted the captain and the door gunner, and only years later did he find out that the captain survived, albeit paralyzed on the left side.

When seasoned veterans like Baltazar or Ballweg left Vietnam, they took precious, hard-won experience with them. The lack of experience was most acute in leadership positions. Some of the men coming in to replace them were combat veterans from previous wars or tours in Vietnam, but most were inexperienced. Despite the efforts of committed and experienced officers and NCOs, the constant shuffling of personnel in and out of units, the frequent changes of command, coupled with declining morale and racial polarization, made it difficult for men to bond together and trust each other and prevented them from developing the small-unit cohesion so necessary to the smooth and efficient functioning of a unit. American combat efficiency was degraded after 1968, and most men just simply wanted to go home.

NOTES

1. Philip Caputo, *A Rumor of War* (New York: Holt, Rinehart, and Winston, 1977).
2. Lieutenant Corporal Winston McElrath, "Our Men in Vietnam," *Sepia,* July 1968, 75.
3. Gonzalo Baltazar, *Oral History Project,* The Vietnam Archive at Texas Tech University. Interviewed by Steve Maxner, March 23, 2001. Retrieved from http://www.virtualarchive.vietnam.ttu.edu/cgi-bin/starfetch. exe?3qUevQOjUtg2mDgIBOhT3hQ7wvenAzlebd@qMS7Av.N9BF7TSM9wvr@vB2M4o7sdoJfUBL5. U3WHS1XkROhq2hvFxK3tPSLj/OH0152.pdf, 33–34.
4. Gerald Kumpf, *Oral History Project,* The Vietnam Archive at Texas Tech University. Interviewed by Richard Verrone, March 10, 2003. Retrieved from http://www.virtualarchive.vietnam.ttu.edu/cgi-bin/star fetch.exe?EWoAfq.tJEBzwDooKsGN8mxwA2X3@q8.Y4@lpzu0qrpNanzPx0Zh6@ZwMPIxL.ex6Y3AV. nGBn7aUH1WFP4otrIS5b2nFx1OwsFzXQ8FRlo/OH0276-1.pdf, 39.
5. Baltazar, *Oral History Project*, 20.
6. Ibid.
7. Albert Childs, *Oral History Project,* The Vietnam Archive at Texas Tech University. Interviewed by Steve Maxner, February 3, 2003. Retrieved from http://www.virtualarchive.vietnam.ttu.edu/cgi-bin/starfetch. exe?px@DCzXFmOuNx2T6g1RlUxXU5JKU.VHLnKVjhB5A.zu78Y18RLhkxS@8DT4FUZiZFMSEp2vq jMbGIa4Bk5SPT9GKohPkmUno/OH0095.pdf, 5.
8. Al Santoli, *Everything We Had* (New York: Ballantine Books, 1981), 92.
9. Kumpf, *Oral History Project*, 32.
10. Lew Moores, "Soldier Devotes Life to Country," *The Cincinnati Enquirer,* November 10, 1997, A-1, A-4.
11. Ron Ballweg, *Oral History Project,* The Vietnam Archive at Texas Tech University. Interviewed by Richard Verrone, May 19, 2003. Retrieved from http://www.virtualarchive.vietnam.ttu.edu/cgi-bin/starfetch. exe?8ef.0OThTHlw@ovB@bMAIW5KtMcM31GAZwYqlEtpvVWLEnlWMsbO6qa0zk8nerqkpky0E2@3. AAMn2RrUMjKQM1MI39jwXFA/OH0296.pdf, 26.
12. Kumpf, *Oral History Project*, 14–15.
13. David H. Hackworth, "The War without End," *Newsweek,* November 22, 1993, 45.
14. Childs, *Oral History Project*, 21.
15. Kumpf, *Oral History Project*, 35.
16. Ibid.
17. Hackworth, "War without End," 47.
18. Kumpf, *Oral History Project*, 35.
19. Caputo, *A Rumor of War,* xvi–xvii.
20. Herman Graham III, *The Brothers' Vietnam War: Black Power, Manhood, and the Military Experience* (Gainesville: University Press of Florida, 2003).
21. Caputo, *A Rumor of War,* xvi.
22. Michael Herr, "Sending the War Home," *Esquire,* June 1983, 268.
23. Baltazar, *Oral History Project*, 33.
24. Kumpf, *Oral History Project*, 37.
25. Gary McKay, *Delta Four: Australian Riflemen in Vietnam* (Crows Nest, NSW, Australia: Allen and Unwin, 1998), 214–15.
26. Kumpf, *Oral History Project*, 37.
27. Childs, *Oral History Project*, 7.
28. Ibid.
29. Kumpf, *Oral History Project*, 31.
30. Ballweg, *Oral History Project*, 16–17.
31. Baltazar, *Oral History Project*, 28.
32. Ballweg, *Oral History Project*, 16–17.
33. Hackworth, "War without End," 45.
34. Lieutenant Colonel K. E. Hamburger, *Leadership in Combat: An Historical Appraisal* (Washington, DC: Department of the Army, 1984), 3.

35. Ibid.

36. Lieutenant General Arthur J. Gregg, Senior Officer *Oral History Project*, U.S. Army Military History Institute, Carlisle Barracks, PA, 1997, 52.

37. Bill Beck, "The Dead Were All Around," *Newsweek,* March 8, 1999, 56.

38. Ibid.

39. Lieutenant General Bernard William Rogers, *Cedar Falls–Junction City: A Turning Point,* Vietnam Studies (Washington, DC: Department of the Army, 1989), 34.

40. Hackworth, "War without End," 44.

41. Russell F. Weigley, "Putting the Poor in Uniform," *The New York Times,* April 11, 1993, 12.

42. Steven Morris, "How Blacks Upset the Marine Corps," *Ebony,* December 1969, 60.

43. Private First Class Jack P. Smith, "Death in the Ia Drang Valley, November 17–18, 1965," *Saturday Evening Post,* 28 January 1967. Reprinted on and retrieved from *Neil Mishalov's Web Site,* http://www.mishalov.com/death_ia_drang_valley.html.

44. Rogers, *Cedar Falls–Junction City,* 59.

45. Ibid., 59.

46. Ibid., 54.

47. John Sacks, "The Education of a Young Lieutenant," *Esquire,* June 1983, 260.

48. Baltazar, *Oral History Project,* 15.

49. Hackworth, "War without End," 47.

50. Baltazar, *Oral History Project,* 15, 19.

51. Hackworth, "War without End," 47.

52. Beck, "Dead Were All Around," 56.

53. Ibid.

54. Hackworth, "War without End," 44–48.

55. Smith, "Death in the Ia Drang Valley."

56. Hackworth, "War without End," 44.

57. Medal of Honor Citation for Private First Class, U.S. Marine Corps, Second Platoon, Company F, Second Battalion, Third Marines, Third Marine Division.

58. Baltazar, *Oral History Project,* 16.

59. Moores, "Soldier Devotes Life," A-4.

60. Herr, "Sending the War Home," 266.

61. Hackworth, "War without End," 44.

62. Baltazar, *Oral History Project,* 19.

63. Smith, "Death in the Ia Drang Valley."

64. Ibid.

65. Ibid.

66. Ibid.

67. Ibid.

68. Allen Thomas Jr., in discussion with the author, Erlanger, Kentucky, 25 July, 2000.

69. Childs, *Oral History Project,* 9.

70. Hackworth, "War without End," 44.

71. U.S. Army Center of Military History, "Medal of Honor Recipients, Vietnam War (A–L)," http://www.army.mil/cmh-pg/mohviet.htm.

72. Thomas Johnson, "Negro Veteran Is Confused and Bitter," *The New York Times,* 29 July, 1968, 14.

73. Vietnam Women's Memorial Project, *Celebration of Patriotism and Courage: Dedication of the Vietnam Women's Memorial, November 10–12, 1993* (Washington, DC: Vietnam Women's Memorial Project, 1993), 35.

74. Kathryn Marshall, *In the Combat Zone: An Oral History of American Women in Vietnam* (Boston: Little, Brown, 1987), 7.

75. Baltazar, *Oral History Project,* 13–14.

76. Kumpf, *Oral History Project,* 14–15.

77. Ibid., 36–37.

78. General Anthony Zinni, interview by Harry Kreisler, Conversations with History, Institute of International Studies, UC Berkeley, March 6, 2001, http:///globetrotter.berkeley.edu/conversations/Zinni/zinni-con3.html.

79. U.S. Department of Defense, *U.S. Casualties in Southeast Asia* (Washington, DC: U.S. Government Printing Office, 1985).

80. Ibid.
81. Hackworth, "War without End," 44.
82. Ballweg, *Oral History Project*, 38.
83. U.S. Department of Defense, *U.S. Casualties.*
84. Ibid.
85. Ian Stewart, "Senator Meets His Rescuer," *The Cincinnati Enquirer,* November 14, 1996, A23.
86. Stewart, "Senator," A23.
87. Millicent Rothrock, "Survival in Captivity," *Greensboro News and Record,* February 24, 1998, B1.
88. P.O.W. Network, "Garwood, Robert Russell," http://www.pownetwork.org/bios/g/g047.htm.
89. "Captain and Mrs. Frederic A. Wyatt (USNR Ret)," in *We Came Home,* ed. Barbara Powers Wyatt (Toluca Lake, CA: P.O.W. Publications, 1977, online edition, http://www.pownetwork.org/bios/m/m102.htm, and P.O.W. Network, "McDaniel, Norman Alexander," http://www.pownetwork.org/bios/m/m102.htm.
90. P.O.W. Network, "Garwood."
91. "Captain and Mrs. Frederic A Wyatt (USNR Ret)," *We Came Home.*
92. James A. Daly and Lee Bergman, *Black Prisoner of War: A Conscientious Objector's Vietnam Memoir* (Lawrence: University Press of Kansas, 2000), 186, 195.
93. Hackworth, "War without End," 48.
94. Baltazar, *Oral History Project*, 18.
95. Ballweg, *Oral History Project*, 32.
96. Ibid., 23.
97. Childs, *Oral History Project*, 22.
98. David White, *Oral History Project,* The Vietnam Archive at Texas Tech University. Interviewed by Richard Verrone, n.d. Retrieved from http://www.virtualarchive.vietnam.ttu.edu/cgi-bin/starfetch.exe?71mIafeP3JsUwk7rv@lU9xasA5uYhgjKNAyaDpYf5Nk.Blkuvd69i.GoLp0Gl4jSbk8HMOoS284C0l6iWWadecNnjn.SRsiy/OH0227.pdf, 26.
99. Ballweg, *Oral History Project*, 30.
100. Gerald Kumpf, 49–50.
101. Ibid., 57–58.
102. Childs, *Oral History Project*, 11.
103. Ballweg, *Oral History Project*, 30.
104. Airman Richard W. Harper, "Our Men in Vietnam," *Sepia,* January 1968, 78–79.
105. Private First Class Michael O. Brown, "Our Men in Vietnam," *Sepia,* June 1968, 58.
106. Floyd Evans, Letter in "Our Men in Vietnam," *Sepia,* February 1968, 71.
107. Ballweg, *Oral History Project*, 45.
108. Herr, "Sending the War Home," 267.
109. Ibid.
110. Childs, *Oral History Project*, 9–10.
111. Herr, "Sending the War Home," 267.
112. Ibid., 268.
113. Horst Faas and Tim Page, *Requiem: By the Photographers Who Died in Vietnam and Indochina* (New York: Random House, 1997), 9–10.
114. Association of the 1st Battalion (Mechanized), 50th Infantry for Vietnam Veterans, "Lessons Learned in Vietnam: 1st Battalion, 50th Infantry," http://www.ichiban1.org/html/history_lessons.htm.
115. Ballweg, *Oral History Project*, 29.
116. Herr, "Sending the War Home," 265.
117. Baltazar, *Oral History Project*, 13.
118. Ibid., 7.
119. Sacks, "Education," 262.
120. Moores, "Soldier Devotes Life," A-1.
121. Baltazar, *Oral History Project*, 14.
122. Ballweg, *Oral History Project*, 13.
123. Baltazar, *Oral History Project*, 29.
124. Ibid.
125. Herr, "Sending the War Home," 265.
126. Kumpf, *Oral History Project*, 33–36.
127. Ballweg, *Oral History Project*, 14.
128. Baltazar, *Oral History Project*, 34.

CHAPTER 5

Soldiers' Issues in the Vietnam War and Afterward

GOING HOME

For military personnel leaving Vietnam, the actual transition from war zone to civilian society could be an abrupt one; some men received their orders home while still out at a remote firebase or just coming in from a patrol. In less than three days, one could go from being heavily armed, dirty, and trying to kill the enemy to sitting in the lobby of an airport in Tacoma or Los Angeles in a pressed and starched dress uniform. One unnamed Vietnam veteran remarked, "When you put people into a pressure cooker, have the sense and decency to set up a cool-down period when you want them to return to standard temperature and pressure. Less than 72 hours from battlefield to Sea-Tac Airport was too heavy for some."[1]

Military personnel going home were processed out at the replacement depot at Long Binh and then bussed to Bien Hao, where they caught the plane home. Most brought souvenirs with them. Ballweg brought back a Chinese Communist rifle. He brought it in legally, and when he later caught a civilian flight from San Francisco to Baltimore, they simply checked the rifle in the cockpit.[2] The same civilian airlines used to bring troops to Vietnam also carried them home. John Ballweg flew home on a TWA 707 airliner. There was still one gauntlet to run before they were safe. Bien Hao had an extremely long runway, around 13,000 feet. The pilot would use most of the runway to build up as much speed as possible, so they would take off like a rocket and build altitude quickly to avoid small arms fire. Ballweg and everybody on his plane cheered when the pilot announced that they had left Vietnamese airspace.

Most veterans could now relax, but for some, even the flight home was still a bit of an ordeal. When David White was evacuated to Japan because of his wounds, his uniforms were left behind, so the navy issued him a brand new blue dress uniform for his trip home. Unfortunately, he had an allergic reaction from the wool on the flight from Japan to San Francisco and spent the trip in misery from a terrible rash. The best relief he ever got was from a small bottle of rubbing alcohol he bought to sooth the rash after he got off the plane.[3]

During Operation Georgia, Marines blow up bunkers and tunnels used by the Viet Cong, May 1966. Courtesy of the National Archives.

The trip home was naturally a long one. The first stop after Vietnam was often Guam, but there were others. Gerald Kumpf went to Okinawa to Hawaii to El Toro when he returned home in September 1966.[4] Gonzalo Baltazar had a quiet trip home. They left from Cam Rahn Bay, flew to Japan, and from there to Fort Lewis, Washington. Ron Ballweg left Vietnam on a Saturday evening and arrived in San Francisco around 5:30 P.M. Saturday evening. He had traveled through two sunsets and had not slept for the entire trip.

APPREHENSION ABOUT THE RECEPTION AT HOME

On arriving back in the United States, personnel were processed through a receiving station, such as El Toro or Oakland, and were given a new uniform and a steak dinner. Most of the returnees were grateful to have survived Vietnam and just wanted a quiet life back home, but because of the turmoil back in civilian society, including antiwar demonstrations and race riots, more than a few were apprehensive about what they would find. Black veterans, in particular, were fearful that they were exchanging one war zone for another. Many returning black veterans did not wear their uniforms off base, especially in the South, but that was due to racism and not hostility by antiwar protesters. African American Sp/4 Hank Lovelady was "just hoping that after my tour I can just go home to a nice quiet life with my family. Really, I wouldn't know how or what to do if I leave here after having been here and safe for so long and then get shot at home in a riot. I'm just hoping we can find peace at home instead of looking to the long, hot summer."[5] Gene Richmond, an African American, also wondered how he would "be treated when I get home? Will I be discriminated against? Will I still be a second-class citizen? Will my family be able to ride at the front of the bus? These are the things I worry about.... Maybe if you print this the white people will see black men also are dying in this war."[6]

As the war became increasingly unpopular in the United States, and emotions mounted on both sides of the issues, Vietnam veterans were very concerned about the way the general population would treat them. Many returnees felt unappreciated by the American public. Army nurse Eddie Meeks remembered that "one of the hardest things was that we weren't allowed to feel proud.... When I was getting ready to go stateside... some nurses who were just coming over told me to be sure to go to the ladies room and change as soon as I got back. Nobody wanted to be reminded, and they didn't want to talk to you about your experience. They hardly knew how."[7]

In army debriefings late in the war, returnees were told that the antiwar movement was hostile and that people would spit on them and call them baby killers. There was some verbal abuse. Someone called John Ballweg a baby killer after coming home from Vietnam. Like many returning veterans, he never argued with them but would simply tell them that they did not know what they were talking about.[8] Gonzalo Baltazar said that when he arrived at Fort Lewis, there were protestors outside the base's chain link fence. "You're happier than heck that you finally made it back to stateside. Then we're getting off the plane and there was a fence around there and there was protestors out there throwing tomatoes at us, yelling at us, 'Baby killers,' and 'Warmongers,' and I thought, man, this is our home country right here. It was pretty disappointing. So, you really get a bitter feeling about the Americans who are knocking us down." By the time he finished processing, flew to Denver, and then drove out to the family farm, it was five o'clock in the morning. "It wasn't a very good homecoming," he remembers.[9] Despite the urban legends, however, few returning veterans reported being spat on. Allen Thomas, a veteran of three tours in Vietnam, explained that it probably was not a good idea to spit on someone just days removed from a war zone.

Some returning veterans were harassed by both supporters and detractors of the war. After his discharge, Gerald Kumpf, still wearing the old khaki uniform because he had no other clothes, decided to hitchhike into town, buy a car, and drive home. A woman stopped and picked him up, but once in the car, she asked him why he was not overseas and then began to berate him because her son was overseas, and "you goddamn hippies are all the same, you're walking around wearing these old uniforms and you don't do anything." Kumpf did not want to argue with her, so he asked to be let out at the next corner and thanked her for the ride. Within minutes, another woman stopped and picked him up, only to tell him that "you goddamn GIs are all the same...over there fighting these wars, you know you're just terrible." It was the first time Kumpf had heard negative criticism of the war, and "it set me back, right there. I thought wow, what the hell is going on here."[10]

While many members of the antiwar movement could be condescending in their treatment of military personnel, most did make a clear distinction between the warrior and the war they were protesting; it was a distinction, however, often lost on the veterans. There were class and political differences separating veterans recently returned from Vietnam and those protesting the war. While the average soldier was more likely to be working class and politically moderate to conservative, the average protestor was just as likely to be middle or upper class, more educated, and more liberal. Christian Appy believed that "on the whole," the attitude of the protestors "towards the soldiers were arrogant, sanctimonious and insensitive to the moral quandaries of those who had to fight."[11]

Most returnees, however, were spared confrontations with hostile protestors. Vietnam veteran Peter Hefron stated, "Frankly, I never had such a problem nor do I know of anyone who did. I passed through both the San Francisco and Boston airports in uniform on a number of occasions during 1968 to 1970 without a problem. Both cities were hot beds of antiwar sentiment. Yet no one confronted me either physically or verbally about my military service." John Ballweg was not harassed because he flew into Travis Air Force Base when he returned home.[12] Arthur Gregg believed that he "always enjoyed a great deal of respect from people for having served in Vietnam. I recall visiting families in my home and my wife's home, and in other places, after I returned in June 1967. I talked with many families." Even families that had lost someone to the war did not display any open bitterness to Gregg.[13] Some even came home to cheerful receptions. Gordon Roberts returned home to Lebanon, Ohio, from Vietnam in 1970 and was welcomed back. "But I guess my saving grace was coming back to a place like Lebanon. A small town, a lot of welcome back." The reality was not hostility but apathy. Most came back alone, and unlike nearly all previous wars, there were no parades or official delegations to welcome them.

Many Vietnam vets believed that the general public was being misinformed about what was actually happening in Vietnam. Like many returning veterans, Kumpf's opinion of the antiwar movement was "mostly negative." Working as a research engineer for the Chemistry Department at the University of Montana, Kumpf heard professors tell their classes what he considered to be "absolute falsehoods" concerning the war.[14] Others thought the movement was unpatriotic. John Ballweg "couldn't stand it. I couldn't stand it at all.... I'm from the old school. My country, right or wrong.... I think they did more harm than good. They divided the country."[15]

Many veterans, however, such as John Jerry, Philip Caputo, and Ron Kovic, came home convinced that the war had been a mistake and joined the antiwar movement. In June 1967, Jan "Barry" Crumb, Mark Donnelly, David Braum, and three other Vietnam vets formed Vietnam Veterans against the War (VVAW) after marching in an antiwar demonstration in New York City that April. The following year, over 1,500 members of the VVAW protested the war and Nixon's nomination at the Republican Convention and were participants in peace demonstrations throughout the country; they occasionally staged their own protests, such as Operation Raw, an acronym for "rapid American withdrawal," in early September 1970, which drew thousands of participants, and Dewey Canyon III in Washington, D.C., in April 1971. That month, VVAW spokesman John Kerry testified against the war for over two hours in front of the Senate Foreign Relations Committee. The VVAW also staged the controversial Winter Soldier hearings on U.S. atrocities in Vietnam. There were other veteran antiwar organizations, but none became as large or as influential as the VVAW. By the end of the war, over 40,000 veterans had joined the VVAW, and, ironically, much like their prowar comrades, they often found themselves the targets of angry civilians; in this case, however, it was supporters of the war outraged by their opposition to the conflict and their alleged collusion with and support of the North Vietnamese.

Many veterans returned home, only to deal with vexing bureaucrats and trivial regulations. Like many returning veterans, Gerald Kumpf had served his time in the military and was eligible for discharge. The problem was that he had only two passable sets of fatigues to wear when he left Vietnam in September 1966 because his dress uniforms and other clothes were allegedly destroyed by a mortar attack while in storage, though it was far more likely that they had probably mildewed or the marines lost them. On Okinawa, they took his old fatigues and burned them and issued him class B fatigues, basically just plain khaki with no rank or insignia. When Kumpf returned to the United States, this caused him "no end of grief" because he was not wearing his lance corporal insignia, putting him in violation of the uniform code. He was also wearing combat boots instead of the regulation shoes. Every officer he passed "was all over my case," leading to "three days of hell." It also complicated his discharge. The discharge officer was not going to issue his discharge papers until Kumpf appeared in his dress uniform as per regulations. Since Kumpf no longer owned a dress uniform, he refused to get one and continued showing up in his khakis. Though it meant spending an extra two days in the marines, Kumpf finally won out, and the frustrated officer finally issued the papers discharging Kumpf from the marines.[16]

RETURNING AS CHANGED INDIVIDUALS

Like veterans of previous conflicts, the men and women who served in Vietnam came back as different individuals, with a different perspective on life. For better or worse, the war had changed them. "The Vietnam War scarred every soldier who served there, and I was no exception," admitted David Hackworth.[17] Ohio had not changed, but Gordon Roberts had. "You age very considerably. You grow a lot; you mature a lot. It takes awhile to adjust back to the norms of your community. It took me awhile."[18]

Some could not forget the war, and more than a few missed it. Many missed friends and were nostalgic for the comradeship and the close ties forged in combat. Some missed the adrenalin rush of combat and others the defined sense of purpose. Many veterans had survivor's guilt and felt terrible that they had survived when so many others had died. Gerald Kumpf was troubled that he came back alive and had never been wounded or in combat in Vietnam; all he did was fix airplanes and keep them flying, in his own estimation. Like many other veterans, Kumpf opened up to another veteran, in this case his own father, and found out that he too had had his bout with survivor's guilt after World War II. David White also felt survivor's guilt due to the death of his replacement. White could have returned to his unit after recovering from his wounds, but he declined to do so due to a combination of depression, "fear and common sense."[19]

Some instinctively still fell back on their combat training and experience. John Ballweg was "jumpy" his first month back. A car backfiring would send him under the table for cover, but he did not have a temper and pretty much just "blended back in."[20]

For most veterans, the memories did fade but remained with them even years later. Years after Vietnam, the sound of thunder reminded Philip Caputo of artillery or a heavy rain of "miserable nights soaking wet out in the field." Walking through woods, he still instinctively looked for trip wires or signs of an impending ambush.[21] Bill Beck could not forget the dead lying all around him in the combat field. It stayed with Beck all his life.[22]

Like veterans of previous wars, it was difficult for Vietnam veterans to discuss their experiences with nonveterans, believing that they could never understand what it was like. Gordon Roberts would sit in the dark in the middle of the night in the family room smoking cigarettes when he first returned from Vietnam. His mother knew that he had a lot to think about, so she never pried or questioned him about his experiences in Vietnam, something for which Roberts was grateful. "That no one really pried helped. I needed, and I think most of us needed, a time to sit back and think a little bit."[23] Like Roberts, Gonzalo Baltazar did not discuss his experiences with his family: "It was something you didn't want to talk about at the time. You wanted your time to think. You really didn't talk about it, and combat veterans, we found out that we didn't have this homecoming that we expected and you couldn't talk to anybody because we were called baby killers and murderers and all that, so most of us just went underground and kept to ourselves, kept quiet because you were already embarrassed by being a Vietnam vet. We were no hero."[24]

Baltazar may not have considered himself a hero, but like the vast majority of men leaving the armed forces, he did so with an honorable discharge. In 1965, the first year of direct American involvement in the war, 678,100 men and women, or 94.3 percent of those leaving military service, did so with honorable discharges, and during the height of the war, in 1968 and 1969, over 96 percent of all those leaving the armed services received honorable discharges. As late as 1970, 95 percent of all African Americans and 97 percent of whites leaving the service received either honorable or general under honorable conditions discharges. Until 1971, the percentage of honorable and general under honorable discharges given out was similar to the percentage given out during World War II, but in 1972, with the war winding down and morale in the armed forces at its worst in decades, 804,470 individuals, or only 90.3 percent of those leaving military service, received honorable discharges, which was the lowest for any year during the war, but another 5.1 percent received general discharges.

POSTTRAUMATIC STRESS DISORDER

Vietnam veterans found adjustment back to civilian life to be very difficult. David White's transition to civilian life went "pretty bad. I was probably pretty bad for a couple of years. I guess too much drinking and whatever," and he was reliving his Vietnam experiences through flashbacks and painful memories. Like many Vietnam veterans, White was suffering from posttraumatic stress disorder (PTSD), defined by the U.S. Department of Veterans Affairs's National Center for PTSD as "a psychiatric disorder that can occur following the experience or witnessing of life-threatening events such as military combat." Symptoms of PTSD include flashbacks, insomnia, depression, and feelings of detachment and estrangement.[25]

Though posttraumatic stress disorder was first recognized as a specific clinical condition only in 1980, it has affected soldiers throughout history. In World Wars I and II, it was known by various names such as shell shock, battle fatigue, or the thousand-yard stare. A 1986–1988 study by the National Vietnam Veterans Readjustment Survey found that overall, 31 percent of male veterans and 27 percent of female veterans experienced PTSD after returning home from Vietnam, and over 15 percent of male veterans and 8.1 percent of women were still diagnosed with it at the time of the report. Anyone serving in a war zone was at risk, but combat veterans were more likely to develop it than those who were not under fire, and minorities were more likely to have PTSD than whites, with roughly 40 percent of black veterans reporting some symptoms of stress disorder, compared to about 20 percent of whites. Many veterans with PTSD experienced problems with the law. Almost half the male veterans in the survey had been jailed or arrested at least once, and over one-third on multiple occasions. Roughly 11 percent had been convicted of a felony. As late as 2004, there were still 161,000 Vietnam veterans receiving disability compensation for PTSD.

A few veterans, like Ballweg, believed that PTSD was not a legitimate disorder and felt that it was an excuse for not adjusting back to civilian life. John Ballweg never "bought into it" and believed that claims of posttraumatic stress disorder were a "crutch." Life was rough, and Ballweg had two divorces and another wife die two years after the marriage, but he never blamed his misfortune on PTSD or Vietnam.[26] David White, like most veterans, worked through his PTSD and other problems and eventually adjusted. He got "straightened out long about '73 or '74" and was married the following year.[27] Other veterans, however, came home to what they thought would be a happy reunion with a wife or girlfriend, only to find that things had changed in a year, and the relationship was over. John Ballweg returned home safely from Vietnam, only to have his wife tell him that their marriage was over; it had little to do with Vietnam, she just did not want to go to his next assignment in Texas.[28] The separation from each other, often for an entire year, and the fact that many veterans returned home different and often troubled individuals suffering from PTSD, was often too much, and Vietnam veterans suffered high divorce rates. The divorce rate among veterans does not appear to be influenced by race, class, or rank in the armed forces but was highest among men that served in combat units with high casualty rates. By 1977, veterans who served in units that had at least a 25 percent casualty rate had a post-Vietnam divorce rate of 30 percent, compared to a 19 percent divorce rate for veterans of units with only modest casualties and a 12 percent rate for units that suffered few or no casualties. On the whole, 20 percent of the combat veterans studied were separated or divorced, in contrast to 14 percent of the noncombat Vietnam veterans.

EMPLOYMENT

Finding employment was another problem for many recently discharged veterans. A few made the transition easily. Gonzalo Baltazar did not have any trouble finding a career after leaving the army, alternating between farming and the post office, finally settling on the latter in 1981.[29] Many returning veterans, however, lacked basic civilian skills. Most had entered the military at a young age and had had little practice dealing with everyday issues. Many had few marketable skills. They could lead an ambush at night or field strip their rifle blindfolded, but few had marketable job skills.

Black veterans usually had a tougher time finding a job than did white veterans. White veterans also had a higher unemployment rate than nonveteran whites, 12.7 percent to 7.4 percent. Black veterans had a 10.5 percent jobless rate, contrasted to a faintly higher rate of 11.3 percent for black nonveterans. White veterans had a low 5.5 percent rate, compared to 5.0 percent for whites who had never served. When one looked at the cumulative numbers for all black veterans between the ages of 20 and 34, the 15.9 percent unemployment rate was only slightly higher than the 15.2 percent rate for nonveterans, but it still lagged far behind the 5.7 percent average for whites, veteran or not.

The issues and problems facing black veterans were known nationally. Part of the dilemma, as usual, was racism. Those with a social conscious were outraged at the treatment accorded black veterans. "I am a white man," wrote William E. McFee, "and I am shocked by the shabby treatment our Negro servicemen are receiving when they return from Vietnam. . . . They seek reasonably respectable jobs in vain." The passionate McFee did not mince words and believed that "there is something damnably wrong in a 'free society' that would permit such unconscionable discrimination and I protest it. It is a disgrace to our country and all we are supposed to stand for."[30] Others talked in alarmist terms, hoping to alert the nation to the possible dangers of ignoring the issue. Journalist Wallace Terry predicted that if we did not "act rapidly and fundamentally on this terrible issue spinning out of Vietnam," meaning what he termed "revolutionary warfare," then "we are in for increments of trouble on the streets of American cities. A new elite of impatient, war-hardened youths is coming home prepared to provide shock troops in a battle for real equal rights—if these are not otherwise accorded."[31] There was an urgent call for action by contemporary observers. "A troublesome question stemming from Vietnam is what to do about Negro GI's returning home," wrote C. L. Sulzberger in the *New York Times* in May 1969. "There must be a national effort to integrate them into an equal society so that each community welcomes that black soldier who went far away and got shot at for his country."[32] The national effort Sulzberger wrote about never materialized.

LESS THAN HONORABLE DISCHARGES

Some veterans found that their search for a decent job was complicated by a less than honorable discharge. The undesirable discharge was the most widely used of the three less than honorable discharges. Early in the war, they made up a relatively small portion of the discharges from military service. In 1965, the Pentagon issued 13,178 undesirable discharges, accounting for only 1.8 percent of the total. As the war progressed, the percentage of undesirable discharges steadily rose. By 1971, there were 29,139 undesirable discharges handed down out of a total of 1,018,822, or 2.9 percent of all discharges that year. In 1973, the last full year of the war, they accounted for 4.1 percent of the total. The number was more than double the 1965 figure, but much of the rise can be explained by the fact that an increasing number of young men were using it as a way to get out of the armed forces, by going to their commanding officers and "confessing" that they were gay, or mentally or emotionally unstable, or anything that was likely to get them booted out of the military. There was an increase to 187 dishonorable discharges the following year, but that was out of a total of 1,016,470 service separations. The last years of the war did see somewhat of an increase. Out of 804,470 enlisted men discharged in 1972, 356 received theirs under dishonorable conditions—not all that many, but still twice the number from three years earlier. Still, despite the controversial nature of the draft and the Vietnam War, there were still relatively few of them. Between 1965 and 1974, there were only 2,218 dishonorable discharges handed down out of more than eight million discharges issued.

The problem was that discharge papers, or Defense Department Form 214, had a separation program number (SPN) on them, detailing the exact nature and type of discharge: an honorable, for example, carried a different SPN than a general or punitive discharge. Theoretically, they were confidential, but many potential employers knew the code numbers for an honorable discharge and would only hire veterans that had one. Most, however, did not know the code for the other types, including those granted under general but honorable conditions, so many employers, including government agencies, lumped them in with the others and mistakenly thought they were all so-called bad paper, or less than honorable discharges. Failing to secure employment, many vets with bad paper discharges turned to crime. Thirty-two percent of the nation's federal prisoners were veterans, according to a 1973 Federal Bureau of Prisons report, and nearly 57 percent of them had received less than honorable discharges. A Veterans Affairs study of 44,000 inmates at 325 major state and federal prisons reached similar conclusions. They found that veterans in general accounted for 25 percent of the total prison population.

Some veterans brought their problems home with them in the form of drug dependencies developed while in the armed forces. Jackie Robinson Jr., the son of the hall of fame baseball player, is a classic example. At age 17, Robinson Jr. quit high school during his junior year and enlisted in the army to "find himself and learn discipline." The younger Robinson spent three years in the military, which included a tour of duty in Vietnam, where he was wounded by shrapnel and awarded a Purple Heart. He also picked up an addiction to heroin, which, like many veterans, he would bring back home with him to civilian life. In 1968, just nine months after he had been honorably discharged from the army, the 21-year-old veteran was arrested by police in Stamford, Connecticut, who found several glassine bags thought to contain heroin, a tobacco pouch of pot, and an Italian .22 caliber handgun in his possession. His father posted $5,000 bail to get him out of jail.[33]

The federal government provided some help to returning veterans. The GI Bill provided monetary help to veterans wishing to attend college or a trade school, to finance a house at affordable rates, or to start up a small business. The benefits were open to all veterans with a discharge under honorable conditions, but the allowances were modest. Single veterans wishing to attend college, for example, were eligible for $130 a month in support, and married veterans received $160 a month. Veterans in need of medical or psychological care could go to a Veterans Affairs (VA) hospital for treatment, but the hospitals, especially in the years following the war, were usually underfunded and understaffed, limiting the quality of care available. Veterans living in rural areas often had no facilities nearby.

AGENT ORANGE

There was one problem, however, the military would not even initially admit to, let alone treat: the effects of a powerful herbicide used in Vietnam named Agent Orange. Agent Orange derived its name from the 55-gallon orange striped barrels it came in and was one of several defoliants used by the U.S. government in Vietnam in an attempt to strip away the forest cover the Vietcong and North Vietnamese used so effectively. The main ingredient in it was phenoxyacetic acid, which kills broad leaf foliage. Phenoxyacetic acid by itself is poisonous, but Agent Orange was also contaminated with dioxins, some of the most toxic chemicals used.

The use of Agent Orange in Vietnam predated the arrival of American combat troops. It and other defoliants were first tested in Vietnam beginning in January 1962, and that year, the U.S. government dumped 15,000 gallons of various herbicides on South Vietnamese jungles, followed by another 59,000 gallons in 1963. Testing ended in 1964 when Agent Orange was selected as the primary defoliant for a massive program known as Project Ranch Hand. That year, 175,000 gallons of herbicides were used on South Vietnam, and another 621,000 gallons were used in 1965. In 1966, over 621,000 gallons were used, mostly in Vietnam, but also in Laos and Thailand. Use of Agent Orange peaked in 1967–1968 and began to level off after that, though the military introduced a newer and deadlier version known as Agent Orange II. The government curtailed use of the herbicide in Vietnam in 1971 amid safety concerns and the high levels of dioxin in men who had been exposed to the defoliant. By then, roughly 20 million gallons of herbicides had been sprayed in South Vietnam, Laos, and Thailand, with Agent Orange accounting for approximately 55 percent of the total. In all, about six million acres of forest were sprayed in Vietnam.

Modified U.S. Air Force C-123K Provider aircraft, carrying 1,000 gallons of herbicide, were the primary method for delivering Agent Orange, though it was also sprayed from helicopters and from trucks or hand sprayed by personnel on the ground. It was mixed with either kerosene or diesel fuel but was applied more heavily and not diluted to the standards set for civilian use back in the United States. The defoliant was dangerous to the men who handled it, but many military personnel were exposed to Agent Orange without realizing it. Spraying often occurred around active operations, with the herbicide settling down as a fine white mist around the troops and contaminating their food and drinking water. Marine Danny Gene Jordan and his unit were doused with Agent Orange sprayed from five C-123s while occupying Hill 549 near Khe Sahn in 1968. The men, their food, and their equipment were literally soaked with the defoliant. Troops did not even have to be near a spraying area to contact the defoliants. Even when sprayed from relatively low altitudes, the poisonous mist could drift upward of six miles, contaminating individuals without them knowing it. Another source of contamination came from the reuse by troops of the orange barrels the defoliant was shipped in. Soldiers in Vietnam used the empty Agent Orange drums for a variety of tasks, including as storage containers for food, as water containers for showers, or even as makeshift barbecue pits. The drums were also used for gasoline and diesel fuel, creating yet another hazard. When the Agent Orange residue in the barrels mixed with the fuel and burned in internal combustion engines, it produced a highly toxic orange aerosol, which killed vegetation along the roads and exposed countless individuals to a more concentrated toxin.

The men involved in Project Ranch Hand displayed a sense of humor concerning their mission. In obvious parody of the Forest Service slogan, a sign over the door of the ready room for Ranch Hand pilots at Tan Son Nhut Airport read "Only You Can Prevent Forests." There was nothing funny, however, about the effects of exposure to the defoliant; it was poisonous, with both immediate and long-term effects. The marines on Hill 549, for example, suffered from nausea and diarrhea for two weeks after their exposure. The worst effects of the herbicide began to show up months and years after the men had returned from Vietnam. Like many men exposed to Agent Orange, Jordan came home from Vietnam with dangerous amounts of dioxin in his system. It was still more than 50 parts per trillion 15 years later, and two of his sons were born with deformed arms and hands. Other victims suffered a wide range of ailments from depression, loss of sex drive, joint pain, non-Hodgkin's lymphoma, Hodgkin's disease, chronic lymphocytic leukemia, and soft-tissue sarcoma.

The U.S. government, the Pentagon, and the manufacturers of Agent Orange all initially denied that the ailments suffered by Vietnam veterans were a result of exposure to the herbicides. Beginning in the mid-1980s, and spurred by the efforts of Admiral Elmo

Zumwalt, whose own son was a victim of Agent Orange, the Department of Defense began accepting some liability for Agent Orange–induced illnesses and allowed treatment at VA hospitals. In 1984, Congress passed Public Law 98-542, providing compensation for soft-tissue sarcoma and requiring Veterans Affairs to establish standards for compensating and aiding Agent Orange victims.

Military personnel are prohibited by law from suing the U.S. government for injuries that occurred during military service, but veterans who became ill from exposure to Agent Orange brought suit in 1978 against the principal makers of Agent Orange. After a long battle, the companies agreed to settle out of court for $180 million. A major class-action suit against the manufacturers of Agent Orange was settled out of court in 1994 when the manufacturers agreed to create a compensation fund for military veterans and their families. That settlement, however, covered only those who became sick before the settlement, but in 2003, the Supreme Court ruled that veterans who became ill after 1994 can still sue the herbicide's manufacturers. In all, approximately 250,000 Vietnam veterans have filed claims against the manufacturers of Agent Orange.

VETERANS ORGANIZATIONS AND THE VIETNAM VET

Vietnam veterans faced many of the same problems encountered by soldiers from previous conflicts, but this did not necessarily translate into solidarity and support, and Vietnam vets of all races found little sympathy or help from veterans of previous wars. Vietnam veterans in general, but black veterans in particular, were unwelcome and not wanted by many veterans organizations and chapters. There was the stigma of losing a war, but older World War II era veterans, who dominated the organizations, had served in a segregated military and wanted to keep their posts and chapters segregated. Some groups had official restrictions in their charters against integration until the mid-1960s. Allen Thomas Jr., for example, was initially rejected by an all-white American Legion post near his neighborhood and advised by its commandant to seek out an all-black post in northern Kentucky. In 1986, Bill O'Neill and a group of Vietnam veterans were asked to leave an American Legion post in Newport News, Virginia, because of the loser stigma and because of race. "We were disinvited by one individual who took it upon himself to show us the door because we had blacks in our group.... Korea and Vietnam vets—they're more familiar with integration. They served in the same units together. But these older guys—segregation was part of their lifestyle. It was part of the military that they knew." African American George C. Duggins and other Vietnam veterans in the mid-1980s were "relegated to the basement" of a Veterans of Foreign Wars chapter in Norfolk, Virginia. They met "without incident" until a World War II veteran found out that many of the Vietnam vets were black, leading to a clash between the two groups.[34] Ultimately, the result of such hostile treatment was to turn Vietnam veterans away from such traditional groups as the American Legion and Veterans of Foreign Wars, at least initially, and to create their own organization, the Vietnam Veterans of America.

STATESIDE ASSIGNMENT

Many veterans still had a military obligation or chose to stay in the armed forces after serving in Vietnam. Returning veterans who still had time left in the military received a 30-day leave after returning home from Vietnam before moving on to their next assignments. Those with only a few months left in the military, however, were often given nothing substantial to do. Baltazar was sent to Fort Hood, which was a return base for returnees from Vietnam that had only a few months to go in their enlistments. Basically, there was nothing for them to do but mark time and play a little ball.

With some exceptions, military personnel returning from Vietnam would be given stateside assignments. Some knew what their next assignment would be even before leaving Vietnam. Major James C. Warren flew 117 combat missions in Vietnam out of Tan Son Nhut Air Base, logging a total of 8,000 hours of flying time in his career, including 1,000 hours of that in combat over three wars. Warren's tour of duty was almost up, and he was already looking forward to "getting back to the world" soon and starting his next assignment, flying C-141s out of Travis Air Force Base in California.[35] Many, like John Ballweg, enjoyed their post-Vietnam assignments. He remained another 15 months in the army after serving in Vietnam. He was assigned to be a helicopter instructor at Fort Walters, Texas, and enjoyed the assignment so much that he spent another year there as a civilian instructor after leaving the army. He had it easy and only worked about five hours a day.

Some received assignments that made them almost regret coming back to the United States. After his first tour in Vietnam in 1968–1969, Albert Childs was operations sergeant for the ROTC program at the University of Delaware. It was not a good assignment. The Weathermen and Students for a Democratic Society were active on campus, and protestors picketed the ROTC building and harassed the staff. The ROTC staff did not wear their uniforms on campus for fear of being attacked. "Well then, in May of '72 I left there and went back to Vietnam, and I was glad to go back to Vietnam because I knew what to expect there."[36]

THE COLLAPSE OF MORALE IN THE ARMED FORCES

Despite the fact that it might easily entail another tour in Vietnam, many men chose to remain in the armed forces. For minorities and poor and working-class whites, a career in the military offered opportunities largely unavailable in the civilian world. And like Albert Childs, many would stay in the military in preference to the chaos and hostility plaguing the United States. But much like American society in the late 1960s and early 1970s, the military would be racked with dissent, violence, and a breakdown in morale and discipline. Many of the problems afflicting the military in this era were products of civilian society, and some were caused by Vietnam, but many problems were caused by the Pentagon's own policies and procedures in response to these new challenges.

Morale was generally high throughout the armed forces, and units generally displayed high effectiveness and cohesion, during the first half of the Vietnam War. Beginning in 1968, however, morale, cohesion, and discipline throughout the U.S. military establishment began to deteriorate, and as the 1970s dawned, the military faced an internal crisis.

There were many reasons for the near-collapse of the armed forces during the later stages of Vietnam, but the most important cause was the war itself. After the 1968 Tet Offensive and President Johnson's subsequent announcement on national TV that he would seek a negotiated peace in Vietnam, few people thought victory in Vietnam was achievable. Survival, not victory, became the main goal for the average soldier or marine. David Hackworth, who commanded a battalion in Vietnam in 1969, observed that "by then, few grunts believed the war was winnable. Their main concern was staying out of body bags."[37] Morale was further undercut by the belief that the grunts were not allowed to properly fight the war because of the numerous limitations imposed on combat operations by both the White House and the Pentagon. Many felt used and abandoned by the nation they had taken an oath to protect. Many soldiers chalked *UUUU* on their helmet covers, which was shorthand for "the unwilling, led by the unqualified, doing the unnecessary for the ungrateful."[38]

Some of the military's own polices worked against them and helped undermine morale. Perhaps the most important would be the one-year rotation policy. Despite the good intentions behind it, once the war was perceived as a lost cause by many of its participants, surviving their 12- or 13-month tours of duty, and not unit cohesion and efficiency, became the utmost priority for many in Vietnam. The rotation of troops in and out of a unit individually also took its toll on unit cohesion. Men that train and serve together know and trust each other and are often skeptical at first about new members to the team. Morale was still high in Gonzalo Baltazar's unit in 1969, for example. "It was pretty good morale because when you train together for eight months you all become pretty good friends. We all knew each other pretty well and we felt a very good trust in each other and we knew who was going to watch your back and who wasn't going to watch your back."[39]

The rotation policy also led to inexperienced leadership in many units. To ensure that officers maximized their experiences in both combat and noncombat situations, officers generally served only six months with a combat unit and six months in an administrative or service assignment during their tours of duty in Vietnam. By the time many of them learned enough to prove capable leaders, they were transferred out and replaced, usually by an inexperienced replacement.

Careerism also impacted the quality of leadership in Vietnam. The fight to move up and win promotions was fierce, and there were a lot of competitors for a very few slots, and the number of available promotions diminished as the war wound down. There were 35,466 second lieutenants in the army in 1968, for example, but only 13,666 three years later. There were a total of 166,173 officers in the army at the time of Tet-68, but only 148,623 in 1971. To eliminate some of the glut, the Defense Department initiated a so-called up or out policy; if you were not worthy of promotion to the next rank, you were basically forced out of the military.

The epitome of success for a career officer is to win promotion to general in the army, air force, or marines, or admiral in the navy. Earning a general's or admiral's star took a combination of skill, luck, politicking, and sheer seniority. It took at least 25 years on average for a newly commissioned officer to make the rank of brigadier general in the army, air force, and marines or rear admiral in the navy. Few would actually make it. In 1967, out of over 4,200 eligible colonels in the army, only 23 were promoted to brigadier general. In 1971, only 49 captains out of over 2,000 eligible for promotion in the navy earned a rear admiral's star.

Serving in combat, or getting your ticket punched, helped facilitate more rapid promotion. Consequently, many of the new officers, especially new junior officers out to prove themselves, were dedicated and enthusiastic, and many were brave to the point of being foolhardy. The attrition rate could be very high. Baltazar's platoon "went through several lieutenants, some got killed, some got wounded, and some couldn't handle it." After the capable and respected Lieutenant Charles Burke left, "we kept going through different platoon leaders because we kept losing them" or because they were so "gung ho they got us in trouble." When taking fire from a certain area, these gung ho young officers wanted to charge in without knowing what was ahead. "Some of these guys were just a little crazy for us." They "didn't care who got killed or anything.... We'd lose those lieutenants."[40]

There were, of course, numerous fine officers during the Vietnam War. Baltazar considered his first platoon commander, Lieutenant Burke, to be the best one he knew in Vietnam. A pilot by training, Burke was "pretty level headed. He kept his cool all the time."[41] John Ballweg assessed leadership at the company and battalion levels as "in general, quite good. Of course, this was their first taste of combat also. But in general we had good leaders.... They did a good job."[42] As a battalion commander in Vietnam, Arthur Gregg had a strong chain of command he could trust. "I had the rare combination of very young officers and mature noncommissioned officers and the combination of the two really made a great battalion." Three of his captains, Chris Crotty, Howard Daniels, and Erv Zouzalik, in particular, were "conspicuously outstanding." Both Daniels and Zouzalik later made full colonel.[43]

Some critics, however, blame poor leadership during the Vietnam War for many of the problems that beset the armed forces. Many of the officers were just incompetent. The rapid expansion of the military and the officer corps to meet both the demands of war and the United State's normal peacetime missions entailed commissioning officers, such as a Lieutenant William Calley, they would not have accepted before Vietnam. More important, there was an undue emphasis on careerism over more traditional military values. Paul L. Savage and Richard R. Gabriel, for example, argued that the traditional warrior ethos of the officer, with its emphasis on honor, was replaced by a managerial model, with an emphasis on efficiency. Others cite the large number of officers. In World War II, for example, officers made up around 5.44 percent of total army strength. In the German army, officers were only 2.86 percent of the total. By the Korean War, officers made up 9 percent of total army strength. In Vietnam, however, officers comprised 15 percent of total army strength. Most were on the larger base camps and generally safe from the enemy. Savage and Gabriel believed that large numbers of relatively high ranking officers at the base camps, enjoying "conspicuously greater privileges and immunity from harm...more so than in any previous war," seriously hurt morale.[44] In fact, they went on to state that "bad leadership seems intimately associated with disintegration: a high desertion rate might be explainable, even a mutiny or two, but when desertions, fragging, mutiny, and drug addiction come together in staggering proportions in a short four or five years, oversimplified references to permissive societies and national 'fragmentation' because of unpopular wars will not suffice as credible explanations."[45] It was a moral as well as a professional failure. Savage and Gabriel claimed that even though most senior military officials knew that our South Vietnamese allies controlled the heroin rackets providing the drug to American servicemen, not a single senior officer protested or resigned in protest over it.[46]

SUBSTANCE ABUSE AND THE MILITARY ESTABLISHMENT

Substance abuse was yet another factor tearing the military apart from the inside. Southeast Asia was a drug user's paradise, with everything from marijuana to cheap heroin plentiful. "Oh, there were a lot of drugs up there," recalled Gonzalo Baltazar. "I seen bags and bags of marijuana that the Vietnamese civilians would sell to the Americans."[47] Early on, drug use was not an issue. Gerald Kumpf said that at Danang, in 1965 and 1966, marijuana was not a problem at that time. "I don't recall anybody ever smoking grass." The unit did have two kids who did heroin, but Kumpf claims that both of them were native New Yorkers and had done the drug before entering the Marine Corps.[48] Likewise, John Ballweg never saw drugs during his August 1966–1967 tour, and alcohol was not yet a problem.[49]

Even later in the war, drugs were not a problem in many units, though recreational users could be found everywhere. Just a few men in Baltazar's platoon smoked pot. He had heard that some men in maintenance and in a machine gun unit used heroin, but no one in his unit did. At that time, there was no real attempt by the chain of command to stop it, and the army never talked to them about it. Marijuana was not the problem in his unit, alcohol was.[50] Even as late as 1972, drugs were not a problem in Albert Childs's unit in Pleiku because "we were all older guys anyway, so drugs were not our thing. Alcohol, well, we'll talk about that."[51]

Like so many other problems affecting the armed forces, the problem with drugs began to escalate after 1968. John Steinbeck IV, son of the famous writer, estimated that three-fourths of the men in Vietnam smoked marijuana during his tour of duty in 1968. "Most young soldiers smoke it, for all sorts of reasons, all the time," he explained. A Defense Department spokesperson disagreed and publicly called Steinbeck's allegations "a gross exaggeration," but he still admitted that marijuana use had "increased" in the military since 1965.[52]

Actual drug use in Vietnam was widespread and hard to estimate, but drug investigations in Vietnam increased from 5,774 in 1969 to 6,432 in 1970.[53] One military official estimated that 10–15 percent of the low-ranking enlisted men used heroin. Pot and heroin use crossed racial lines and led to fraternization between so-called heads of both races.[54] In the later stages of the war, probably around half to two-thirds of the enlisted men in Vietnam used marijuana, and 5–10 percent were, at least, casual users of heroin.[55] One army study estimated that as many as 28.5 percent of the troops had used heroin.[56] Drugs were also big business in Vietnam. At Cam Ranh Bay, 43 members of the base security detachment were caught and arrested in a narcotics sting on base, and in 1970, an air force major and pilot was caught trying to smuggle $8 million worth of heroin out of Vietnam in his aircraft. He was apprehended at Tan Son Nhut Air Base.

The drug problem was not confined to the troops in Vietnam, but was widespread throughout the military establishment. In the United States, drugs were cheap and easy to find. For example, over 1,400 out of 36,000, or roughly 4 percent of the soldiers stationed at Fort Bragg, North Carolina, the army's third largest base, admitted using hard drugs, mostly LSD or heroin. In 1971, a copyrighted article in the *Annapolis Capitol* claimed that upward of 1,000 midshipmen at the Naval Academy used marijuana. Eight midshipmen were busted for dealing drugs at the academy, and midshipmen admitted confidentially that pot was easy to find at the academy. Drug use flourished in the navy as much as it did in the jungles of Vietnam. In 1966, the navy discharged 166 seamen on drug-related charges. Three years later, in 1969, the number had swelled to 3,800 sailors discharged on drug-related charges, and in 1970, over 5,000 seamen were kicked out of the navy for illegal drug use. That same year, the army conducted 17,742 drug investigations, and the air force 2,715.

The problem was just as bad among the troops stationed in Europe. Colonel Thomas B. Hauschild of the U.S. Army European Command estimated that 46 percent of the 200,000 American military personnel stationed in Europe had used illegal drugs at least once in the last year. A survey of one battalion stationed in Germany found that half of the soldiers smoked pot regularly, and half of them had also used hard drugs recently.

Throughout the military establishment, the typical drug abuser tended to be white, young, and enlisted, though army investigators concluded that drug use was slightly higher among African Americans than whites in general and, interestingly, higher among technicians than combat or service troops.[57] Officers were also occasionally involved. In 1971, for example, an air force colonel was busted, court-martialled, and kicked out of the service for having pot parties with his troops.

DESERTION AND GOING AWOL

Another problem that plagued the entire U.S. military establishment was desertion and soldiers who were AWOL. The difference between the two was actually minimal. Military personnel who were late for reporting to duty or failed to show up for several days were considered AWOL, whereas desertion is defined by the U.S. armed forces as being absent for 30 days or more without authorization, usually with the intent of never returning to duty. Desertions occur in every war, and the desertion rate in the early stages of Vietnam was similar to desertion rates in both World War II and Korea. The peak desertion rate of 63 men per 1,000 in 1945 for World War II was not reached in Vietnam until 1971, and until that year, the desertion rate for the Vietnam War was actually lower than for the Korean conflict. Beginning in 1968, however, the desertion rate began to climb. From 1968 to 1971, there was a 20 percent increase in the navy and a 60 percent increase in the army of desertion rates. The Marine Corps had a slightly higher incidence of desertion, and the air force the lowest, but overall, the armed forces were losing substantial numbers of men. In 1970, for example, 65,643 men deserted from the U.S. Army, which is the equivalent of four infantry divisions. In 1971, there were 98,324 incidents of desertion, or a rate of 142.2 per 1,000 troops. According to the Department of Defense, there were a total of 503,926 desertions from the U.S. military between July 1, 1966, and December 31, 1973.

Like many aspects of Vietnam, there are a lot of misconceptions regarding desertion during the war. The data indicate that whatever reasons led to an increase in desertion rates, increased combat losses were not among them; the desertion rate rose even as combat fatalities in the war declined. Even assignment to Vietnam was not a major cause of desertion. The vast majority of deserters went AWOL from duty assignments in the United States, and men were more likely to desert after a tour of duty in Vietnam, and not before. Terry Whitmore, who cited both racism and opposition to the war as his reasons for deserting, was typical in deserting after he had been to Vietnam. In fact, only about 3 percent of army deserters did so while still in country. There were practical reasons involved in that there were few places in Vietnam where a deserter could go to hide. Aside from places like Soul Alley in Saigon, and a maybe a handful of the other bigger cities, the only other real option was not a particularly attractive one to most deserters: defect to the Vietcong and live with them out in the bush—only a few did.

Some deserters undoubtedly did leave the military for political or philosophical reasons, and many African Americans cited racism as their primary reason for desertion. Don Williams, cochairman of the Afro-American Deserters Committee in Stockholm, Sweden, in 1968, said that his "main reason—and I cannot stress this enough—for my own defection is the injustices committed against my people in the U.S." An African American living in Paris, France, who wanted to be identified only as "Frenchie" claimed in the *Black Panther* that "blacks in the army have more reason to leave than whites" and cited racism as his reason for deserting his unit in West Germany. Many cited both racism and their opposition to the war in Vietnam as the reasons they deserted. Ray Jones, a 21-year-old private from Pontiac, Michigan, the first American soldier to desert the armed forces and seek asylum in Sweden, claimed that he left to protest racial discrimination and the war in Vietnam. Opposition to the war was also cited by many deserters, leading some, like Kenneth Dupre, who was a member of the militant American Serviceman's Union (ASU), to go AWOL, rather than serve in Vietnam.

Despite Whitmore and other deserters who claimed racism or opposition to the war as their main reasons, few men actually deserted for political reasons. The estimates vary, but all of them are relatively low. William Westmoreland cites a figure of 10 percent, and 14 percent of those later interviewed during the Ford amnesty program claimed that they deserted for political reasons. The vast majority of deserters, as in previous conflicts, did so for purely personal reasons. In fact, the profile of the average deserter was the same regardless of race, and their reasons did not differ significantly from deserters in previous wars. Most of them had voluntarily enlisted and were not reluctant draftees. They were 19 or younger when they had enlisted and were likely to have less than a high school education. Most had a history of disciplinary problems and repeated clashes with the chain of command before they went AWOL. It was more likely a failing marriage, inability to adjust to the discipline of military life, or a run in with a sergeant or commanding officer that led them to desert.

The vast majority of deserters remained in the United States, and only around 2,400 deserters sought refuge in a foreign country, primarily Canada, Mexico, and Sweden, which willingly accepted and aided deserters, setting them up in living quarters and helping them find employment. But many of them would have second thoughts, especially if they had deserted for ideological or political reasons, and about 600 would voluntarily return to U.S. custody. Ray Jones, for example, had made a new life for himself in Stockholm, with his German-born wife, Gabrielle, and their three-month-old son, and he was employed teaching jazz ballet at a dance studio. He was happy in Sweden, but he also believed that he had an obligation to speak out against the war and racism in the armed forces. "I was free in Sweden. . . . I had a wonderful life there," he explained, "but it would have been the biggest mistake of my life if I had stayed. I went voluntarily and came back the same way." Despite facing a 10-year prison sentence for desertion, Jones decided to return, and in the spring of 1968, and accompanied by his wife and son, he surrendered himself to U.S. military authorities in Frankfurt, West Germany.[58]

DISCONTENT AND THE RISE OF BLACK MILITANCY

One of the most important issues affecting morale and discipline in the armed forces in the later stages of the Vietnam War was the rise of black militancy in the ranks. Many African Americans like Colin Powell or Allen Thomas Jr. still believed that the armed forces offered the best chance for advancement for African Americans and appreciated the opportunities a career in the military afforded them. But thousands of younger blacks entering the armed services beginning in the mid-1960s were convinced that the military was just as racist as the rest of American society. The civil rights movement had been successful in eliminating many of the evils of Jim Crow, most notably with the passage of the Civil Rights Act of 1964 and the Voting Rights Act of 1965. But there was still much to be done; institutional racism may have been dealt a death blow, but individual racism was still a potent factor, and much of black America lived in poverty. The movement had raised hopes and expectations and galvanized African Americans to crusade for justice, but obviously, it could not cure all the ills facing African Americans, leaving many blacks, particularly younger African Americans, disillusioned and angry. Once inducted into the armed forces, they felt isolated and oppressed in an institution dominated by whites and believed that they were being used as cannon fodder in Vietnam.

To their credit, the various armed services, after initially defying President Harry Truman's 1948 Executive Order 9981 mandating equal opportunity regardless of race, embraced integration and equal opportunity, thus becoming a model for civilian society to emulate. By 1968, the Department of Defense would even boast that institutional racism had been totally eliminated from the armed forces. But the concerns of African Americans about the persistence of both institutional and personal racism in the military were well founded. In many areas, such as testing and placement, promotion, and military justice, vestiges of institutional racism remained.

INEQUITIES IN THE MILITARY JUSTICE SYSTEM

African Americans were very concerned about inequities in the military justice system. Justice is administered in the armed forces on two distinct levels. The first and less serious of the two is known as nonjudicial punishment. Nonjudicial punishment, also known as an Article 15 in the army and air force and as a captain's mast in the navy and marines, has no real civilian equivalent. An Article 15 is generally given for minor offenses, such as reporting late to a duty station or a uniform code violation. Any officer or NCO can write up an individual for nonjudicial punishment, but the case is heard by the accused offender's commanding officer, who also is the dispensary of any punishment or reprimand handed down. The accused is allowed to bring a representative with him to the hearing to speak on his behalf, if he so chooses, but this individual is generally a junior officer and not a lawyer. The commanding officer's decision is final, and there is no appeal. Most military personnel believe that it is useless to fight the system and usually accept punishment.

Punishment of an offence was at the discretion of the commanding officer and could entail only a written reprimand in one's official record or, at worst, 30 days' correctional custody in the stockade, or 45 days of extra duty, or 60 days' restriction and forfeiture of one-half a month's pay for two months. In addition, E-4s or below could be reduced to the lowest enlisted grade, E-1, and an E-5 or above could be demoted one grade. Gonzalo Baltazar, for example, was given an Article 15 in 1969 for putting two MPs in the hospital following a fight at the EM club at Fort Hood. His 30-day leave before going to Vietnam was reduced to only 9 days, and instead of taking the ship over, he ended up going to Vietnam on one of the airliners—under escort.[59]

Blacks were convinced that the system was being abused by racists and that a double standard existed in the administration of nonjudicial punishment. An NAACP investigation into the administration of military justice in the European command found that black soldiers were "convinced that white soldiers are not punished for behavior which, on the part of a black, would bring an Article 15 action. Whites, they said, were not dealt with for wearing long hair while blacks were punished for long hair. There seemed to be two sets of rules: one for whites and the other for blacks."[60] Statistics seem to support the charge. African Americans comprised only 27.5 percent of the 193rd Infantry Brigade stationed in West Germany in 1970–1971, for example, but received 39 percent of the Article 15s in that unit, numbers that were typical for other units stationed in Europe.[61]

Personal accounts also indicate that white racists abused the justice system. Major Michael F. Colacicco had to relieve one of his platoon sergeants in Vietnam in 1971 for targeting black soldiers for Article 15s. "I started to get a string of people coming before me for Article 15's for failure to make work call formations....They were all black. Of course, in conducting the Article 15 investigations, I found out it was because the platoon sergeant was going through and waking up white soldiers and not waking up the black soldiers. He would pick on...particular people he didn't like, who all happened to be black."[62]

African Americans claimed that they were written up for Article 15s for minor infractions, whereas whites were usually not. One black enlisted man testified before Congress that he was given nonjudicial punishment of 14 days restriction and 14 days extra duty for wearing a slave bracelet, for example. African Americans were singled out by racist supervisors for Article 15s, but the discretionary authority given officers and NCOs in the dispensation of nonjudicial punishment meant that many whites were also written up for extremely petty infractions as well. Because of an extremely busy flight schedule, Gerald Kumpf had not gotten a haircut in three weeks, and his hair was longer than regulation. He was ordered by one officer to get a haircut by a certain time, and then given other duties by yet another officer that kept him from getting the required haircut. In retaliation, the first officer had a so-called junk on the bunk inspection for Kumpf, where he had to put all of his personal articles out on his bunk for inspection. The officer found an ink pen marked U.S. government in his locker, threatened to court-martial him, but gave him an Article 15 instead for possessing unauthorized government property, busting him one full rank, among other penalties. Luckily for Kumpf, he had his rank restored six or seven months later when the officer in question was given a Section Eight, or psychological discharge, from the marines.[63]

The number of Article 15s varied from unit to unit and depending on circumstances. Commanding officers often used nonjudicial punishment to restore discipline. In October 1969, Thomas Peoples assumed command of an ordnance company at Cam Rahn Bay composed largely of black soldiers who had just been released from Long Binh Stockade and was forced to make use of the justice system to restore order and efficiency to the company. Peoples presided over 54 Article 15 hearings and four courts-martial but had "very little discipline problems" afterward.[64] Some units were already well disciplined and had few problems. Arthur Gregg had few discipline problems in the 96th Quartermaster Battalion in Vietnam in 1966–1967. He could recall only one field grade Article 15 and one court-martial during his year in command.[65] Some units reported fewer cases of nonjudicial punishment because discipline and punishment were often handed out informally and physically. In many units, the platoon sergeant simply took the miscreant behind the barracks and beat him. Ironically, many men actually preferred such informal punishment to official methods of discipline because it kept the offense out of their service records, which could cost them their rank or hurt their chance for promotion.[66]

Racism was certainly a factor in the number of Article 15s handed down, but there were other factors at work as well, such as drug abuse, and the number of Article 15s given out by the army correspondingly rose as discipline broke down. In 1967, there were 46,392 cases of nonjudicial punishment in Vietnam, rising to 59,178 in 1968, and another 66,702 in 1969. This can partially be explained by the rise in troop levels in 1968, but the number of nonjudicial punishments adjudicated remained high in 1970, at 64,534, and another 41,237 in 1971 when American units were disengaging from Vietnam under

Vietnamization. Interestingly, the number of courts-martial held in Vietnam during the war generally rose and fell with the number of troops stationed in country. In 1965, there were only a total of 814 general, summary, or special courts-martial in Vietnam. At the height of American involvement in 1968, there were 9,219 courts-martial held, and 9,922 in 1969. Afterward, the number began to decline along with American troop levels. There were 5,861 in 1970, 4,462 in 1971, and only 1,072 in 1972.

Except during combat, or if a ship was out at sea, an enlisted person did have the right to request a court-martial instead of an Article 15 or captain's mast. Most did not do so because the punishment could be far more severe than an Article 15 if found guilty at a court-martial. A court-martial is similar to a civilian trial in many respects. The accused has the right to an attorney, and there is a jury, but it was not necessarily composed of the defendant's peers. Most juries and all court-martial boards were composed of officers. There were other key differences as well. The defendant could be held in a military stockade for up to 30 days without being charged, had no right to bail, and, under normal circumstances, could not appeal the outcome of a court-martial.

Most courts-martial were for relatively serious offenses, such as murder, theft, or rape, or violation of the Articles of War, such as looting or deserting in the face of the enemy. For those convicted at court-martial, the penalties could be fairly severe, including reduction to the lowest rank, forfeiture of all pay, years in prison, often at hard labor, and, in the case of rape, murder, treason, mutiny, or "misbehavior before the enemy," which is defined as cowardice or desertion in the face of the enemy, willfully casting away arms or ammunition to avoid combat and quitting "his place of duty to plunder or pillage," under Article 99 of the Uniform Code of Military Justice, the death penalty could be imposed.[67]

Military prisoners convicted of the equivalent of civilian felonies, such as rape or murder, made up only a small percentage of those incarcerated for crime. Seventy-five percent of all military prisoners were in prison for military offenses, being AWOL or insubordination, for example. Behavior that was considered militant and subversive often brought unduly long prison sentences. Nation of Islam members Lance Corporal William Harvey Jr. and Private First Class George Daniels of the Marine Corps were sentenced to 6 and 10 years, respectively, at hard labor by courts-martial in 1969. Daniels was convicted of violating the 1940 Smith Act, originally passed to suppress Nazis in the United States, which made it a felony to "cause insubordination, disloyalty, mutiny or refusal of duty," and his compatriot for violating similar provisions of the Uniform Code of Military Justice.

SERVING TIME IN A MILITARY STOCKADE

Defendants sentenced to prison served their time at one of the military stockades such as Leavenworth or Mannheim Stockade, the largest U.S. military prison in West Germany. Conditions in these stockades were often very brutal and were as bad or worse than some of the more notorious civilian prisons. *Time* magazine in 1971 characterized Mannheim Stockade as "almost a carbon copy of the worst civilian prison facilities in the U.S.," where "few if any prisoners...are rehabilitated."[68] Overcrowding was a typical problem; at the stockade known as LBJ in Vietnam, in 1968, there were nearly 740 inmates jammed into a facility originally designed to hold only 500 prisoners. Often the cells seemed like something out of the Dark Ages. The cement block maximum-security cells at Da Nang Brig were cold and dungeon-like, measuring only seven by seven feet. The bad living conditions were sometimes accompanied by brutal and sadistic treatment by the guards. Marine guards were accused of hog-tying and beating difficult inmates at the Camp Pendleton, California, brig, and inmates at the Quantico brig across the country in Virginia rioted over the cruel treatment inflicted on them by marine guards at that facility.

African Americans accounted for a disproportionately high number of military prison inmates during the Vietnam War. Forty percent of the prisoners incarcerated at the seven U.S. military prisons in Europe were black, as were 50 percent of the inmates at Long Binh in 1969. It was the same at stateside bases. Only 16 percent of the marines stationed at Quantico, for example, were black, but they accounted for half of that base's prison population. In 1971, African Americans made up slightly less than 32 percent of all army confinements, 21 percent of all marine prisoners, over 53 percent of all prisoners in the air force, and slightly more than 16 percent of all confinements for the navy.

African Americans were convinced that racism had something to do with the high number of African Americans given nonjudicial punishments, courts-martial, and prison time, and several investigations by different agencies supported this contention. The Congressional Black Caucus found that an "Article 15 punishment administered at the discretion of individual commanders for 'minor' offenses has without doubt resulted in irreparable damage to the service careers of blacks vastly out of proportion to black enrollment in the military."[69] Studies conducted within the armed forces reached the same conclusions. An air force Air Training Command investigation confirmed the existence of a racially based discriminatory pattern. More important, the members of the Department of Defense's Task Force on Military Justice were "convinced that the black or Spanish speaking enlisted man is often singled out for punishment by white authority figures where his white counterpart is not. There is enough evidence of intentional discrimination by individuals to convince the task force that selective punishment is in many cases racially motivated."[70]

Many whites, however, discounted black complaints and argued that African Americans perceived racism when none was intended or existed, and often used charges of prejudice to cover for their own failures. In Vietnam, in 1969, there was one black soldier in Gonzalo Baltazar's unit he considered racist. "He was black and had a lot of problems with race and everything and he thought everybody was racist and prejudiced towards him. There was a lot of that in Vietnam."[71] Some black officers and NCOs agreed that racism was often cited as an excuse for poor performance or behavior. "Unfortunately, the colored soldier bases his complaints on his race too frequently," claimed Colonel Willard C. Stewart. "He uses it as a crutch."[72]

Of course, some African Americans did use racism as a crutch or an excuse, and as an extension of American society, the military was undoubtedly influenced by trends and events in civilian society, but racism within the armed forces was a real problem and sometimes of the military's own making. Blacks had viewed the military as one of the more racially egalitarian institutions in America, but the militant attitudes of many younger recruits, coupled with the failure of military authorities to address adequately many of the legitimate concerns of black military personnel, convinced many that the armed forces were just as bigoted as the rest of America. Private Joseph Daryl Miles considered the army "the most racist institution I've seen. . . . We got a whole lot of freedom on the battlefield, a whole lot of democracy in the foxhole, a whole lot of equality to die."[73] Another black soldier claimed that the "army is the most racist pig organization you ever seen."[74] Black officers tended to be far more conservative and promilitary than most African Americans in the military, but some of them lashed out as well against the system. In Vietnam, in 1968, 20-year army veteran Major Lavell Merritt, in an article published in the *New York Times,* accused the army of being a "racist organization ... that denied equality and justice to its black personnel."[75]

RACIAL SOLIDARITY AND BLACK POWER

The black response was a rise in racial solidarity and black power militancy in the armed forces. African Americans called each other bloods, souls, soul brothers, or brothers and usually greeted each other with a sign of racial solidarity, such as a so-called black power salute, which was a raised clenched fist, or by a ritualized handshake known as a dap. The term *dap* is a corruption of Vietnamese slang for "beautiful" and originated among the brothers fighting in Southeast Asia. Each step during dapping had a specific meaning, and though there were some movements that were basic to dapping, there was no set procedure, and an individual dap could take but a few seconds or last upward of several minutes. African Americans in the armed forces also wore or carried items proclaiming their racial pride that black was beautiful. Many carried ebony walking sticks, usually adorned with a clenched fist for a knob, known as a black power cane. So-called slave bracelets, woven out of bootlaces and worn around the wrist, were very common. Soldiers of all races chalked sayings and slogans on their helmet liners or flak jackets. Many of the sayings had an antiwar theme, such as "Fuck the War" or "Give Peace a Chance," and some could be sarcastic; more than a few grunts in Vietnam chalked "LBJ's Hired Gun," for example. African Americans often chose racial themes, such as "Soul Brother" or "Black Is Beautiful," to adorn their equipment, reflecting their pride and solidarity.

The majority of African Americans embracing racial solidarity and black power were not subversives or hostile or threatening to whites, and most bloods that segregated themselves basically sought to avoid trouble and be left alone by racist whites. Air force sergeant Jack Smedley just wanted "to relax, really relax" when he was off duty and did not "want to listen with half an ear to hear if some drunken whites are going to call him a nigger."[76] "Chuck's all right until he gets a beer under his belt, and then its Nigger this and Nigger that," added another black soldier in Vietnam.[77] Many African Americans had white friends. "We are not antiwhite and don't bar whites if they dig us," remarked marine officer and Vietnam veteran Dwight Rawls. "I got some white friends who are 'For Real' studs, and hell, they could call me anything they want, because I know they are for real," explained one African American in Vietnam. "I know some Chucks who I'd most likely punch in the mouth if they said good morning to me because I know they are some wrong studs."[78]

Most of the self-segregation occurred during off duty hours, and few whites or blacks seemed to have a problem working together. "The black guys always hung around with the blacks and the whites hung around with the whites," noted Captain Stewart H. Barnhoft, a white officer commanding an engineering company at Chu Lai, Vietnam, in 1971, but "on duty everybody tended to work fairly well together."[79] Black officers had no trouble working with their fellow white officers and often socialized in integrated settings, but African Americans often socialized at all-black events as well. Korean and Vietnam War veteran Lieutenant Colonel Maurice L. Adams mixed freely with whites but noted that he and other black officers "often sit apart just to look at each other in our pride."[80] "We had our own parties, put on soul food nights, and played Aretha Franklin records," Colin Powell recalled. For black officers, it was the best of both worlds. "Blacks could hang around with the brothers in their free time, and no one gave it any more thought than the fact that West Pointers, tankers, or engineers went off by themselves. That was exactly the kind of integration we had been fighting for, to be permitted our blackness and also to be able to make it in a mostly white world."[81]

RACIAL HOSTILITY

Though the majority of African Americans considered their solidarity and self-segregation as protection against racism, many whites increasingly saw such behavior as hateful and hostile. One white Green Beret stated that "blacks pretty much stuck to themselves and hated everyone else." Black militants told their white commanding general in Germany that he was a pig and that all whites were pigs. Most of the black prisoners at the Danang Stockade were hard-core militants and "thoroughly full of hate for all whiteys," according to the brig's executive officer.[82] Gerald Kumpf considered the two African Americans from an army supply unit that came over to play poker with them to be racist and troublemakers. "The blacks were definitely anti-white and it was over a poker game and they come in doing all kinds of bad-mouthing on whitey and things like that.... They hated white guys... and they were out for blood." Kumpf claimed that they caught the two blacks cheating, and a fight broke out. Kumpf did not get involved because he was a "pacifist."[83] In 1972, the Department of Defense's Task Force on the Administration of Military Justice saw "evidence of blacks separating themselves from their non-black comrades in hostile ways, going beyond affirming their racial and cultural solidarity."[84]

Racial hostility and friction were increasing in the military, and there were enough racists and militants on both sides to provoke trouble. Gonzalo Baltazar recalled that "in Vietnam there was a lot of racism. I never knew... I came from a small town. I didn't know what racism was as far as black. I knew what racism was as far as Mexicans because in school I ran into a lot of racism between the whites and the Mexicans, but I never knew a black so I didn't think much of it. But a lot of these guys came from Detroit and Chicago, blacks and whites, well there was lot of racism between them." In Vietnam, he thought to himself, "Man, we're fighting two wars over here right now" due to the name-calling and racial friction.[85] Name-calling and stereotyping were common on both sides of the racial divide. A lot of blacks referred to whites using derogatory names, calling them Chucks, honkies, Caucasians, beasts, dudes, pigs, foreigners, and rabbits. Whites reciprocated with pejoratives such as coon, spear chucker, boy, spook, and the ever traditional nigger. "Niggers eat shit" and "I'd prefer a gook to a nigger" and other expressions of racist graffiti frequently decorated the walls of bars and latrines throughout Vietnam. The problem obviously was not limited to the bathrooms of Southeast Asia but occurred throughout the military establishment. Common suggestions in the Camp Lejeune suggestion box included "Keep those niggers off the [dance] floor" and "Coons please go back to Africa."[86] Some whites mocked the black power salute, or reciprocated with invented white power salutes, while others enacted exaggerated daps.

CULTURAL EXPRESSIONS AND RACIAL TENSION

Dapping, in particular, proved to be the cause of a lot of racial friction. Some whites, like army captain John Ellis, were understanding and patient and realized that the dap "was a very meaningful thing to young blacks. It meant a lot to them and sometimes, like in anything like that, what starts out to be meaningful sort of gets made into something sort of ridiculous."[87] Most whites, however, viewed it as provocative and believed that many blacks engaged in time-consuming daps simply to annoy them, particularly in chow line. "Well, the favorite time for blacks to do that was in line in the mess hall, and sometimes they would go into a five or ten minute dapping period," recalled Captain Vernon Conner, adding that "the whites would not be real thrilled about waiting in line while a couple of the bro's went through their dapping procedures."[88] The Department of Defense's Task Force on the Administration of Military Justice found that "dapping has become a source of considerable friction both between the black serviceman and his white counterparts and between him and the military system. It seems to provoke a reaction of white anger out of proportion to its own importance."[89]

Whites could also be provocative in their choices of cultural pride and expressions. If dapping angered many whites, the use of Confederate flags in Vietnam drove African Americans to the point of distraction. Many whites viewed the flag as a symbol of southern pride and not of a racist legacy, but few things infuriated blacks more than this symbol of racial oppression flying over hooches, fire bases, and even over major installations in Vietnam. The flag of the former confederacy was ubiquitous. On Christmas day in 1965, six whites carried a rebel flag and paraded in front of over 1,500 troops attending a Bob Hope USO show. Several officers and NCOs later posed for pictures under the flag. One black soldier present observed angrily that the display made him feel "like an outsider."[90] The *Crisis,* the journal of the NAACP, expressed how most black people felt about the Stars and Bars when it referred to the Confederate flag as "the tattered banner of that evil and misbegotten system," a "despicable" symbol "of a dead and dishonorable past," adding that "the Stars and Bars and the Swastika are equally the emblem of a false doctrine of racial supremacy."[91]

Much like 1968 was a pivotal year in the course of the war, it was also the turning point in terms of racial violence in the military in that all the elements needed to spark open racial warfare were now present. The use of the draft to facilitate the expansion of the armed forces brought in thousands of disaffected and radicalized individuals straight from a civilian society bitterly divided by war in Vietnam, the civil rights movement, and the rise of black militancy. The influx of tens of thousands of new recruits, coupled with the military's own rotation policies, worked against unit cohesion and ensured that many military installations were overcrowded with transients heading to new assignments. Most were strangers to each other, not comrades in arms they had trained and served with, and there was little familiarity or trust between officers and enlisted men or between black and white. Finally, the erosion of morale, spotty leadership, and the weakening of discipline created an environment that allowed militancy, racism, and insubordination to flourish.

THE ASSASSINATION OF DR. MARTIN LUTHER KING JR.

There was some racial violence in the military before 1968, but most of it was between two or just a few individuals. That changed after the assassination of Dr. Martin Luther King Jr. on April 4, 1968, in Memphis, Tennessee. The assassination of America's foremost civil rights crusader and apostle for peace left a lot of black military personnel stunned and saddened. Twenty-one-year-old Specialist 4 Reginald Daniels said that King "was a man we believed in, we trusted in. If anybody was the liberator, he was the man."[92] Sergeant James H. House was out in the field on a sweep with his unit when news of Dr. King's assassination came over the radio. It left him shocked. "Often we pay no attention to radio," he explained, "but this bulletin was the news of the death of Dr. Martin Luther King Jr.... It was really a shock, not only to me but to everybody who stands for peace. It made us all realize that now is the time to unite for peace."[93]

Many whites were as shocked and saddened as African Americans were by the news. "Speaking for myself, I'm appalled," remarked white airman first class Logan Hill to a *New York Times* reporter. Petty Officer Third Class John Brackett, who served in Vietnam in 1968–1969, had a "couple of good friends who were white and not racist, and that helped."[94]

Others, however, were apathetic, even callous about King's murder. "We feel sorry they got King," explained an anonymous white military policeman. "He's a martyr now and his people will probably follow the Rap Browns and Stokely Carmichaels." Another white explained, "We have 300 Americans dying here each week... King was one man. What about the people out here that are dying?" Other whites expressed satisfaction that King was dead. Airman Logan had "talked to some people who thought it was a pretty good thing,"[95] and John Brackett remembered the "overt joy expressed by some of my white colleagues that this 'trouble-maker' had been eliminated."[96] Some whites celebrated King's assassination openly by donning makeshift white Ku Klux Klan robes or burning crosses, and at Cam Rahn Bay, they hoisted a Confederate flag over the naval headquarters building.

King's death, and the manner in which some whites reacted to it, led to violence. There was rioting in over 100 cities, and army troops were called out to assist the National Guard in quelling the disturbances. There was sporadic violence within the military as well, but it was largely confined to fights between individuals. King's death changed things for many African Americans, and many became disillusioned and angry.

"Almost everywhere here you can see the unity which exists among the Negro soldiers," observed one black soldier. "After the assassination of Dr. M. L. King you could also feel the malcontent."[97]

RACIAL VIOLENCE AND THE ARMED FORCES

Signs of growing racial violence in the armed forces surfaced in August 1968, when black inmates rioted at the navy brig at Danang, as did prisoners later that month at the huge Long Binh Stockade outside Saigon. Large military installations saw a rise in racial violence. At Camp Lejeune, in 1968, there were over 160 recorded racial assaults and "an explosive situation of major proportions has been created and continues to be aggravated," warned a committee investigating the violence. One white marine at Lejeune mused that "violence is our only meeting ground now."[98]

The predictions of violence came true at Camp Lejeune the night of July 20, 1969, when a large interracial gang fight broke out at a send-off party for the First Battalion, Sixth Marines, leaving to join the Sixth Fleet at Rota, Spain. Sporadic violence between whites and blacks climaxed around 11:00 P.M. when, yelling "white beasts" and "we are going to mess up some beasts tonight," around 30 black and Latino marines engaged a slightly smaller group of whites in a general brawl in front of the enlisted men's club. Dozens of men were injured, and two white marines were hospitalized with stab wounds and another with a serious head injury. The one fatality was an innocent victim, a 20-year-old white corporal from Mississippi named Edward Bankston, who apparently had not taken part in the fighting.

The so-called Rumble at Camp Lejeune proved to be the first of several large-scale racial confrontations on military bases that year. Ten days later, there was a confrontation between whites and blacks at Millington Naval Air Station near Memphis, Tennessee. The fight started when whites confronted a group of African Americans returning from a night out at the bars. One white yelled out, "Here come those drunken niggers now," which led to a 15-minute free-for-all that started at a barracks and ended at a nearby bar. No one was seriously hurt, but four black marines were arrested and charged with rioting and conspiracy.[99] In August, a fight erupted at Kaneohe Marine Corps Air Station in Hawaii after approximately 50 African Americans gave a black power salute during the lowering of the colors. For over four hours, an estimated 250 marines fought each other armed with sticks, pipes, and entrenching tools, leaving 16 injured, 3 of whom were hospitalized. In Vietnam, two white colonels were injured that year during a major race riot at the naval installation at Cam Ranh Bay.[100]

In the next few years, rioting or racial warfare occurred at numerous bases, including Fort Bragg, Fort Hood, and Fort McClellan in the United States, and overseas from South Korea and Okinawa to West Germany and Labrador, Canada. Despite the varied locations, there was a definite pattern. Most of the racial warfare occurred on or near large installations and often began in the enlisted men's clubs or nearby bars and places of entertainment. Alcohol was almost always involved. Sometimes it was over women, but often, it was over music and was generally triggered by a racial slur or challenge. In addition to the large-scale fighting, the brawl at Fort Bragg, North Carolina, involved over 200 whites and blacks, for example, and low-intensity warfare, in which individuals or small groups would seek out members of the opposite race, was endemic. At Cam Ranh Bay in 1970–1971, Major Thomas Cecil witnessed an endless secession of "small gang wars going back and forth between companies. Blacks against whites, whites would attack blacks, Hispanics would attack blacks, and it was a constant give and take which just went on."[101] In October 1972, the aircraft carriers *Kitty Hawk* and *Constellation* both experienced a wave of racial violence in which groups of disgruntled black sailors waylaid and beat whites.

COMBAT UNITS AND THE LACK OF RACIAL VIOLENCE

Despite the intensity and widespread nature of the racial violence permeating the military, there was virtually no racial conflict within combat units in Vietnam. Marine Corps historians Henry Shaw and Ralph Donnelly wrote, "There were racial incidents and confrontations in rear areas in Vietnam," but "these disruptions did not extend to the sectors of fighting where the color of a person's skin was of no import to his role as a combat Marine."[102] An army study conducted in 1969 reached the same conclusions, albeit stating it somewhat in reverse, claiming that "polarization of the races...[was] more obvious in those areas where groups were not in direct contact with an armed enemy."

Experienced journalists also noted the distinction. "As it happens in any situation of great stress, racial differences between blacks and whites have disappeared on the fighting fronts," wrote veteran Vietnam reporter Thomas Johnson in August 1968, noting that "at the front, the main thing is to stay alive and you do this most often by depending on the man next to you."[103] Writing in May 1969, veteran reporter Wallace Terry could refer to race relations in Vietnam as "not as critical" as they were in the United States, where they were "immensely significant."[104] Even in 1970, as morale in the U.S. military

Marines of Company G, 2nd Battalion, 7th Marines, during Operation Allen Brook, a search-and-destroy operation that began in May 1968. Courtesy of the U.S. Marine Corps.

was bottoming out and racial warfare was threatening to tear the now fragile racial cohesion of the armed forces apart, the *Baltimore Afro-American* could confidently report that there was a "total absence of racial unrest" at the frontline firebases.[105]

There were several reasons why combat units were almost universally spared the racial warfare so prevalent in other sectors of the military establishment. To begin with, the men in these units faced death together; to possibly get out alive, the men of a unit had to depend on each other and cover each other's back. "When you got bullets flying...no one knows what color you are," observed Leon Mizelle, an African American, who fought in Vietnam with the 196th Infantry in 1965–1966.[106] "I never really felt there was any tension," recalled Major William G. Riederer, who commanded two different companies in Vietnam in 1969. "We pretty much operated on everybody pull their own and everybody was liable to go out and get shot and everybody would go out and get shot at."[107] Major Richard H. Torovosky had no racial problems in his unit in 1970–1971 because after "sleeping together, fighting together, being dirty together, and them playing together," the men were very close and had no trouble "getting along" with each other.[108]

This feeling of all being in there together usually fostered deep feelings of camaraderie, concern, and friendship among the unit's personnel. First Lieutenant Gasanove Stephens, an African American, who was the leader of Third Platoon, "Evil Troop," Second Squadron, 11th Armored Division, from August 1967 until he was wounded in action on February 3, 1968, stated that his "platoon contained all races, yet during my time as platoon leader there was never any kind of prejudice in any way. Every man seemed to be dedicated to the cause and always treated each other as brothers." Stephens lost three men during his tour of duty, a "Texas Negro and...two Caucasians" and was deeply hurt by their deaths and mourned them all equally.[109] Eugene White became very good friends with his black platoon sergeant. "The rapport that we developed between us was tremendous. I think that I would go to the mat for him, and he would go to the mat for me." White was transferred and took command of a company of his own, but the two men remained in contact, and when they ran into each other in Vietnam, "it was just like two really old friends seeing each other and happy to see one another."[110] Captain Tony Mavroudis, a close friend of Colin Powell's, during an interview for an NBC documentary *Same Mud, Same Blood* on African Americans in Vietnam, told reporter Frank McGee that race did not matter out in the jungle. "It doesn't exist. We're all soldiers. The only color we know is khaki and green, the color of the mud and the color of the blood is all the same."[111] Five days after the interview aired, Mavroudis stepped on a land mine and was killed.

Though a large number of military personnel believed that race relations were better in Vietnam, especially in combat units, than they were elsewhere in the military establishment or the civilian world, these feelings were not universal. There were many who believed that racism and racial antagonism were just as prevalent in combat units as in other formations. Among many of both races, there was still a lack of respect. Private First Class Donnel Jones recalled having "the honor of saving the life of a white man who later called me a black nigger."[112] Charles Porter was convinced that it was only the fighting prowess of African Americans that was keeping the whites from dying and losing the war. "But I must say this, the only thing keeping the white GI's alive is us soul brothers. If we weren't here, Charlie would have cleaned up just about everything long ago," he mused.[113] Others doubted whether the bonds of comradeship forged in war were genuine and strong enough to survive without the threat of death and the need to cooperate. One black army lieutenant colonel bitterly observed in 1969 that "the threat of death changes many things, but comradeship doesn't last after you get" back "to the village."[114]

Even those that failed to form friendships across racial lines still realized that the key to survival in a combat zone depended on cooperation. If you wanted to survive your tour of duty, you worked together, and this also contributed to keeping racial antagonism from flaring up and threatening the entire unit. William Miller, a 30-year veteran with combat stints in both Korea and Vietnam, claimed that there were still racial barriers out in the field. "When you reach the foxhole, it doesn't go away," but "it gets masked over because you have to cover your back."[115]

Highly trained and specialized units, airborne units in particular, reported virtually no racial strife or violence. Major Patrick Carder had few problems because his outfit was "what could have been considered a rather elite company. All the personnel in the company were Airborne, and were all parachute riggers. Because the requirements for parachute rigger school required individuals to have a pretty high I.Q. just to get in, the people were fairly smart and didn't get into the racial problems. They tended to join together regardless of race, color, or creed."[116] Max V. Terrien, serving in the First Air Cavalry, "didn't have any racial strife problems" because "morale was good," and everyone in the reconnaissance and surveillance company "was hand-picked, and they knew they were hand-picked."[117] Captain Victor E. Miller also commanded a company of air cavalry in Vietnam, and while he had a bit of a drug problem, he had no racial strife to speak of in his unit. "I was in an airborne outfit, and most of the kids were pretty motivated anyway, and we didn't have really too much of that."[118] In an army interview conducted in 1982, Major Richard H. Torovosky wanted to "comment specifically on drug abuse and racial strife, mainly from the fact that I don't think they were in" his elite air assault company, which specialized in counterguerrilla operations, adding that all his men were excellent soldiers.[119]

COMBAT REFUSALS

Combat units in Vietnam did have their share of problems. In the later stages of the war, individuals, and sometimes entire units, refused to engage the enemy. In 1968, 68 American soldiers out of seven total divisions in Vietnam refused to go into combat. A year later, in 1969, an entire company of the 196th Light Infantry Brigade refused orders and sat down in spite of their commander's entreaties. The incident was filmed by a CBS news team. Later that year, a company from the First Air Cavalry Division disobeyed direct orders and "flatly refused" to advance down a dangerous road.[120] By 1970, combat refusals were so common and discipline so lax that one American stationed at Cu Chi nonchalantly remarked that "if a man is ordered to go to such and such a place, he no longer goes through the hassle of refusing; he just packs his shirt and goes to visit some buddies at another base camp."[121] There were at least 35 more combat refusals in the division that year. Many were never prosecuted. One of the punitive enlistees in Gonzalo Baltazar's platoon went AWOL after a major battle because he could not take it. He managed to get back home to Detroit, where a counselor talked him into going back to Vietnam. He was not punished when he returned, just made a jeep driver for the rest of his tour of duty. "There was no discipline."[122]

FRAGGING

Attempts by officers to restore or enforce discipline in their commands often led to attempts on their lives, known as fragging in Vietnam. Fragging was a deliberate attempt to kill, maim, or intimidate someone in the American or allied armed forces and took its name from the favorite weapon of choice, the fragmentation grenade. Grenades were an excellent choice for murder because they were ubiquitous in Vietnam, and because there was no ballistics test for one, it left little incriminating evidence. Grenades and claymore mines could also be rigged as booby traps, meaning that the assailant did not even have to be in the immediate vicinity when the attack occurred. Though anyone could be the target of a fragging, the intended victim was usually an officer or NCO, and the perpetrator an enlisted person.

Killing one's own officers is nothing new in warfare. During World War I, for example, the army prosecuted almost 370 cases of violence aimed at a superior officer or NCO, but this was out of an army that numbered over 4.7 million men. The ratios were also relatively low for World War II and Korea. What separated Vietnam from these earlier conflicts was the sheer number of attempted fraggings and the fact that the army had to coin a term for the phenomenon. The number of attempted fraggings early in the Vietnam War is not known because the army did not begin to track them until 1969. There were some. Lloyd Hudson, an African American who served in the 101st Airborne in 1965–1966, knew "people who got shot because of racial tensions."[123] But because morale was still relatively high, the number of attempted fraggings early in the war was likely to be very low. David White, for example, who served in Vietnam in 1968–1969, never heard of a fragging while he was over there and did not even hear the term itself until he was out of the service years later.[124] Beginning in 1969, however, army records list 23 men killed and 191 injured in 126 known attempted fraggings, including 30 incidents listed as possible assaults.[125] Officers and NCOs were the targets in 70 cases. An independent congressional investigation found 239 fraggings for that year. There were 271 reported fraggings in 1970, leaving 34 killed and 306 injured. Officers and NCOs were the intended victims in 154 cases.[126] The congressional investigation again found more fraggings than the army, claiming that there were at least 386 attempts that year. Enlisted men, ARVN, and allied personnel were also the targets of fraggings. There were 40 actual or possible fraggings on enlisted men in 1970, for example, along with 20 Vietnamese. The year 1971 was the worst for fraggings, with 333 incidents reported, but there were only 12 dead and 198 injured, 158 of whom were officers and NCOs.[127] The number of fraggings sharply decreased as the United States disengaged from Vietnam. The Department of Defense reported only 58 actual or possible fraggings in 1972, which left 3 dead and 19 wounded. The army documented a total of 788 fraggings or attempted fraggings from 1969 to 1972, and the congressional investigation over 1,000, but this was probably only the tip of a deadly iceberg. Officers in the Judge Advocate General Corps estimated that only about 10 percent of attempted fraggings ended up in court-martial.

Attempting to impose discipline on a unit was just one of many reasons disgruntled soldiers endeavored to kill their superior officers. Officers and NCOs that tried to suppress the use or sale of drugs in their units were often targets of fraggings. Captain Vernon Connor believed that the attempt on his life at Long Binh, in 1970, stemmed from his attempts to clean up drug traffic in his company, for example.

Race was yet another factor, and black enlisted personnel often fragged officers or NCOs perceived as racist. By May 1971, the *Pittsburgh Courier* reported that many white officers in Vietnam were cowed by threats of fragging from discontented blacks.[128] One African American in Baltazar's unit, for example, was court-martialled and sentenced to 30 years' hard labor at Leavenworth for a racially motivated fragging of a white sergeant, and militant Melvin X. Smith received a life sentence in 1971 for shooting two whites.

Another reason was faulty or callous command decisions that resulted in excessive or needless casualties. Even for soldiers that never attempted it, the thought certainly crossed many of their minds. John Ballweg blamed an overambitious captain for the death of 18-year-old Junior Evans, the youngest pilot in the army at that time. The helicopters were returning from a mission when they took fire from a lone Vietcong down in the bush. Ballweg believed that they should never have gone after a lone individual, but Evans took a round in the head and died 11 hours later. When Ballweg found out "what had happened they had to hold me back because I was going to go and take care of this captain who should have never turned to return fire from one little Charlie running around.... I would have just torn him apart, literally.... He wanted a medal and he wanted the recognition and that would help toward promotion."[129] Ballweg suppressed his desire to go after the officer in question, but many others did not. Soldiers in Vietnam posted a $10,000 reward for anyone who would frag Lieutenant Colonel Weldon Honeycutt, the officer who had ordered the disastrous and costly assaults on Hamburger Hill in the A Shau Valley in 1969. Honeycutt returned safely to the United States in spite of several attempts on his life.

The grunts in combat units hated overzealous junior officers in particular, nicknamed "John Waynes," who endangered their men in needless firefights, either out of enthusiasm to get the job done, or eagerness to get promoted. Some junior officers were just anxious to do their duty. They performed well in combat but were often too quick to prove their courage, recklessly rushing unwisely into situations without thinking ahead. Others, however, were simply reckless.

Despite the high numbers of attempts, the army claimed in 1972 that fragging was not a serious problem, nor was it racially motivated. In hearings on attempts to subvert the U.S. armed forces, former chief of personnel and administration for MACV, Brigadier General Lawrence Greene, characterized the situation as not serious, telling the congressional committee that fraggings could be attributed to "personality" and "personal factors," such as bad news from home or a "buddy getting killed," bringing out "latent characteristics," and not as a sign that morale in general, or race relations in particular, had reached crisis proportions in the armed forces.[130]

If the senior leadership chose to downplay the problem, officers in Vietnam certainly took it seriously enough. Just being an authority figure was often enough to get one fragged, regardless of race. During his second tour in Vietnam at Duc Pho in 1968–1969, Colin Powell "was living in a large tent and I moved my cot every night, partly to thwart Viet Cong informants...but also because I did not rule out attacks on authority from within the battalion itself."[131] When Captain Henry Parker took command of his company in November 1969, he was informed that his predecessor had been fragged, and there was at least one attempt on his life. Captain Richard Bevington, who commanded a company at Camp Evans in 1970–1971, had so little trust in his own men that he slept with a loaded .45 under his pillow. Captain Thomas Cecil, who was stationed at Cam Rahn Bay from September 1970 to May 1971, was so worried about attacks on his life that during his last month in Vietnam, he slept in the military intelligence (MI) bunker, and only his battalion commander knew where he was at night.

CIVILIAN INFLUENCE AND RADICALISM IN THE ARMED FORCES

Military officials were convinced that the racial problems and violence within the armed services was the result of outside civilian influences and problems being brought into the military by young inductees. Echoing the belief held among senior officers, General William Westmoreland was convinced that "attitudes and beliefs developed before they enter the services" led to racial violence and dissention in the armed forces.[132] It was not just the white officers that believed this. Lieutenant Colonel Kenneth Berthoud, one of the highest-ranking African Americans in the army during the war, counseled, "Remember they feel they've got where they have only by solidarity....They come in with the idea of brother-above-all."[133]

Young whites in the military, especially some of the draftees, were radicalized as well. Though college was correctly viewed as a haven from military service, many men were drafted after dropping out or graduating from school, and many brought the radicalism permeating higher education with them into the ranks. Some belonged to so-called Old Left organizations, such as the Communist Party USA or the Socialist Workers Party, and they would help influence the movement. But most young white radicals ideologically belonged to what they termed the "New Left," evoking socialist principles and idolizing young, dashing revolutionaries such as Che Guevara, while showing a distain for dogmatic Stalinism and distrusting the Soviet Union as much as they distrusted their own government.

Along with their occasional allies, the Black Nationalists, white radicals were busy proselytizing and organizing within the ranks, and by 1971, there were at least

14 dissident organizations operating within the armed forces, including the Black Nationalist Movement for a Democratic Military (MDM) and the socialist American Serviceman's Union (ASU). Collectively, they were known as the GI movement to their supporters, or RITA, an acronym for "Resistance in the Army," to military officials, but there was a wide range of differences among the various groups. Two of the organizations were made up exclusively of officers, and there were six or more veterans groups, including Vietnam Veterans against the War, Flower of the Dragon, and the Winter Soldier Organization. Several of the organizations existed at only one installation, and most for only a brief period of time, but a few, like the ASU, attracted a sizeable following. At its height in 1970, the ASU claimed over 10,000 members at over 100 stateside and 60 overseas bases as well as on 50 navy vessels. It was generally well funded by outside dissident groups and printed its own underground newspaper, the *Bond.*

UNDERGROUND NEWSPAPERS

The dissidents used a variety of printed material to get their message out to the military rank and file, but their most important method of disseminating material was through the underground newspapers, a term used loosely to describe the plethora of counterculture and generally antimilitary publications that abounded in the late 1960s and 1970s, most of which were neither illegal nor underground. Some, such as the *Black Voice* at Fort McClellan, were black nationalist papers published for an African American readership, but the vast majority of the newspapers were generated by predominately white organizations espousing either New Left or more traditional revolutionary Marxist doctrines. Between 1967 and 1972, there were an estimated 245 underground newspapers published by or for military personnel. At any given time, there were 40–50 a year in publication, with titles *Travesty* at Travis Air Force Base, the *Fatigue Press* at Fort Hood, or one of three newspapers at Fort Knox, including *In Formation.* There were at least two papers in both Japan and Okinawa, and service personnel in Europe could read *Act,* which was published out of Paris, France. In May 1970, Brigadier General S.L.A. Marshall, a special aid to Westmoreland charged with studying the issue, estimated that there were currently 65 in publication, but that appears to have been the high-water mark, and the number began to decline quickly after that. By August 1970, just three months later, Marshall claimed that there were now only 30 still in publication.

A few, like the *Bond,* boasted a respectable readership; the ASU claimed over 25,000 readers an edition in 1969, but most did not have a wide distribution or much influence on enlisted personnel. An army survey at Long Binh, for instance, found that only 1 serviceperson out of 200 had even seen a publication he thought might "foster racial tension" between blacks and whites.

There are also questions as to how much armed resistance the various radical groups actually engaged in. The radicals unquestionably encouraged revolution and sabotage from within. In a universal call not only to the Black Panthers in the ranks, but to all African American GIs, party communications director Kathleen Cleaver wrote in the *Black Panther* on December 14, 1970, that "right inside of the U.S. imperialist beast's Army, you are strategically placed to begin the process of destroying him from within.... You don't have to wait...to begin to fight.... Sabotage from within until you get into a position to destroy from without! We need you, your military skills, your military equipment and your courage for our own struggle." Some of the groups were involved in serious revolutionary activity. The MDM and Black Berets, for example, stole weapons from military arsenals and stockpiled them for the coming revolution. They were also suspected in the torching of two mess halls at Fort Ord on August 12, 1970, and at other installations where these groups had active chapters. Often their claims of striking violent blows against the empire could not be verified. Activist Andrew Stapp, for instance, would later claim that the ASU had "a meaningful role at both Long Binh and Danang where the men revolted and fought the brass over abominable stockade conditions and racist terror unleashed on the prisoners," but there is no evidence for it, and the prisoners that rioted claimed that they did so over racist conditions and brutal treatment, not due to any exhortations by Stapp or any other activist.[134] All in all, and in spite of these actions and the rousing calls to revolution, the damage done to the military, physically or in terms of efficiency, appears to be minimal.

THE MILITARY PERSONNEL SECURITY PROGRAM

Faced with severe morale, racial, and drug problems and deteriorating discipline, military authorities responded by imprisoning or discharging radicals and militants. The military's internal apparatus for identifying and flagging subversives was the Military Personnel Security Program, established by Department of Defense Directive 5210.9 on June 19, 1956. The armed forces authority to suppress subversive activity within the armed forces came from Department of Defense Directive 1325.6, titled "Guidelines for Handling Dissident and Protest Activities among Members of the Armed Forces," issued by Secretary of Defense Melvin Laird on September 12, 1969. Laird stressed that "the service member's right of expression should be preserved to the maximum extent possible," but that this had to be "consistent with good order and discipline and the national security," and since "no Commander should be indifferent to conduct which, if allowed to proceed unchecked, would destroy the effectiveness of his unit," commanding offices were given authority to curb militants and their activities.[135] The Department of Defense guidelines allowed commanding officers to ban underground publications and discipline personnel engaged in activities detrimental to the armed forces such as peace marches or racial demonstrations. They could also declare establishments, such as coffeehouses, off-limits to military personnel.

Much of the military crackdown focused on ending racial violence. Provocative gestures or actions, such as dapping, were banned by numerous base and unit commanders, and the navy prohibited it throughout the service. Service personnel, especially minorities, involved in racial violence were punished. At Camp Lejeune, the Marine Corps arrested and brought charges against 44 men in connection with the racial brawl that occurred there on July 20–21, 1969. Charges against 24 of the defendants were eventually dropped, leaving 18 African Americans and two Puerto Ricans awaiting court-martial, where 5 won acquittal, and 1 deserted before going to trial, but 14 were found guilty of a range of charges, including involuntary manslaughter—which brought a sentence of nine years at hard labor—rioting, disobedience, and assault. One other casualty of the brawl was the battalion's commander, who was relieved of duty, Lieutenant Colonel Hurdle L. Maxwell, the first African American to command a marine combat battalion.

Another focus of the crackdown was purging the armed forces of the radicals leading the movement from within. In September 1969, for example, antiwar activists privates Eugene Rudder and Joseph F. Coles were court-martialled for distributing the banned newspaper *Short-Times* at Fort Jackson and given undesirable discharges, as was Andrew Pulley of GIs United, who was dishonorably discharged for his radical activities.[136] The navy opted for a comprehensive program for weeding out dissidents and troublemakers. Under NAVOP 231, issued in December 1972, the navy officially adopted a program under which seamen "who are an administrative burden to their commands because of repeated disciplinary infractions" could request general discharges under honorable conditions in the best interests of both the individual and the navy. The program proved so successful that the navy extended it indefinitely past its original February 1973 cutoff date. Those the military could not kick out were sent where they could do little harm. Radical leader Joseph Miles, for example, found himself transferred to a small, remote radar station in Alaska.

The Department of Defense also took steps to curb drug abuse in the ranks. On December 31, 1969, the Pentagon announced that it would begin to test randomly all military personnel for drug use as soon as effective measures to do so were available. It took the Defense Department longer than anticipated, but a random drug-testing program was in place finally by April 1972.

REFORM IN THE ARMED FORCES

Military leaders were also aware of the need for basic reform and took steps to correct many of the legitimate problems facing service personnel. One of the most crucial was reform in the military justice system, particularly the nonjudicial punishment process. For example, officers now had to document and cite justification for all Article 15s. The Pentagon established race relations councils, and race relations became part of an officer's fitness report. Chief of naval operations Admiral Elmo Zumwalt eased or abolished many of the Mickey Mouse regulations sailors complained about and retained black officers to advise him on racial reforms in the navy.

Some of the reforms led to increased opportunity for women in the armed forces. In November 1967, President Lyndon Johnson signed Public Law 90-130, which abolished the 2 percent ceiling of the number of women in the armed forces and removed promotional ceilings, allowing women to reach the higher ranks in the armed forces. On June 11, 1970, Anna Hays became the first woman and first army nurse to be promoted to brigadier general. In 1975, the three service academies were opened to women, and three years later, women were formally constituted into the regular establishment with abolishment of the Women's Army Corps. By 1991, the 35,000 women serving in Desert Storm made up 12 percent of American personnel serving in that war.

The military addressed many key concerns regarding both gender and racial discrimination in the armed forces, and most veterans believed that conditions, if not morale and discipline, steadily improved in the postwar years, but it took time. Despite the reforms, and the fact that many of the radicals and troublemakers left the service after the war, some problems lingered for several years, especially racial friction. Sociologist Charles Moskos found that "the early years of the all-volunteer force were in some cases worse, especially since we weren't at war." Troop morale was at an "all time low," and the end of the draft meant the end of college-educated soldiers in the ranks. Military recruits came from "the poorest and toughest element of America, white and black. Drugs and hooliganism infested the barracks."[137] Between 1975 and 1978, racial gang fights in barracks, attacks on individuals, and other forms of racial violence occurred throughout the military establishment. Some places, such as Germany and individual bases such as Camp Lejeune, North Carolina, were reported to be particularly bad.

A resurgence of white supremacist groups active within the ranks also threatened the racial stability of the military establishment. In 1979, the Pentagon became alarmed over a dramatic increase in Ku Klux Klan activity among off duty service personnel. That summer, three white sailors wearing sheets and hoods sparked a black power demonstration on the aircraft carrier *Independence* in the Mediterranean Sea. There were Klan members allegedly on at least two other ships in the Atlantic fleet. In 1980, the army relieved five military policemen and self-confessed Klansmen at Fort Monroe, Virginia.

By the early 1980s, however, the wartime and postwar reforms were finally having their desired effect, and the racial climate in the military had changed. African Americans, and, to a much lesser degree, women, were now fully part of the command structure, and higher recruiting standards emphasizing education over bonuses for enlistment finally began making a difference. Army captain David Doctor, a tank company and then later headquarters company commander in Germany in the early 1980s, stated that he "never had a problem" with a racist soldier when he was in the military.[138] The military was so successful in combating racism that Charles Moskos could claim with authority that there was not single major racial incident in the Gulf War, Bosnia, or Somalia.

Other lessons from the Vietnam War, however, proved more difficult and painful for the military to institutionalize. Initially, the armed forces preferred to forget about Vietnam and did not take immediate steps to institutionalize the lessons learned in Southeast Asia. Colonel David Hackworth has argued that "after the war, U.S. military leadership, humiliated by defeat, simply buried the experience. For almost two decades, service schools avoided teaching the lessons of Vietnam and trained primarily for the pleasantly familiar 'big battle war' on the plains of Europe."[139] The lessons from Vietnam were eventually worked into the curriculum. Training scenarios on guerilla warfare at West Point, for example, were based on the Vietnam experience until 2005, when they were replaced by exercises based on the war in Iraq.

AFTER THE WAR

The postwar era saw varying levels of success for veterans of the war. William Westmoreland is often blamed for losing the Vietnam War but still enjoyed a very successful career. After stepping down as the commander in chief of the MACV in 1968, he went on to hold the highest position in the army, chief of staff, until his retirement in 1972. Two years later, he tried his luck at electoral politics but lost his bid for the governorship of his native state of South Carolina. Vietnam would continue to have an influence over his life. In 1976, he published his memoirs, *A Soldier Reports,* and in 1982, he sued CBS over their assertion that he had purposely inflated the enemy body count and other allegations of lies and misconduct. The case went to trial, but after 18 weeks, the aging general dropped his suit on February 13, 1985. Westmoreland died in 2005.

Admiral Elmo Zumwalt served as chief of naval operations until his retirement from the Navy on July 1, 1974. Like Westmoreland, he dabbled in politics, running unsuccessfully as a Democratic candidate for the Senate from Virginia in 1976. Zumwalt wrote two books, served on several boards of directors, and was president of the American Medical Building Corporation in Milwaukee, Wisconsin. Zumwalt was 79 when he died on January 2, 2000.

Many of those that stayed in the armed forces after the war had successful careers. Albert Childs stayed in the armed service, as did Allen Thomas, and both retired senior

A Joint Services Honor Guard participates in the dedication ceremony for the Vietnam Memorial, 1982. Courtesy of the Department of Defense.

sergeants. Thomas lives in Erlanger, Kentucky, and is active in church, civic, and veterans' organizations. He is a member of Vietnam Veterans of America and post commander of his local chapter of the Veterans of Foreign Wars. Gerald Kumpf served in the U.S. Marine Corps from 1961 until 1966 and in the U.S. Air Force from 1967 until 1982. With the air force, he rotated in and out of Southeast Asia over the next 15 years in Taiwan, Okinawa, Thailand, Guam, the Philippines, and South Korea. During this time, Gerald served as an aircraft instrument technician, avionics systems technician, airborne avionics systems technician, and avionics systems superintendent. General Wallace H. Nutting, who served two tours in Vietnam, went on to command the Third Armored Division in Germany and later served as commander of the U.S. Southern Command. Anthony Zinni, who also served two tours in Vietnam with the Marine Corps, went on to earn the rank of general and serve as commander in chief of the Central Command.[140] Arthur Gregg, who commanded the 96th Quartermaster Battalion in Vietnam from 1966 to 1967, held numerous high posts in the quartermaster corps and retired as a lieutenant general. Harry Dukes, who assumed command from Gregg of the 96th Quartermaster Battalion in Vietnam in 1967, reached the rank of major general and was quartermaster general of the U.S. Army.

Many veterans left the armed forces, only to return later. Alfonza Wright left the navy and had a good job at a steel mill in Baltimore but enlisted and made the army a career. After retirement, Sergeant Wright went on to earn bachelor's and master's degrees and work as a counselor and with paroled felons in South Carolina. Medal of Honor winner Gordon Roberts returned home from Vietnam in 1970, attended college, and also earned bachelor's and master's degrees. He worked for the Warren County, Ohio, juvenile court, did drug and alcohol counseling, and made an unsuccessful bid at

Congress before rejoining the army in the early 1990s. He was commissioned an officer and was a major as of 1999.

Some returned to infamy. Marine corporal Robert Garwood, captured by the Vietcong on September 28, 1965, came home in 1979 claiming that he had been held a prisoner. The Marine Corps, however, immediately charged him with collaboration and assault on a fellow POW, and he was convicted at court-martial and dishonorably discharged. He is the only serviceman to be charged with these crimes from the Vietnam War. In 1998, the Department of Defense changed Garwood's status from Returnee to AWOL/Deserter/Collaborator.

Most of the ships and military hardware used during the Vietnam War are retired as well, but there is one notable veteran still serving. As of early 2005, the USS *Kitty Hawk,* scene of violent racial warfare in October 1972, was still in service as the forward deployed carrier of the Pacific fleet, based in Japan.

Most veterans went home to resume normal lives. Gonzalo Baltazar farmed for a while before starting a career with the post office in 1982. Some successfully entered the political arena. John McCain, the young navy pilot shot down over Hanoi in October 1967, entered politics and became a Republican senator from Arizona and a presidential candidate. John Kerry also went on to a successful career in the Senate and was the Democratic candidate for president in 2004. Many veterans found success in civilian life as reporters and writers. Two-tour Vietnam veteran David Hackworth retired a colonel and went on to become a leading military theorist and historian. Marine lieutenant Philip Caputo wrote one of the most outstanding memoirs of the Vietnam War, *A Rumor of War,* joined the antiwar movement, and became a correspondent for the *Chicago Tribune,* where he was part of a Pulitzer Prize–winning team for investigative journalism in 1972. In 1975, he covered the fall of Saigon. During his career as a journalist, he was kidnapped by Palestinian terrorists and won the Overseas Press Club's George Polk Citation for his reporting on that experience. Adam Smith, who served with Special Forces in Vietnam as an enlisted man in 1955, became a noted economist and author of several books, including *The Money Game, Supermoney,* and others. Jack Smith, who was wounded at Ia Drang, left the army in late 1967 and earned a degree in history in 1971 at Carnegie Mellon University in Pittsburgh, and another BA from Oxford University, in England, in 1974. Smith began working for ABC in 1984 and became an Emmy Award–winning reporter, writer, and principal correspondent for several programs, including *This Week with David Brinkley.* Smith returned to his battlefield in Vietnam in 1993 as a reporter for *Nightline* and *Day One.*

Whether one remained in the military or sought success in the civilian sector, most Vietnam veterans felt shunned and unappreciated by their fellow countrymen, receiving no thanks or recognition for their service, and often sacrifice, in Southeast Asia. In 1981, however, a design for a Vietnam veterans memorial in Washington, D.C., was approved. Submitted by a 21-year-old Yale student from Athens, Ohio, Maya Ying Lin, her design for a black granite wall inscribed with the names of those killed in the war was chosen over 1,421 other designs submitted. The Vietnam Veterans Memorial was officially dedicated on November 13, 1983, but two months later, in January 1984, the Memorial Commission decided to add a flagstaff and a figurative sculpture by Frederick Hart of three fighting men to the memorial, in deference to complaints by veterans that the memorial was too abstract. The statue of two white and one black servicemen was installed in the fall of 1984, and on November 11, 1984, President Ronald Reagan accepted the monument on behalf of the American people. The over 11,000 women who served in

Vietnam also got their memorial, although much later than their male colleagues. In November 1993, the Women's Vietnam Memorial was dedicated in Washington, D.C., near the wall.

Having made peace with their own country, many veterans sought closure with their former enemies as well. Jack Smith was one of thousands of Vietnam War veterans who returned to Vietnam. Gonzalo Baltazar went back in 1999 and was pleasantly surprised to find that "those people are happy. . . . There was peace over there. Even though it was a communist country, they seem to be enjoying life. I wish we would have never got involved." The Vietnamese people were great and treated the Americans well, even members of the Vietnamese armed forces they met.[141] David Hackworth returned to the Mekong delta 25 years after serving there in 1969. He claimed that 24 years later, he could still "hear the fallen men cry, Medic! Medic! Medic!"[142] "Today, the shell scorched earth where Joe Holleman and Dennis Richards died is rich with rice, and the bunker line where Roger Keppel was shot in the chest is now a peaceful banana grove," he observed. "The mines, booby traps and fighting positions are all gone. The men of the Viet Cong have hung up their Aks, and built a new hamlet over that field where more than 100 soldiers fell."[143]

Many veterans, like Hackworth and McCain, bear no animosity toward their former enemies. John McCain became one of the leading advocates for reconciliation with Vietnam and, in November 1996, returned to Vietnam during a tour of Asia. He met with the now 79-year-old Mai Van On, who had saved his life 29 years earlier. Hackworth also supports closer ties with Vietnam. Hackworth "never hated the Vietnamese" and "saw no point in continuing America's policy of official hostility to Vietnam."[144] "Warriors seldom hate each other," he mused. "They know they're pawns in a killing game."[145]

David Hackworth, like many writers, however, believes that to understand truly the Vietnam experience and exorcise its ghosts from both the military establishment and the veterans that fought the war, we must face some uncomfortable truths and learn the true lessons of that war. "To close the book on Vietnam," Hackworth contends, "we must understand that America lost on the battlefield not because of peace protests at Berkeley or failures of nerve in the Congress, but because our military leadership thought bombs could beat a people's hunger for independence. The price for that lack of moral courage to tell the politicians that it was a bad war fought with a flawed strategy was death for thousands of young Americans."[146]

NOTES

1. Association of the 1st Battalion (Mechanized), 50th Infantry for Vietnam Veterans, "Lessons Learned in Vietnam: 1st Battalion, 50th Infantry," http://www.ichiban1.org/html/history_lessons.htm.

2. Ron Ballweg, *Oral History Project,* The Vietnam Archive at Texas Tech University. Interviewed by Richard Verrone, May 19, 2003. Retrieved from http://www.virtualarchive.vietnam.ttu.edu/cgi-bin/star fetch.exe?8ef.0OThTHlw@ovB@bMAIW5KtMcM31GAZwYqlEtpvVWLEnlWMsbO6qa0zk 8nerqkpky0E2@3.AAMn2RrUMjKQM1MI39jwXFA/OH0296.pdf, 42.

3. David White, *Oral History Project,* The Vietnam Archive at Texas Tech University. Interviewed by Richard Verrone, n.d. Retrieved from http://www.virtualarchive.vietnam.ttu.edu/cgi-bin/starfetch. exe?71mIafeP3JsUwk7rv@lU9xasA5uYhgjKNAyaDpYf5Nk.Blkuvd69i.GoLp0Gl4jSbk8HMOoS284 C0l6iWWadecNnjn.SRsiy/OH0227.pdf, 25.

4. Gerald Kumpf, *Oral History Project,* The Vietnam Archive at Texas Tech University. Interviewed by Richard Verrone, March 10, 2003. Retrieved from http://www.virtualarchive.vietnam.ttu.edu/cgi-bin/ starfetch.exe?EWoAfq.tJEBzwDooKsGN8mxwA2X3@q8.Y4@lpzu0qrpNanzPx0Zh6@ZwMPIxL. ex6Y3AV.nGBn7aUH1WFP4otrIS5b2nFx1OwsFzXQ8FRlo/OH0276-1.pdf, 41.

5. Sp/4 Hank Lovelady, "Our Men in Vietnam," *Sepia,* July 1968, 75.

6. Sp/3 Gene Richmond, "Our Men in Vietnam," *Sepia,* July 1968, 74.

7. Eddie Meeks, "Nursing the Dying," *Newsweek,* March 8, 1999, 61.

8. Ballweg, *Oral History Project,* 44.

9. Gonzalo Baltazar, *Oral History Project,* The Vietnam Archive at Texas Tech University. Interviewed by Steve Maxner, March 23, 2001. Retrieved from http://www.virtualarchive.vietnam.ttu.edu/cgi-bin/starfetch. exe?3qUevQOjUtg2mDgIBOhT3hQ7wvenAzlebd@qMS7Av.N9BF7TSM9wvr@vB2M4o7sdoJfUBL5. U3WHS1XkROhq2hvFxK3tPSLj/OH0152.pdf, 36–37.

10. Kumpf, *Oral History Project,* 42.

11. Russell F. Weigley, "Putting the Poor in Uniform," *The New York Times,* April 11, 1993, 12.

12. Ballweg, *Oral History Project,* 42.

13. Lieutenant General Arthur J. Gregg, *Senior Officer Oral History Project,* U.S. Army Military History Institute, Carlisle Barracks, PA, 1997, 68.

14. Kumpf, *Oral History Project,* 43–44.

15. Ballweg, *Oral History Project,* 44.

16. Kumpf, *Oral History Project,* 41–42.

17. David H. Hackworth, "The War without End," *Newsweek,* November 22, 1993, 45.

18. Lew Moores, "Soldier Devotes Life to Country," *The Cincinnati Enquirer,* November 10, 1997, A-4.

19. White, *Oral History Project,* 27.

20. Ballweg, *Oral History Project,* 42.

21. Philip Caputo, *A Rumor of War* (New York: Holt, Rinehart, and Winston, 1977), xiv–xv.

22. Bill Beck, "The Dead Were All Around," *Newsweek,* March 8, 1999, 56.

23. Moores, "Soldier Devotes Life," A-4.

24. Baltazar, *Oral History Project,* 37.

25. National Center for PTSD, "What Is Posttraumatic Stress Disorder?," http://www.ncptsd.va.gov/ ncmain/ncdocs/fact_shts/fs_what_is_ptsd.html.

26. Ballweg, *Oral History Project.*

27. White, *Oral History Project,* 27.

28. Ballweg, *Oral History Project,* 42.

29. Baltazar, *Oral History Project,* 37.

30. William E. McFee, "Shabby Treatment," letter to the editor, *The Cincinnati Enquirer,* December 1, 1967, 8.

31. Wallace Terry, "Bringing the War Home," *Black Scholar,* November 1970, 7–8.

32. C. L. Sulzberger, "Foreign Affairs: The Spin-Out," *The New York Times,* May 21, 1969, 46.

33. "Tragic Case of Jackie Robinson's Son," Roundup, *Sepia,* May 1968, 32, and "Are Our G.I.'s on Dope?" *Sepia,* July 1968, 10–12.

34. Mark St. John Erickson, "Blacks Break into Ranks of Vet Groups," *Newport News–Hampton, Virginia Daily Press,* Williamsburg ed., July 27, 1998, A5.

35. Major James C. Warren, "Our Men in Vietnam," *Sepia,* April 1968, 75.

36. Albert Childs, *Oral History Project,* The Vietnam Archive at Texas Tech University. Interviewed by Steve Maxner, February 3, 2003. Retrieved from http://www.virtualarchive.vietnam.ttu.edu/cgi-bin/starfetch. exe?px@DCzXFmOuNx2T6g1RlUxXU5JKU.VHLnKVjhB5A.zu78Y18RLhkxS@8DT4FUZiZFMSEp2vq jMbGIa4Bk5SPT9GKohPkmUno/OH0095.pdf, 17.

37. Hackworth, "War without End," 44.

38. Arnold R. Isaacs, *Without Honor: Defeat in Vietnam and Cambodia* (Baltimore: Johns Hopkins University Press, 1983), 125.

39. Baltazar, *Oral History Project,* 10.

40. Ibid., 17–18.

41. Ibid., 17.

42. Ballweg, *Oral History Project,* 28.

43. Gregg, *Senior Officer Oral History Project,* 60.

44. Paul L. Savage and Richard A. Gabriel, "Cohesion and Disintegration in the American Army: An Alternative Perspective," in *The Military in America from the Colonial Era to the Present,* ed. Peter Kartsen (New York: MacMillan, 1980), 413.

45. Ibid., 413.

46. Ibid.

47. Baltazar, *Oral History Project,* 31.

48. Kumpf, *Oral History Project*, 38.

49. Ballweg, *Oral History Project*, 35–36.

50. Baltazar, *Oral History Project*, 31.

51. Childs, *Oral History Project*, 20.

52. "Are Our G.I.'s on Dope?," 10–12.

53. Herman Graham III, *The Brothers' Vietnam War: Black Power, Manhood, and the Military Experience* (Gainesville: University Press of Florida, 2003), 63.

54. Ibid.

55. Charles C. Moskos Jr., "The American Combat Soldier in Vietnam," *Journal of Social Issues 31*(4), (1975), 33.

56. Savage and Gabriel, "Cohesion and Disintegration."

57. Lawrence M. Baskir and William Strauss, *Chance and Circumstance: The Draft, the War, and the Vietnam Generation* (New York: Random House, 1978), 134–35, and Major Thomas Cecil, *Senior Officer Oral History Project,* U.S. Army Military History Institute, Carlisle Barracks, PA, 1982 30.

58. "G.I. in Sweden Returns to Army," Roundup, *Sepia,* May 1968, 32.

59. Baltazar, *Oral History Project*, 10.

60. National Association for the Advancement of Colored People, *The Search for Military Justice,* (New York: NAACP, 1971) 6.

61. Honorable Louis Stokes, "Racism in the Military: The Congressional Black Caucus Report, 15 May, 1972," 82nd Cong., 2nd sess., *Congressional Record 118* (October 14, 1972): 36,584.

62. Major Michael F. Colacicco, *Senior Officer Oral History Project,* U.S. Army Military History Institute, Carlisle Barracks, PA, 1982, 10–11.

63. Kumpf, *Oral History Project.*

64. Major Thomas Peoples, *Senior Officer Oral History Project,* U.S. Army Military History Institute, Carlisle Barracks, PA, 1982, 47.

65. Gregg, *Senior Officer Oral History Project.*

66. Caputo, *A Rumor of War.*

67. Edward Souders, "Racism in the Military," unpublished, New York: Safe Return, January, 1974, p. 3., Citizen Soldier Files, 7033 Box 8, file 59, Vietnam War Veteran's Archive, Department of Manuscripts and Archives, Ithaca: New York, Cornell University Library, 6, and Department of Defense (DOD), *Manual for Courts-Martial,* vol. A-2 (Washington: U.S. Government Printing Office, 1969), 5–7, 26–33, and DOD, *Task Force on the Administration of Military Justice,* vol. 1 (Washington: U.S. Government Printing Office, 1972), 9.

68. "Military Prisons: About Face," *Time,* May 17, 1971, 63.

69. Stokes, "Black Caucus Report," 36,583–86.

70. DOD, *Task Force,* vol. 1, 63.

71. Baltazar, *Oral History Project*, 12.

72. Curtis Daniell, "Germany: Trouble Spot for Black GI's" *Ebony,* August, 1968, 127.

73. "GI Transferrred," *The Black Liberator,* July 1969, 3.

74. "GI's Complain about Bias in Armed Services," *The Pittsburgh Courier,* May 8, 1971, 9.

75. "Army Denounced by Negro Major," *New York Times,* October 14, 1968, 3.

76. Sol Stern, "When the Black GI Comes Back from Vietnam," *New York Times Magazine,* March 24, 1968, 42, and Thomas Johnson, "The U.S. Negro in Vietnam," *New York Times,* April 29, 1968, 16, and Thomas Johnson, "Negro Expatriates Finding Wide Opportunity in Asia," *New York Times,* April 30, 1969, 18.

77. Stokes, "Black Caucus Report," 36, 589, and Thomas Johnson, "Negroes in the Nam," *Ebony,* August 1968, 38.

78. Thomas Johnson, "Negro Expatriates Finding Wide Opportunity in Asia," *The New York Times,* April 30, 1969, 18, and, Thomas Johnson, "The U.S. Negro in Vietnam," *New York Times,* April 29, 1968, 16.

79. Major Stewart H. Barnhoft, *Company Officer Oral History Project,* U.S. Military History Institute, Carlisle Barracks, PA, 1982, 6.

80. Garven Dalglish, "Black and Back from Vietnam," *The Cincinnati Enquirer Magazine,* July 19, 1970, 11.

81. Colin Powell, *My American Journey* (New York: Random House, 1995), 124.

82. Baskir and Strauss, *Chance and Circumstance,* 137, and Lieutenant Charles Anderson File, letter dated November 15, 1968, 1, #7028, Box 1, File #1, Cornell University Archives, Ithaca, NY.

83. Ballweg, *Oral History Project*, 40.

84. DOD, *Task Force,* vol. 1, 61–62.

85. Baltazar, *Oral History Project*, 30.

86. "Lejeune Described As Worse than Mississippi," *The Pittsburgh Courier,* August 30, 1969, 1.

87. DOD, *Task Force*, vol. 1, 60–61, and "GI's Complain about Bias in Armed Services," *The Pittsburgh Courier*, May 8, 1971, 9, and Major John J. Ellis, *Senior Officer Oral History Project*, 1982, U.S. Army Military History Institute, Carlisle Barracks, PA, 5.

88. Lieutenant Colonel Vernon L. Conner, *Company Officer Oral History Project*, U.S. Army Military History Institute, Carlisle Barracks, PA, 1982, 46.

89. DOD, *Task Force*, vol. 1, 61.

90. "No Dixie Flag in Armed Forces," *The Baltimore Afro-American*, February 19, 1966, 3, and "From a G.I.," *The Black Panther*, July 26, 1969, 6.

91. "Requiem for Dixie," *The Crisis*, March 1969, 112.

92. Bernard Weinraub, "Rioting Disquiets G.I.'s in Vietnam," *The New York Times*, April 8, 1968, 35.

93. Sergeant James H. House, "From Viet Nam," letters to the editor, *Sepia*, August 1968, 6.

94. James E. Westheider, *Fighting on Two Fronts: African Americans and the Vietnam War* (New York: New York University Press, 1997), 98.

95. Weinraub, "Rioting," 35.

96. James E. Westheider, "African Americans and the Vietnam War," in *The Blackwell Companion to the Vietnam War*, eds. Marilyn Young and Robert Buzzanco (Boston: Blackwell, 2002), 343.

97. Clinton H. Hunt, in discussion with the author, Cincinnati, Ohio, September 21, 1991, and Pfc. Morocco Coleman, "The Prince of Peace," letters to the editor, *Ebony*, August 1968, 17.

98. Shaw and Donnelly, *Blacks in the Marine Corps*, 72, and Flora Lewis, "The Rumble at Camp Lejeune," *The Atlantic*, January 1970, 26, 38, and "White v. Black Confrontations Are Increasing," *The Pittsburgh Courier*, August 23, 1969, 14.

99. "Black GI's," *The Black Liberator*, December 1969, 2, and "4 Marines Convicted of Assault Not Rioting," *The Baltimore Afro-American*, February 14, 1970, 18, and "Memphis," *The Crisis*, March 1970, 116.

100. Cecil, *Senior Officer Oral History Project*.

101. Ibid., 2.

102. Shaw and Donnelly, *Blacks in the Marine Corps*, 73.

103. Johnson, "Negroes in the Nam," 36.

104. Sulzberger, "Foreign Affairs," 46.

105. "Study Sees more Bloodshed," *The Baltimore Afro-American*, January 31, 1970, 3.

106. William H. McMichael, "A War on Two Fronts," *Newport News–Hampton, Virginia Daily Press*, Williamsburg ed., July 27, 1998, 1, A-6.

107. Major William G. Riederer, *Senior Officer Oral History Project*, U.S. Army Military History Institute, Carlisle Barracks, PA, 1982, 6.

108. Major Richard H. Torovsky, *Senior Officer Oral History Project*, U.S. Army Military History Institute, Carlisle Barracks, PA, 1982, 5–6.

109. First Lieutenant Gasanove Stephens, "Our Men in Vietnam," Sepia, June 1968, 58.

110. Major Eugene J. White Interview, *Senior Officer Oral History Project*, U.S. Army Military History Institute, Carlisle Barracks, PA, 1982, 12.

111. Powell, *My American Journey*, 125.

112. Private First Class Donnel Jones, "Racism in Vietnam," letter to the editor, *Sepia*, August 1968, 6.

113. Charles Porter, letters to the editor, *Sepia*, March 1968, 6.

114. Zalin B. Grant, "Whites Against Blacks in Vietnam," *The New Republic*, January 18, 1969, 16.

115. McMichael, "A War on Two Fronts," A-6.

116. Major Patric Carder, *Senior Officer Oral History Project*, U.S. Army Military History Institute, Carlisle Barracks, PA, 1982, 4.

117. Major Maxwell V. Terrien, *Senior Officer Oral History Project*, U.S. Army Military History Institute, Carlisle Barracks, PA, 1982, 3–4.

118. Major Victor E. Miller, *Senior Officer Oral History Project*, U.S. Army Military History Institute, Carlisle Barracks, PA, 1982.

119. Torovsky, *Senior Officer Oral History Project*, 5–6.

120. Baskir and Strauss, *Chance and Circumstance*, 61, and Colonel Robert D. Heinl Jr., "The Collapse of the Armed Forces," *Armed Forces Journal*, June 7, 1971, 32. 121. Heinl, "Collapse," 32.

122. Baltazar, *Oral History Project*, 11.

123. McMichael, "A War on Two Fronts," A-6.

124. White, *Oral History Project*, 24.

125. McMichael, "A War on Two Fronts," 1, A4–A6.

126. Savage and Gabriel, "Cohesion and Disintegration," 418.

127. Ibid.

128. "GI's Complain about Bias in Armed Services," *The Pittsburgh Courier,* May 8, 1971, 9.

129. Ballweg, *Oral History Project*, 27–28.

130. Committee on Internal Security, House of Representatives, *Investigation of Attempts to Subvert the United States Armed Forces,* part 2 (Washington, DC: U.S. Government Printing Office, 1972, 6993.

131. Powell, *My American Journey,* 133.

132. Lewis, "Rumble at Camp Lejeune," 39, and General William Westmoreland, *Report of the Chief of Staff of the United States Army, 1 July 1968–30 June 1972* (Washington: Department of the Army, 1977), 62.

133. Lewis, "Rumble at Camp Lejeune," 39.

134. Ibid.

135. Melvin Laird, "Guidelines for Handling Dissident and Protest Activities among Members of the Armed Forces," Department of Defense Directive 1325.6, September 12, 1969.

136. Ben A. Franklin, "War Resistance by GI's Is Urged," *The New York Times,* November 14, 1969, 11.

137. McMichael, "A War on Two Fronts," A-5.

138. William H. McMichael, "In Fight against Bias, Victory Is Never Secure," *Newport News–Hampton, Virginia Daily Press,* July 28, 1998, A4.

139. Hackworth, "War without End," 48.

140. General Anthony Zinni, interview by Harry Kreisler, Conversations with History, Institute of International Studies, UC Berkeley, March 6, 2001, http:///globetrotter.berkeley.edu/conversations/Zinni/zinni-con3.html.

141. Baltazar, *Oral History Project*, 39.

142. Hackworth, "War without End," 44.

143. Ibid., 44.

144. Ibid., 45.

145. Ibid., 47.

146. Ibid., 48.

Bibliography

GENERAL STUDIES OF THE VIETNAM WAR

Davidson, Phillip B., *Vietnam at War: The History, 1946–1975* (Novato, CA: Presidio Press, 1988).

Herring, George S., *America's Longest War: The United States and Vietnam, 1950–1975* (New York: McGraw-Hill, 2001).

Karnow, Stanley, *Vietnam: A History* (New York: Viking Press, 1983).

Kolko, Gabriel, *Anatomy of a War* (New York: New Press, 1985).

Moss, George Donelson, *Vietnam: An American Ordeal*, 3rd ed. (Upper Saddle River, NJ: Prentice Hall, 1998).

Palmer, Bruce, *The Twenty-five Year War* (New York: Simon and Schuster, 1984).

The Vietnam Center, Texas Tech University, "The Vietnam Project," http://star.vietnam.ttu.edu. Includes archives, an oral history project, interviews with numerous Vietnam veterans, teachers' resources, a collection of military personnel graffiti from bunk canvases and ship logs on ships supporting the war effort, and other resources.

Young, Marilyn, *The Vietnam Wars, 1945–1990* (New York: HarperCollins, 1991).

GENERAL ANTHOLOGIES

McMahon, Robert J., *Major Problems in the History of the Vietnam War*, 2nd ed. (Lexington, MA: D. C. Heath, 1995).

Young, Marilyn, and Robert Buzzanco, eds., *The Blackwell Companion to the Vietnam War* (New York: Blackwell, 2002).

REFERENCES

Anderson, David L., *Columbia Guide to the Vietnam War* (New York: Columbia University Press, 2002).

Kelley, Michael P., *Where We Were in Vietnam: A Comprehensive Guide to the Firebases, Military Installations, and Naval Vessels of the Vietnam War, 1945–1975* (Central Point, OR: Hellgate Press, 2002).

Kutler, Stanley, ed., *Encyclopedia of the Vietnam War* (New York: Oxford Books, 1998).

Olson, James, ed., *Dictionary of the Vietnam War* (New York: Peter Bedrick Books, 1987).

Summers, Harry, *Vietnam War Almanac* (Novato, CA: Presidio Press, 1985).

———, *Historical Atlas of the Vietnam War* (New York: Houghton Mifflin, 1996).

Tucker, Spencer, ed., *Encyclopedia of the Vietnam War* (Santa Barbara, CA: ABC-CLIO, 1998).

Army Doctrine and Operations

Bergerud, Eric M., *Red Thunder, Tropic Lightning: The World of a Combat Division in Vietnam* (Boulder, CO: Westview Press, 1993).

Cable, Larry E., *Conflict of Myths: The Development of American Counterinsurgency Doctrine and the Vietnam War* (New York: New York University Press, 1986).

Hamburger, Kenneth E., *Leadership in Combat: An Historical Appraisal* (Washington, DC: Department of the Army, 1984).

Krepinevich, Andrew W., Jr., *The Army and Vietnam* (Baltimore: Johns Hopkins University Press, 1986).

Levine, Beth, "Headlong into Underground Battle," *Military History 51* (January 1987): 43–48.

Matthews, Lloyd J., and Dale E. Brown, eds., *Assessing the Vietnam War* (Washington, DC: Pergamon-Brassey's International Defense, 1987).

McKay, Gary, *Delta Four: Australian Riflemen in Vietnam* (Crows Nest, NSW, Australia: Allen and Unwin, 1996).

———, *In Good Company: One Man's War in Vietnam* (Crows Nest, NSW, Australia: Allen and Unwin, 1998).

Moskos, Charles C., Jr., *The American Enlisted Man* (New York: Russell Sage Foundation, 1970).

Stanton, Shelby L., *The Rise and Fall of an American Army: U.S. Ground Forces in Vietnam, 1965–1973* (Novato, CA: Presidio Press, 1985).

Summers, Harry G., *On Strategy: A Critical Analysis of the Vietnam War* (Novato, CA: Presidio Press, 1982).

The Air War

Clodfelter, Mark, *The Limits of Airpower: The American Bombing of North Vietnam* (New York: The Free Press, 1989).

Eschmann, Karl J., *Linebacker: The Untold Story of the Air Raids over North Vietnam* (New York: Ivy Books, 1989).

Office of U.S. Air Force History, *The United States Air Force in Southeast Asia, 1961–1973* (Washington, DC: Government Printing Office, 1986).

Thompson, Wayne, *To Hanoi and Back: The United States Air Force and North Vietnam, 1966–1973* (Washington, DC: Smithsonian Institution Press, 2000).

U.S. Navy

Marolda, Edward J., *By Sea, Air, and Land: An Illustrated History of the U.S. Navy and the War in Southeast Asia* (Washington, DC: Naval Historical Center, 1992).

Marolda, Edward J., and Oscar P. Fitzgerald, *The United States Navy and the Vietnam Conflict*, vol. 2, *From Military Assistance to Combat, 1959–1965* (Washington, DC: Naval Historical Center, 1986).

Mersky, Peter B., and Norman Polmar, *The Naval Air War in Vietnam* (Mt. Pleasant, SC: Nautical and Aviation, 1981).

Major Battles and Events

Anderson, David L., ed., *Facing My Lai: Moving beyond the Massacre* (Lawrence: University Press of Kansas, 1998).

Moore, Harold G., and Joseph Galloway, *We Were Soldiers Once... and Young: Ia Drang—The Battle That Changed the War in Vietnam* (New York: Random House, 1993).

Oberdorfer, Don, *Tet: The Turning Point in the Vietnam War* (New York: Da Capo Press, 1984).

Olsen, James S., and Randy Roberts, *My Lai: A Brief History with Documents* (Boston: Bedford Books, 1999).

Rogers, Bernard William, *Cedar Falls-Junction City: A Turning Point,* Vietnam Studies (Washington, DC: Department of the Army, 1989).

Spector, Ronald, *After Tet: The Bloodiest Year in Vietnam* (New York: Free Press, 1993).

Turley, G. H., *The Easter Offensive* (Novato, CA: Presidio Press, 1985).

Personal Accounts, Biographies, and Memoirs

Atkinson, Rick, *The Long Gray Line* (New York: Henry Holt, 1989).

Brennan, Matthew, *Brennan's War: Vietnam 1965–1969* (Novato, CA: Presidio Press, 1985).

Caputo, Philip, *A Rumor of War* (New York: Holt, Rinehart, and Winston, 1977).

Krulak, Victor, *First to Fight: An Inside View of the U.S. Marine Corps* (Washington, DC: Naval Institute Press, 1984).

Contains several fine biographies.

Parks, David, *GI Diary,* reprint ed. (Washington, DC: Howard University Press, 1982).

Powell, Colin, and Joseph E. Persico, *My American Journey* (New York: Random House, 1995).

Santoli, Al, *Everything We Had* (New York: Ballantine Books, 1981).

Sheehan, Neil, *A Bright Shining Lie: John Paul Vann and America in Vietnam* (New York: Random House, 1988).

Sorley, Lewis, *Thunderbolt: General Creighton Abrams and the Army of His Times* (New York: Simon and Schuster, 1992).

A fine biography.

Stoffey, Bob, *Cleared Hot!: A Marine Combat Pilot's Vietnam Diary* (New York: St. Martin's Press, 1999).

Westmoreland, William C., *A Soldier Reports* (Garden City, NY: Doubleday, 1976).

Prisoners of War

Daly, James A., and Lee Bergman, *Black Prisoner of War: A Conscientious Objector's Vietnam Memoir* (Lawrence: University Press of Kansas, 2000).

McCain, John, *Faith of My Fathers: A Family Memoir* (New York: Random House, 1999).

McConnell, Malcolm, *Into the Mouth of the Cat* (East Rutherford, NJ: New American Library of Canada, 1986).

Women

Freedman, Dan, ed., *Nurses in Vietnam: The Forgotten Veterans* (Austin: Texas Monthly Press, 1987).

Marshall, Kathryn, *In the Combat Zone: An Oral History of American Women in Vietnam* (Boston: Little, Brown, 1987).

Norman, Elizabeth, *Women at War: The Story of Fifty Military Nurses Who Served in Vietnam* (Philadelphia: University of Pennsylvania Press, 1990).

Walker, Keith, *A Piece of My Heart: The Stories of 26 Women Who Served in Vietnam* (Novato, CA: Presidio Press, 1985).

African Americans and Vietnam

Goff, Stanley, and Robert Sanders, *Brothers: Black Soldiers in the Nam* (New York: Berkeley Books, 1982).

Graham, Herman, III, *The Brothers' Vietnam War: Black Power, Manhood, and the Military Experience* (Gainesville: University Press of Florida, 2003).

Mullen, Robert, *Blacks in America's Wars: The Shift in Attitudes from the Revolutionary War to Vietnam* (New York: Pathfinder Press, 1973).

Shapiro, Herbet, "The Vietnam War and the American Civil Rights Movement," *Journal of Ethnic Studies* 16 (1989): 117–41.

Terry, Wallace, *Bloods: An Oral History of the Vietnam War* (New York: Random House, 1984).

Westheider, James E., *Fighting on Two Fronts: African Americans and the Vietnam War* (New York: New York University Press, 1997).

———, "Sgt. Allen Thomas, Jr.: A Black Soldier in Vietnam," in *Portraits of African American Life Since 1865*, ed. Nina Mjagkij (Wilmington, DE: Scholarly Resources, 2003). Examines the experiences of a veteran of three tours in Vietnam.

The Draft

Appy, Christian G., *Working-Class War: American Combat Soldiers and Vietnam* (Chapel Hill: University of North Carolina Press, 1993).

Baskir, Lawrence M., and William Strauss, *Chance and Circumstance: The Draft, the War, and the Vietnam Generation* (New York: Random House, 1978).

Bingham, Howard L., and Max Wallace, *Muhammad Ali's Greatest Fight* (New York: M. Evans, 2000).

Ferber, Michael, and Stoughton Lynd, *The Resistance* (Boston: Beacon Press, 1971).

Foley, Michael S., *Confronting the War Machine: Draft Resistance during the Vietnam War* (Chapel Hill: University of North Carolina Press, 2003).

Taylor, Clyde, *Vietnam and Black America: An Anthology of Protest and Resistance* (Garden City, NY: Anchor Press, 1973).

Morale and Dissent

Bell, D. Bruce, and Beverly W. Bell, "Desertion and Antiwar Protest," *Armed Forces and Society,* May 1977, 433–43.

Boyle, Richard, *Flower of the Dragon: The Breakdown of the U.S. Army in Vietnam* (San Francisco: Ramparts Press, 1972).

Glenn, Taylor, Kelly Mack, and Josh Blackwelder, "USO Shows in the Vietnam War," http://www.newberry.k12.sc.us/mchs/uso.htm.

Heinl, Robert D., Jr., "The Collapse of the Armed Forces," *Armed Forces Journal,* June 7, 1971, 31–37.

Henderson, William Darryl, *The Hollow Army* (New York: Greenwood Press, 1990).

Moskos, Charles C., Jr., "The American Combat Soldier in Vietnam," *Journal of Social Issues,* 31 (1975): 25–37.

Moser, Richard, *The New Winter Soldiers: GI and Veteran Dissent during the Vietnam Era* (New Brunswick, NJ: Rutgers University Press, 1996).

Savage, Paul L., and Richard A. Gabriel, "Cohesion and Disintegration in the American Army: An Alternative Perspective," in *The Military in America from the Colonial Era to the Present,* ed. Peter Kartsen (New York: MacMillan, 1980).

Shils, Edward, "A Profile of the Military Deserter," *Armed Forces and Society,* May 1977, 429.

United Service Organizations, "66th Anniversary Factsheets," http://uso.mediaroom.com/index. php?s=pageB.

Whitmore, Terry, *Memphis-Nam-Sweden: The Autobiography of a Black American Exile* (Oxford: University Press of Mississippi, 1997).

The Media and the War

Bates, Milton J., *Reporting Vietnam: American Journalism 1959–1969,* part I, Library Classics of the United States (New York: Penguin Books, 1998).

Braestrup, Peter, *Big Story* (Boulder, CO: Westview Press, 1977).

Hammond, William H., *Reporting Vietnam: Media and Military at War* (Lawrence: University Press of Kansas, 2000).

Herr, Michael, *Dispatches* (New York: Alfred E. Knopf, 1977).

Wyatt, Clarence R., *Paper Soldiers: The American Press and the Vietnam War* (Chicago: University of Chicago Press, 1995).

Veterans

Bonior, David E., *The Vietnam Veteran: A History of Neglect* (New York: Praeger, 1984).

Camp, Norman M., Robert H. Stretch, and William C. Marshall, *Stress, Strain, and Vietnam: An Annotated Bibliography of Two Decades of Psychiatric and Social Sciences Literature Reflecting the Effect of the War on the American Soldier* (Westport, CT: Greenwood Press, 1988).

Vietnamese Military Forces

Bartholome-Feis, Dixee R., *The OSS and Ho Chi Minh* (Lawrence: University Press of Kansas, 2006).

Chanoff, David, and Doan Van Toai, *Portrait of the Enemy* (New York: Random House, 1986).

Clarke, Jeffrey C., *Advice and Support: The Final Years, 1965–1973* (Washington, DC: Government Printing Office, 1988).

Halberstam, David, *Ho* (New York: McGraw-Hill, 1987).

Lanning, Michael Lee, and Dan Cragg, *Inside the VC and NVA* (New York: Ivy Books, 1992).

Pike, Douglas, *PAVN: People's Army of Vietnam* (Novato, CA: Presidio Press, 1986).

Truong Nhu Tang, *A Vietcong Memoir* (San Diego, CA: Harcourt Brace, 1985).

INDEX

Stackpole Military History Series

Real battles. Real soldiers. Real stories.

Stackpole Military History Series

Real battles. Real soldiers. Real stories.

Stackpole Military History Series

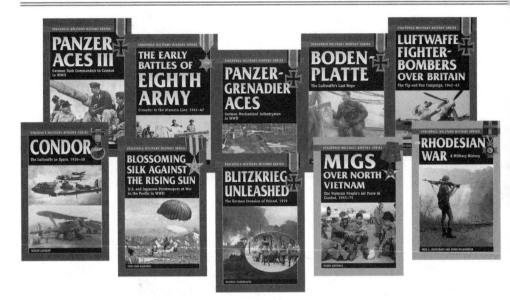

Real battles. Real soldiers. Real stories.

STACKPOLE MILITARY HISTORY SERIES

LUFTWAFFE FIGHTERS & BOMBERS
The Battle of Britain
CHRIS GOSS

STACKPOLE MILITARY HISTORY SERIES

NIGHT FLYER/ MOSQUITO PATHFINDER
Night Operations in WWII

STACKPOLE MILITARY HISTORY SERIES

POLAND BETRAYED
The Nazi-Soviet Invasions of 1939
DAVID G. WILLIAMSON

STACKPOLE MILITARY HISTORY SERIES

THE SIEGE OF KÜSTRIN
Gateway to Berlin, 1945

STACKPOLE MILITARY HISTORY SERIES

AIRBORNE COMBAT
The Glider War/Fighting Gliders of WWII

NEW for Spring 2011

STACKPOLE MILITARY HISTORY SERIES

ARNHEM 1944
The Airborne Battle
MARTIN MIDDLEBROOK

STACKPOLE MILITARY HISTORY SERIES

EUROPE IN FLAMES
Understanding WWII
EDITED BY HAROLD J. GOLDBERG

STACKPOLE MILITARY HISTORY SERIES

FIGHTING IN VIETNAM
The Experiences of the U.S. Soldier
JAMES WESTHEIDER

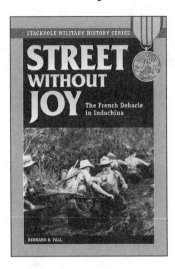

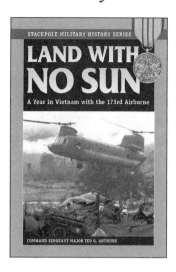

Stackpole Military History Series

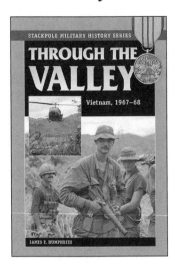

THROUGH THE VALLEY
VIETNAM, 1967–68
Col. James F. Humphries

In the remote northern provinces of South Vietnam—
a region of long-forgotten villages and steep hills—
the U.S. Americal Division and 196th Light Infantry
Brigade fought a series of battles against the North
Vietnamese and Vietcong in 1967–68: Hiep Duc, Nhi Ha,
Hill 406, and others. These pitched engagements, marked
by fierce close combat, have gone virtually unreported in
the decades since, but Col. James F. Humphries brings
them into sharp focus, chronicling the efforts of these
proud American units against a stubborn enemy and
reconstructing what it was like to fight in Vietnam.

$19.95 • Paperback • 6 x 9 • 384 pages • 47 b/w photos, 24 maps

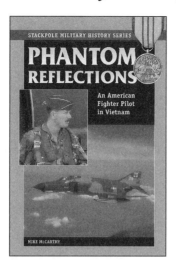

Stackpole Military History Series

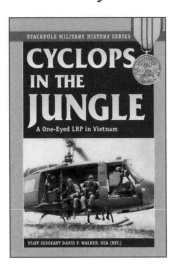

CYCLOPS IN THE JUNGLE
A ONE-EYED LRP IN VIETNAM
Staff Sergeant David P. Walker, USA (Ret.)

Dave Walker enlisted in the U.S. Army at seventeen, full
of patriotism and eager to play his part in Vietnam.
Trained for long-range patrol (LRP) operations, he
received a debilitating shrapnel wound to his eye barely
a month after arriving in Vietnam. Medically discharged
and sent home to a country he decreasingly recognized,
Walker—now missing an eye—maneuvered his way back
to the jungles of Vietnam, where he survived another
eighteen months conducting patrols and special
operations with an elite Ranger unit.

$18.95 • Paperback • 6 x 9 • 240 pages • 30 b/w photos

Stackpole Military History Series

EXPENDABLE WARRIORS
THE BATTLE OF KHE SANH AND THE VIETNAM WAR
Bruce B. G. Clarke

On January 21, 1968, nine days before the Tet Offensive, thousands of North Vietnamese soldiers attacked the U.S. Marine base at Khe Sanh in remote northwestern South Vietnam. The ensuing siege ended seventy-seven days later in a tactical victory for the United States, which eventually abandoned the base, making it a heartbreaking and controversial symbol of American involvement in Vietnam. Bruce Clarke participated in the battle as a young U.S. Army officer, and his book combines his firsthand experiences and archival research to describe the saga of Khe Sanh.

$18.95 • Paperback • 6 x 9 • 208 pages • 11 b/w photos, 5 maps

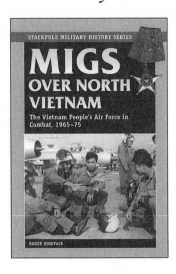

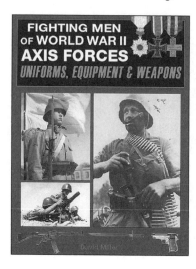 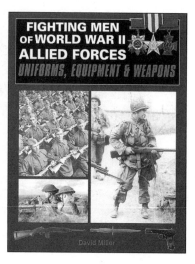